FRANCE

BELGIUM & THE NETHERLANDS
1997

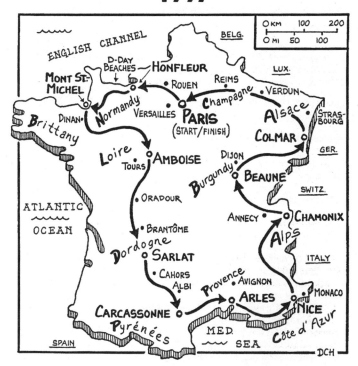

Rick Steves and Steve Smith

John Muir Publications
Santa Fe, New Mexico

Other JMP travel guidebooks by Rick Steves
Asia Through the Back Door (with Bob Effertz)
Europe Through the Back Door
Europe 101: History and Art for the Traveler (with Gene Openshaw)
Mona Winks: Self-Guided Tours of Europe's Top Museums
    (with Gene Openshaw)
Rick Steves' Baltics & Russia (with Ian Watson)
Rick Steves' Europe
Rick Steves' Germany, Austria & Switzerland
Rick Steves' Great Britain & Ireland
Rick Steves' Italy
Rick Steves' Scandinavia
Rick Steves' Spain & Portugal
Rick Steves' Phrase Books: German, French, Italian,
    Spanish/Portuguese, and French/German/Italian

Thanks to Steve's wife, Karen Lewis, for her help on covering the cuisine of France.

John Muir Publications, P.O. Box 613, Santa Fe, NM 87504
Copyright © 1997, 1996, 1995 by Rick Steves and Steve Smith
Cover © 1997 by John Muir Publications
All rights reserved.

Printed in the United States of America
First printing February 1997

Previously published as *2 to 22 Days in France* © 1989, 1991, 1992, 1993, 1994

For the latest on Rick's lectures, guidebooks, tours, and PBS-TV series, contact Europe Through the Back Door, Box 2009, Edmonds WA 98020, tel. 206/771-8303, fax 206/771-0833, online at ricksteves@aol.com, or on the Web at http://www.ricksteves.com.

ISSN 1084-4406
ISBN 1-56261-327-8

Europe Through the Back Door Editor Risa Laib
John Muir Publications Editors Dianna Delling, Chris Hayhurst, Heidi Utz
Production Nikki Rooker, Janine Lehmann
Maps Dave Hoerlein
Cover Design Cowgirls Design, Kathryn Lloyd-Strongin
Design Linda Braun
Typesetting John Ericksen
Printer Banta Company
Cover Photo Provence, France; Leo de Wys Inc./DeWys/TPL

Distributed to the book trade by
Publishers Group West
Emeryville, California

Top Destinations in France, Belgium, and the Netherlands

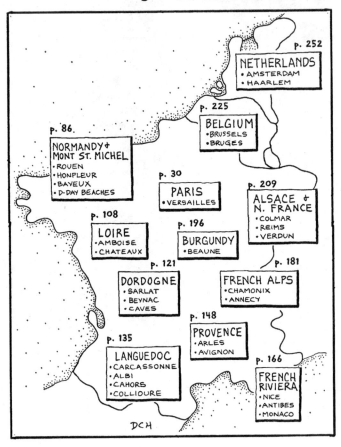

p. 252
NETHERLANDS
•AMSTERDAM
•HAARLEM

p. 225
BELGIUM
•BRUSSELS
•BRUGES

p. 86
NORMANDY &
MONT ST. MICHEL
•ROUEN
•HONFLEUR
•BAYEUX
•D-DAY BEACHES

p. 30
PARIS
•VERSAILLES

p. 209
ALSACE &
N. FRANCE
•COLMAR
•REIMS
•VERDUN

p. 108
LOIRE
•AMBOISE
•CHATEAUX

p. 196
BURGUNDY
•BEAUNE

p. 121
DORDOGNE
•SARLAT
•BEYNAC
•CAVES

p. 181
FRENCH ALPS
•CHAMONIX
•ANNECY

p. 148
PROVENCE
•ARLES
•AVIGNON

p. 135
LANGUEDOC
•CARCASSONNE
•ALBI
•CAHORS
•COLLIOURE

p. 166
FRENCH
RIVIERA
•NICE
•ANTIBES
•MONACO

DCH

CONTENTS

INTRODUCTION

Our compliments. You've made a great choice. France is Europe's most diverse, tasty, and in many ways, exciting country to explore.

France is as big as Texas, with 58 million people and 460 different cheeses. *Diversité* is a French *forté:* this country features three distinct mountain ranges—the Alps, Pyrénées, and Massif Central—remarkably different Atlantic and Mediterranean coastlines, cosmopolitan cities, and sleepy villages. From its Swisslike Alps to its Italianesque Riviera, and from the Spanish Pyrénées to das German Alsace, you can stay in France, feel like you've sampled much of Europe, and never be more than a short stroll from a good *vin rouge*.

And for extra travel thrills, this book takes you north through the best of Belgium and the Netherlands. Surrounded by mega-Europe, the Low Countries ("low" because nearly half the land is below sea level) are easy to overlook. But we've spliced it into our France guide so that your travel memories can include some Bruges lace, Belgian waffles, a dike hike, and a few Dutch masters. If ever an area was a travel cliché come true, it's the Low Countries.

After years of researching and tour guiding together, Rick Steves has teamed up with Francophile Steve Smith to write this book. Together we give you the region's top destinations and tips on how to use your time and money most efficiently. France, Belgium, and the Netherlands are a many-faceted cultural fondue. Each of our recommended destinations is a dripping forkful (complete with instructions to enjoy the full flavor without burning your tongue).

This book covers the predictable biggies and mixes in a healthy dose of "Back Door" intimacy. Along with the Eiffel Tower, Mont St. Michel, and the French Riviera, you'll take a bike tour of the Loire, marvel at 15,000-year-old cave paintings, and walk the walls of a medieval fortress city. You'll find a *magnifique* castle perch to catch a Dordogne Valley sunset,

ride Europe's highest mountain lift, and touch the quiet
Romanesque soul of village Burgundy.

Rick Steves' France, Belgium, and the Netherlands is a tour
guide in your pocket—actually, two tour guides in your pocket.
Places covered are balanced to include the most famous cities
and intimate villages, from jet-setting beach resorts to the traditional heartland. We've been very selective, including only
the most exciting sights. For example, there are *beaucoup* beautiful châteaus surrounding Loire. We recommend the best
three. The best is, of course, only our opinion. But after 20
busy years of travel writing, lecturing, tour guiding, and Fran-
cophilia between us, we've developed a sixth sense for what
tickles the traveler's fancy.

This Information Is Accurate and Up-to-Date

This book is updated every year. Most publishers of guidebooks that cover a region from top to bottom can afford an
update only every two or three years (and even then, it's often
by letter). Since this book is selective, covering only the places
we think make the top month of sightseeing, we can update it
each summer. Even with an annual update, things change. But
if you're traveling with the current edition of this book, we
guarantee you're using the most up-to-date information available. This book will help you have an inexpensive, hassle-free
trip. *Use this year's edition.* Saving a few bucks by traveling on
old information is not smart. If you're packing an old book,
you'll learn the seriousness of your mistake . . . in Europe.
Your trip costs at least $10 per waking hour. Your time is valu-
able. This guidebook saves lots of time.

Planning Your Trip

This book is organized by destinations. Each of these destinations is a minivacation on its own, filled with exciting sights and
homey, affordable places to stay. For each chapter, you'll find:

Planning Your Time, a suggested schedule with thoughts
on how to best use your limited time.

Orientation material, including tourist information, city
transportation, and an easy-to-read map designed to make the
text clear and your arrival smooth.

Sights with ratings: ▲▲▲—Don't miss; ▲▲—Try hard
to see; ▲—Worthwhile if you can make it; No rating—Worth
knowing about.

Sleeping and **Eating,** with addresses and phone numbers of our favorite budget hotels and restaurants.

And **Transportation Connections** to nearby destinations by train and route tips for drivers.

The handy Appendix includes a climate chart, campground listings, telephone tips, and French survival phrases.

Browse through this book, choose your favorite destinations, and link them up. Then have a great trip! You'll travel like a temporary local, getting the absolute most out of every mile, minute, and dollar. You won't waste time on mediocre sights because, unlike other guidebooks, we cover only the best. Since your major financial pitfall is lousy expensive hotels, we've worked hard to assemble the best accommodations values for each stop. And, as you travel the route we know and love, we're happy you'll be meeting some of our favorite European people.

Trip Costs

Five components make up your trip costs: airfare, surface transportation, room and board, sightseeing, and shopping/entertainment/miscellany.

Airfare: Don't try to sort through the mess. Find and use a good travel agent. A basic round-trip U.S.A.–Paris flight costs $700–$1,100, depending on where you fly from and when. Always consider saving time and money in Europe by flying "open jaws" (into one city and out of another). Flying into Amsterdam and out of Paris costs roughly the same as flying round-trip to Paris. You can get cheaper round-trip flights to London or Amsterdam, but the cost of additional train tickets (to get you back to London or Amsterdam for your flight home) will eliminate most of your savings.

Surface Transportation: For a three-week whirlwind trip of our recommended destinations in France, allow $500 per person for public transportation (trains and key buses), or $650 per person for a three-week car rental (based on two people sharing), tolls, gas, and insurance. Car rental is cheapest if arranged from the U.S.A. Train passes are normally available only outside of Europe. You may save money by simply buying tickets as you go (see Transportation, below).

Room and Board: You can thrive in France and the Low Countries on $60 a day per person for room and board. With good information, even Paris is affordable. A $60-a-day budget allows $10 for lunch, $15 for dinner, and $35 for lodging (based on two people splitting the cost of a $70 double room that includes breakfast). That's doable. Students and tightwads do it on $40 ($20 per bed, $15–$20 for meals and snacks). But budget sleeping and eating require the skills and information covered later in this chapter.

Sightseeing: In big cities, figure $5–$8 per major sight (Louvre-$8, Anne Frank House-$6), $2 for minor ones (climbing church towers), $10 for guided walks, $25 for bus tours and splurge experiences (concerts in Paris' Sainte-Chapelle or the Chamonix gondola). An overall average of $15 a day works for most. Don't skimp here. After all, this category directly powers most of the experiences all the other expenses are designed to make possible.

Shopping/Entertainment/Miscellany: This can vary from nearly nothing to a small fortune. Figure $2 per ice cream cone, coffee, or soft drink, and $10 to $30 for evening entertainment. Good budget travelers find that this category has little to do with assembling a trip full of life-long and wonderful memories.

Exchange Rates
We've priced things in this book in the local currency:
    5 French francs (F) = about $1
    30 Belgian francs (BF) = about $1
    1 Dutch guilder (f) = about 70 cents

Prices, Times, and Discounts
The prices in this book, as well as the hours and telephone numbers, are accurate as of late 1996. Europe is always changing, and we know you'll understand that this, like any other guidebook, starts to yellow even before it's printed.

In Europe—and in this book—you'll be using the 24-hour clock. After 12:00 noon, keep going—13:00, 14:00, and so on. For anything over 12, subtract 12 and add p.m. (for example, 14:00 is 2 p.m.).

This book lists peak-season hours for sightseeing attractions. Off-season, expect generally shorter hours and more lunchtime breaks.

While discounts for sights and transportation are not listed in this book, seniors (60 and over), students (with International Student Identification Cards), and youths (under 18) often get big discounts—but only by asking.

When to Go

Late spring and fall are best. Wildflowers proliferate in May and June, while September brings the grape harvest and drier weather. In late October, France glistens in fall colors. Europeans vacation in July and August, jamming the Riviera and the Alps (August is worst). While many French businesses close in August, the traveler hardly notices. Winter travel is OK—you'll find gray, generally mild weather in the south, cold weather in the north, and rain everywhere. While Holland is a festival of flowers in the spring, the Low Countries have considerably shorter summers and drearier winters than southern France. Sights and tourist-information offices keep shorter hours, and some tourist activities (like English-language castle tours) vanish altogether.

Sightseeing Priorities

Depending on the length of your trip, here are our recommended priorities. The material in this book could keep you wonderfully entertained for a month in France, Belgium, and the Netherlands.

France:

3 days:	Paris, Versailles
5 days, add:	Normandy
7 days, add:	Loire
10 days, add:	Dordogne, Carcassonne
14 days, add:	Burgundy, Provence
18 days, add:	Riviera, Chamonix
21 days, add:	Alsace, Champagne

(This includes everything on the three-week route to match the map that follows.)

Belgium and the Netherlands: With cheap flights from the U.S.A., minimal culture shock, almost no language barrier, and a super-well-organized tourist trade, the Low Countries are a good place to start a European trip.

2 days:	Amsterdam, Haarlem
3–4 days, add:	Bruges
5–6 days, add:	Brussels
7 days, add:	Side trips from Amsterdam (e.g., Arnhem)

Whirlwind (Kamikaze) Three-Week Tour of France by Car

Day

1   Fly into Paris, pick up car, visit Giverny and/or Rouen, overnight in Honfleur (save Paris sightseeing for end of trip).

2   9:00, depart Honfleur; 10:00, Caen WWII museum; 12:00, drive to Arromanches for lunch and museum; 15:00, American cemetery; 16:00, Point du Hoc; 17:00, German cemetery, dinner and overnight in Bayeux.

3   9:00, Bayeux tapestry and church; 13:30, Mont St. Michel; 16:00, drive to Dinan; 17:00, arrive in Dinan for one Brittany stop; sleep in Dinan.

4   10:00, depart Dinan, drive to Loire; 14:00, tour Chambord; 17:00, arrive in Amboise; sleep in Amboise.

5   8:45, depart; 9:00, Chenonceaux; 11:30, Cheverny château and lunch; 14:00, (possible stop in Chaumont) back in Amboise for Leonardo's house and free time in town; sleep in Amboise.

Whirlwind Three-Week Tour of France

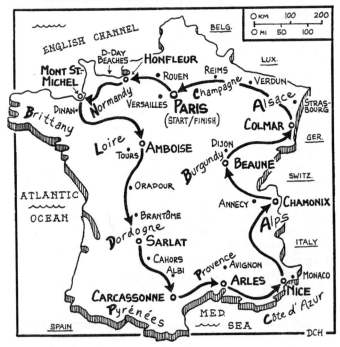

6   8:30, depart, morning stop in Chauvingy, lunch at Mortemart; 13:30, Oradour-sur-Glane; 14:30, drive to Beynac; 17:30, tour Beynac castle; dinner and overnight in Beynac.

7   9:00, free browse and maybe market in Sarlat; 12:00, Font de Gaume tour; 14:00, more caves or canoe extravaganza; dinner and sleep in Beynac.

8   9:00, depart Beynac; 10:00, short stop at Cahors bridge; 12:30, arrive Albi, couscous lunch; 14:00, tour church and Toulouse-Lautrec museum; 16:00, depart for Carcassonne; 18:00, explore, have dinner, and sleep in Carcassonne.

9   10:30, depart; 11:00, Lastours castles; 15:30, Pont du Gard; 16:30, drive to Arles; 17:30, set up for evening in Arles.

10   All day for Arles and Avignon, evening back in Arles.

11   8:30, depart; 9:00, les Baux; 11:00, depart; 12:00, lunch and wander in Isle sur la Sorgue; 14:00, Luberon hilltown drive; 16:00, depart for Nice; 19:00, arrive Nice or Antibes.

12   Sightsee in Nice and Monaco, sleep again in Nice or Antibes.

13   Morning free, 12:00 drive north, sleep at Clelles.

14   Morning drive north, stop in Annecy, afternoon arrive in Chamonix. With clear weather do Aiguille du Midi.

15   All day for Alps.

Key Drive Times

Paris–Giverny: 1.5 hrs	Carcassonne–Peyrepertuse: 2 hrs
Giverny–Rouen: 1 hr	Peyrepertuse–Collioure: 1.5 hrs
Rouen–Honfleur: 1.5 hrs	Carcassonne–Pont du Gard/Arles: 3 hrs
Honfleur–Caen: 1 hr	Arles/Avignon–Nice: 3.5 hrs
Caen–Bayeux: .5 hr	Nice–Clelles: 5 hrs
Bayeux–Mont St. Michel: 1.5 hrs	Clelles–Annecy: 2 hrs
Mont St. Michel–Dinan: 1 hr	Annecy–Chamonix: 1 hr
Dinan–Amboise: 4.5 hrs	Chamonix–Beaune: 4 hrs
Amboise–Oradour: 3.5 hrs	Beaune–Colmar: 3.5 hrs
Oradour–Beynac: 2.5 hrs	Colmar–Verdun: 4 hrs
Beynac–Albi: 3 hrs	Verdun–Reims: 1 hr
Albi–Carcassonne: 2 hrs	Reims–Paris: 1.5 hrs

16   9:00, depart; 12:00, lunch in Brancion; 14:00, depart; 15:00, arrive in Beaune for Hotel Dieu and wine tasting; sleep in Beaune.
17   9:00, depart for Burgundy village treats or get to Alsace early. Arrive in Colmar after 3.5-hour drive.
18   9:00, Unterlinden museum; 10:00, free in town; 14:00, Wine Road villages; evening back in Colmar.
19   8:00, depart; 12:00, lunch and tour Verdun battlefield; 15:00, depart; 16:00, arrive Reims, church and champagne; 18:00, turn in car at Reims, picnic dinner celebration on train; 21:00, collapse in Paris hotel.
20   Sightsee Paris.
21   Sightsee Paris, tour over.

Red Tape and Business Hours
You need a passport but no visa or shots to travel in France, Belgium, and the Netherlands.

In any season, you'll find much of rural France closed from 12:00–14:00. Lunch is sacred. On Monday many businesses are closed until 14:00, and often all day. Many small markets, *boulangeries* (bakeries), and the like are open Sunday morning until 12:00. Beware: many sights stop admitting people 30 minutes before they close.

PTT (Postal, Telegraph, and Telephone) offices' hours vary, though most are open 8:00–19:00 weekdays and 8:00–12:00 Saturday. (Small-town PTTs close for lunch 12:00–14:00.) Stamps are also sold at the *tabac* (tobacco shop).

Banking
Bring traveler's checks in dollars along with some plastic (ATM, credit, or debit cards).

Regular banks have the best rates for cashing traveler's checks. For a large exchange, it pays to compare rates and fees. The Bank of France (Banque de France) offers the best rates but is generally located only in larger cities. Post offices, train stations, and tourist offices usually change money if you can't get to a bank. Post offices (which take cash or American Express checks) give a good rate, have longer hours, and charge no fee.

To get a cash advance from bank machines (generally the best way to get cash in francs), you'll need a four-digit PIN (numbers only, no letters) with your Visa or MasterCard. Some ATM bankcards will work at some banks, though Visa and MasterCard are more reliable. Before you go, verify with your bank that your card will work. You're well advised to bring two copies of the same card; demagnetization seems to be a common problem. And beware that the distances between these machines can be great (no problem in Paris), and bring traveler's checks as backup.

Just like at home, credit (or debit) cards work easily at larger hotels, restaurants, and shops, but smaller businesses prefer payment in local currency. Smart travelers function with hard local cash.

Don't be petty about changing money. The greatest avoidable money-changing expense is having to waste time every few days returning to a bank. Change ten days' or two weeks' worth of money, get big bills, stuff it in your money belt, and travel!

French banking hours vary, though most are open 9:00–16:30 Tuesday–Friday. Some branches open Saturday morning, and many close on Monday.

The Language Barrier

You've no doubt heard that the French are "mean and cold and refuse to speak English." This is an out-of-date preconception left over from the de Gaulle days. The French are as friendly as any other people. Parisians are no more disagreeable than New Yorkers. And, without any doubt, the French speak more English than Americans speak French. Be reasonable in your expectations: Small-town French postal clerks are every bit as speedy, cheery, and multilingual as ours are back home.

With an understanding of French culture, you're less likely to misinterpret the French people. The French take great pride in their culture, clinging to their belief in cultural superiority despite the fact that they're no longer a world superpower. Let's face it, it's tough to keep on smiling when you've been crushed by a Big Mac, lashed by Levis, and drowned in instant coffee. To the French, America must seem a lot like Ross Perot in a good mood. The French are cold only if you decide to see them that way. Look for friendliness and give them the benefit of the doubt. The fine points of culture, not rugged Yankee individualism, are respected here.

Communication difficulties in France are exaggerated. To hurdle the language barrier, bring a small English/French dictionary, a phrase book (look for ours), a menu reader, and a good supply of patience. If you learn only five phrases, learn and use these: *bonjour* (good day), *merçi* (thank you), *pardon* (pardon me), *s'il vous plaît* (please), and *au revoir* (goodbye). The French place great importance on politeness.

The French are language perfectionists—they take their language (and other languages) seriously. Often, they speak more English than they let on. This isn't a tourist-baiting tactic but timidity on their part to speak another language less than fluently. Start any conversation with *"Bonjour, Madame/ Monsieur. Parlez-vous anglais?"* and hope they speak more English than you speak French. In transactions, a small notepad and pen minimize misunderstandings about prices—have vendors write the price down.

In Belgium and the Netherlands, forget the language barrier. Except in smaller untouristy towns, most young or well-educated people speak English (along with other languages). In southern Belgium, French is foremost, and in northern Belgium and the Netherlands it's Dutch, but English is a close second.

Travel Smart

Upon arrival in a new town, lay the groundwork for a smooth departure. Reread this book as you travel, and visit local tourist information offices. Buy a phone card and use it for reservations and confirmations. Enjoy the friendliness of the local people. Ask questions. Most locals are eager to point you in their idea of the right direction and tell you about their town's history. Wear your money belt, pack a pocket-size notepad to organize your thoughts, and see simplicity as a virtue. Those who expect to travel smart, do. Plan ahead for banking, laundry, post office chores, and picnics. Maximize rootedness by minimizing one-night stands. Mix intense and relaxed periods. Every trip (and every traveler) needs at least a few slack days. Pace yourself. Assume you will return.

As you read through this book, note special days (festivals, colorful market days, and days when sights are closed). Sundays have pros and cons, as they do for travelers in the U.S.A. (special events and weekly markets, limited hours, shops and banks closed, limited public transportation, no rush hours). Saturdays are virtually weekdays (with most places open until lunchtime). Popular places are even more popular on weekends.

Tourist Information

The tourist information office is your best first stop in any new city. If you're arriving in town after they close, try calling ahead or picking up a map in a neighboring town. In this book, we'll refer to a tourist office as a TI (for Tourist Information). Throughout France and the Low Countries, you'll find TIs are usually well-organized and English-speaking. Most will help you find a room by calling hotels (for a small fee) or giving you a complete listing of bed and breakfasts available. Towns with much tourism generally have English-speaking guides available for private hire (about $100 for a 90-minute guided town walk).

The French call their TIs by different names—Syndicat d'Initiative, Office de Tourisme, Bureau de Tourisme, or Information Touristique. French TIs are often closed 12:00–14:00.

Tourist Offices, U.S.A. Addresses

Each country's national tourist office in the U.S.A. is a wealth of information. Before your trip, request any specific information you may want (such as city maps and schedules of upcoming festivals). The Worldwide Web offers much, much more information for travelers adept at cyberspace. For the latest in Paris, log on to http://www.Pariscope.Fr/.

France: Strangely, the French office in the U.S.A. has only a 95-cents-per-minute toll number: 900/990-0040. You can write to 444 Madison Ave., 16th Floor, New York, NY, 10022; or 9454 Wilshire Boulevard, Beverly Hills, CA 90212.

Belgium: 780 Third Ave., Suite 1501, New York, NY 10017 (tel. 212/758-8130, fax 212/355-7675).

Netherlands: 225 N. Michigan Ave., #1854, Chicago, IL 60601 (tel. 888/GO-HOLLAND for automated response, 312/819-1500 for real person).

Recommended Guidebooks

Consider some supplemental travel information, especially if you're traveling beyond our recommended destinations. Considering the improvements they'll make in your $3,000 vacation, $25 or $35 for extra maps and books is money well spent. One simple budget tip can easily save the price of an extra guidebook.

France: *The Lonely Planet Guide to France* is well-researched and packed with good maps and hotel recommendations for low to moderate budget travelers. The highly opinionated *Let's Go: France* (St. Martin's Press) is great for students and vagabonds. The popular skinny green Michelin Guides are dry but informative, especially if you're driving. They're known for their city and sightseeing maps, concise and helpful information on all major sights, and good cultural and historical background. English editions, covering most of the regions you'll want to visit, are sold in France for about $12. (They cost $20 in the U.S.A.) The *Paris Access* guide is loaded with helpful information and neighborhood walking tours for those who plan a longer visit. Of the multitude of other guidebooks on France and Paris, many are high on facts and low on opinion, guts, or personality.

Belgium and the Netherlands: For the same reason that this region only appears as an add-on to our France book, the Low Countries seem to fall through the cracks in most travel publishers' catalogs. You'll find skimpy chapters in the big all-Europe books or too much information in the various city or country guidebooks covering the region.

Rick Steves' Books and Videos

Rick Steves' Europe Through the Back Door (John Muir Publications, 1997) gives you budget travel tips on minimizing jet lag, packing light, planning your itinerary, traveling by car or train, finding budget beds without reservations, changing money, avoiding rip-offs, outsmarting thieves, hurdling the language barrier, staying healthy, taking great photographs, using your bidet, and lots more. The book also includes chapters on 40 of Rick's favorite "Back Doors."

Rick Steves' Country Guides are a series of eight guidebooks covering Europe, Britain/Ireland, Italy, Spain/Portugal, Germany/Austria/Switzerland, Scandinavia, and the Baltics/Russia, just as this one covers France, Belgium, and the Netherlands. These are updated annually and come out in January.

Europe 101: History and Art for the Traveler (cowritten with Gene Openshaw, John Muir Publications, 1996) gives you the story of Europe's people, history, and art. Written for smart people who were sleeping in their history and art classes before they knew they were going to Europe, *101* really helps Europe's sights come alive.

Mona Winks (also cowritten with Gene Openshaw, John Muir Publications, 1996) gives you fun, easy-to-follow self-guided tours of Europe's top 20 museums, including Amsterdam's Rijksmuseum and Van Gogh Museum, and Paris' Louvre, Orsay Museum, Pompidou Modern Art Museum, and Palace of Versailles, along with an historic Paris walk.

Our newest book is *Rick Steves' French Phrase Book* (John Muir Publications, 1997), which gives you the words and survival phrases you'll need while traveling in France and much of Belgium.

My television series, *Travels in Europe with Rick Steves*, includes eight half-hour shows on France, Belgium, and the Netherlands. These may reair on your local PBS station or the Travel Channel, and they're also available as information-packed videotapes, along with my two-hour slideshow lecture on France (call us at 206/771-8303 for our free newsletter/catalog). Two more France shows should be released with my fourth series late in 1997.

Maps
The maps in this book, drawn by Dave Hoerlein, are concise and simple. Dave, who is well-traveled in France and the Low Countries, has designed the maps to help you locate recommended places and get to the tourist offices, where you'll find more in-depth maps (often free) of the cities or regions.

Don't skimp on maps. Excellent Michelin maps are available throughout France (for 28F, half the U.S.A. price) at bookstores, newsstands, and gas stations. Train travelers can do fine with Michelin's #989 France map (1:1,000,000). For serious navigation, pick up the yellow 1:200,000 scale maps. Drivers should consider the soft-cover Michelin France atlas (the entire country at 1:200,000, well-organized in a $20 book with an index and maps of major cities). Learn the Michelin key to get the most sightseeing value out of their maps.

Transportation

By Car or Train?
Cars are best for three or more traveling together (especially families with small kids), those packing heavy, and those scouring the countryside. Trains and buses are best for solo travelers, blitz tourists, and city-to-city travelers.

Trains

Train stations are almost always centrally located in cities, making hotel hunting and sightseeing easier. Schedules change by season, weekend, and weekday. Verify any train schedule shown in this book.

France's rail system (SNCF) sets the pace in Europe. Its super TGV system has inspired bullet trains throughout the world. The TGV runs on its own track at 170 to 220 mph. Rails are fused into one long continuous track for a faster and smoother ride. The TGV has changed commuting patterns in much of France and put most of the country within day-trip distance of Paris. The new Eurostar English Channel tunnel train to Britain is just another link in the grand European train system of the 21st century.

While Eurailpasses work well, those traveling solely within France will save money with a France Railpass (available outside of France only, through your travel agent or ETBD—call 206/771-8303 for our free railpass guide). For about the cost of a Paris–Avignon–Paris ticket, you get any three days of travel (within a month) anywhere in France and

Cost of Public Transportation

1997 FRANCE FLEXIPASS

	1st class	2nd class
Any 3 days in a month*	$198	$160
Additional days (max 6)	30	30
France Flexi Companion**148.⁵⁰ ea.	..	120 ea.

*Kids 4-11 half fare.
**3 days in a month, 2 people traveling together on all journeys, extra days (6 max) $30 ea. No "Companion" kids discounts.

FRANCE RAIL 'N DRIVE PASS

Any 3 days of rail and 2 days of car in a month.

car category	1st class	2nd class	extra car day
A-Economy	$189	$159	$44
B-Small	209	179	64
C-Medium	229	199	84
D-Small automatic	219	189	74

France:
Point-to-point 2nd class rail fares in $US.

Rail 'n Drive prices are approximate per person, two traveling together. Solo travelers pay about $100 extra, third and fourth members of a group need only buy the equivalent flexi railpass. Extra rail days (maximum of 6) cost $30 first class or $30 second class per day. You can add up to 6 extra car days.

can add up to six additional days for the cost of a two-hour ride each. (The Flexi Saver pass gives two traveling together a 25 percent discount.) Each day of use allows you to take as many trips as you want in a 24-hour period (you could go from Paris to Chartres, see the cathedral, then continue to Avignon, stay a few hours, and end in Nice). Buy second-class tickets in France for shorter trips and spend your valuable rail-pass days wisely.

If traveling sans railpass, inquire about the many point-to-point discount fares possible (youths, those over 60, married couples, families, and others qualify).

Reservations are generally unnecessary except for the TGV trains (20F and up) and for *couchettes* (berths, 100F) on night trains. Even railpass holders need reservations for the TGV "bullet trains." Validate *(composter)* all train tickets and reservations in the orange machines located before the plat-forms. (Watch others and imitate.)

Cars, Rail 'n' Drive Passes, and Buses

Car rental is cheapest if arranged in advance through your hometown travel agent. The best rates are weekly with unlim-ited mileage, or leasing (see below). You can pick up and drop off just about anywhere, any time. Big companies have offices in most cities. Small rental companies can be cheaper but aren't as flexible.

When you drive a rental car, you are liable for its replace-ment value. CDW insurance (Collision-Damage Waiver) gives you the piece of mind that comes with a zero-deductible cover-age—for about $14 a day. A few "gold" credit cards provide this coverage for free if you use their card for the rental (quiz your credit card company on the worst-case scenario). You can buy CDW coverage from Travel Guard for $4 a day. (Your travel agent has details.)

For a trip of three weeks or more, leasing is a bargain. By technically buying and then selling back the car, you save lots of money on insurance (CDW is included) and tax. Leas-ing requires a 22-day minimum contract, which you arrange in the U.S.A.

You can rent a car on the spot just about anywhere. In many cases this is a worthwhile splurge. All you need is your American license and money (about 300F, or $60, for a day with 100 km).

In the Netherlands, Campanje offers cut-rate camper and Vanagon rentals (Box 9332, 3506 GH Utrecht, Netherlands, tel. 31/30/244-7070, fax 31/30/242-0981 E-mail campanje@worldaccess.nl). They have a creative program offering short-term, long-term, camping gear, rent and buy/sell-back deals.

Rail 'n' drive passes let you economically mix car and train travel (available outside of France only, through your travel agent or ETBD at 206/771-8303). Generally, big city connections are best done by train, and rural regions are best scoured with the freewheeling mobility of a car. With a rail 'n' drive pass, you get an economic "flexi" railpass and the chance to add on a few "flexi" car days at the weekly car rental rate rather than the budget-busting daily rate. This allows you to combine rail and drive into one pass—you can take advantage of the high speed and comfort of the TGV trains for longer trips, and rent a car for as little as one day at a time for those regions that are difficult to get around in sans car (like the Loire, the Dordogne, and Provence), all for a very reasonable package price. Within the same country, you can pick a car up in one city and drop it off in another city with no problem.

Another good car/train solution is combining a one-way car rental from Paris to Nice (seeing Normandy, the Loire, the Dordogne, Carcassonne, and Provence) with a railpass back to Paris (via Chamonix, Burgundy, and the Alsace). This allows you to take advantage of weekly car rental rates (for the parts of France most deserving of a car) and France's cheap railpass deals.

Regional buses take over where the trains stop. You can get almost anywhere by rail and bus if you're well-organized and patient. Review our bus schedule information and always verify times at the tourist office or bus station, calling ahead when possible. On Sunday regional bus service virtually disappears.

Regional minivan excursions offer organized day tours of regions where bus and train service is virtually useless. For the D-Day beaches, châteaus of the Loire Valley, sightseeing in the Dordogne Valley, and wine tasting in Burgundy, we identify small companies providing this extraordinarily helpful service at reasonable rates.

Driving

The hardest thing about driving in France is not stopping at every mouth-watering bakery and *pâtisserie* you pass.

International driver's licenses are not necessary. Seat belts are mandatory, and children under age 10 must be in the back seat. Gas is expensive: about $4 per gallon. It's most expensive on autoroutes (you'll save about $4 a tank by filling up at a supermarket).

Go metric. A liter is about a quart, four to a gallon. A kilometer is six-tenths of a mile. I figure kilometers to miles by cutting them in half and adding back 10 percent of the original (120 km: 60 + 12 = 72 miles, 300 km: 150 + 30 = 180 miles).

Four hours of autoroute tolls cost about $20, but the alternative to these super "feeways" is often being marooned in rural traffic. Autoroutes usually save enough time, gas, and nausea to justify the splurge. Mix scenic country road rambling with high-speed "autorouting."

Roads in France are classified into departmental (D), national (N), and autoroutes (A). D routes (usually yellow lines on maps) are slow and often the most scenic. N routes (usually red lines) are the fastest after autoroutes (orange lines). Green road signs are for national routes, blue for autoroutes. There are plenty of good facilities, gas stations, and rest stops along most French roads.

Here are a few French road tips: In city centers, traffic merging from the right normally has the right of way (*priorité à droite*). Approach intersections cautiously. When navigating through cities, stow the map and follow the signs to *centre-ville* (downtown), and from there to the tourist-information office. When leaving (or just passing through), follow the *Toutes Directions* or *Autres Directions* (meaning anywhere else) signs until you see a sign for your specific destination. Be careful of sluggish tractors on country roads. While the French are eating (12:00–14:00), many sights (and gas stations) are closed, so you can make great time driving. The French drive fast and love to tailgate.

Parking is a headache in the larger cities, and theft is a problem throughout France. Pay to park at well-patrolled lots or use the parking meters, which are usually free 12:30–14:00 and 19:00–9:00, and in August. Keep a pile of 1F and 2F coins in your ashtray for parking meters, public restrooms, and laundromat dryers.

Biking

Throughout France and the Low Countries, you'll find areas where public transportation is limited and bicycle touring is an excellent idea. We've listed bike rental shops where appropriate. The TI will always have the best listing. For a good touring bike, allow about $14 for a half day and $18 for a full day.

Telephones and Mail

Make local and long distance calls from the public phones on the street. A super-efficient vandal-resistant, card-operated system has virtually replaced coin-operated public phones throughout Europe. The coin-free card system is a breeze to use. Each country offers phone cards, good for use only within its borders. Buy a phone card, available at any post office, train station, and most newsstands and tobacco shops (*tabac* in France). When you use the card (simply take the phone off the hook, insert the card, and wait for a dial tone), the price of the call (local or international) is automatically deducted. Buy a card at the beginning of your trip and use it for hotel reservations, calling tourist information offices, and phoning home.

France: France has a new dial-direct ten-digit telephone system. There are no area codes. To call to or from anywhere in France, including Paris, you dial the ten numbers directly. In late 1996, the old eight-digit numbers each gained two new numbers at the start. If you encounter an old eight-digit number, update it by simply adding that region's two lead numbers to it (Paris-01; northwest France's Loire, Normandy, and Brittany numbers now start with 02; northeast France's Burgundy and Alsace, 03; southeast France's Provence, Riviera, and the Alps, 04; southwest France's Dordogne, 05).

To dial out of France, you must start your call with its international code: 00. To call France from another country, start with the international access code of the country you're calling from (00 for most European countries and 011 from America), then dial France's country code (33), then drop the lead 0 of the ten-digit local number and dial the remaining nine digits. For example, the number of our favorite hotel in Paris is 01 47 05 49 15. To call it from home, dial 011-33-1 47 05 49 15. For a listing of international access codes and country codes, see the Appendix.

In France, the cheapest phone card (*une petite*) costs 40F; the most expensive (*une grande*) is 90F.

Belgium and the Netherlands: Both countries use area codes throughout. In this book, you'll find the area code under the Sleeping header in each chapter. For instance, Bruges' area code is 050. To call Bruges long distance from within Belgium, dial 050, then the local number. When calling from another country, drop the first zero in the area code. Calling Bruges from Amsterdam, you'd dial 09 (Netherlands' international access code), 32 (Belgium's country code), 50 (Bruges' area code without the zero), then the local number.

U.S.A. Direct Services: Calling home from Europe is easy from any kind of phone if you have an AT&T, MCI, or Sprint calling card. Each card company has a toll-free number in each European country that puts you in touch with an English-speaking operator. The operator takes your card number and the number you want to call, puts you through, and bills your home phone number for the call (at the cheaper U.S.A. rate of about $3 for the first minute and a dollar a minute after that, plus a $2.50 service charge). You'll save money on calls of three minutes or more. Hanging up when you hear an answering machine is a $5 expense. Use a small-value coin or a French, Belgian, or Dutch phone card to call home for five seconds—long enough to say "call me," or to make sure an answering machine is off so you can call back, using your U.S.A. Direct number to connect with a person. European time is six/nine hours ahead of the east/west coast of the U.S.A. For a list of AT&T, MCI, and Sprint calling card operators, see the Appendix. U.S.A. Direct services are a rip-off for calls between European countries. Call direct using coins or a European phone card.

Mail: To arrange for mail delivery, reserve a few hotels along your route in advance and give their addresses to friends, or use American Express Company's mail services (available to anyone who has at least one Amex traveler's check). Allow ten days for a letter to arrive. Phoning is so easy that we've dispensed with mail stops altogether.

Sleeping

In France and the Low Countries, accommodations are a good value and easy to find. Choose from one- or two-star hotels, bed and breakfasts, youth hostels, and campgrounds. We like places that are clean, small, central, traditional, inexpensive, friendly, and not listed in other guidebooks. Most places we list have at least five of these seven virtues.

Sleep Code

To give maximum information with a minimum of space, we use these codes to describe accommodations listed in this book. Prices listed are per room, not per person.

S = Single room (or price for one person in a double).

D = Double or Twin. French double beds can be very small.

T = Triple (generally a double bed with a single).

Q = Quad (usually two double beds).

b = Private bathroom with toilet and shower or tub

t = Private toilet only. (The shower is down the hall.)

s = Private shower or tub only. (The toilet is down the hall.)

CC = Accepts credit cards (Visa, MasterCard, American Express). If CC isn't mentioned, assume you'll need to pay cash.

SE = Speaks English. This code is used only when it seems predictable that you'll encounter English-speaking staff.

NSE = Does not speak English. Used only when it's unlikely you'll encounter English-speaking staff.

* = French hotel rating system, ranging from zero to four stars.

According to this code, a couple staying at a "Db-250F, CC:V, SE" hotel would pay a total of 250 French francs (or about $50) for a double room with a private bathroom. The hotel accepts Visa or French cash in payment, and the staff speaks English.

Hotels

In this book, the price for a double room will normally range from $25 (very simple, toilet and shower down the hall) to $140 (maximum plumbing and more), with most clustering around $60. Rates are higher in Paris and in more touristy cities. A triple and a double are often the same room, with a small double bed and a sliver single, so a third person sleeps very cheaply. Most hotels have a few singles, triples, and quads. While groups sleep cheap, traveling alone can be expensive—a single room usually costs about the same as a double. Rooms are safe. Still, keep cameras and money out of sight. In Europe towels aren't routinely replaced every day; drip-dry and conserve.

French receptionists are often reluctant to mention the cheaper rooms. Study the room price list posted at the desk.

Understand it. You'll save about $15 on the average if you ask for (and they have) a room *sans douche* (without shower, rather than *avec douche*, with shower) and just use the public shower down the hall. A room with a bathtub (*salle de bain*) costs $5 to $10 more than a room with a shower (*douche*). A double bed (*grand lit*) is $5 to $10 cheaper than twins (*deux petits lits*). Hotels are inclined to give you a room with a tub (which the French prefer). If you prefer a double bed and a shower, you need to ask for it—and you'll save up to $20. If you'll take twins or a double, ask for a *chambre pour deux* (room for two) to avoid being needlessly turned away.

The French have a simple hotel rating system (zero through four stars) depending on the amenities offered. We like the one- or two-star hotels. More than two stars gets you expensive and unnecessary amenities. Unclassified hotels (no stars) can be bargains or depressing dumps. Look before you leap, and lay before you pay. You'll almost always have the option of breakfast at your hotel—pleasant, convenient, but— at 25F to 50F—often double the price of the corner café. While hotels hope you'll spring for their breakfast, this is optional unless otherwise noted. In places where demand exceeds supply, many French hotels require their summertime guests to take half-pension; that is, breakfast and either lunch or dinner. It adds around 100F per person and can be a poor value. The yellow *logis de France* sign posted at the door indicates a particularly good value.

France is littered with inexpensive, sterile, ultra-modern hotels, usually located on cheap land just outside of town. The antiseptically clean Formule 1 chain is most popular. While far from quaint, these can be a fine value (140F–165F per room for up to three people).

If that French Lincoln-log pillow isn't your idea of comfort, American-style pillows (and extra blankets) are usually in the closet or available on request. Ask for *"Un oreiller, s'il vous plaît"* (un oar-ray-yay, see-voo-play).

Making Reservations

It's possible to travel at any time of year without reservations, but given the high stakes, erratic accommodations values, and the quality of the gems we've found for this book, we'd highly recommend calling ahead for rooms a day or two in advance as you travel. When tourist crowds are down, you might make a habit of calling between 9:00 and 10:00 on the day you plan to arrive, when the hotel knows who'll be checking out and just which rooms will be available. We've taken great pains to list telephone numbers with long-distance instructions (see Telephones and Mail, above, and the Appendix). Use the telephone and the convenient telephone cards. Most hotels listed are accustomed to English-only speakers. A hotel receptionist will trust you and hold a room until 17:00 (5:00 p.m.) without a deposit, though some will ask for a credit card number. Honor (or cancel by phone) your reservations. Long distance is cheap and easy from public phone booths. Don't let these people down—we promised you'd call and cancel if for some reason you won't show up. Don't needlessly confirm rooms through the tourist office; they'll take a commission.

If you know exactly which dates you need and really want a particular place, reserve a room well in advance before you leave home. This is especially important for Paris, which can be jammed during conventions (May, June, September, and October are worst). To reserve from home, call, fax, or write the hotel. Phone and fax costs are reasonable, and simple English is usually fine. To fax, use the form in the Appendix. If you're writing, add the zip code and confirm the need and method for a deposit. A two-night stay in August would be "2 nights, 16/8/97 to 18/8/97"—European hotel jargon uses your day of departure. You'll often receive a letter back requesting one night's deposit. A credit card will usually be accepted as a deposit, though you may need to send a signed traveler's check or a bank draft in the local currency. If your credit card is the deposit, you can pay with your card or cash when you arrive. If you don't show up, you'll be billed for one night. Reconfirm your reservations a day in advance for safety. (By the way, we personally visited 90 percent of the hotels listed in this book in May of 1996. At least 90 percent of those visited had available rooms to show us.)

Bed & Breakfasts

B&Bs offer double the cultural intimacy for less than most hotel rooms. TIs have listings for each town.

France: *Chambres d'Hôte (CH)* are found mainly in the smaller towns and countryside. They are listed by the owner's family name. While some post small *Chambres* or *Chambres d'Hôte* signs in their front windows, many are found only through the local tourist office. Doubles with breakfast cost around 200F (breakfast may or may not be included—ask). This is a great way to get beneath the surface with French locals. While your hosts will rarely speak English, they will almost always be enthusiastic and a delight to share a home with.

Belgium and the Netherlands: B&Bs in the Low Countries are common in well-touristed areas. Hosts are usually English-speaking and interesting conversationalists. Local TIs can book you into a B&B much cheaper than a hotel. B&Bs are more important for budget travelers here than in France.

Hostels

Hostels charge about $14 per bed. Get a hostel card before you go. Travelers of any age are welcome if they don't mind dorm-style accommodations or meeting other travelers. Travelers without a hostel card can generally spend the night for a small extra "one-night membership" fee. Cheap meals are sometimes available, and kitchen facilities are usually provided for do-it-yourselfers. Expect crowds in the summer, snoring, and lots of youth groups in the spring. Family rooms are sometimes available on request, but it's basically boys' dorms and girls' dorms. You usually can't check in before 17:00 and must be out by 10:00. There is often a 23:00 curfew. Official hostels are marked with a triangular sign that shows a house and a tree. In France ask for an *auberge de jeunesse*.

Camping

In Europe camping is more of a social than an environmental experience. It's a great way for American travelers to make European friends. Camping costs about $12 per camp site per night, and almost every destination recommended in this book has a campground within a reasonable walk or bus ride from the town center and train station. A tent and sleeping bag are all you need. Many campgrounds have small grocery stores and washing machines, and some even come with discos and miniature golf. Hot showers are better at campgrounds than at many hotels. Local tourist information offices have camping information. Serious campers should use the *Michelin Camping Guide*, available in most French bookstores, or the more thorough *Guide Officiel Camping/Caravaning (Fédération Française de Camping et de Caravaning)*.

Eating in France

The French eat long and well. Two-hour lunches, three-hour dinners, and endless hours sitting in outdoor cafés are the norm. They have a legislated 39-hour workweek and a self-imposed 35-hour eat-week. The French spend much of their five annual weeks of paid vacation around the dinner table. Local cafés, cuisine, and wines become a highlight of any French adventure—sightseeing for your palate. Even if the rest of you is sleeping in cheap hotels, let your tastebuds travel first-class in France. (They can go coach in England.) You can eat well without going broke, but choose carefully: you're just as likely to blow a small fortune on a mediocre meal as you are to dine wonderfully for $15.

Restaurants

You can order *à la carte* like the locals do, or get the no-brainer *menu*, which is a fixed-price meal offering three or four courses—and generally a good value. The fixed-price menu gives you your choice of soup, appetizer, or salad; choice of three or four main courses (*plats*) with vegetables; cheese course and/or a choice of desserts. Service is included, but wine or drinks are extra. (Remember, in France an *entrée* is a first course and *le plat* is the main course.) *Le plat* or *le plat du jour* is just the main course with vegetables (usually 50F to 70F). For a light, healthy, fast and inexpensive option in a pricey restaurant (or a restaurant offering more ambiance than value), the various salads are 40F to 50F well spent. Soft drinks and beer cost 8F–20F ($1.50–$4), and a bottle or carafe of house wine—which is invariably good enough for Rick, if not always Steve—costs 30F–70F ($6–$14). Service is always included.

French Café Culture

French cafés (or *brasserie*) provide reasonable light meals and a refuge from museum and church overload. They are carefully positioned viewpoints from which to watch the river of local life flow by. It's easier for the novice to sit and feel comfortable in a café when you know the system.

Cafés charge different prices for the same drink depending upon where you want to be seated. Prices are posted: *comptoir* (counter/bar) and the more expensive *salle* (seated). The standard menu items are the *Croque Monsieur* (grilled cheese sandwich) and *Croque Madame* (Monsieur with a fried egg on top). The *salade compose* (com-po-zay) is a hearty chef's salad. Sandwiches are least expensive but plain. To get more than a piece of ham (*jambon*) on a baguette, order a sandwich *jambon-crudite* (crew-dee-tay), which means garnished with lettuce, tomatoes, cucumbers, and so on. Omelettes come lonely on a plate with a basket of bread. The *plat du jour* (daily special) is your fast, hearty 50F hot plate (main course and vegetables). Whatever you order, remember bread is free (to get more just hold up your bread basket and ask, "*encore s'il vous plait*"), and the words for tap water are *une carafe d'eau* (oon caraf doe). House wine at the bar is cheap (5F–10F per glass, cheapest by the *pichet*), and the local beer is cheaper on tap (*une pression*) than in the bottle (*bouteille*). While prices include service, tip, and tax, it's polite to leave the coins for a drink or meal well served.

Breakfast

Petit déjeuner (peh-tee day-zhu-nay) is typically *café au lait* (espresso with hot milk), hot chocolate, or tea; a roll with butter and marmalade; and a croissant. Don't expect much variety for breakfast, but the bread is fresh and the coffee is great. While available at your hotel (25F–50F), breakfasts are cheaper at the corner café. It's entirely acceptable to buy a croissant or roll at a nearby bakery and eat it with your (single) cup of coffee (no refills) at a café. If the morning egg urge gets the best of you, drop into a café and order *une omelette* or *oeufs sur le plat* (fried eggs). You could also buy or bring plastic bowls and spoons from home, buy a box of French cereal and a small box of milk, and eat in your room before heading out for coffee. We carry a package of Vache Qui Rit (Laughing Cow) cheese and fruit to supplement the morning jelly.

Lunch

For lunch—*déjeuner* (day-zhuh-nay)—we picnic or munch a take-away *boulangerie* sandwich. French picnics can be first-class affairs and adventures in high cuisine. Be daring. Try the smelly cheeses, ugly pâtés, sissy quiches, and minuscule yogurts. Local shopkeepers are accustomed to selling small quantities of produce. Try the tasty salads to go and ask for *une fourchette en plastique* (a plastic fork).

Gather supplies early; you'll probably visit several small stores to assemble a complete meal, and many close at noon.

Look for a *boulangerie* (bakery), a *crémerie* (cheeses), a *charcuterie* (deli items, meats, and pâtés), an *épicerie* or *alimentation* (small grocery with veggies, drinks, and so on), and a *pâtisserie* (delicious pastries). Open-air markets (*marchés*) are fun and photogenic. Local *supermarchés* offer less color and cost, more efficiency, and adequate quality. Department stores often have supermarkets in the basement. On the outskirts of cities, you'll find the monster *hypermarchés*. Drop in for a glimpse of hyper-France in action.

If not picnicking, look for food stands selling take-out sandwiches and drinks, or *crêperies* or *brasseries* for fast and easy sit-down restaurant food. *Brasseries* are cafés serving basic fare such as omelets, chicken, and fries, as well as simple sandwiches and hearty salads. Look for their *plat du jour*, the daily special. Many French restaurants offer good value, three- to five-course menus at lunch only. The same menu is often 30F more at dinner. Drivers find roadside *frites* trailers selling fries, hot snacks, drinks, and so on. (See Café Culture, above.)

Dinner

For *dîner* (dee-nay), choose restaurants filled with locals, not places with big neon signs boasting, "We Speak English." When you're on the road, look for the red and blue *Relais Routier* decal, indicating that the place is recommended by the truckers' union. If the menu (*la carte*) isn't posted outside, move along. Also look for set-price *menus*. Ask the waiter for help deciphering *la carte*. Go with his recommendations and anything *de la maison* (of the house). Galloping gourmets should bring a menu translator (the *Marling Menu Master* is excellent). Remember, if you ask for a *menu*, you'll get a meal (*la carte* is the list of what's cooking), and if you ask for an *entrée*, you'll get an appetizer. The wines are often listed in a separate *carte des vins*. Tipping (*pourboire*) is unnecessary, though if you enjoyed the service, it's polite to leave a few francs.

Drinks

In stores, unrefrigerated soft drinks and beer are one-third the price of cold drinks. Milk and boxed fruit juice are the cheapest drinks. Avoid buying drinks to go at streetside stands; you'll find them far cheaper in a shop. Try to keep a water bottle with you. Water quenches your thirst better and cheaper than anything you'll find in a store or café. We drink tap water throughout France and the Low Countries.

To get a free pitcher of tap water at a French restaurant, ask for *une carafe d'eau*. Otherwise, you may unwittingly buy bottled water. (*L'eau du robinet* is tap water in French.) When ordering a beer at a café or restaurant, ask for *une pression* or *un demi* (draft beer), which is cheaper than bottled. When ordering table wine at a café or restaurant, ask for a pitcher, *un pichet* (pee-shay), again cheaper than a bottle. If all you want is a glass of wine, ask for *un verre de vin*. Wine-wise, you could drink away your children's inheritance if you're not careful. The most famous wines are the most expensive, while lesser-known taste-alikes remain a bargain (see our regional suggestions for ideas). If you like brandy, try Armagnac, cognac's cheaper twin brother. *Pastis*, the standard *apéritif*, is a sweet anise or licorice drink which comes on the rocks with a glass of water. Cut it to taste with lots of water. France's best beer is Alsatian; try Krônenburg or the heavier Pelfort. For a fun, bright, nonalcoholic drink, order *un diabolo menthe* (7-Up with mint syrup). The ice cubes melted after the last Yankee tour group left.

Stranger in a Strange Land

We travel all the way to Europe to enjoy differences—to become temporary locals. You'll experience frustrations. Certain truths that we find "God-given" or "self-evident," like cold beer, ice in drinks, bottomless cups of coffee, hot showers, body odor smelling bad, and bigger being better, are suddenly not so true. One of the benefits of travel is the eye-opening realization that there are logical, civil, and even better alternatives. The fact that Americans treat time as a commodity can lead to frustrations when dealing with other cultures. For instance, while an American "spends" or "wastes" time, a French person merely "passes" it. A willingness to go local (and at a local tempo) ensures that you'll enjoy a full dose of European hospitality.

If there is a negative aspect to the European image of Americans, we can appear big, loud, aggressive, impolite, rich, and a bit naive. While Europeans look bemusedly at some of our Yankee excesses—and worriedly at others—they nearly always afford us individual travelers all the warmth we deserve.

Back Door Manners

While updating this book, we heard over and over again that our readers are considerate and fun to have as guests. Thank you for traveling as temporary locals who are sensitive to the culture. It's fun to follow you in our travels.

Tours of France by Rick Steves and Steve Smith

At Europe Through the Back Door, we organize and lead tours covering the highlights of this book: our favorite three weeks in France. These depart each year from April through October, are limited to 25 people per group, have two guides, big buses with lots of empty seats, and come in "fully guided," "bus, bed, and breakfast" (less structured and cheaper) and "slow dance with France" flavors. For details, call us at 206/771-8303.

Send Us a Postcard, Drop Us a Line

If you enjoy a successful trip with the help of this book and would like to share your discoveries, please send any tips, recommendations, criticisms, or corrections to us at Europe Through the Back Door, Box 2009, Edmonds, WA 98020. We personally read and value all feedback. Sending us a postcard or trip report gets you on our free newsletter list.

For our latest travel information, tap into our web site: http://www.ricksteves.com, or find us on America Online (key word: Rick Steves). Our E-mail address is ricksteves@aol.com. Anyone is welcome to request a free issue of our Back Door quarterly newsletter.

Judging from all the positive feedback and happy postcards we receive from travelers who have used this book, it's safe to assume you're on your way to a great vacation—independent, inexpensive, and with the finesse of an experienced traveler.

From this point, "we" (your co-authors) will shed our respective egos and become "I."

Thanks, and *bon voyage!*

BACK DOOR TRAVEL PHILOSOPHY
As Taught in *Rick Steves' Europe Through the Back Door*

Travel is intensified living—maximum thrills per minute and one of the last great sources of legal adventure. Travel is freedom. It's recess, and we need it.

Experiencing the real Europe requires catching it by surprise, going casual . . . "Through the Back Door."

Affording travel is a matter of priorities. (Make do with the old car.) You can travel—simply, safely, and comfortably—anywhere in Europe for $60 a day plus transportation costs. In many ways, spending more money only builds a thicker wall between you and what you came to see. Europe is a cultural carnival, and time after time, you'll find that its best acts are free and the best seats are the cheap ones.

A tight budget forces you to travel close to the ground, meeting and communicating with the people, not relying on service with a purchased smile. Never sacrifice sleep, nutrition, safety, or cleanliness in the name of budget. Simply enjoy the local-style alternatives to expensive hotels and restaurants.

Extroverts have more fun. If your trip is low on magic moments, kick yourself and make things happen. If you don't enjoy a place, maybe you don't know enough about it. Seek the truth. Recognize tourist traps. Give a culture the benefit of your open mind. See things as different but not better or worse. Any culture has much to share.

Of course, travel, like the world, is a series of hills and valleys. Be fanatically positive and militantly optimistic. If something's not to your liking, change your liking. Travel is addicting. It can make you a happier American, as well as a citizen of the world. Our Earth is home to nearly 6 billion equally important people. It's humbling to travel and find that people don't envy Americans. They like us, but with all due respect, they wouldn't trade passports.

Globetrotting destroys ethnocentricity. It helps you understand and appreciate different cultures. Travel changes people. It broadens perspectives and teaches new ways to measure quality of life. Many travelers toss aside their hometown blinders. Their prized souvenirs are the strands of different cultures they decide to knit into their own character. The world is a cultural yarn shop. And Back Door Travelers are weaving the ultimate tapestry. Come on, join in!

PARIS

Paris offers sweeping boulevards, sleepy parks, world-class art galleries, chatty crêpe stands, Napoleon's body, sleek shopping malls, the Eiffel Tower, and people-watching from outdoor cafés. Climb the Notre-Dame and the Eiffel Tower, cruise the Seine and the Champs-Élysées, and master the Louvre and Orsay museums. Save some after-dark energy for one of the world's most romantic cities. Many people fall in love with Paris. Some see the essentials and flee, overwhelmed by the huge city. With the proper approach and a good orientation, you'll fall head over heels for Europe's capital city.

Planning Your Time
Best of Paris in Two Days
Day 1
Morning: Historic walk featuring Île de la Cité, Notre-Dame, Latin Quarter, and Sainte-Chapelle.

Afternoon: Métro to Arc de Triomphe and walk down the Champs-Élysées and through the Tuilleries. Tour the Louvre late, when it's less crowded and half-price.

Day 2
Morning: Pick up your art history where the Louvre left off by touring the Orsay Gallery. For more Impressionism, visit the Rodin Museum (enjoy a picnic lunch in its garden). Historians may prefer paying homage to Napoleon and his military museum at Les Invalides across the street. Poets will enjoy a moveable feast for lunch on the rue Cler.

Paris

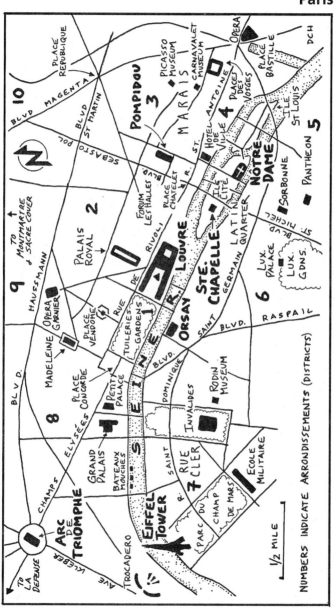

Afternoon: Métro to Bastille to do the Marais walk (described later in this chapter).
Alternative options: Take the Marais walk in the morning, and see the Orsay after lunch. At 15:00, take an RER trip efficiently from Orsay to Versailles to see the palace and its park late without the crowds.
Twilight: Métro to Trocadero for a closer look at the Eiffel Tower.
Touristy night options: Seine cruise, Montmartre, Latin Quarter. The Pompidou Modern Art Gallery is the only museum open late.

Orientation

Paris is split in half by the Seine River, divided into 20 *arrondissements* (proud and independent governmental jurisdictions), and circled by a ring-road freeway (the *périphérique*). You'll find Paris easier to negotiate if you know which side of the river you're on, which *arrondissement* you're in, and which subway (Métro) stop you're closest to. Remember, if you're north of the river (above on any city map), you're on the Right Bank (*rive droite*), and if you're south of it, you're on the Left Bank (*rive gauche*).

Arrondissements are numbered, starting at Notre-Dame (ground zero) and moving in a clockwise spiral out to the ring road. The last two digits in a Parisian postal code are the *arrondissement* number, and the notation for the Métro stop is "Mo." In Parisian jargon, Napoleon's tomb is on *la rive gauche* (the Left Bank) in the 7ème (*arrondissement*), postal code 75007, Mo: Invalides. Paris Métro stops are a standard aid in giving directions.

Tourist Information

Avoid the Paris TIs—long lines, short information, and a 5F charge for maps. This book, the *Pariscope* magazine (described below), and one of the freebie maps available at any hotel are all you need for a short visit. The main TI is at 127 avenue des Champs-Élysées (open 9:00–20:00), but the TIs at the Eiffel Tower and train stations are handier. You'll find TIs at these train stations: Gares de Lyon, Montparnasse, Austerlitz, Nord, and Est. Hours: 8:00–20:00, except at Austerlitz, which closes at 15:00 during off-season.

The *Pariscope* weekly magazine (or one of its clones, 3F, at any newsstand) lists museum hours, concerts and musical festivals, plays, movies, nightclubs, and special art exhibits. For a complete list of museum hours and scheduled English museum tours, pick up the free *Musées, Monuments Historiques, et Expositions* booklet from any museum.

While it's easy to pick up free maps of Paris once you've arrived (your hotel has them), they don't show all the streets, and you may want the huge Michelin #10 map of Paris. For an extended stay, consider the pocket-size *Paris par Arrondissement* map book, as well as two fine guidebooks: *Michelin Green Guide* (somewhat scholarly) and the more readable *Paris Access Guide*.

There are many English-language bookstores in Paris where you can pick up guidebooks (for nearly double their American price). A few are: Shakespeare and Co. (lots of used travel books, 37 rue de la Boucherie, across the river from Notre-Dame, 12:00–24:00), W. H. Smith (248 rue de Rivoli), and Brentanos (37 avenue de L'Opéra).

The American Church is a nerve center for the American èmigrè community and distributes the *Free Voice*, a handy monthly English-language newspaper, with useful reviews of current events in Paris, and *France—U.S.A. Contacts*, an advertisement paper, full of useful information for those looking for work or long-term housing (facing the river between Eiffel and Orsay at 65 quai d'Orsay, Métro: Invalides).

Arrival in Paris

By Train: Paris has six train stations, all connected by Métro and bus, most with banks and tourist information offices. The train station you arrive at (or leave from) depends on where you came from (or where you're going). The Gare de l'Est serves the east; the Gare du Nord and Gare St. Lazare serve northern and central Europe; the Gare d'Austerlitz and Gare du Lyon cover southern Europe, and the newly revamped Gare Montparnasse handles western France and TGV service to France's southwest. (Any train station can give you schedule information, make reservations, and sell tickets for any destination.) From any station, enter the Métro and head to the stop nearest your hotel. Buying tickets is handier at your neighborhood travel agency—worth their small fee (SNCF signs in their window indicate they sell train tickets). For schedule information, tel. 01 36 35 35 35 (2.50F/minute).

By Plane: For detailed information on getting from Paris's airports to downtown Paris (and vice versa), see Transportation Connections at the end of this chapter.

Helpful Hints

Museums: The Louvre and many other museums are closed on Tuesday, and the Orsay and Rodin museums, and Versailles are closed Monday. Most offer reduced prices and shorter hours on Sunday. Many begin closing rooms 30 minutes before the actual closing time. For the fewest crowds, visit very early, at lunch, or very late. The best Impressionist art museums are the Orsay, Marmottan, and L'Orangerie (all described below). Most museums have shorter hours October–March. French holidays (Jan. 1, May 1, May 8, July 14, Nov. 1, Nov. 11, and Dec. 25) can really mess up your sightseeing plans.

Mona Winks: This guidebook (by Rick Steves and Gene Openshaw) is particularly heavy on Paris, with extensive self-guided walking tours of the Louvre, the Orsay, the Pompidou Gallery, Versailles, and the Historic Core of Paris.

The Paris Museum Pass: In Paris there are two classes of sightseers: those with this pass and those without. Serious sightseers save time (no lines) and money by getting this pass. Sold at museums, main Métro stations, and tourist offices, it pays for itself in two admissions and gets you into sights with no lining up (one day-70F, three consecutive days-140F, five consecutive days-200F). Included sights (and admission prices without the pass) you're likely to visit are: Louvre (45F), Orsay (36F), Sainte-Chapelle (32F), Arc de Triumphe (32F), Army Museum and Napoleon's Tomb (35F), Pompidou Gallery (35F), Carnavalet Museum (28F), Conciergerie (28F), Sewer Tour (25F), Cluny Museum (28F), Notre-Dame towers (27F) and crypt (27F), L'Orangerie (28F), Picasso Museum (28F), Rodin Museum (28F), House of Victor Hugo (25F), and the elevator to the top of the Grand Arche de La Defense (40F). Outside Paris, the pass covers the Palace of Versailles (45F) and its Grand Trianon (25F) and Château Chantilly (35F). Notable sights not covered: Marmottan Museum, Eiffel Tower, Montparnasse Tower, the ladies of Pigalle, and Disneyland Paris. Tally it up—but remember, a major advantage of the pass is that you skip to the front of all lines—saving hours of waiting in the summer. And with the pass, you'll pop painlessly into sights that you're walking by (even for a few minutes) that you'd otherwise probably skip (e.g., Notre-Dame crypt, Cluny Museum, Victor Hugo's place). The free museum and monuments directory that comes with your pass is handy, with the latest hours, phone numbers, and specifics on which kids pay. The cut-off age for free entry varies from 5 to 18. Most major, serious art museums let young people up to 18 in for free. For some reason, anyone over age 5 has to pay to tour the sewers. Note: pass holders still have to stand in security check lines.

    Toilets: Carry small change for pay toilets, or walk into any outdoor café like you own the place and find the toilet in the back. Remember, the toilets in museums are free and generally the best you'll find. Modern super-sanitary street booths provide both relief and a memory.

    Theft Alert: Use your money belt, and never carry a wallet in your back pocket or a purse over your shoulder. Thieves target tourists at tourist areas, in subway stations, and on the Métro.

    Telephone Cards: Pick up the essential France *tèlécarte* at any *tabac*, post office, or tourist office (*une petite carte* is 40F; *une grande* is 90F). Smart travelers check things by telephone. Most public phones use these cards.

    Useful Telephone Numbers: American Hospital, 01 46 41 25 25; American pharmacy, 01 47 42 49 40 (Opéra); Police, 17; U.S. Embassy, 01 43 12 22 22; Paris and France directory assistance, 12; AT&T operator, 19 00 11; MCI, 19 00 19; Sprint, 19 00 87. (See Appendix for additional numbers.)

Getting Around Paris

By Métro: Europe's best subway is divided into two systems—the Métro (puddle-jumping everywhere in the city) and the RER (which makes giant speedy leaps around town and connects suburban destinations). You'll be using the Métro for almost all your trips. In Paris you're never more than a ten-minute walk from a Métro station. One ticket takes you anywhere in the system with unlimited transfers. Save 40 percent by buying a *carnet* (car-nay) of ten tickets for 46F at any Métro station (a single ticket is 7.50F). Métro tickets work on city buses, though one ticket cannot be used as a transfer between subway and bus.

    The *Formule 1* pass (30F) allows unlimited travel for a single day on all bus and Métro lines. If you're staying longer, the *Carte d'Orange* pass gives you free run of the bus and Métro system for one week (67F and a photo, ask for the *Carte d'Orange*

Coupon Vert) or a month (230F, ask for the *Carte d'Orange Coupon Orange*). The weekly pass begins Monday and ends Sunday, and the monthly pass begins the first day of the month and ends the last day of that month, so midweek or midmonth purchases are generally not worthwhile. All passes can be purchased at any Métro station (most have photo booths).

To get to your destination, determine which "Mo." stop is closest to your destination and which line(s) will get you there. The lines have numbers, but they're best known by their *direction* or end-of-the-line stop. (For example, the Saint-Denis/Châtillon line runs between Saint-Denis in the north and Châtillon in the south.)

Once in the Métro station, you'll see blue-on-white signs directing you to the train going in your direction (e.g., *direction: Saint-Denis*). Insert your ticket in the automatic turnstile, pass through, reclaim and *keep your ticket until you exit the system* (fare inspectors accept no excuses from anyone). Transfers are free and can be made wherever lines cross. When you transfer, look for the orange *correspondance* (connections) signs when you exit your first train, then follow the proper "direction" sign.

Before you *sortie* (exit), check the helpful *plan du quartier* (map of the neighborhood) to get your bearings, locate your destination, and decide which *sortie* you want. At stops with several *sorties*, you can save lots of walking by choosing the best exit. Remember your essential Métro words: *direction, correspondance* (connections), *sortie* (exit), *carnet* (cheap set of ten tickets), and *donnez-moi mon porte-monnaie!* (Give me back my wallet!) Thieves thrive in the Métro.

By RER: The **RER** (Réseau Express Régionale, pronounced ehr-uh-ehr) suburban train system (thick lines on your subway map identified by letters A, B, C, etc.) works like the Métro but is much speedier because it makes only a few stops within the city. One Métro ticket is all you need for RER rides within Paris. You can transfer between the Métro and RER systems with the same ticket, and unlike the Métro, you need to insert your ticket in a turnstile to exit the RER system. To travel outside the city (to Versailles or the airport, for example), you'll need to buy another ticket at the station window before boarding, and make sure your stop is served by checking the signs over the train platform (not all trains serve all stops).

By City Bus: The trickier bus system is worth figuring out. Métro tickets are good on both bus and Métro, though you can't use the same ticket to transfer between the two systems. One ticket gets you anywhere in central Paris, but if you leave the city center (shown as section 1 onboard the bus diagram), you must validate a second ticket. While the Métro shuts down about 00:45, some buses continue much later. Schedules are posted at bus stops.

Big system maps, posted at each bus and Métro stop, display the routes. Individual route diagrams show the exact route of the lines serving that stop. Major stops are painted on the side of each bus. Enter through the front doors. Punch your Métro ticket in the machine behind the driver, or pay the higher cash fare. Get off the bus using the rear door. Even if you're not certain you've figured it out, do some joyriding (outside of rush hour). Lines #24, #63, and #69 are Paris' most scenic routes and make a great introduction to the city. Bus #69 is particularly handy, running between the Eiffel Tower, the recommended hotels around rue Cler, the Orsay Gallery, the Louvre, the Marais/Bastille area (more recommended hotels), and the Père Lachaise Cemetery.

By Taxi: Parisian taxis are almost reasonable. A ten-minute ride costs about 50F (versus 5F to get anywhere in town on the Métro). You can try waving one down, but it's easier to ask for the nearest taxi stand (*"oo-ay la tet de stah-see-oh taxi"*) or ask your hotel to call for you. Sunday and night rates are higher, and if you call from your hotel, the meter starts as soon as the call is received. Taxis are tough to find on Friday and Saturday night, especially after the Métro closes.

Sights—The "Historic Core of Paris" Walk

These sights are best done as described in this "best first four hours in Paris historic walk." Start your visit where the city did—on the Île de la Cité—facing the Notre-Dame and following the dotted line on the "Heart of Paris" map. (This information is distilled from the Historic Paris Walk chapter in *Mona Winks* by Gene Openshaw and Rick Steves.) To get to the Notre-Dame, ride the Métro to Cité, Hotel de Ville, or St-Michel and walk to the big square facing the . . .

▲▲**Notre-Dame Cathedral**—The 700-year-old cathedral is packed with history and tourists. Study its sculpture (Notre-Dame's forte) and windows, take in a Mass, eavesdrop on guides, and walk all around the outside. (Open daily 8:00–18:45; treasury

Heart of Paris

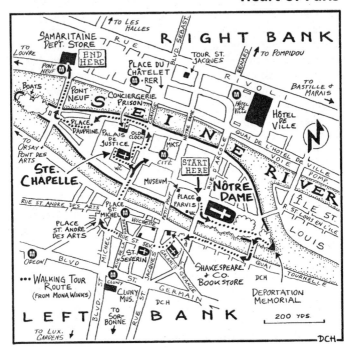

15F, open 9:30–17:30. Ask about the free English tours, normally Wednesday and Thursday at noon. Clean 2.50F toilets in front of the church near Charlemagne's statue.) Sunday Masses are at 8:00, 8:45, 10:00, 11:30, 12:30, and 18:30. Climb to the top for a great gargoyle's-eye view of the city (entrance on outside, north tower open 9:30–17:30, closed at lunch and earlier off-season, Métro: Cité). You get more than 400 stairs for only 27F.

The **Cathedral facade** is the worth a close look. The church is dedicated to "Our Lady" ("Notre-Dame"). Mary is center stage—cradling Jesus, surrounded by the halo of the rose window. Adam is on the left, and Eve is on the right.

Below Mary and above the arches is a row of 28 statues known as the Kings of Judah. During the French Revolution, these Biblical kings were mistaken for the hated French kings. The citizens stormed the church, crying, "Off with their heads." All were decapitated but have since been recapitated.

Speaking of decapitation, look at the carving above the doorway on the left. The man with his head in his hands is St. Denis. Back when there was a Roman temple on this spot, Christianity began making converts. The fourth-century bishop of Roman Paris, Denis, was beheaded. But these early Christians were hard to keep down. The man who would become St. Denis got up, tucked his head under his arm, and headed north until he found just the right place to meet his maker: Montmartre, which means "mountain of the martyr." The Parisians were convinced of this miracle, Christianity gained ground, and a church soon replaced the pagan temple.

Medieval art was OK if it embellished the house of God and told Bible stories. For a fine example, move to the base of the central column (at the foot of Mary, about where the head of St. Denis could spit if he was real good). Working around from the left, find God telling a barely created Eve, "Have fun but no apples." Next, the the sexiest serpent I've ever seen makes apples *à la mode*. Finally, Adam and Eve, now ashamed of their nakedness, are expelled by an angel. This is a tiny example (featuring a story most of us know) in a church covered with meaning.

Now move to the right and study the carving above the central portal. It's the end of the world, and Christ sits on the throne of Judgment (just under the arches, holding his hands up). Below him, an angel and a demon weigh souls in the balance. The "good" stand to the left, looking up to heaven. The "bad" ones to the right are chained up and led off to . . .Versailles on a Tuesday. The "ugly" ones must be the crazy sculpted demons to the right, at the base of the arch.

Wander through the interior. You'll be routed around the ambulatory, much as medieval pilgrims would have been. Don't miss the rose windows filling each of the transepts. Back outside, walk around the church through the park on the riverside for a close look at the flying buttresses.

The neo-Gothic 90-meter spire is a product of the 1860 reconstruction. Around its base are apostles and evangelists (the green men) as well as Viollet-le-Duc, the architect in charge of the work. Notice how the apostles look outward, blessing the city, while the architect (at top, seen from behind the church) looks up, admiring his spire.

The archaeological crypt is worth your time and money if you're interested in Roman Paris (enter 100 yards in front of

church, 27F, daily 10:00–18:00). You'll see Roman ruins, trace
the street plan of the medieval village, and see diagrams of how
the earliest Paris grew and grew, all thoughtfully explained in
English.

If you're hungry near Notre-Dame, the only grocery store
on the Île de la Cité is tucked away on tiny rue Chanoinesse
running parallel to the church, 1 block north (9:00–13:30,
16:00–20:30, closed Sunday). Plan a picnic for the quiet bench-
filled park immediately behind the church (public WC).

Behind the Notre-Dame, squeeze through the tourist
buses, cross the street, and enter the iron gate into the park at
the tip of the island.

▲▲**Deportation Memorial ("Mémorial de la Déporta-
tion")**—This memorial to the 200,000 French victims of the
Nazi concentration camps draws you into their experience. As
you descend the steps, the city around you disappears. Surrounded by walls, you have become a prisoner. Your only freedom is your view of the sky and the tantalizing glimpse of the
river below.

Enter the dark, single-file chamber ahead. Inside, the circular plaque in the floor reads, "They descended into the
mouth of the earth and they did not return."

A hallway stretches in front of you, lined with 200,000
lighted crystals, one for each French citizen that died. Flicker-
ing at the far end is the eternal flame of hope. The tomb of the
unknown deportee lies at your feet. Above, the inscription
reads, "Dedicated to the living memory of the 200,000 French
deportees sleeping in the night and the fog, exterminated in
the Nazi concentration camps."

Above the exit as you leave is the message you'll find at all
Nazi sights: "Forgive but never forget." (Free, open daily
8:30–21:45, weekends and holidays from 9:00, less off-season,
east tip of the island near Île St. Louis, behind Notre-Dame,
Métro: Cité.)

Île St-Louis—Back on street level, look across the river to the
Île St-Louis. If the Île de la Cité is a tug laden with the history
of Paris, it's towing this classy little residential dinghy laden
only with boutiques, characteristic restaurants, and famous sorbet shops. This island wasn't developed until much later (18th
century). What was a swampy mess is now harmonious
Parisian architecture. The pedestrian bridge (Pont Saint Louis)
connects the two islands leading right to rue Saint Louis en

l'Île. This spine of the island is lined with interesting shops. A short stroll takes you to the famous Bertillon ice cream parlour (#31). Loop back to the pedestrian bridge along the parklike quays (walk north to the river and turn left). This riverside walk is about as peaceful and romantic as Paris gets.

Before walking to the opposite end of the Île de la Cité, loop through the Latin Quarter (as indicated on the map). From the Deportation Memorial, cross the bridge onto the Left Bank and enjoy the riverside view of the Notre-Dame for a block or two. At the little park, venture inland a few blocks, basically arcing through the Latin Quarter and returning to the island three bridges down at place St-Michel.

▲**The Latin Quarter**—This area, which gets its name from the language used here when it was an exclusive medieval university district, lies between the Luxembourg Gardens and the Seine, centering around the Sorbonne University and boulevards St. Germain and St. Michel. This is the core of the Left Bank—it's crowded with international eateries, far-out bookshops, street singers, and jazz clubs. For colorful wandering and café-sitting, afternoons and evenings are best. (Métro: St. Michel.)

Along rue Saint-Severin you can still see the shadow of the medieval sewer system. (The street slopes into a central channel of bricks.) In the days before plumbing and toilets, when people still went to the river or neighborhood wells for their water, "flushing" meant throwing it out the window. Certain times of day were flushing times. Maids on the fourth floor would holler *"Garde de l'eau!"* ("Look out for the water!") and heave it into the streets, where it would eventually wash down into the Seine.

The **Cluny Museum,** a treasure trove of medieval art, fills the old Roman baths, offering close-up looks at stained glass, Notre-Dame carvings, fine goldsmithing and jewelry, and rooms of tapestries—the best of which is the exquisite *Lady with the Unicorn.* In five panels, a delicate-as-medieval-can-be noble lady introduces a delighted unicorn to the senses of taste, hearing, sight, smell, and touch (28F, daily 9:15–17:45, closed Tuesday, near the corner of boulevards St-Michel and St-Germain, tel. 01 43 25 62 00, Métro: Cluny).

Place St-Michel (facing the St-Michel bridge) is the traditional core of the Left Bank's artsy, liberal, hippie, Bohemian district of poets, philosophers, winos, and tourists. In less commercial times, place St-Michel was a gathering point for the city's malcontents and misfits. Here, in 1871, the citizens took the streets from the government troops, set up barricades *Les Miz*–style, and established the Paris Commune. In World War II, the locals rose up against their Nazi oppressors (read the plaques by the St. Michael fountain). And in the spring of 1968, a time of social upheaval all over the world, young students, battling riot batons and tear gas, took over the square and demanded change.

From place St-Michel, look across the river and find the spire of Sainte-Chapelle church and its weathervane angel. Cross the river on the Pont St-Michel and continue along boulevard du Palais. On your left you'll see the high-security doorway to Sainte-Chapelle. But first, carry on another 30 meters and turn right at a wide pedestrian street, the rue de Lutece.

Cité "Métropolitain" Stop—Of the 141 original turn-of-the-century subway entrances, this is one of 17 survivors now preserved as a national art treasure. The curvy, plant-like ironwork is a textbook example of Art Nouveau, the style that rebelled against the erector-set squareness of the Industrial Age (e.g., Mr. Eiffel's tower).

The flower market right there on place Louis Lepine is a pleasant detour. On Sundays this square chirps with a busy bird market. And across the way is the Prefecture de Police, where Inspector Clouseau of Pink Panther fame used to work, and where the local resistance fighters took the first building in August 1944 from the Nazis, leading to the allied liberation of Paris a week later.

Pause here to admire the view. Sainte-Chapelle is a pearl in an ugly architectural oyster, part of a complex of buildings that includes the Palace of Justice (to the right of Sainte-Chapelle, behind the fancy gates). Return to the entrance of Sainte-Chapelle. You'll need to pass through a metal detector to get in. Toilets are ahead, on the left. The line into the church may be long. (Museum card holders can go directly in; pick up the excellent English info sheet.) Enter the humble ground floor . . .

▲▲▲**Sainte-Chapelle**—The triumph of Gothic church architecture is a cathedral of glass like no other. It was speedily built from 1242 to 1248 for St. Louis IX (France's only canonized king) to house the supposed Crown of Thorns. Its architectural harmony is due to the fact that it was completed under the direction of one architect in only six years—unheard of in Gothic times. Notre-Dame took more than 200 years.

The design clearly shows an Old Regime approach to worship. The basement was for staff and other common folk. Royal Christians worshipped upstairs. The paint job, a 19th-century restoration, helps you imagine how grand this small jeweled chapel was.

Climb the spiral staircase to the *Chapelle Haute.* Fill the place with choral music, crank up the sunshine, face the top of the altar, really believe that the Crown of Thorns was there, and this becomes one awesome space.

"Let there be light." In the Bible, it's clear: light is divine. Light shining through stained glass was a symbol of God's grace shining down to earth. Gothic architects used their new technology to turn dark stone buildings into lanterns of light. The glory of Gothic shines brighter here than in any other church.

There are 15 separate panels of stained glass (6,500 square feet—two-thirds of it 13th-century original), with more than 1,100 different scenes, mostly from the Bible. In medieval times, scenes like these helped teach Bible stories to the illiterate.

The altar was raised up high, to better display the relic around which this chapel was built—the Crown of Thorns. The supposed Crown cost King Louis three times as much as this church. Today it is kept in the Notre-Dame Treasury and shown only on Good Friday.

Louis' little private viewing window is in the wall to the right of the altar. Louis, both saintly and shy, liked to go to church without dealing with the rigors of public royal life. Here he could worship still dressed in his jammies.

Lay your camera on the ground and shoot the ceiling. Those pure and simple ribs growing out of the slender columns are the essence of Gothic.

Books in the gift shop explain the stained glass in English. There are concerts (120F) almost every summer evening. (32F, daily 9:30–18:00 even Tuesday, off-season 10:00–16:30. Call 48 01 91 35 for concert information. Handy free public toilets just outside, Métro: Cité.)

Palais du Cité—Back outside, as you walk around the church exterior, look down and notice how much Paris has risen in the 800 years since Sainte-Chapelle was built. You're in a huge complex of buildings that has housed the local government since ancient Roman times. It was the site of the original Gothic palace of the early kings of France. The only surviving medieval parts are the Sainte-Chapelle church and the Conciergerie prison.

Most of the site is now covered by the giant Palais de Justice, home of France's supreme court (built in 1776). *"Liberté, Egalité, Fraternité"* over the doors is a reminder that this was also the headquarters of the revolutionary government.

Now pass through the big iron gate to the noisy boulevard du Palais and turn left (toward the right bank). On the corner is the site of the oldest public clock (1334) in the city. While the present clock is said to be Baroque, it somehow still manages to keep accurate time.

Turn left onto Quai de l'Horologe and walk along the river. The round medieval tower just ahead marks the entrance to the Conciergerie. Pop in to visit the courtyard and lobby (free). Step past the serious-looking guard into the courtyard.
Conciergerie—The Conciergerie, a former prison, is a gloomy place. Kings used it to torture and execute failed assassins. The leaders of the Revolution put it to similar good use. The tower next to the entrance, called "the babbler," was named for the painful sounds that leaked from it.

Look at the stark lettering above the doorways. This was a no-nonsense revolutionary time. Everything, even lettering, was subjected to the test of reason. No frills or we chop 'em off.

Step inside (the lobby, with an English-language history display, is free). Marie-Antoinette was imprisoned here. During a busy eight-month period in the Revolution, she was one of 2,600 prisoners kept here on their way to the guillotine. The interior (28F, daily 9:30–18:30, 10:00–17:00 in winter, good English), with its huge vaulted and pillared rooms, echoes with history but is pretty barren. You can see Marie-Antoinette's cell, housing a collection of her mementoes. In another room, a list of those made "a foot shorter at the top" by the "national razor" includes ex-King Louis XVI, Charlotte Corday (who murdered Marat in his bathtub), and the chief revolutionary who got a taste of his own medicine, Maximilien Robespierre.

Back outside, wink at the flak-vested guard, turn left, listen for babbles, and continue your walk along the river. Across the river you can see the rooftop observatory—flags flapping—of the Samaritaine Department store, where this walk will end. At the first corner, veer left past France's supreme court building and into a sleepy triangular square called place Dauphine. Marvel at how such quaintness could be lodged in the midst of such greatness as you walk through the park to the end of the island. At the equestrian statue of Henry IV, turn right onto the bridge and take refuge in one of the nooks on the Eiffel Tower side.

Pont Neuf—This "new bridge" is now Paris' oldest. Built during Henry IV's reign (around 1600), its 12 arches span the widest part of the river. The fine view includes the park on the tip of the island (note Seine tour boats), the Orsay Gallery, and the Louvre. These turrets were originally for vendors and street entertainers. In the days of Henry IV, who originated the promise of "a chicken in every pot," this would have been a lively scene.

Directly over the river, the first building you'll hit on the Right Bank is the venerable old department store, Samaritaine.

▲**Samaritaine Department Store Viewpoint**—Enter the store and go to the rooftop. Ride the glass elevator from near the Pont Neuf entrance to ninth floor (you'll be greeted by a WC, check out the sink). Pass the tenth floor *terrasse* for the 11th-floor *panorama* (tight spiral staircase; watch your head). Quiz yourself. Working counterclockwise, find: the Eiffel Tower, Invalides/ Napoleon's Tomb, Montparnasse Tower, Henry IV statue on the tip of the island, Sorbonne University, the dome of the Panthéon, Sainte-Chapelle, Notre-Dame, Hôtel de Ville (city hall), Pompidou Center, Sacré-Coeur, Opéra, and Louvre. The Champs-Élysées leads to the Arc de Triomphe. Shadowing that—even bigger, while two times as distant—is the Grand Arche la Defense. You'll find light, scenic meals on the breezy terrace and a supermarket in the basement. (Rooftop view is free, open daily, tel. 01 40 41 20 20. Métro: Pont Neuf.)

Sights—Paris' Museum Neighborhood

(These four museums are close together and listed in walking order.)

▲▲▲**The Louvre**—This is Europe's oldest, biggest, greatest, and maybe most-crowded museum. Don't try to cover the museum thoroughly. The 33F, 90-minute English-language tours, which leave six times daily except Sunday, boil this overwhelming museum down to size (tour tel. 01 40 20 52 09). Clever new 30F digital audio tours give you a receiver and a directory of about 130 masterpieces, allowing you to dial a (rather dull) commentary on included works as you stumble upon them. Rick's museum guidebook, *Mona Winks* (buy in U.S.A.), includes a self-guided tour of the Louvre. Pick up the free *Louvre Handbook in English* at the information desk under the pyramid as you enter.

If you can't get a guide, start in the Denon wing and visit these highlights (in this order): Michelangelo's *Slaves*, Ancient Greek and Roman (Parthenon frieze, *Venus de Milo*, Pompeii mosaics, Etruscan sarcophagi, Roman portrait busts, Nike of Samothrace); Apollo Gallery (jewels); French and Italian paintings in the Grande Galerie (a quarter-mile long and worth the hike); the *Mona Lisa* and her Italian Renaissance roommates; the nearby neoclassical collection *(Coronation of Napoleon)*; and the Romantic collection, with works by Delacroix *(Liberty at the Barricades*—see your 100F note) and Géricault *(Raft of the Medusa)*.

Admission 45F until 15:00, 26F after 15:00 and all day Sunday, free if you're under 18. Open daily 9:00–18:00; Wednesday until 21:30; closed Tuesday. You can enter the pyramid for free until 21:30. Go in at night and see it glow. Tel. 01 40 20 53 17 or 01 40 20 51 51 for recorded information. Métro: Palais-Royal/Musée du Louvre. Note: the old "Louvre" Métro stop called "Louvre Rivoli" no longer goes to the Louvre.

The newly renovated Richelieu wing and underground shopping mall extension add the finishing touches to *Le Grand Louvre Project* (that started in 1989 with the pyramid entrance). To explore this most recent extension of the Louvre, enter through the pyramid, then walk toward the inverted pyramid and uncover a post office, a Virgin Megastore, a dizzying assortment of eateries (up the escalator), and the Palais Royal Métro entrance. Stairs at the far end take you right into the Tuileries Gardens. (If there's a long line at the pyramid, these stairs may sneak you in much quicker.)

▲L'Orangerie—This small, quiet, and often-overlooked museum houses Monet's water lilies, many famous Renoirs, and a scattering of other Impressionist works. The two breezy round rooms of water lilies are two of the most enjoyable rooms in Paris (28F, open 9:45–17:00, closed Tuesday, located in the Tuileries Gardens near the place de la Concorde. Métro: Concorde).

Jeu de Paume—This one-time home to the Impressionist art collection (now located in the Musée d'Orsay) hosts rotating exhibits of top contemporary artists (35F, open 12:00–19:00, weekends 10:00–19:00, closed Monday, on place de la Concorde, just inside the Tuileries gardens on the rue de Rivoli side. Métro: Concorde).

▲▲▲**Orsay Museum**—This is Paris' 19th-century art museum (actually, art from 1848–1914), including Europe's greatest collection of Impressionist works (call for 36F English tour schedule, usually daily at 11:00, not Sunday). Start on the ground floor. The "pretty" conservative establishment art is on the right. Then cross left into the brutally truthful and, at that time, very shocking art of the realist rebels and Manet. Then ride the escalators at the far end (detouring at the top for a grand museum view) to the series of Impressionist rooms (Monet, Renoir, Dégas, et al.). Don't miss the Grand Ballroom (room 52, Arts et Decors de la IIIème Republique) and Art Nouveau on the mezzanine level. The museum is housed in a former train station (Gare d'Orsay) across the river and ten minutes downstream from the Louvre. (36F, 24F for the young and old, under 18 free, open late June through late September and all Sundays 9:00–18:00, other days 10:00–18:00, Thursday until 21:45, closed Monday, most crowded around 11:00 and 14:00; city museum passes are sold in the basement; if there's a long line you can skip it by buying one there; 1 rue Bellechasse, tel. 01 40 49 48 14, reception tel. 01 40 49 48 48; Métro: Solferino or, better, the RER: Musée d'Orsay. Note: From here it's a convenient straight shot to Versailles on the RER.)

Sights—Southwest Paris

▲▲▲**Eiffel Tower**—Crowded and expensive but worth the trouble. The higher you go, the more you pay. I think the view from the 400-foot-high second level is plenty. *Pilier Nord* (the north pillar) has the biggest elevator—with the fastest moving line. The Restaurant Belle France serves decent 100F meals (first level). Don't miss the entertaining free movie on the history of the tower on the first level. Heck of a view. It costs 20F to go to the first level, 40F to the second, and 56F to go all the way for the 1,000-foot view (not included with museum pass). On a budget? You can climb the stairs to the second level for only 12F (open daily 9:00–24:00, off-season 9:30–23:00, tel. 01 44 11 23 23, Métro: Trocadero, RER: Champs de Mars). Arrive by 9:00 for fewer crowds. For another great view, especially at night, enjoy the tower (and the wild rollerblading scene) by approaching via the Trocadero Métro stop. Have a picnic dinner in front of the tower in the Champs de Mars park after the grass guards have left.

The Paris Sewer Tour (Egouts)—This quick and easy visit takes you along a few hundred yards of underground water tunnel lined with interesting displays, well-described in English, explaining the evolution of the huge city's sewer system. Don't miss the slide show just beyond the gift shop (25F, 11:00–17:00, closed Thursday and Friday, where the Pont de l'Alma hits the Left Bank, tel. 01 47 05 10 29).

▲▲Napoleon's Tomb and the Army Museum—The emperor lies majestically dead inside several coffins under a grand dome—a goose-bumping pilgrimage for historians. Napoleon is surrounded by the tombs of other French war heroes and Europe's greatest military museum, in the Hôtel des Invalides. Follow signs to "crypt," where you'll find Roman Empire–style reliefs listing the accomplishments of Napoleon's administration. The restored dome glitters with 26 pounds of gold (35F, daily 10:00–18:00, off-season 17:00, tel. 01 44 42 37 67, Métros: La Tour Maubourg or Varennes).

▲▲Rodin Museum—This user-friendly museum is filled with passionate works by the greatest sculptor since Michelangelo. See *The Kiss, The Thinker, The Gates of Hell*, and many more. Don't miss the room full of work by Rodin's student and mistress, Camille Claudel. (28F, 18F on Sunday, 5F for gardens only, which may be Paris' best deal as many works are well-displayed in the gardens. Open 9:30–17:45, closed Monday and at 17:00 off-season, 77 rue de Varennes, tel. 01 44 18 61 10, Métro: Varennes, near Napoleon's Tomb.) Good self-serve cafeteria and idyllic picnic spots in back garden.

▲▲The Marmottan—In this intimate, less-visited museum you'll find more than 100 paintings by Claude Monet (thanks to his son Michel), including the *Impressions of a Sunrise* painting that gave the movement its start—and name. (35F, open 10:00–17:30, closed Monday, 2 rue Louis Boilly, tel. 01 42 24 07 02, Métro: La Muette and follow the museum signs 6 blocks through a park to the museum. Note: This private museum is not included in the museum pass.)

Sights—Southeast Paris

▲**Latin Quarter**—See the "Historic Core of Paris" walk above.

St-Germain-des-Prés—A church was first built on this site in A.D. 452. The church you see today was constructed in 1163. The area around the church hops at night with fire-eaters, mimes, and scads of artists. (Métro: St-Germain-des-Prés)

▲**St. Sulpice Organ Concert**—For pipe-organ enthusiasts, this is a delight. The Grand-Orgue at St. Sulpice has a rich history, with a line of 12 world-class organists (including Widor and Dupre) going back 300 years. Marcel Dupre started the tradition of opening the loft to visitors after the 10:30 service on Sundays. The friendly-in-three-languages Daniel Roth continues to welcome guests as he plays five keyboards at once. The 10:30 Sunday Mass is followed by a 20-minute recital (11:40). At 12:00 the unmarked little door (left of entry as you face the rear) opens, and visitors scamper like sixteenth notes up spiral stairs to a world of 6,000 pipes, where they can watch the master perform—friends warming his bench, and a committee scrambling to pull and push the 110 stops. (Métro: St. Sulpice or Mabillon)

▲**Luxembourg Gardens**—Paris' most beautiful, interesting, and enjoyable garden/park/recreational area is a great place to watch Parisians at rest and play. Check out the card players (near the tennis courts), find a free chair near the main pond, and take a breather. Notice any pigeons? A poor Ernest Hemingway used to hand-hunt (read: strangle) them here. The grand neoclassical-domed Panthéon (now a mausoleum housing the tombs of several great Frenchmen) is a block away. The park is open until dusk. Métro: Odéon. If you enjoy the Luxembourg Gardens and want to see more, visit **Parc Monceau** (Métro: Monceau) and the **Jardin des Plantes** (Métro: Jussieu).

▲**Montparnasse Tower**—This 59-floor superscraper—cheaper and easier to get to the top of than the Eiffel Tower—offers arguably Paris' best view, since the Eiffel Tower is in it and the Montparnasse tower isn't. Buy the photo guide to the city, then go to the rooftop and orient yourself. This is a fine way to understand the lay of this magnificent urban land (42F, open daily, summer 9:30–23:00, off-season 10:00–22:00, disappointing after dark, entrance on rue l'Arrivé, Métro: Montparnasse). This is efficient when combined with a day trip to Chartres, which begins at the Montparnasse train station.

Sights—Northwest Paris

▲▲**Place de la Concorde and the Champs-Élysées**—This famous boulevard is Paris' backbone and greatest concentration of traffic. All of France seems to converge on the place de la Concorde, the city's largest square. It was here that the guillotine took the lives of thousands—including King Louis XVI. Back then it was called the place de la Revolution.

Catherine de Medici wanted a place to drive her carriage, so she started draining the swamp that would become the Champs-Élysées. Napoleon put on the final touches, and it's been the place to be seen ever since. The Tour de France bicycle race ends here, as do all parades (French or foe) of any significance. While the boulevard has become a bit hamburgerized, a walk here is a must. Take the Métro to the Arc de Triomphe (Métro: Étoile) and saunter down the Champs-Élysées (Métros: FDR, Étoile, or George V).

▲▲▲**Arc de Triomphe**—Napoleon had the magnificent Arc de Triomphe constructed to commemorate his victory at the Battle of Austerlitz. It was finished in 1836, just in time to be a part of the emperor's funeral parade. Today it commemorates heroes of past wars. There's no triumphal arch bigger (50 meters high, 40 meters wide). And, with 12 converging boulevards, there's no traffic circle more thrilling to experience—either behind the wheel or on foot (take the underpass). Eleven major boulevards feed into the place Charles de Gaulle (Étoile) that surrounds the arch. Study the traffic "system." Underneath the arch is the eternal flame and tomb of the unknown soldier. An elevator leads to a cute museum about the arch and a grand view from the top (32F, daily 9:00–18:30, tel. 01 43 80 31 31, Métro: Étoile).

▲**Grande Arche, La Defense**—This modern architectural wonder is the pride of contemporary Paris. The centerpiece of "Paris-Manhattan," as locals call La Defense, is the Grande Arche. Built to celebrate the 200th anniversary of the 1789 French Revolution, the place is big—38 floors on more than 200 acres. It holds offices for 30,000 people. Notre-Dame Cathedral could fit under its arch. Take the Métro or RER to

La Defense, then follow signs to Grande Arche. Great city views from the Arche elevator (40F includes a film on its construction, daily 9:00–20:00, 9:00–19:00 off-season, tel. 01 49 07 27 57. Métro: La Defense).

Sights—North and Northeast Paris

Note: For more information on this area, see the self-guided Marais walk, below.

▲▲**Pompidou Center**—Europe's greatest collection of far-out modern art, the **Musée National d'Art Moderne** is housed in this colorfully exoskeletal building. After so many Madonnas and Children, a piano smashed to bits and glued to the wall is refreshing. It's a social center with lots of people, street theater, and activity inside and out—a perpetual street fair. Ride the escalator for a free city view from the café terrace on top and don't miss the free exhibits on the ground floor. (35F, 24F for the young and old. Open Monday–Friday 12:00–22:00; Saturday, Sunday, and most holidays 10:00–22:00; closed Tuesday, tel. 01 44 78 12 33, Métro: Rambuteau.) For more on the Pompidou neighborhood Beaubourg, read the described Marais walk, below.

▲**Picasso Museum (Hôtel de Salé)**—The largest collection in the world of Pablo Picasso's paintings, sculpture, sketches, and ceramics, as well as his personal collection of Impressionist art. It's well-explained in English and ▲▲▲ if you're a fan. (28F, open 9:30–18:00, until 22:00 on Wednesday, closed Tuesday, 5 rue Thorigny, tel. 01 42 71 25 21, Métro: St. Paul or Rambuteau.)

▲**Père Lachaise Cemetery**—Littered with the tombstones of many of the city's most illustrious dead, this is your best one-stop look at the fascinating and romantic world of the "permanent Parisians." The place is confusing, but maps (from the guardhouse or the cemetery flower shops) will direct you to the graves of Chopin, Molière, and even the American rock star Jim Morrison (who died in Paris). In section 92, a series of statues memorializing the war makes the French war experience a bit more real (10F maps at flower store near entry, closes at dusk, Métro: Père Lachaise or bus #69).

▲▲**Sacré-Coeur and Montmartre**—This Byzantine-looking church, while only 100 years old, is impressive. It was built as a "praise the Lord anyway" gesture, after the French were humiliated by the Germans in a brief war in 1871. The church is open daily until 23:00. The place du Tertre (a block from the church) was the haunt of Toulouse-Lautrec and the original Bohemians. Today, it's mobbed by tourists and unoriginal Bohemians, but still fun. Watch the artists, tip the street singers, have a dessert crêpe, and wander down the rue Lepic to the two remaining windmills (there were once 30). Rue des Saules leads to Paris' only vineyard. Plaster of Paris comes from the gypsum found on this *mont*. Place Blanche is the white place near where they used to load it, sloppily. Métros: Anvers (use the funicular to avoid stairs, one Métro ticket) or the closer but less scenic Abbesses. A taxi up may be worth the splurge.

Pigalle—Paris' red-light district, the infamous "Pig Alley," is at the foot of Butte Montmartre. Ooh la la. More shocking than dangerous. Stick to the bigger streets, hang on to your wallet, and exercise good judgment. Can-can can cost a fortune, as can con artists in topless bars. After dark, countless tour buses line the streets, reminding us that tour guides make big bucks by bringing their groups to touristic nightclubs like the famous Moulin Rouge (Métro: Pigalle).

Disappointments *de* Paris

While Paris can drive you in Seine with superlatives, here are a few negatives to help you manage with limited time:

La Madeleine is a big stark neoclassical church with a postcard facade and a postbox interior. The famous aristocratic deli behind the church, Fauchon, is elegant, but so are many others handier to your hotel.

The old Opéra Garnier has a great Chagall-painted ceiling but is in a pedestrian-mean area. Don't go to American Express (behind the Opéra) just to change money. You'll get a better rate at the Bank of France.

Paris' Panthéon (nothing like Rome's) is another stark neoclassical ediface filled with mortal remains of great Frenchmen who mean little to the average American tourist.

The Bastille is Paris' most famous nonsight. The square is there, but confused tourists look everywhere and can't find the famous prison of Revolution fame. The building's gone and the square is good only as a jumping-off point for the Marais walk (see below).

Montmartre, the once-artsy now-touristy original haunt of the Bohemians, is overrun with big-bus tourists and those who live off of them. The view—from the steps of Sacré-Coeur—is marred by hustlers.

And the Latin Quarter is a frail shadow of its characteristic self. It's more Tunisian, Greek, and Woolworth's than old-time Paris. The café life that turned on Hemingway and endeared Boul Miche and Boulevard St-Germain to so many poets is also trampled by modern commercialism.

Best Shopping

Forum des Halles is a huge subterranean shopping center. Fun, mod, colorful but without a soul (Métro: Halles). The Lafayette Galleries behind the opera house is your best elegant, Old World, one-stop, Parisian department store/shopping center. Also, visit the Printemps store and the historic as well as handy Samaritaine department store in several buildings near Pont Neuf. Ritzy shops surround the Ritz Hotel at place Vendôme (Métro: Tuileries).

More Paris Walks

Before setting out on each of these walks, mark your route on the free tourist map at your hotel. (Your receptionist can help.) Be certain you splice in visits to the recommended sights you'll pass along the way.

▲**First Evening Orientation Walk**—If you just landed in Europe, an evening walk will show you some of Paris' delights and keep your jet-laggy body moving until a reasonable European bedtime. Bring a map and, when you run out of steam, hop the nearest Métro and head home.

Start with a Métro ride to the "Louvre Rivoli" stop (not the Palais-Royal/Musée du Louvre stop). This art-filled subway station offers a tiny sneak preview of the culture Paris offers. Exiting the station you get more art: the Métro entrance itself is Art Nouveau. Walk along the imposing facade of the Louvre palace (on your right), with a spindly Gothic church on your left to the river. Fake left to the Île de la Cité, then jog right and cross the pedestrian-only bridge (Pont des Arts). Grab a bench. Savor this spot. If facing the history-laden Île de la Cité, turn around and you'll see the Eiffel Tower. Just to its right, the Orsay Museum still looks like a train station. Further right, the Louvre seems to go on forever.

Cross to the dome which welcomes you to the Left Bank. This is the Palais de l'Institut de France, part of which is the

Académie Française. Circle the building on the right, past the statue of the all-knowing Voltaire. Then angle up the modern art gallery–lined rue de Seine. Consider a stop at the very Parisian La Palette café. If you've yet to encounter a Turkish-type toilet . . . a block beyond La Palette, turn right on rue Jacob. After about 3 blocks, turn left following rue Bonaparte to the church of Germain-des-Pres, with the oldest bell tower in Paris. Explore this Romanesque landmark (from 1163, English info sheet inside). One of Paris' most expensive and famous cafés , Les Deux Magots, faces the church. (Ernest Hemingway hung out here while writing *The Sun Also Rises*, back when they didn't charge $12 for a glass of champagne.)

Follow the famous boulevard St-Germain (with the church on your left and the Montparnasse skyscraper towering in the distance on your right) for about 4 blocks. This lively café and shopping scene is typical of the Left Bank. At the five-screen cinema and Métro stop, turn right on Carrefour de l'Odéon, which leads straight to the temple-like Theatre de l'Odéon. Behind that is Paris' most beautiful park, the Luxembourg Gardens. Grab a chair by the center fountain and contemplate where you are—Paris. (The recommended Polidor Restaurant is nearby. The handiest Métro stop from here is Luxembourg or Odéon, back where you left boulevard St-Germain.)

▲**Eiffel Tower/Rue Cler/Rodin Museum/Orsay Museum Walk**—Take the Métro to Trocadero. Exit the subway following the *Sortie Tour Eiffel* signs to one of Europe's great views (gloriously floodlit at night). From here, the tower seems to straddle the military school (École Militaire). Napoleon lies, hand tucked under a rib, beneath the golden dome of Les Invalides to the left. From the Trocadero terrace balcony, enjoy the lively people scene with tourists, hustlers, and dare-devil rollerbladers. The Naval Museum (one of Europe's best, with lots of ship models) and the National Museum of French Monuments (fascinating for art enthusiasts, with plaster life-size models of sculpture from France's greatest medieval churches) are both right here in the Chaillot Palace (each free with museum pass).

Hike across the river to the Eiffel Tower. Ride the elevator up to the second level of the tower. Then walk away from the river through the park. Follow the third cross street (rue de Grenelle) left and turn right on rue Cler for a rare bit of vil-

lage Paris (shops closed 13:00–16:00 and on Monday; for recommended hotels and restaurants, see Sleeping and Eating,
below).

Assemble a picnic on the rue Cler, then turn left on the
avenue de la Motte Piquet to the grand esplanade des
Invalides, a fine picnic spot. The Hôtel des Invalides, with
Napoleon's Tomb and the Army museum, is on your right.
Cross the esplanade, turn right on boulevard des Invalides, and
look for the Rodin Museum (Hôtel Biron) on the left. Tour
the great sculpture museum. You can picnic or eat in the
pricey cafeteria surrounded by Rodin's works in the elegant
backyard.

Now it's on to the crowd-pleaser of Paris' museums, the
d'Orsay. Turn right out of the Rodin Museum and take a quick
left on rue de Bourgogne. Follow it to the Assemblée
Nationale, where you'll turn right on rue de l'Université, then
cross boulevard St-Germain, and follow signs to the Musée
d'Orsay. If you still have energy after touring the Musée d'Orsay, walk away from the river and hook up with Paris' best
people-watching, shopping, and café street, the boulevard
St-Germain.

▲▲Bastille/Marais/Beaubourg Walk—This walk takes you
through one of Paris' most characteristic quarters. When in
Paris, the natural inclination is to concentrate only on the big
sights. But to experience Paris, you need to experience a vital
neighborhood. This one is a good one, containing more prerevolutionary buildings than anywhere else in town. It's Paris
at its best, with the body of yesterday and the pulse of today.
Ride the Métro to Bastille and follow the dotted path outlined
on the Marais map. (As a recommended home neighborhood,
you'll find the map and lots of good hotels and eateries listed
later in this chapter.)

At the **Bastille,** there are more revolutionary images in
the Métro station murals than on the square. Exit following
signs to rue Saint Antoine. Ascend onto a noisy square domi-
nated by the bronze *Colonne de Juillet* (July Column). Victims
of the revolutions of 1830 and 1848 are buried in a vault 55
meters below this guilded statue of liberty. The actual Bastille,
a royal fortress-then-prison that once symbolized old regime
tyranny and now symbolizes the Parisian emancipation, is long
gone. While only a brick outline of the fortress' round turrets
survives (under the traffic, at the Métro exit where rue Saint

Antoine hits the square), the story of the Bastille is indelibly etched on the city's psyche.

For centuries the Bastille was used to defend the city (mostly from its own people). On July 14, 1789, the people of Paris stormed the prison, releasing its seven prisoners and hoping to find arms. They demolished the brick fortress and decorated their pikes with the heads of a few big wigs. Shedding blood, the leaders of the gang made sure it would be tough to turn back the tides of revolution. Ever since, the French have celebrated July 14th as their independence day—Bastille Day.

The flashy glass and grey **Opéra-Bastille** dominates the square. Designed by the Canadian architect Carlos Ott, this latest Parisian grand project was opened with great fanfare by François Mitterrand on the 200th Bastille Day, July 14, 1989.

Turn your back to the statue and (passing the Bank of France—which pays top franc for dollars—on your right, opposite a fine map of the area on your left) head straight down the busy rue Saint Antoine about 4 blocks into the Marais.

The **Marais,** still filled with prerevolutionary lanes and buildings, is more characteristic than touristy (unlike the Latin Quarter). It is Paris at its medieval best. This is how much of the city looked until, in the mid-1800s, Napoleon III had Baron Haussmann blast through the boulevards (open and wide enough for the guns and marching ranks of the army, too wide for revolutionary barricades), creating modern Paris.

Leave rue Saint Antoine at #62, turn right through two elegant courtyards of Hotel de Sully (62 rue Saint Antoine, open until 19:00, good Marais map on corridor wall). Originally a swamp *(marais)*, during the reign of Henry IV, it became hometown of the French aristocracy. In the 17th century, big shots built their private mansions—like this one—close to Henry's place des Vosges. Today these *hôtels*, with their tranquil garden courtyards, house museums, libraries, and national institutions. The aristocrats are gone, but the Marais—which, until recently, was a dumpy Bohemian quarter—is now a thriving, trendy but real-feeling community and a joy to explore.

To get to the **place des Vosges**, continue through the Hotel de Sully. The small door on the far right corner of the second courtyard pops you out into one of Paris' finest squares. Walk to the center, where Louis XIII sits on a horse surrounded by locals enjoying their fine community park. Children frolic in the sandbox, lovers warm benches, and pigeons guard their fountains, while trees shade this retreat from the glare of the big city. Henry IV built this centerpiece of the Marais in 1605. As hoped, this turned the Marais into Paris' most exclusive neighborhood. Victor Hugo lived at #6 (corner closest the Bastille, open to the public, admission fee).

To leave the square, walk behind Louis' horse to the arcade. Follow it left past art galleries and antique shops onto the boutique-filled rue des Francs Bourgeois (frank boo-szh-wah). Browse 2 blocks off the place des Vosges to corner of rue de Sévigné, where you'll see the Musée Carnavalet (on right).

The **Carnavalet (History of Paris) Museum**, housed inside a fine example of a Marais mansion, complete with classy courtyards and statues, features paintings of Parisian scenes, French Revolution paraphernalia, old Parisian store signs, a guillotine, a model of 16th-century Île de la Cité (notice the bridge houses), and rooms full of 15th-century Parisian furniture. Unfortunately, explanations are in French only (28F, open 10:00–17:30, closed Monday, 23 rue de Sévigné, tel. 01 42 72 21 13, Métro: St. Paul).

To continue the Marais walk, go another block along rue des Francs Bourgeois (peeking through the gate on the right) and turn left at the post office (Picasso museum, described above, is on right). From rue Pavée, bend right onto rue Rosiers, which runs straight for 3 blocks through Paris' lively (except on Saturday) Jewish Quarter.

The **Jewish Quarter** is lined with colorful shops and kosher eateries. Jo Goldenberg's delicatessen/restaurant (first corner on left, at #7—scene of a terrorist bombing in darker times) is worth poking into. You'll be tempted by kosher pizza and plenty of falafel-to-go (to go = *emporter*) joints. Rue Rosiers deadends into rue du Vieille du Temple. Turn right.

Frank Bourgeois is waiting at the great corner postcard/ print shop. He leads left past the national archives (becoming rue Rambuteau; first block of the street is lined with cheap eateries). The pipes and glass of the **Pompidou Center** reintroduce you to our century. Pass that huge building on your left to join the fray in front of the center (also called the Centre Beaubourg). Survey this popular spot from the top of the sloping square. Looking at the broad side of the controversial building, you'll see the digital *Le Genitron* (far right) counting down the seconds to the new millenium. A tubular series of escalators leads up the building (free, entry from inside, fine view terrace with café on top, modern Pompidou art gallery on fourth floor—described above).

The Centre Georges Pompidou follows with gusto the 20th-century architectural axiom "form follows function." To get a more spacious and functional interior, the guts of this exoskeletal building are draped on the outside—color coded: vibrant red for people lifts, cool blue for air conditioning, eco-green for plumbing, don't-touch-it yellow for electrical stuff, and white for bones. Explore the always-titillating interior. The ground floor and three-floor library (second-floor entrance) are free. The Centre's many contemporary exhibits make it the most visited sight in Paris. Back outside, wander to the *Homage to Stravinsky* fountain behind Le Genitron (to the right as you face it). Jean Tingley designed this new-wave fountain as a tribute to Stravinsky . . . every fountain represents one of his hard-to-hum scores.

With your back to Le Genitron, walk the cobbled pedestrian mall, crossing the busy boulevard Sebastopol to the ivy-covered pavillions of Les Halles. After 800 years as Paris' down-and-dirty central produce market, this was replaced by a glitzy but soul-less modern shopping center in the late 1970s. The most endearing layer of the mall is its grassy rooftop park. The fine Gothic Saint Eustache church overlooking this contemporary scene has a famous 8,000-pipe organ. The Louvre and Notre-Dame are just a short walk away. The mall is served by Paris' busiest Métro hub (the Chatelet-Les Halles station).

Near Paris: Versailles

▲▲▲**The Palace of Versailles**—Every king's dream, Versailles was the residence of the French king and the cultural heartbeat of Europe for about 100 years—until the Revolution of 1789 ended the notion that God deputized some people to rule for Him on Earth. Louis XIV spent half a year's income of Europe's richest country turning his dad's hunting lodge into a palace fit for a divine monarch. Louis XV and Louis XVI spent much of the 18th century gilding Louis XIV's lily. About 50 years after the royal family was evicted, King Louis Philippe opened the palace as a museum in 1837. Europe's next-best palaces are Versailles wannabes.

Versailles

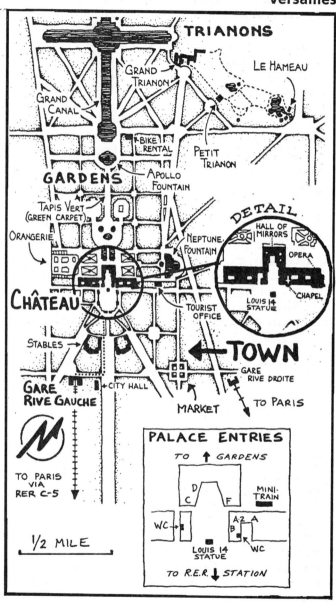

TRIANONS

LE HAMEAU

GRAND TRIANON

GRAND CANAL

BIKE RENTAL

PETIT TRIANON

GARDENS

APOLLO FOUNTAIN

TAPIS VERT (GREEN CARPET)

ORANGERIE

NEPTUNE FOUNTAIN

DETAIL

HALL OF MIRRORS

OPERA

CHAPEL

LOUIS 14 STATUE

CHÂTEAU

TOURIST OFFICE

STABLES

TOWN

GARE RIVE DROITE

CITY HALL

GARE RIVE GAUCHE

MARKET

TO PARIS

TO PARIS VIA RER C-5

½ MILE

PALACE ENTRIES

TO ↑ GARDENS

D

C   F

MINI-TRAIN

WC

A·2 A

B

WC

LOUIS 14 STATUE

TO R.E.R. ↓ STATION

Information: There's a helpful tourist information office across the street from Versailles' R.G. station (tel. 01 39 50 36 22), and two information desks on the approach to the palace. The useful brochure, "Versailles Orientation Guide," explains your sightseeing options.

Tickets: Your choices are the main palace with a basic self-guided walk, several main-palace sections tourable only with guided walks, and two smaller palaces in the backyard. Thus, admissions are complicated. In the main palace, the self-guided one-way palace romp, including the Hall of Mirrors, costs 45F (35F after 15:30, on Sunday, or for those under 26). To take a private tour through the other sections, you'll need to pay the 45F base price, then add 25F for a one-hour guided tour, 37F for a 90-minute guided tour, or 25F for a self-guided Walkman-cassette tour.

Hours: Tuesday–Sunday 9:00–18:30, October–April 9:00–17:30, last entry 30 minutes before closing, closed Monday, information tel. 01 30 84 76 18 or 01 30 84 74 00. Crowds are a problem from 10:00 to 15:00. Tuesday and Sunday are most crowded. If you dislike crowds, arrive after 15:30, pay a reduced admission charge, tour the main palace, and tour the gardens after the palace closes. The palace is great late. On my last visit, at 18:00, I was the only tourist in the Hall of Mirrors, even on a Tuesday.

For the basic self-guided tour, join the line at entrance A. Enter the palace and take a one-way walk through the state apartments from the "King's Wing," through the magnificent Hall of Mirrors, and out via the "Queen's Wing."

The Hall of Mirrors was the ultimate hall of the day— 250 feet long, 17 arched mirrors matching 17 windows with royal garden views, 24 gilded candelabra, eight busts of Roman emperors, and eight classical-style statues (seven of them actually ancient originals). The ceiling is decorated with stories of Louis' triumphs. Imagine this place filled with silk gowns and powdered wigs, lit by thousands of candles. The mirrors—a luxurious rarity at the time—were a reflection of a time when aristocrats felt good about their looks and their fortunes. In another age altogether, this was the room in which the Treaty of Versailles was signed, ending World War I.

Before going downstairs at the end, take a historic stroll clockwise around the long room filled with the great battles of France murals. If you don't have *Mona Winks*, the guide-book called *The Châteaux, The Gardens, and Trianon* gives a room-by-room rundown.

For a private tour, pay the base-price admission at the same time you pay for your tour (entrance D). The 60- or 90-minute tours, led by an English-speaking art historian, take you through sections of Versailles not included in the base-price visit. Groups are limited to 30. Of the several tours offered, the 90-minute version covering Louis XV and Louis XVI's apartments and the opera is best. Pay and get your tour appointment at entrance D. Tour times are normally all allotted for the day by 13:00. Tours leave from entrance F. If the line's long and you're in a hurry, the self-guided Walkman-cassette tour of the King's Chamber (25F, entrance C, last entry at 15:00) covers Louis XIV's rooms and is a good option. If you're waiting for your tour time, have done a tour or have a Paris Museum pass, you can go directly into the main palace with no line at the A2 gate.

The Palace Gardens: The gardens offer a world of royal amusements. Outside the palace is the L'Orangerie. Louis, the only one who could grow oranges in Paris, had an orange grove on wheels that could be wheeled in and out of his green-houses according to the weather. A promenade leads from the palace to the Grand Canal, an artificial lake that, in Louis' day, was a mini-sea with nine ships, including a 32-cannon warship. France's royalty used to float up and down the canal in Venetian gondolas.

While Louis cleverly used palace life at Versailles to "domesticate" his nobility, turning otherwise meddlesome nobles into groveling socialites, all this pomp and ceremony hampered the royal family, as well. For an escape from the public life at Versailles, they built more intimate palaces as retreats in their garden. Before the Revolution, there was plenty of space to retreat—the grounds were enclosed by a 25-mile-long fence.

The beautifully restored **Grand Trianon Palace** is as sumptuous as the main palace but much smaller. With its pastel pink colonnade and more human scale, this is the place where you may experience a little Louis envy.

The nearby **Petit Trianon**, Marie Antoinette's favorite residence, is a neoclassical gem (1769) worth wandering through on your way to the *hameau* (hamlet).

You can almost see princesses bobbing gaily in the branches as you walk through the enchanting forest, past the white marble temple of love (1778) to the queen's fake-peasant hamlet. Palace life really got to Marie Antoinette. Sort of a back-to-basics queen, she retreated further and further from her blue-blooded reality. Her happiest days were at the hamlet, under a bonnet, tending her perfumed sheep and her manicured gardens in a thatch-happy wonderland.

Getting around the gardens: It's a 30-minute hike from the palace, down the canal, past the two mini-palaces to the hamlet. You can rent bikes (30F/hr). The pokey tourist train (31F, 5/hr, 4 stops, you can hop on and off as you like, nearly worthless commentary) is handy for the very slow or very tired.

Garden admissions: Except for fountain Sundays, the gardens are free and open from 7:00 to sunset (as late as 21:30). Grand and Petit Trianon are open May–September 10:00–18:00 (off-season 10:00–17:00, closed Monday, Grand Trianon-25F, Petit Trianon-15F, 30F for both). The park is picnic-perfect. Food is not allowed into the palace, but those with a picnic can check bags (and picnics) at doors A or C. There's a decent restaurant on the canal in the gardens.

Fountain Spectacles: Every Sunday, May–October, music fills the king's backyard and the garden's fountains are in full squirt (two at 11:15 and all fountains at 15:30, 25F garden admission on these days only). Louis had his engineers literally reroute a river to fuel these fountains. Even by today's standards they are impressive.

Getting to Versailles: Versailles, 12 miles from downtown Paris, is an easy direct 30-minute ride on the RER train. While two other trains go to Versailles, RER is the most efficient for the tourist. Métro to any RER-C station (Austerlitz, St-Michel, Orsay, Invalides, Pont de l'Alma, or Champs de Mars/Tour Eiffel) and follow the RER signs to trains (usually named VICK) bound for Versailles R.G. (Rive Gauche station). Do not ride Versailles C.H. trains; they stop at a different Versailles station, farther from the palace. (24F round-trip, covered by railpasses, 30 minutes each way; trains run every 15 minutes; most but not all trains go to Versailles R.G. Check the stops listed on signs over the platform and confirm with a local. From the Versailles R.G. station, which is the end of the RER line, it's a ten-minute walk to the palace.)

The Town of Versailles: After the palace closes and the tourists go, the prosperous little town of Versailles feels extremely normal and wonderfully French. The central market (place du Marche, leaving the RER station, turn right and walk ten minutes) thrives on Tuesday, Friday, and Saturday. Consider the wisdom of picking up or dropping your rental car here rather than in Paris. The Hertz and Avis offices are at the Gare des Chantiers (train station served by Paris' Montparnasse station), a six-minute walk from the RER station.

For a laid-back alternative to Paris within easy reach of the big city (30 minutes by RER, 5/hour), with free and safe parking, this can be a good overnight stop. **Hôtel Le Cheval Rouge****, built in 1676 as Louis XIV's stables, now houses tourists comfortably. It's a block behind the place du Marche in a quaint corner of town on a large quiet courtyard (Ds-255F, Db-310F–390F, extra bed-90F, CC:VM, 18 rue Andre Chenier, 78000 Versailles, tel. 01 39 50 03 03, fax 01 39 50 61 27). **Ibis Versailles****, a slick business-class place, offers absolutely all the comfort with none of the character (Db-380F–480F, CC:VMA, across from the RER station, 4 ave du Gen de Gaulle, 78000 Versailles, tel. 01 39 53 03 03, fax 01 39 50 06 31, SE). **Hotel du Palais**, facing the RER station, has cheap and handy beds. It's a pink and funky place, dumpy enough to earn no stars but proud enough to put candy on the beds (D-170F, Ds-200F, Db-240F, Tb-270F, miles of stairs, 6 place Lyautey, tel. 01 39 50 39 29, fax 01 39 50 80 44, NSE). **Hotel d'Angleterre**** is a well-worn old place near the palace (Db-300F–350F, extra bed-60F, CC:VM, first-floor rooms are best, 2 rue de Fontenay, tel. 01 39 51 43 50, fax 01 39 51 45 63).

More Side Trips from Paris

▲▲▲**Chartres**—In 1194, a terrible fire destroyed the church at Chartres with the much-venerated veil of Mary. With almost unbelievable good fortune, the monks found the veil miraculously preserved in the ashes. And money poured in for the building of a bigger and better cathedral. Bigger and better it was, as the grand new church was decorated with 2,000 carved figures and some of France's best stained glass. The cathedral feels too large for the city because it was designed to accommodate huge crowds of pilgrims. One of those pilgrims, an impressed Napoleon, declared after a visit in 1811,

Paris Area

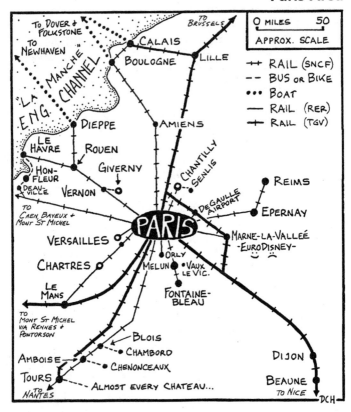

"Chartres is no place for an atheist." Rodin called it "the Acropolis of France." British Francophile Malcolm Miller or his impressive assistant give great "Appreciation of Gothic" tours daily (except Sunday and off-season, usually at noon and 14:45, verify in advance, call the TI at 02 37 21 50 00). Each 30F tour is different; many stay for both tours. Just show up at the church (open 7:00–19:00).

Find time to explore Chartres' pleasant center city and discover the picnic-perfect park behind the cathedral. The helpful TI is next to the cathedral and has a map with a self-guided tour of Chartres (open 9:30–18:45). Chartres is a one-hour train trip from Paris (hourly departures from the Gare Montparnasse, about 140F round-trip) and is a delightful overnight stop.

For good-value rooms and a well-respected restaurant, find the **Hôtel le Boeuf Couronne****, a few blocks up from the train station (D-160F, Db-285F, Tb-300F, CC:VM, 15 place Chatelet, tel. 02 37 18 06 06, fax 02 37 21 72 13).

▲▲**Château of Chantilly** (shan-tee-yee)—One of France's best château experiences is just 30 minutes and 40F by RER train from Paris's Gare du Nord station, and then a 20-minute walk. This château has it all: moat, drawbridge, sculpted gardens, little hamlet (the prototype for the more famous *hameau* at Versailles), lavish interior that rivals Versailles', world-class art collection (including two Raphaels), and manageable crowds. (35F includes required French-language tour, 15F for gardens only, open daily except Tuesday 10:00–18:00, off-season 10:30–12:45 and 14:00–17:00, tel. 01 44 57 08 00.) Horse lovers will enjoy the nearby stables (expensive), built for a prince who believed he'd be reincarnated as a horse. The quaint and impressively preserved medieval town of Senlis is a 30-minute bus ride from the Chantilly station.

▲**Giverny**—Monet spent 43 of his most creative years (1883–1926) here at the Camp David of Impressionism. Monet's gardens and home are split by a busy road. Buy your ticket, walk through the gardens, and take the underpass into the artist's famous lily-pad land. The path leads you over the Japanese Bridge, under weeping willows, and past countless scenes that leave artists aching for an easel. For Monet fans, it's strangely nostalgic. Back on the other side, continue your visit with a wander through his more robust and structured garden and his mildly interesting home. The gift shop at the exit is the actual skylit studio Monet used to paint his water-lily masterpieces.

Lines can be horrendous, and once you're inside, the tour groups can trample any magic still left in those lily pads. While it's well worth a stop if you're driving by, without a car or during peak season, most splash-in-the-pan Impressionist fans would be better off at the Orsay Gallery, L'Orangerie, and Marmottan Museums back in Paris (35F, 25F for gardens only, open April 1–October 31 10:00–18:00, closed Monday and off-season, tel. 02 32 51 28 21). Take the Rouen train from Paris' Gare St. Lazare station to Vernon, a pleasant Normandy town. To get from the Vernon train station to Monet's garden (4 km away), take the Vernon–Giverny bus (5/day), hitch, taxi (60F), or rent a bike at the station (55F; busy road). The big tour companies do a Giverny day trip from Paris for around $60.

The new **American Impressionist Art Museum** (100 yards down the lane from Monet's place) is devoted to American artists who followed Claude to Giverny. Giverny had a great influence on American artists of Monet's day. This bright, modern gallery is well-explained in English, has a good little Mary Cassatt section, and gives Americans a rare chance to see French people appreciating our artists (same price and hours as Monet's home).

▲▲**Vaux-le-Vicomte**—This château is considered the prototype for Versailles. In fact, when its owner, Nicolas Fouquet, gave a grand party, Louis XIV was so jealous that he arrested the host and proceeded with the construction of the bigger and costlier (but not necessarily more splendid) palace of Versailles. Vaux-le-Vicomte is a joy to tour, elegantly furnished, surrounded by royal gardens, and not crowded. It's difficult to get to without a car. Take the train from Paris' Gare de Lyon (*Départs Banelieve*) to Melun. Rent a bike (crummy ride on a busy road) or taxi (about 70F) the 6 km to the château. (A steep 56F admission, gardens only 30F, open daily 10:00–18:00. Special candlelit visits cost 68F and are on Saturday May–October 20:30–23:00, and Friday and Saturday in July and August. The fountains run April–October on the second and last Saturday of each month 15:00–18:00, tel. 01 64 14 41 90.)

▲▲**Disneyland Paris**—Europe's Disneyland is basically a modern remake of the one in California, with most of the same rides and smiles. The main difference is that Mickey Mouse speaks French (and you can buy wine with your lunch). My kids went ducky. Locals love it. It's worth a day if Paris is handier than Florida or California. Crowds are a problem. Avoid Saturday, Sunday, Wednesday, school holidays, and July and August, if you can. The park is occasionally so crowded that they close the gates at 60,000 people (tel. 01 64 74 30 00 for the latest). After dinner the crowds are gone, and you'll walk right on to rides that had a 45-minute wait three hours earlier. Food service is fun but expensive. Save money with a picnic. Disney brochures are in every Paris hotel. The RER (37F each way, direct from downtown Paris to Station Marne-la-Vallee in 30 minutes) drops you right into the park. The last train to Paris leaves shortly after midnight. (195F for adults, 150F for kids 3–11, 25F less in spring and fall. Open daily 9:00–23:00 late June through early September and Saturday and Sunday off-season, shoulder-season weekdays 9:00–

19:00, off-season 10:00–18:00, tel. 01 60 30 60 30 for park and hotel reservations.) To sleep reasonably at the huge Disney complex, try **Hotel Sante Fe** (550F family rooms for two to four people, 450F off-season; ask for their hotel and park package deal). If all this ain't enough, a new Planet Hollywood restaurant opened just outside the park a five-minute walk from the RER stop.

Sleeping in Paris
(5F = about $1)

Sleep Code: **S** = Single, **D** = Double/Twin, **T** = Triple, **Q** = Quad, **b** = bathroom, **t** = toilet only, **s** = shower only, **CC** = Credit Card (Visa, MasterCard, Amex), **SE** = Speaks English, **NSE** = No English, * = French hotel rating system (0–4 stars).

Quad rooms usually have two double beds. Recommended hotels have an elevator unless otherwise noted. Because double beds and showers are cheaper than twin beds and baths, rooms prices vary within each hotel. To keep things manageable, I've focused on three safe, handy, and colorful neighborhoods (listing good hotels, restaurants, and helpful hints for each).

French hotels are rated by stars. One star is simple, two has most of the basic comforts, and three is, for this book, plush (stars are indicated here by an *). Old, characteristic, budget Parisian hotels have always been cramped. Retrofitted with elevators, toilets, and private showers, they are even more cramped. Almost every hotel accepts Visa and MasterCard. Few take American Express.

While you can save up to 100F by finding the increasingly rare room without a shower, these rooms are often smaller and charge around 20F for down-the-hall showers. Breakfasts cost 20F–40F extra. Café or picnic breakfasts are cheaper. Singles (except for the rare closet-type rooms that fit only one twin bed) are simply doubles inhabited by one person, renting for only a little less than a double.

Conventions clog Paris in September (worst), October, May, and June. Reserve in advance during these months. July and August are no problem. Most hotels accept telephone reservations with a credit-card number and prefer a faxed follow-up to be sure everything is in order. Most require prepayment for reservations. A credit-card number is easiest.

Paris, Rue Cler Neighborhood

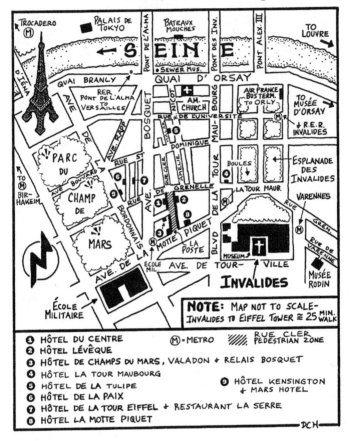

① HÔTEL DU CENTRE
② HÔTEL LÉVÊQUE
③ HÔTEL DE CHAMPS DU MARS, VALADON & RELAIS BOSQUET
④ HÔTEL LA TOUR MAUBOURG
⑤ HÔTEL DE LA TULIPE
⑥ HÔTEL DE LA PAIX
⑦ HÔTEL DE LA TOUR EIFFEL & RESTAURANT LA SERRE
⑧ HÔTEL LA MOTTE PIQUET

Ⓜ = METRO   ////// RUE CLER PEDESTRIAN ZONE

⑨ HÔTEL KENSINGTON & MARS HOTEL

Get advice for safe parking. Meters are free in August. Garages are plentiful (about 140F per day, with special rates through some hotels).

Sleeping in the Rue Cler Neighborhood
(7th district, Métro: École Militaire, postal code: 75007)
Rue Cler, a villagelike pedestrian street, is safe, tidy, and makes me feel like I must have been a poodle in a previous life. How such coziness lodged itself between the high-powered government/business district and the expensive Eiffel Tower and Invalides areas, I'll never know. Living here ranks with the top museums as one of the city's great experiences.

On rue Cler, you can eat and browse your way through a street full of tart shops, colorful outdoor produce stalls, cheeseries, and fish vendors. From rue Cler, it's a short stroll to the Eiffel Tower, Les Invalides, the Seine, and the Orsay and Rodin museums. Warning: The first two hotels are over-run with my readers.

Hôtel Leveque* is simple, clean, and well-run, with a helpful staff and a singing maid. It's the best budget deal with the best location on the block (S-195F–225F, D-195F–225F, Ds-295F, Db-320F–365F, Tb-430F, CC:VM, down-the-hall showers are free, but one shower labels hot with the color blue, 29 rue Cler, tel. 01 47 05 49 15, fax 01 45 50 49 36 for reservation confirmations, the friendly staff speaks English, except for cheery Michele, who is very creative at communicating). Lots of stairs, dark drab carpet, no elevator, right in the traffic-free thick of things.

Hôtel du Champs de Mars**, with its cheery pastel rooms and sincerely helpful English-speaking owners, Françoise and Stephane, is rue Cler's top two-star option. The hotel has a Provence-style small-town warmth from top to bottom (Db-390F–420F, Tb-505F, CC:VM, 30 yards off rue Cler at 7 rue du Champs de Mars, tel. 01 45 51 52 30, fax 01 45 51 64 36).

Hôtel du Centre*, across the street from Leveque, is another simple hotel with a charming location (D-225F–250F, Db-360F–390F, Tb-460F, TV, showers 10F, CC:VMA, 24 rue Cler, tel. 01 47 05 52 33, fax 01 40 62 95 66).

Hôtel la Motte Piquet**, with a plush lobby and basic, comfortable rooms, is high on gadgets and low on charm (Db-330F–430F, third person-100F, CC:VM, 30 avenue de la Motte Piquet, on the corner of rue Cler, tel. 01 47 05 09 57, fax 01 47 05 74 36).

Hôtel Relais Bosquet***, bright, spacious, and newly renovated, is my most upscale and comfortable listing in the area (Db-575F–810F, CC:VMA, 19 rue du Champs de Mars, tel. 01 47 05 25 45, fax 01 45 55 08 24, SE).

Hôtel Le Valadon**, on a very quiet street with a plain lobby and spacious comfy rooms, has a shy Parisian cuteness (Db-400F, Tb-450F, 16 rue Valadon, tel. 01 47 53 89 85, fax 01 44 18 90 56, NSE).

Hôtel de la Tour Eiffel**, with petite, wicker-pleasant rooms, is like a small wilting salad with lots of dressing

(Sb-320F, Db-370F, Tb-470F, CC:VMA, 17 rue de l'Exposition, tel. 01 47 05 14 75, fax 01 47 53 99 46, Muriel SE).

Hôtel de l'Alma*** is a tight and tidy place with 32 delightful look-alike rooms all with modern plumbing, TV, and minibar (Sb-400F, Db-450F, breakfast included, this price—below their listed price—seems unrealistic but is promised to my readers through 1997; no triples but a kid's bed can be moved in for free, popular with Spanish and Russian groups, CC:VMA, 32 rue de l'Exposition, tel. 01 47 05 45 70, fax 01 45 51 84 47, SE).

Hôtel La Tour Maubourg***, with a grand public living room and spacious bedrooms, feels like a trés elegant manor house. Overlooking a cheery green within sight of Napoleon's tomb (Sb-510F–570F, Db-670F–820F, suites for up to four about 1,000F, prices include breakfast, CC:VM, immediately at the La Tour Maubourg Métro stop, 150 rue de Grenelle, tel. 01 47 05 16 16, fax 01 47 05 16 14, SE).

Mars Hôtel** has a richly decorated lobby, spacious—if well-worn—rooms, and a beam-me-up-Maurice coffin-sized elevator. The front rooms look out on the Eiffel Tower (large Sb-300F, Db-350F, Twin-b-400F, CC:VM, 117 avenue de la Bourdonnais, tel. 01 47 05 42 30, fax 01 47 05 45 91).

Hôtel Kensington**, very near the Mars Hotel, is bigger, more professional, and a fair value (St-310F, Db-385F–490F, extra bed 80F, CC:VMA, 79 avenue de La Bourdonnais, tel. 01 47 05 74 00, fax 01 47 05 25 81).

These places are lesser values but, in this fine area, reasonable last choices: **Hôtel Eiffel Rive Gauche**** (Dt-260F, Db-360F–465F, 6 rue du Gros-Caillou, tel. 01 45 51 24 56, fax 01 45 51 11 77), **Hôtel de la Tulipe**** (Db-500F–550F, wood-beamed with a leafy courtyard, no elevator, 33 rue Malar, tel. 01 45 51 67 21, fax 01 47 53 96 37), **Hôtel Royal Phare**** (Db-310F–400F, facing the École Militaire Métro stop, 40 avenue de la Motte Piquet, tel. 01 47 05 57 30, fax 01 45 51 64 41), and **Hôtel de la Paix**** (S-160F, Ds-305F, Db-385F, Tb-460F, well-worn, quiet, run very agreeably by English-speaking Noël, no elevator, 19 rue du Gros-Caillou, tel. 01 45 51 86 17).

Rue Cler Helpful Hints: Become a local at a rue Cler café for breakfast, or join the afternoon crowd for *une bière pression* (a draft beer). Cute shops and bakeries line rue Cler. Self-serve laundromats are at 16 rue Cler and just off rue Cler at 167 rue de Grenelle. The Métro station (École Militaire) and a post office with phone booths are at the end of rue Cler, on avenue de la Motte Piquet. Your neighborhood TI is at the Eiffel Tower (open May–September 11:00–18:00, tel. 01 45 51 22 15). There's a small late-night grocery on rue de Grenelle, just off rue Cler. The Bank Populaire (across from the Hôtel Leveque) changes money.

At 65 quai d'Orsay, you'll find the American Church and College, the community center for Americans living in Paris. The interdenominational service at 11:00 on Sunday, the coffee hour after church, and the free Sunday concerts (18:00) are a great way to make some friends and get a taste of émigré life in Paris. Stop by and pick up copies of the *Free Voice* and *France–U.S.A. Contacts* newspapers (tel. 01 47 05 07 99). Information is available for those in need of housing or work through the community of 30,000 Americans living in Paris.

Afternoon *boules* (lawn bowling) on the esplanade des Invalides is a relaxing spectator sport. Look for the dirt area to the upper right as you face the Invalides.

Rue Cler is a moveable feast. The entire street is clogged with connoisseurs of good eating. Only the health-food store is not busy. For a magical picnic dinner, assemble it in no fewer than six shops on rue Cler and lounge on the best grass in Paris (the police don't mind after dark) with the dogs, Frisbees, a floodlit Eiffel Tower, and a cool breeze in the Parc du Champs de Mars. (More eating specifics below.)

For an after-dinner cruise on the Seine, it's just a short walk to the river to the Bâteaux Mouches.

Sleeping in the Marais Neighborhood
(4th district, Métro: St. Paul, postal code: 75004)

Those interested in a more Soho/Greenwich, gentrified, urban-jungle locale would enjoy making the Marais their Parisian home. The Marais is a cheaper and more happening locale than rue Cler. Narrow medieval Paris at its finest, only 15 years ago it was a forgotten Parisian backwater. Now the Marais is one of Paris' most popular residential areas. It's a short walk to Notre-Dame, Île St. Louis, and the Latin Quarter. The St. Paul Métro stop puts you right in the heart of the Marais.

Castex Hôtel** is pleasant, clean, cheery, quiet, and run by the very friendly Bouchand family (son Blaise, pronounced

Paris, Marais Neighborhood

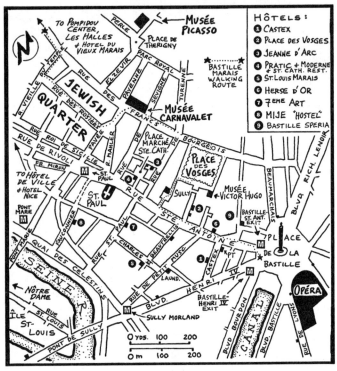

"blaze," speaks English). This place is a great value, with the distinctly un-Parisian characteristic of seeming like it wants your business (Ss-220F, Sb-240F–270F, Ds-300F–320F, Db-320F– 340F, Tb-440F, CC:VM, no elevator, 5 rue Castex, just off place de la Bastille and rue Saint Antoine, Métro: Bastille, tel. 01 42 72 31 52, fax 01 42 72 57 91). Reserve by phone and leave your credit-card number. Closed in August. The security code marked on your key opens the front door after hours.

Grand Hôtel Jeanne d'Arc**, a cozy and friendly place with an elegant breakfast room on a quiet street, is a haven for connoisseurs of the Marais (small Db-305F, Db-390F–460F, Tb-515F, Qb-570F, extra bed 75F, CC:VM, 3 rue Jarente, tel. 01 48 87 62 11, fax 01 48 87 37 31, SE). Sixth-floor rooms have a view. Corner rooms are wonderfully bright in the city of light.

Hotel Bastille Speria*** feels warm and family-run while offering a serious business-type service. Perfectly located, its spacious lobby and 45 rooms are mod, cheery, and pastel. It's English language–friendly, from the *Herald Tribune*s in the lobby, to the history of the Bastille in the elevator (Sb-516F, Db-558F–622F, Tb-758F, CC:VMA, fold-out sofas let two kids stow away for free in larger doubles, 1 rue de la Bastille, tel. 01 42 72 04 01, fax 01 42 72 56 38, Michelle SE).

Hôtel de la Place des Vosges**, quasi-classy with a linoleum antique feel, charges the limit for its 16 rooms but is ideally located on a quiet street (Db-380F–550F, CC:VMA, 12 rue de Biraque, just off the elegant place des Vosges and just as snooty, tel. 01 42 72 60 46, fax 01 42 72 02 64).

Hotel de la Herse D'Or is industrial-strength, three-coats-of-paint simple, with a great location, tortured floor plan, and hard-to-beat prices (S-160F, D-200F, Db-240F, showers 10F, no elevator, no CC, 20 rue St. Antoine, tel. 01 48 87 84 09).

Hôtel Pratic* has a slightly Arabic feel in its cramped lobby. The tidy rooms are simple but not confined, stairs are many, and it's right on a great people-friendly square (S-150F, D-230F, Ds-275F, Db-340F, showers 10F, no elevator, no CC, 9 rue d'Ormesson, 75004 Paris, tel. 01 48 87 80 47, fax 01 48 87 40 04).

The bare-bones and dumpy **Hôtel Moderne**, next to the Hôtel Pratic, might be better than a youth hostel if you need privacy. The only thing "moderne" about it is the name—which is illegible on the broken sign (D-160F, Ds-220F, no elevator, 3 rue Caron, tel. 01 48 87 97 05).

Hôtel de 7ème Art** is a Hollywood-nostalgia place (run by young, hip Marais types) with dull rooms, a full service café/bar, and Charlie Chaplin murals (Db-410F–470F, CC:VMA, 20 rue St. Paul, tel. 01 42 77 04 03, fax 01 42 77 69 10).

Hôtel de Nice** is a cozy "Marie Antoinette does tie-dye" place with lots of thoughtful touches on the Marais' busy main drag (Sb-350F, Db-400F, Tb-500F, CC:VM, 42 bis rue de Rivoli, tel. 01 42 78 55 29, fax 01 42 78 36 07). Twin rooms, which cost the same as doubles, are roomier but on the street side (effective double-pane windows).

Hotel de Vieux Marais** offers comfortable rooms tucked away on a quiet street near the Pompidou Center

(Sb-400F, Db-510F–550F, Tb-665F, CC:VM, off rue du Temple, 8 rue du Platre, tel. 01 42 78 47 22, fax 01 42 78 34 32).

MIJE "Youth Hostels": The Maison Internationale de la Jeunesse des Étudiants (MIJE) runs three classy old residences in the Marais for travelers under age 30. Each offers simple, clean, single-sex, mostly two- and four-bed rooms for 120F per bed, including shower and breakfast. Rooms are locked 12:00–16:00 and at 1:00 a.m. MIJE Fourcy (6 rue de Fourcy, just south of the rue Rivoli), MIJE Fauconnier (11 rue Fauconnier), and the best, MIJE Maubisson (12 rue des Barres), share one telephone number (01 42 74 23 45) and Métro stop (St. Paul). Reservations taken only one week ahead. MIJE Fourcy offers 36F and 52F dinners.

Marais Helpful Hints: Place des Vosges, Paris' oldest square, the new Bastille opera house, and the Jewish Quarter (rue des Rosiers) are all nearby. The Marais' main drag, rue Saint Antoine, starts at the Bastille and leads west towards the hopping Beaubourg/Les Halles area. Paris' biggest and best budget department store is BHV, next to the Hôtel de Ville. Marais post offices are on rue Castex, and on the corner of rues Pavée and Francs Bourgeois. (See the Marais walk described above for neighborhood details.)

The nearest TI is in the Gare de Lyon (arrival level open 8:00–20:00, tel. 01 43 43 33 24). Neighborhood laundromats are at 96 rue Saint Antoine, 40 rue de Roi de Sicile, and 23 rue de Petit Musc. The Bank of France (where rue St. Antoine hits the place de la Bastille, 9:00–11:45 and 13:30–15:30 Monday–Friday) changes money, offering great rates and minimal headaches. Most banks, shops, and other services are on the rue St. Antoine between Métro stops St. Paul and Bastille.

Bus 69 rolls you scenically from the Marais (rue St. Antoine) to the recommended rue Cler neighborhood via the Louvre and Orsay museums.

Sleeping in the Contrescarpe Neighborhood
(5th district, Métro: Place Monge, postal code: 75005)

This neighborhood—just over the hill from the Latin Quarter, five minutes from the Panthéon, and an easy walk to Notre-Dame, Île de la Cité, Île St. Louis, Luxembourg Gardens, and the grand boulevards St-Germain and St-Michel—is close to the action. The rue Mouffetard and place Contrescarpe are the heart and soul of this area. Rue Mouffetard is a market street by day and restaurant row by night.

The **Hôtel des Grandes Écoles****, slightly upscale, offers an idyllic, peaceful oasis with three buildings protecting its own garden courtyard (Db-500F–700F, Tb-700F–850F, Qb-850F–950F, 75 rue de Cardinal Lemoine, tel. 01 43 26 79 23, fax 01 43 25 28 15; popular, so call well in advance).

Hôtel Central* has a romantic location, a steep and slippery, castlelike stairway, simple rooms (all with shower) and so-so beds (Ss-155F–180F, Ds-220F–250F, no elevator, toilets down the hall, 6 rue Descartes, tel. 01 46 33 57 93, NSE). Nothing fancy but very Parisian and a good budget option.

The low-energy, bare-bones **Hôtel du Commerce** is run by Monsieur Mattuzzi, who must be a pirate gone good (no stars, S-140F, D-150F, Ds-160F, Ts-220F, Qs-270F, showers 15F, no elevator, takes no reservations, call at 10:00 and he'll say *"oui"* or *"non,"* 14 rue de La Montagne Sainte-Geneviève, Métro: Place Maubert, tel. 01 43 54 89 69, NSE). This 300-year-old place (with vinyl that looks it) is a great rock-bottom deal and as safe as any dive next to a police station can be. In the morning, the landlady will knock and chirp, *"Restez-vous?"* ("Are you staying tonight?").

Hotel de l'Esperance** gives you nearly three stars for the price of two. It's quiet, polished, and very comfortable, with thoughtfully appointed rooms complete with canopy beds, hair dryers, and cable TV (Db-450F–550F, 70F for extra bed, CC:VM, 15 rue Pascal, Métro: Censier-Daubenton, tel. 01 47 07 10 99, fax 01 43 37 56 19, SE).

Hotel Pascal* offers spotless, simple rooms with tiny bathrooms and some particularly French (read "small") double beds (Db-250F, no elevator, 20 rue Pascal, Métro: Censier-Daubenton, tel. 01 47 07 41 92, fax 01 45 65 93 31).

The **Hotel de France****, on a busy street, has good modern rooms and hard-working owners (Sb-350F, Db-400F, CC:VM, 108 rue Monge, Métro: Censier-Daubenton, tel. 01 47 07 19 04, fax 01 43 36 62 34). Its best and quietest rooms are *sur le cour* (on the courtyard).

Y&H Hostel offers a great location, easygoing management, depressing showers, and generally squalid conditions. (100F-beds, 15F for sheets, four- to eight-bed rooms, closed 11:00–17:00, no reservations, 80 rue Mouffetard, tel. 01 45 35 09 53.)

Contrescarpe Helpful Hints: The neighborhood TI is in the Gare d'Austerlitz (Monday–Saturday 8:00–15:00). The post office (PTT) is between rue Mouffetard and rue Monge at 10 rue de l'Épée du Bois. Place Monge hosts a colorful outdoor market (Wednesday, Friday, and Sunday until 13:00). The street market at the bottom of rue Mouffetard (5 blocks down past the place Contrescarpe) bustles daily (8:00–12:00 and 15:30–19:00), and the heart of this neighborhood, the place Contrescarpe, hops in the afternoon and after dark. Best midday café sitting is at the Café Le Mouffetard (corner of rue Mouffetard and rue de l'Arbalete). After dark, do your sipping at any café on the place Contrescarpe.

The Jardin des Plantes is close by and great for afternoon walks, but the smaller gardens at the École Polytechnique, next to the Hotel Central, are closer. The doorway at 49 rue Monge leads to a hidden Roman arena (*Arènes de Lutèce*). Today, *boules* players occupy the stage, while couples cuddle on the cheaper seats. Walk over to the Panthéon, admire it from the outside, and go into the wildly beautiful St. Étienne-du-Mont church.

Eating in Paris

Paris is France's wine and cuisine melting pot. While it lacks a style of its own, it draws from the best of France. Paris could hold a gourmet's Olympics—and import nothing.

Picnic or go to snack bars for quick lunches and linger longer over dinner. You can eat very well, restaurant-style, for 100F–130F. Ask your hotel to recommend a small nearby restaurant in the 60F–100F range. Famous places are often overpriced, overcrowded, and overrated. Find a quiet neighborhood and wander, or follow a local recommendation. Don't arrive before 19:00. Small local favorites get crowded after 21:00.

Cafeterias and Picnics

Many Parisian department stores have huge supermarkets hiding in the basement and top-floor cafeterias offering not really cheap but low-risk, low-stress, what-you-see-is-what-you-get meals. For picnics, you'll find handy little groceries (*épiceries*) and delis (*charcuteries*) all over town (but rarely near famous sights). Good picnic fixings include roasted chicken, half-liter boxes of demi-crème (2 percent) milk, drinkable yogurt, fresh bakery goods, melons, and exotic pâtés and cheeses. Great take-out deli-type foods like gourmet salads and quiches abound. Boulangeries make good cheap miniquiches and sandwiches. While wine is taboo in public places in the U.S., it's *pas de problème* (no problem) in France. The general budget eating tips in this book's introduction will save piles of francs in Paris.

Good Picnic Spots: The pedestrian bridge, Pont des Arts, with unmatched views and plentiful benches, and the park under the Eiffel Tower are my favorite dinner-picnic places. Bring your own dinner feast and watch the riverboats or the Eiffel Tower light up the city for you. The Palais Royal (across the street from the Louvre) is a good spot for a peaceful and royal picnic. Also try the little triangular Henry IV Park on the west tip of the Île de la Cité, people-watching at the Pompidou Center, the elegant place des Vosges (closes at dusk), the Rodin Museum gardens, and the Luxembourg Gardens.

Restaurants
The Parisian eating scene is kept at a rolling boil. Entire books (and lives) are dedicated to the subject. If you are traveling outside Paris, save your splurges for the countryside, where you'll enjoy better cooking for less money. I've listed places that fit a busy sightseeing schedule conveniently and places near recommended hotels. If you'd like to visit a district specifically to eat, consider the many romantic restaurants that line the cozy Île St. Louis' main street and the colorful, touristic but fun string of eateries along rue Mouffetard behind the Panthéon.

Restaurants in Rue Cler Neighborhood
The rue Cler neighborhood isn't famous for its restaurants. That's why I eat here. Several small family-run places serve great dinner menus for 100F–150F.

For a special dinner, a handful of fine places are on rues de l'Exposition and Augerau, between rue St. Dominique and rue de Grenelle. **Restaurant La Serre** has a wonderful ambiance and food worth the splurge (*plats* from 50F to 70F, open daily from 19:00, often a wait after 21:00, great onion soup, 29 rue de l'Exposition, tel. 01 45 55 20 96, Marie-Alice and Philippe SE). The more subdued **La Maison de Cosima** offers creative French cuisine (one 140F menu with several choices offered, 20 rue de l'Exposition, tel. 01 45 51 37 71, Helene SE).

La Varanque, a friendly, unpretentious little place, is a good budget bet with 50F plats and a 74F menu (27 rue Augereau, tel. 01 47 05 51 22). **Au Café de Mars** is a contemporary Parisian café/restaurant with good Franco-Californian cuisine and fair prices (also on rue Augerau, tel. 01 47 05 05 91, SE).

On the other side of rue Cler: **Au Petit Paname** (9 rue Amelie, closed Saturday, tel. 01 45 56 98 98) and **Restaurant Leo le Lion** (110F menu, 1 block off rue Cler at 23 rue Duvivier, tel. 01 45 51 41 77) are classy nooks popular with locals. **L'Ami de Jean** is a lively place to sample Basque cuisine (27 rue Malar, closed Sunday, tel. 01 47 05 86 89). The dressy **Thoumieux** is a bustling and very traditional *brasserie* (79 rue St. Dominique, tel. 01 47 05 49 75). The **Ambassade du Sud-Ouest**, a wine store/restaurant, specializes in French Southwest cuisine (such as *daubes de canard*, 46 ave. de la Bour-donnais, tel. 01 45 55 59 59).

Rue Cler gives fast-food a good name. The street, a festi-val of food, is lined with people whose lives seem to be devoted to their specialty: stacking polished produce, rotisserie chicken, crêpes, or cheese squares. An Asian deli (**Traiteur Asie**, across from Hôtel Leveque) has tasty low-stress, low-price take-out treats. Its two tables offer the cheapest place to sit, eat, and enjoy the rue Cler ambiance. For quiche, cheese pie, or a pear/chocolate tart, try Tarte Julie's (take-out or stools, 28 rue Cler). The *boulangerie* on the corner of rue de Champs de Mars is the place for a fresh baguette, sandwich, tiny quiche, or *pain au chocolat* (try one). The **Café du Marche** (corner rue Cler and rue Champs du Mars), with the best seats on rue Cler, serves hearty salads and great 50F lunch and dinner plates. **Café La Roussillon** also offers a quintessential café experi-ence. Peopled and decorated *belle epoche*, you can sip a 7F wine at the bar and grab a light lunch at a table (hearty 50F plates and salads, corner of Grenelle and Cler). The tiny rue Grenelle grocery store next door is open nightly until mid-night. The **Real McCoy** is a little shop selling American food and sandwiches (194 rue de Grenelle).

The almost no-name **Maison Altmayer** is a hole-in-the-wall place for a drink quietly festooned with reality (next to Hôtel Eiffel Rive Gauche at 6 rue du Gros Caillou, open 9:00–19:30). Cafés like this originated (and this one still func-tions) as a place where locals enjoyed a drink while their heat-ing wood, coal, or gas was prepared for delivery.

Restaurants in the Marais Neighborhood

The windows of the Marais are filled with munching sophisti-
cates. The epicenter is the tiny square where rue Caron and
rue d'Ormesson intersect, midway between the St. Paul Métro
stop and the place des Vosges. I like **Le Marais Ste. Catherine** at 5 rue Caron (100F menu, daily from 19:00, extra seating
in their candlelit cellar, tel. 01 42 72 39 94). **Auberge de Jarente** (just off that square at 7 rue Jarente, closed Sunday and
Monday, tel. 01 42 77 49 35) is popular, atmospheric, and reasonable. For more conspicuous elegance, a coffee or splurge
dinner on the place des Vosges is good (locals like **Ma Bourgogne**, no CC, daily, tel. 01 42 78 44 64).

Hobos picnic on the place des Vosges itself, trying not to
make the local mothers with children nervous (closes at dusk).
While gourmet take-out places do a brisk business all along rue
Saint Antoine, those hobos stretch their francs at the supermarket in the basement of the Monoprix department store
(closest to place des Vosges on rue Saint Antoine).

For a fast, cheap, and healthy food fix, eat at the
Chinese/Japanese **Delice House**. Two can split 200 grams of
chicken curry (or whatever, 25F) and a heaping helping of rice
(20F). Lots of seating, with pitchers of water at the ground-
floor tables and a roomier upstairs (81 rue Saint Antoine, open
until 21:00).

Near the Hôtel Castex, the restaurant **La Poste** and the
Crêperie across the street (13 rue Castex) are both inexpensive, closed on Sunday, and good values. The **Le Paradis de
Fruit** serves salads and organic foods to a young local crowd
(on the small square at rues Tournelle and St. Antoine). The
couscous restaurant next door, **La Perle** (till wee hours), is
good and cheap. **L'Énoteca** has lively reasonable Italian cuisine in a relaxed, open setting (across from Hôtel du 7ème Art
at 20 rue St. Paul, closed Sunday, tel. 01 42 78 91 44).

For breakfast at half the hotel price, warm a stool at the
tiny *boulangerie/pâtisserie* where the hotels buy their croissants
(a block off place Bastille, corner of rue Saint Antoine and rue
de Lesdiguieres, coffee machine-3F, 10F baby quiches, 5F *pain
au chocolat*). There's a midnight minigrocery across the street.

Restaurants in the Latin Quarter

La Petite Bouclerie is a cozy place with classy family cooking
(70F menu, closed Monday, 33 rue de la Harpe, center of

touristy Latin Quarter, tel. 01 43 54 18 03). The popular
Restaurant Polidor is an old turn-of-the-century-style place,
with great *cuisine bourgeois*, a vigorous local crowd, and a historic
toilet. Arrive at 19:00 to get a seat in the restaurant (65F *plat du
jour*, 100F menus, 41 rue Monsieur le Prince, midway between
Odéon and Luxembourg Métro stops, tel. 01 43 26 95 34).

Restaurants on the Île St. Louis

Cruise the island's main street for a variety of good options. All
listings below are on the rue St. Louis en l'Île. I like the cozy
Relais de L'Îsle (120F menu, #37, tel. 01 46 34 72 89) and for
a minisplurge, my favorite is **Le Tastevin** (150F menu, #46,
tel. 01 43 54 17 31). For crazy (but touristy and expensive) cellar atmosphere and hearty fun food, feast at **La Taverne du
Sergeant Recruiter**. The "Sergeant Recruiter" used to get
young Parisians drunk and stuffed here, then sign them into
the army. It's all-you-can-eat, including wine and service, for
190F (open Monday–Saturday from 19:00, #41, tel. 01 43 54
75 42). There's a just-this-side-of-a-food-fight clone next door
at **Nos Ancêtres Les Gaulois** ("Our Ancestors the Gauls,"
190F, open daily at 19:00, tel. 01 46 33 66 07). For a memorable picnic dinner ten minutes from the Marais, cross the
river to Île St. Louis and find a river-level bench on the tip facing Île de la Cité. Don't leave the island without tasting the
best sorbet and ice cream in Paris at any place advertising *les
glaces Berthillon*.

Restaurants near the Pompidou Center

The **Mélodine** self-service is right at the Rambuteau Métro
stop. **Dame Tartine** overlooks the *Homage to Stravinsky* fountain, serves a young clientele, and offers excellent, cheap, lively
meals. The popular **Café de la Cité** fills one long line of tables
with locals enjoying their 44F lunches and 65F dinner specials
(22 rue Rambuteau, tel. 01 48 04 30 74).

Restaurants in Other Paris Locations

Three gourmet working-class fixtures in Paris are **Le Chartier**
(7 rue du Faubourge Montmartre, Métro: Montmartre), **Le
Commerce** (51 rue du Commerce, Métro: Commerce), and
Le Drouot (103 rue de Richelieu, Métro: Richelieu-Drouot).
Each wraps very cheap and basic food in a bustling, unpreten-
tious atmosphere.

Parisian Entertainment

A Tour of Pariscope

Newstands sell weekly magazines listing all the events and happenings in Paris. *Pariscope* (3F) or *L'Officiel des Spectacles* (2F) are cheap and essential if you want to know what's happening. Pick one up and page through it. For a head start, *Pariscope* has a web site (http://www.Pariscope.Fr/).

Each begins with culture news. Skip the bulky "Theatres" and *"Diners/Spectacles"* sections and anything listed as *"des environs"* (outside of Paris). *"Musique"* or *"Concerts Classiques"* follow, listing each day's events (program, location, time, and price). Venues with phone numbers and addresses are listed in an *"Adresses des Salles"* sidebar. Touristic venues (such as Sainte-Chapelle and Église de la Madeleine) are often featured in display ads. Operas, Traditional Music, Ballet/Dance, and Jazz/Pop/Rock listings follow.

Half of these magazines are devoted to Cinema—a Paris forte. After the *"Films Nouveaux"* section trumpets new releases, the *"Films en Exclusivite"* pages list all the films playing in town. While a code marks films as *"Historique," "Karate," "Erotisme,"* and so on, the key mark for tourists is "vo," which means *version original* (American films would have their English soundtracks and French subtitles). Films are listed alphabetically, with theaters and their *arrondissements* at the end of each entry. Later films are listed by neighborhood (*arrondissement*) and by *genre*. To find a showing near your hotel, simply match the *arrondissement*. (But don't hesitate to hop on the Métro for the film you want.) Film festivals are also listed.

Pariscope has a small English "Time Out" section listing the week's events. The *"Musées"* sections (*Monuments, Jardins, Autres Curiosites, Promenades, Activites Sportives, Piscines*) give the latest hours and phone numbers of the sights, gardens, assorted curiosities, boat tours, sports, swimming pools, etc. *Clubs de Loisirs* are various athletic and social clubs. *Pour les Jeunes* is for young people (kids' films, animations/cartoons, marionettes, circuses, and amusement parks such as Asterix and Disney). *Conferences* are mostly lectures. For cancan mischief, look under *"Paris la nuit,"* "cabarets," or *"spectacles erotiques."*

Finally, you'll find a TV listing. Paris has four countrywide stations: TF1, France 2, France 3, and the new *"Arte"*

station (a German/French cultural channel). M6 is filled with
American series. Canal Plus (channel 4) is a cable channel that
airs an American news show at 7:00 a.m. and an American
sports event on Sunday evening.

Jazz Clubs
The **Caveau de la Huchette** is the handiest characteristic old
jazz club for visitors, filling an ancient Latin Quarter cellar with
live jazz and frenzied dancing every night (60F weekday, 70F
weekend admission, 30F drinks, open 21:30– 02:30 or later,
closed Monday, 5 rue de la Huchette, 75005 Paris, tel. 01 43 26
65 05). You'll also find several well-reputed clubs bordering the
Forum shopping center in Les Halles area on the rue Berger.

Transportation Connections—Paris
Paris is Europe's transportation hub. You'll find trains and buses
(day and night) to most any French or European destination.
Paris has six central rail stations, each serving different regions.
   Gare St. Lazare: Serves Upper Normandy. To **Rouen**
(15/day, 1 hr), **Honfleur** (6/day, 3 hrs, via Lisieux then bus),
Bayeux (9/day, 2.5 hrs), **Caen** (12/day, 2 hrs).
   Gare Montparnasse: Serves Lower Normandy and Brit-
tany, and offers TGV service to the Loire Valley and south-
western France. To **Chartres** (10/day, 1 hr), **Mont St. Michel**
(2/day, 4.5 hrs, via Rennes), **Dinan** (7/day, 3.5 hrs via Rennes),
Bordeaux (14/day, 3.5 hrs), **Toulouse** (7/day, 5 hrs), **Albi** (6.5
hrs, via Toulouse), **Carcassonne** (6.5 hrs, via Toulouse),
Tours (14/day, 1 hr).
   Gare d'Austerlitz: Provides non-TGV service to the
Loire Valley, southwestern France, Spain, and Portugal. To
Amboise (8/day, 2.5 hrs), **Sarlat** (5/day, 5.5 hrs), **Cahors**
(5/day, 7 hrs), **Barcelona** (3/day, 13 hrs), **Madrid** (5/day, 16
hrs), **Lisbon** (1/day, 24 hrs).
   Gare du Nord: Serves northern France and international
destinations. To **Brussels** (10/day, 3.5 hrs), **Amsterdam** (10/day,
5.5 hrs), **Copenhagen** (3/day, 16 hrs), **Koblenz** on the Rhine
(3/day, 7 hrs), **London** via the Eurostar Chunnel (5/day, 3 hrs).
   Gare de l'Est: Serves eastern France and points east.
To **Colmar** (10/day, 6.5 hours), **Strasbourg** (13/day, 4.5
hours), **Reims** (8/day, 2 hrs), **Verdun** (5/day, 3 hrs),
Munich (4/day, 8.5 hrs), **Vienna** (3/day, 13 hrs), **Zurich**
(4/day, 6 hrs).

Gare du Lyon: Offers TGV and regular service to south-eastern France, Italy, and other international destinations. To **Beaune** (8/day, 2–3 hrs), **Dijon** (13/day, 1.5 hrs), **Lyon** (12/day, 2.5 hrs), **Avignon** (10/day, 4 hrs), **Arles** (10/day, 5 hrs), **Nice** (8/day, 7 hrs), **Venice** (5/day, 11 hrs), **Rome** (3/day, 15 hrs), **Bern** (5/day, 5 hrs).

Buses: Long-distance bus lines provide a cheaper, if less comfortable and less flexible, alternative transportation to major European cities. The principal bus station in Paris is the Gare Routière du Paris-Gallieni at Métro Gallieni, avenue du General de Gaulle, in the suburb of Bagnolet (tel. 01 49 72 51 51). Eurolines buses depart from here.

Charles de Gaulle Airport

There are three main terminals, T-1, T-2, and T-9. Air France uses T-2, charters dominate T-9, and most airlines serving the U.S.A. use T-1. The three terminals are connected every few minutes by a free shuttle bus called a *navette* (gate 26, T-1).

At Terminal 1 you'll find an American Express cash machine, an automatic bill changer (at baggage claim 30), and a bank exchange window (at baggage claim 18). The TI (open until 23:00) at the "Meeting Point" has free Paris city maps and sightseeing information. You can buy a *télécarte* (phone card) at the Relais H at the Meeting Point and pick up French currency at the bank or ATM machine near gate 16 (barely acceptable rates). Car rental offices are found on the arrival level between gates 10–22, and a handy SNCF (train) office is at gate 22. For flight information, call 01 48 62 22 80.

Transportation Between Paris and Charles de Gaulle Airport: Three efficient public-transportation routes link the airport's T-1 terminal and central Paris. The free shuttle bus (*navette*) runs between gate 28 and the **RER Roissy Rail** station, where a train zips you into Paris' subway system (Métro) in 30 minutes (45F, stops at Gare du Nord, Chatelet, St-Michel, and Luxembourg Gardens). The **Roissy Bus** runs every 15 minutes between gate 32 and the old Paris Opéra (stop is on the rue Scribe, in front of the American Express), costs 40F (use the automatic ticket machine), and takes 40 minutes but can be jammed. The **Air France Bus** leaves every 15 minutes from gate 34 and serves the Arc de Triomphe and the Porte Maillot in about 40 minutes for 55F, and the Mont-parnasse Tower in 60 minutes for 65F. For most people the

RER Roissy Rail works best. A taxi ride with luggage costs about 230F (taxi stand, often with long waits, at gate 16).

The Roissy bus, Air France buses, and RER trains described above also connect T-2 and Paris with the same frequency and for the same prices as from T-1.

Transportation between Charles de Gaulle Airport and Other Destinations in France: A new TGV (tay-jay-vay) rail station (located at T-2) links this airport at blistering speeds with Lille to the north and Lyon, Avignon, Nîmes, Marseille, and Montpellier to the south, without passing through Paris. You can transfer easily from these cities to many other French and European destinations.

Sleeping at or near Charles de Gaulle Airport: Those with early flights may want to sleep in terminal 1 at **Cocoon** (60 "cabins," Sb-250F, Db-300F, CC:VM, tel. 01 48 62 06 16, fax 01 48 62 56 97). Take the elevator down to "boutique level" or walk down from the departure level; it's near the Burger King. You get 16 hours of silence buried under the check-in level with TV and toilet. The **Hôtel IBIS** (at the Roissy Rail station; free shuttle bus to either terminal takes two minutes) offers more normal accommodations (Db-400F, CC:VM, tel. 01 49 19 19 19, fax 01 49 19 19 21).

If you've rented a car and want to stay near the airport, consider the pleasant city of Senlis, 15 minutes by car. **Hostellerie de la Porte Bellon** is comfortable (Sb-210F, Db-360F–410F, CC:VM, 51 rue Bellon, tel. 01 44 53 03 05, fax 01 44 53 29 94).

Orly Airport

This airport feels small. It's easier than de Gaulle. After customs and baggage claim (near gate H), you'll see the ADP counter, a quasi–tourist office that offers free city maps and sightseeing information. Near the ADP you'll find a CFF exchange desk (decent rates, no commission for traveler's checks), a Paris Métro info and ticket desk, and a SNCF French rail desk (sells train tickets and even Eurailpasses). Downstairs, a handy mall has all the shops you could want (sandwich bar, bank—lousy rates, newsstand—buy *télécarte* phone card, and post office—great rates for cash or AmExCo traveler's checks). For flight information, call 01 49 75 15 15.

Transportation Between Paris and Orly Airport: The **Air France Bus**, which runs between gate F and Paris'

Invalides Métro stop (40F, every 15 minutes, 30-minute trip), is best for those staying in the rue Cler neighborhood. For the Marais neighborhood and other Paris destinations, take the **Jetbus** (22F, bus #285, every 15 minutes) from near gate F to the the Villejuif Métro stop, buy a *carnet* of 10 Métro tickets, and you're in the Métro system. Get off at the Sully Morland stop for Marais area hotels. There are several other bus/Métro options. Allow 150F for a taxi into central Paris—one partner can stand in line while the other does arrival chores.

   Sleeping near Orly Airport: The only reasonable hotel is the IBIS (Db-400F, tel. 01 46 87 33 50, fax 01 46 87 29 92), with free shuttle service to the terminal. Chartres and Versailles are convenient to Orly by car, but beware of rush hour on the freeways. Check my hotel listings under these sights.

NORMANDY

These are lands of lush green rolling hills, apple orchards, dramatic coastlines, half-timbered homes, and thatched roofs. Parisians call Normandy "the 21st *arrondissement*." It's their escape—the nearest beach. The British call this close enough for a weekend away.

Viking Norsemen settled here in the ninth century, giving Normandy its name. William the Conqueror invaded England from Normandy in the 11th century. To see his victory commemorated in a remarkable tapestry, weave Bayeux into your trip. In Rouen, France's all-time inspirational leader, Joan of Arc (Jeanne d'Arc), was convicted of heresy and burned at the stake by the English, against whom she had rallied France during the Hundred Years' War.

The rugged coast of Normandy harbors tiny fishing villages like little Honfleur, which today has more charm than fish. The cliff-edged coast, two hours south of Honfleur, was the scene of a WWII battle that changed the course of history. South of the D-Day beaches, on the border of Brittany, is the almost surreal island abbey of Mont St. Michel, rising serene and majestic, oblivious to its tides of tourists.

Planning Your Time
Three Days in Normandy by Car:
Day 1 Depart Paris by 8:15. Be in line at Giverny for the 10:00 opening, afternoon walk in Rouen, evening in Honfleur.

Normandy

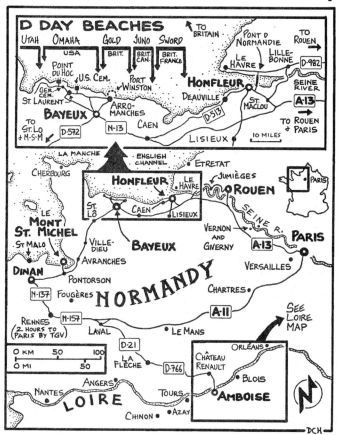

Day 2 Depart Honfleur by 9:00. Caen Battle of Normandy Museum/Memorial at 10:00. 13:00, Arromanches for lunch and museum; 15:00, American cemetery; 16:00, Pointe du Hoc Ranger Memorial; 17:00, German cemetery; 18:00, Bayeux hotel.

Day 3 Bayeux tapestry in morning, Mont St. Michel in afternoon, overnight in Dinan or (if you're really pushed for time) drive to Loire Valley.

Without a car and without a lot of time, consider skipping Giverny and Honfleur.

Cuisine Scene—Normandy

Known as the land of the four C's (Calvados, Camembert, cider, and *crème*), Normandy's cuisine specializes in cream sauces, organ meats (kidneys, sweetbreads, and tripe—the "gizzard salads" are great), and seafood (*fruit de mer*). Dairy products are big here. Local cheeses are Camembert (mild to very strong), Brillat-Savarin (buttery), Livarot (spicy and pungent), Pavé d'Auge (spicy and tangy), and Pont l'Evéque (earthy flavor). Normandy is famous for its powerful Calvados apple brandy, Benedictine brandy (made by local monks), and three kinds of alcoholic apple ciders (*cidre* can be *doux*—sweet, *brut*—dry, or *bouche*—sparkling and the strongest).

ROUEN

This 2,000-year-old city of 100,000 people mixes dazzling Gothic architecture, exquisite half-timbered houses, and contemporary bustle like no other in Europe. A one-time powerhouse, medieval Rouen walked a political tightrope between England and France. It was an English base during the Hundred Years' War. William the Conqueror lived here, and Joan of Arc was burned here.

Tourist Information: The TI, in a fine Renaissance building, faces the cathedral. Pick up their map highlighting an ideal walking tour (open May–September 15, Monday–Saturday 9:00–19:00, Sunday 9:00–12:30 and 14:30–18:00; off-season Monday–Saturday 9:00–18:30, Sunday 10:00–13:00, tel. 02 32 08 32 40).

Arrival in Rouen

By Train: Rue Jeanne d'Arc cuts from Rouen's station straight through the town center to the Seine River. Upon arrival, walk down rue Jeanne d'Arc to rue du Gros Horloge, the medieval center's pedestrian mall that connects the Old Market and Jeanne d'Arc church (on the right) with the cathedral and TI (on the left). To go directly to the start of the Rouen walking tour, described below, turn right on rue du Gros Horloge (you'll see the sweeping roof of the modern Eglise Jeanne d' Arc).

By Car: Follow signs to *centre-ville* and Rive Droite and park along the river (metered) or in the pay lot next to the cathedral.

Sights—Rouen

▲▲▲**Rouen Walking Tour**—For a good quick dose of Rouen's Gothic and half-timbered wonders, begin at the Jeanne d'Arc church and follow the route described below (most sights close 12:00–14:00). With the town's lacy Gothic skyline and half-timbered building solidly on vertical hold, it's hard to imagine the town devastated by WWII bombs. Its restoration attests to the French commitment to their people-friendly city centers (rather than to suburban sprawl).

The striking half-timbered houses (14th to 19th centuries) that line Rouen's streets remind us that there's more oak than stone in this region. Cantilevered floors were standard until about 1520. These top-heavy designs made sense because city land was limited, property taxes were based on ground-floor square footage, and the cantilevering minimized unsupported spans on upper floors.

Église Jeanne d'Arc—This modern church is a tribute to Jeanne d'Arc. Nineteen-year-old Jeanne was burned at the stake on this square in 1431. The church, completed in 1979, feels Scandinavian inside and out—reminding us again of Normandy's Nordic roots. Pick up an English pamphlet describing the church (closed 12:00–14:00). A WC is 30 yards from the church doors. Next door, under a modern roof, is a great outdoor morning market for picnic fixings—until 12:30. (For the story of Jeanne d'Arc and a rundown on the Hundred Years' War, see the Appendix.)

Rue du Gros Horloge—This has been Rouen's main pedestrian and shopping street since Roman times. It links the Église Jeanne d'Arc (church) and the Cathédrale Notre Dame, and shows off the impressive Renaissance (1528) public clock, le Gros Horloge. Admire the clock and sculpture in the arch from below but skip the 10F climb to the top.

Palace of Justice—Take the first left after the old clock and in a block you'll see the impressive Flamboyant Gothic Palace of Justice (largely restored after WWII bombing, though the western facade remains littered with pockmarks from German guns). Returning to the rue du Gros Horloge, turn left and continue to the . . .

Cathédrale Notre Dame—The exterior is considered one of France's most beautiful, a fine example of the last overripe stage of Gothic architecture called "*flamboyant*"—flamelike. Make a marvel-at-the-Gothic circuit inside, stopping halfway down the

Rouen

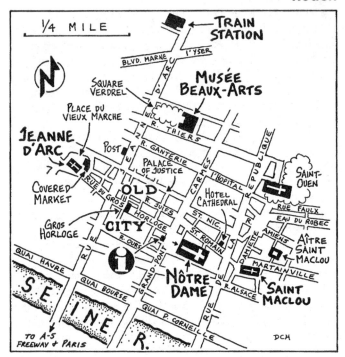

nave on the right to see photos showing the severe World War II bomb damage. This is the church Monet painted at various times of day from the apartment he rented for this purpose opposite the cathedral. You can see some of these paintings at the Musée d'Orsay in Paris.

Leave the cathedral via the left (northern) transept, enjoy the Gothic facade behind you, then turn right to rue St. Romain. This fine old medieval lane leads a few blocks to the St. Maclou Church. A plaque on your right (under the ruined Gothic arch) identifies the site of an old chapel where Joan of Arc was sentenced to death—and where she was proclaimed innocent 25 years later. Take a look down rue des Chanoines (next left) for a half-timbered fantasy. Rue St. Romain leads to the . . .

St. Maclou Church—Study the unique bowed facade. Inside, walk to the end of the choir and look back at the stained glass framed by the suspended crucifix.

Leaving the church, turn right and right (giving the boys on the corner a wide berth) and wander past a fine wall of half-timbered buildings fronting rue Martainville. Within a block a passageway on the left leads to . . .

Aître St. Maclou—Wander all the way into this half-timbered courtyard/graveyard/cloister. This was a cemetery for 14th-century plague victims. Notice the ghoulish carvings lurking around you. It's now an art school. Peek in on the young artists.

Return to the center via the half-timbered antique shops of rue Damiette and Rouen's third fine Gothic church, St. Ouen. A thousand-year-old Danish rune stone stands by the church door, reminding locals of their Nordic heritage. From there, rue Hôpital takes you back to rue Jeanne d'Arc and the station.

The town's other sights, such as the **Musée des Beaux Arts** (paintings from all periods, including works by Caravaggio, Rubens, Veronese, Steen, Géricault, Ingres, Delacroix, and the Impressionists), are described in the free TI Rouen map.

Sights—Near Rouen

▲**La Route des Anciennes Abbayes**—The route of the ancient abbeys (follow the D-982 west of Rouen if driving, or inquire about buses at the TI) is punctuated with abbeys, apple trees, Seine River views, and pastoral scenery. Monks are the guides at l'Abbaye de St. Wandrille, and Jumièges offers France's most romantic ruined abbey. Get details at Rouen's TI.

Sleeping and Eating in Rouen
(5F = about $1)
Stay at the ideal **Hôtel de la Cathédrale** (Sb-250F–305F, Db-300F–355F, 12 rue St. Romain, tel. 02 35 71 57 95, fax 02 35 70 15 54). Rouen's best moderately priced seafood restaurant is **La Mirabelle**, across from Église Jeanne d'Arc (tel. 02 35 71 58 21), though you'll find many inexpensive alternatives between St. Maclou and St. Ouen churches.

Transportation Connections—Rouen
Rouen is well served by trains from Paris, through Amiens to other points north, and through Caen to other destinations west and south.

By train to: Paris' Gare St. Lazare (nearly hrly, 75 min), **Bayeux** (8/day, 3 hrs, transfer in Caen), **Mont St. Michel** (6/day, 4 hrs, via Caen and Pontorson; short bus ride from

Pontorson to Mont St. Michel), **Honfleur** (6/day, 90 min to Lisieux, then bus to Honfleur, hrly, 30 min). The *Inter Normandie* buses (tel. 02 31 44 77 44) to Honfleur are a quicker but less frequent alternative (2/day, 2 hrs, transfer in Pont Audemer). Inquire at either TI.

HONFLEUR

Honfleur (ohn-fluer) actually feels as picturesque as it looks. Its cozy harbor, surrounded by skinny, soaring houses, was a favorite of 16th-century sailors and 19th-century Impressionists. Today Honfleur, eclipsed by the gargantuan port of Le Havre, just across the Seine, happily uses its past as a bar stool and sits on it. All of Honfleur's interesting streets and activities are packed together within a few minutes' walk of the old port (Vieux Bassin).

Tourist Information: The helpful, English-speaking TI is hidden a few blocks just off the Vieux Bassin, on the lower building side of the harbor. Pick up their handy town map and any information you need on Normandy (open daily Easter–October 9:00–12:30 and 14:00–18:30, 10:00– 16:00 on Sunday, off-season 9:00–12:00 and 14:00–17:30, closed Sunday, place Arthur Boudin, tel. 02 31 89 23 30).

Arrival in Honfleur

By Bus: The bus stop is a five-minute walk north of the old port (Vieux Bassin). Walk up the rue des Fosses and turn right on rue de la Ville to reach the TI, or continue straight to the old port and hotels.

By Car: Follow *centre-ville* signs, then park as close to the old port (Vieux Bassin) as possible. Parking lots are just north of the old port, though you can probably park very near your hotel. Parking is free from 19:00–9:00.

Sights—Honfleur

Honfleur is low on sights but high on ambiance. (Arriving late afternoon and leaving after breakfast is not a bad plan for drivers.) Skinny half-timbered buildings crowd around the harbor, remembering the 16th- and 17th-century days of discovery, when sloops set out to unknown New World corners; and 19th-century days, when artists reveled in their new-found freedom to look beyond mere physical things, making light and color their subject. Snoop around the streets behind place Berthelot and the Église Ste. Catherine for some of Nor-

Honfleur

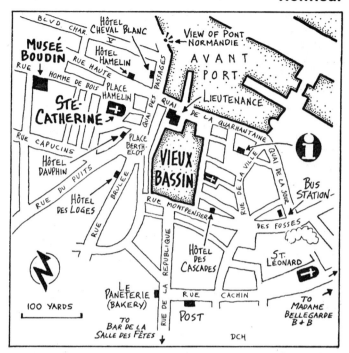

mandy's oldest half-timbered homes and interesting art galleries. Honfleur escaped the bombs of WWII.

▲**Église Ste. Catherine**—As you step inside this church your first thought is, "If you could turn it over it would float." This unique church was built in the 15th century, logically, in this ship-building town, by naval architects. Rough-hewn wood beams give it a feel-good warmth you don't find in stone churches. In the last months of WWII, a bomb fell through the roof but didn't explode. The exterior is a wonderful conglomeration of wood shingle, brick, and half-timbered construction.

The church's bell tower was built across the square to lighten the load on the roof of the wooden church and to minimize fire hazards. (Tower and church open 9:00–12:00 and 14:00–18:00, summer 9:00–18:30.) The church is free. There's only one room with a few church artifacts open in the tower—not worth the 10F.

Eugène Boudin Museum—This pleasant museum houses a variety of early Impressionist paintings and Normand costumes (20F, open 10:00–12:00 and 14:00–18:00, closed Tuesday, rue de l'Homme de Bois).

Saturday Morning Farmers' Market—The area around the Église Ste. Catherine is transformed into a colorful market each Saturday morning.

▲**Normandie Bridge**—The new 2.1-km-long Pont de Normandie is the longest suspension bridge in the world (until a Japanese bridge, which will beat it by 40 meters, is completed). This is a key piece of a super-freeway which, by the year 2000, will link the Atlantic ports from Belgium to Spain. Honfleur's TI has a fine brochure with all the engineering details. You can view the bridge from Honfleur (impressive when floodlit) or drive over and visit the free Exhibition Hall (under the toll booth on the Le Havre side, daily 8:00–19:00). The Seine finishes its windy 500-mile journey here. From its source it drops only 1,500 feet. It flows so slowly that in certain places, a stiff breeze can send it flowing "upstream."

Sleeping in Honfleur
(5F = about $1, postal code: 14600)
Sleep Code: **S** = Single, **D** = Double/Twin, **T** = Triple, **Q** = Quad, **b** = bathroom, **t** = toilet only, **s** = shower only, **CC** = Credit Card (**V**isa, **M**asterCard, **A**mex), **SE** = Speaks English, **NSE** = No English, * = Hotel rating (0–4 stars).

Honfleur is crowded on weekends, holidays, and in the summer, when many hotels require half-pension. I've listed places which normally don't. English is widely spoken in this town where local merchants post banners saying, "We welcome our liberators."

Hôtel Dauphin** is your best midrange bet, with a family feel, homey lounge/breakfast room, Escher-esque floorplan, great plumbing, and delightfully funky rooms, some with open beam ceilings (Db-300F–350F, Tb-350F–600F, no elevator, some smoke-free rooms, CC:VM, a block off the harbor at 10 place Berthelot, tel. 02 31 89 15 53, fax 02 31 89 92 06).

Hôtel des Loges** is quiet and comfortable (Db-295F–410F, Tb-330F, CC:VM, 18 rue Brûlée, tel. 02 31 89 38 26).

Hôtel des Cascades* is comfortable, well-located—a block off the harbor—with a tangled-fishnet floor plan (Db-

200F–300F, add 50F for a third person, only 10F for a fourth, dinner required during summer weekends, CC:VM, facing rue Montpensier at 17 place Thiers, tel. 02 31 89 05 83, fax 02 31 89 32 13, Melanie SE).

Hôtel Hamelin* is a basic budget value, even though half-pension is required. The rooms are small but clean, all have showers, toilets are down the hall (Ss-180F–230F, Ds-180F–230F, Ts-300F, half-pension is extra but cheap, 16 place Hamlein, tel. and fax 02 31 89 16 25).

Hôtel Le Cheval Blanc*** is a good three-star splurge, with port views from every room and the only elevator I saw in town. It's a big, borderline-musty, half-timbered place with no restaurant (Db-474F–600F, add 100F per person for triple and quad, prices include breakfast, CC:VM, quai de Passagers, tel. 02 31 81 65 00, fax 02 31 89 52 80).

Chambres d'hôte offer a good option here (the TI has a list), though most are at least 1 mile from the center of Honfleur. Try the bargain rooms above the very local **Bar de la Salle des Fêtes,** where French is spoken with a smile (Db-170F, place Albert Sorel, half a mile out rue de la République, tel. 02 31 89 19 69). **Madame Bellegarde** offers quiet, simple, and comfortable rooms (D-176F, Ts-290F, private shower and toilet down the hall, a ten-minute walk from the tourist office, just uphill from the church St. Leonard in non-touristed Honfleur, 54 rue St. Leonard, no sign in window, tel. 02 31 89 06 52).

Eating in Honfleur
Eat seafood. I like the restaurants located along the rue de l'Homme de Bois. Savor a slow meal at **La Tortue** (moderately priced, 36 rue de l'Homme de Bois, tel. 02 31 89 04 93), or better yet, enjoy Honfleur's best seafood in the cozy **Au Petit Mareyeur** (4 place Hamlein, tel. 02 31 98 84 23 for necessary reservations). The old harbor is ideal for evening picnics, especially as the sun sets. Try the steps in front of the port's bureau (La Lieutenance). **Le Paneterie** (26 rue de la République) is Honfleur's best *boulangerie-pâtisserie.*

Transportation Connections—Honfleur
Buses connect Honfleur with Lisieux, where you'll catch a train to other points. Train and bus service is usually coordinated.

To: **Bayeux** (6/day, 2.5 hrs; bus to Caen, then train to

Bayeux); **Paris'** Gare St. Lazare (5/day, 3 hrs; bus to Lisieux, train to Paris; buses from Honfleur meet most trains).

BAYEUX
Only 6 miles from the D-Day beaches, Bayeux (bye-yuh) was the first city liberated after the landing and makes an ideal base for visiting the D-Day sights. Even without its famous tapestry and proximity to the D-Day beaches, Bayeux would be worth a visit for its pleasant *centre-ville* and imposing cathedral. Navigating in Bayeux is a breeze on foot or by car. Look for the church spires and follow the signs to *centre-ville* or *Tapisserie* to reach the city center.

   Tourist Information: Pick up a town map at the friendly TI on the bridge (Pont St. Jean) leading to the pedestrian street rue St. Jean (Monday–Saturday 9:00–12:00 and 14:00–18:00, on Sunday June to mid-September 10:00–12:00 and 15:00–18:00, tel. 02 31 92 16 26, fax 02 31 92 01 79).

Bayeux History—The Battle of Hastings
1066 is probably the most memorable date of the Middle Ages because of this pivotal battle. England's King Ethelred was about to die sans heir, and the question was who would succeed him: Harold, an English noble, or William, the Duke of Normandy? Harold was captured during a battle in Normandy. To gain his freedom he promised William that, when the ailing King Ethelred died, he would allow William to ascend the throne. Shortly after that oath was taken, Harold was back in England, Ethelred died, and Harold grabbed the throne. William, known as William the Bastard, invaded England to claim the throne he figured was rightfully his. Harold met him in southern England at the town of Hastings, where their forces fought a fierce 14-hour battle. Harold was killed and his Saxon forces routed. William, now "the Conqueror," marched on London to claim his throne, becoming King of England as well as Duke of Normandy. (The advent of a Norman king of England muddied the political waters, setting in motion 400 years of conflict between England and France not to be resolved until the end of the Hundred Years' War in 1453.)

   The Norman Conquest of England brought England into the European mainstream. The Normans established a strong central English government. They brought with them the Romanesque style of architecture (e.g., the Tower of London and

Durham cathedral) that the English call "Norman." Historians speculate that, had William not succeeded, England would have remained on the fringe of Europe (like Scandinavia), and French culture (and language) would have prevailed in the New World.

Sights—Bayeux

▲▲▲**Bayeux Tapestry**—Actually woolen embroidery on linen cloth, this document—precious to historians—is a 70-meter cartoon telling the story of William the Conqueror's rise from Duke of Normandy to King of England and his victory over Harold at the Battle of Hastings. Long and skinny, it was designed to hang from the nave of Bayeux's cathedral.

Your visit has three parts (explaining the basic story of the battle three times—which was about right for me): First you'll walk through a "mood-setting images on sails" room into a replica of the tapestry with extensive explanations and a room designed to set the cultural scene for the battle. Next, a 15-minute AV show in the cinema gives a relaxing dramatization of the event. Finally you'll get to the real McCoy. It's worth the 5F and wait for the headphones, which give a top-notch fast-moving 20-minute scene-by-scene narration complete with period music. If you lose your place, you'll find subtitles in Latin. Remember, this is a piece of Norman propaganda—the English (the bad guys—referred to as *les goddamns*, after a phrase the French kept hearing them say) are shown with moustaches and long hair; the French (*les* good guys) are clean-cut and clean-shaven (35F, open daily May 15–September 15, 9:00–19:00, otherwise 9:00–12:30 and 14:00–18:00; a half-hour later in April and October; tel. 02 31 92 05 48). When buying your ticket, get the English film showtimes. If you're rushed and the cinema schedule doesn't match yours, skip the AV show. Cinemagoers pile into the tapestry with a crowd of 200. Cinema-skippers may have fewer crowds.

▲**Bayeux Cathedral**—Enjoy the view of the nave from the top of the steps as you enter the church. The tapestry originally hung here. Imagine it proudly circling the congregation, draped around the nave from the miniarches just below the big bright upper windows of the clerestory. The nave's huge round lower arches are Romanesque (11th century) and decorated with the same zig-zag pattern that characterizes this "Norman" art in England. But this nave is much brighter because of the later

Gothic windows of the top half of the nave. The finest example of 13th-century "Norman Gothic" is in the choir (the fancy area behind the central altar). For maximum 1066 atmosphere, step into the crypt (below the central altar). Study the frescoed angels and the ornately carved (Roman-style acanthus leaves and grey meanies) 11th-century capitals (free, 9:00–18:00).

Bayeux Memorial Museum/Battle of Normandy—This museum offers a fine overview of the Battle of Normandy, featuring tanks, jeeps, uniforms, and countless informative displays (30F, open daily June–August, 9:00–19:00, off-season closes from 12:30–14:00; on the Bayeux's ring road, 20 minutes on foot from the center).

Sleeping in Bayeux
(5F = about $1, postal code: 14400)

Bayeux has several good budget hotels. The most convenient for train travelers is the trés local and friendly **Hôtel de la Gare***, with simple, spotless rooms, at the train station (S-90F, D-100F, Db-210F–290F, T-140F, Tb-300F, Q-180F, tel. 02 31 92 10 70, fax 02 31 51 95 99). **Hôtel Notre Dame***, ideally situated right across from the cathedral, has comfortable rooms with wall-to-ceiling carpeting and asks that you dine at its moderately priced classy restaurant (D-160F, Db-270F, Tb-360F, Qb-465F, showers 20F if not in room, CC:VM, 44 rue des Cuisiniers, tel. 02 31 92 87 24, fax 02 31 92 67 11). **Hôtel de Reine Mathilde****, located right downtown, has modern and very comfortable rooms (Sb-260F, Db-270F–290F, Tb-340F– 390F, Qb-430F, CC:VM, 23 rue Larcher, tel. 02 31 92 08 13, fax 02 31 92 09 93). Travelers on any budget will appreciate the friendly welcome, inexpensive rooms, and cheap meals at the **Family Home Youth Hostel and Bed and Breakfast** (90F dorm bed with membership, 100F without, Sb-170F, D-200F, Db-230F in cozy bed-and-breakfast rooms, 65F dinner in wood-beamed dining room with wine included, 3 blocks in front of cathedral at 39 rue General de Dais, tel. 02 31 92 15 22, fax 02 31 92 55 72).

Sleeping near Bayeux: When driving in this area, I prefer the rural *chambre d'hôte* option. **Madame Sebire**'s rooms are cheap, comfortable, cozy, and located in the tiny village of Ryes at the Ferme du Clos Neuf (between Bayeux and Arromanches, Db-200F, breakfast included but minimal English, postal code 14400, tel. 02 31 22 32 34). For more *chambre d'hôte* listings, inquire at the Bayeux or Arromanches TI. Dead-center in Arromanches, the **Pappagall, Hotel d'Arromanches** is sans doubt the best value (Db-230F low season, 280F high season, 2 rue Colonel Rene Michel, 14117 Arromanches, tel. 02 31 22 36 26, fax 02 31 22 23 29). It sports a cozy bar and cheery, well-reputed restaurant.

Eating in Bayeux

Bayeux's old city centers around the pedestrian street rue St. Jean, which is lined with *crêperies*, cafés, and restaurants. The restaurants at the **Hôtel Notre Dame** and **Le Petit Normand** (both 80F menus, 35 rue Larcher) have fine reputations.

Transportation Connections—Bayeux

Rail service connects Bayeux with major cities, and limited bus service is available to the D-Day beaches.

   To: Paris' St. Lazare (12 trains/day, 2.5 hrs); **D-Day Beaches** (6 buses/day, 22 min, depart Bayeux train station or place St. Patrice in city center, arrive Arromanches, site of artificial harbor); **Mont St. Michel** (3 trains/day, 2 hrs to Pontorson, the nearest train station) from Pontorson, catch a bus (6/day, 10 min), taxi (70F, tel. 02 33 60 26 89), or bike (rent at Pontorson's station) to Mont St. Michel.

D-DAY BEACHES

Stretching 75 miles along the Atlantic coast north of Bayeux (from Sainte Marie du Mont to Ouistreham), you'll find museums, monuments, cemeteries, and battle remains left in tribute to the courage of the WWII British, Canadian, and American armies who successfully carried out the largest military operation in history. It was on these beautiful beaches, at the crack of dawn, June 6, 1944, that the Allies finally gained a foothold in France, and Nazi Europe began to crumble.

"The first twenty-four hours of the invasion will be decisive . . . the fate of Germany depends on the outcome . . . for the Allies, as well as Germany, it will be the longest day."

—Field Marshall Erwin Rommel to his aide, April 22, 1944, from *The Longest Day*.

Getting Around the D-Day Beaches

A car is ideal (the TI lists local agencies), though biking is an option for those with time and energy (rent a bike in Bayeux at M. Roue's shop for 80F, boulevard W. Churchill, tel. 02 31 92 27 75; or at the Family Home, 60F, see Sleeping in Bayeux). Buses connect Bayeux and Arromanches (see Bayeux Transportation Connections, above) to allow you to see the most impressive D-Day (*Jour J* in French) sights; or better, consider a minivan tour. Several companies offer tours of the D-Day beaches from Bayeux for about 150F per person (includes Arromanches museum entry). Jean-Marc Bacon of Normandy Tours (Hôtel de la Gare) does it in a minivan with a friendly personal touch (tel. 02 31 92 10 70, fax 02 31 51 95 99). Bus Fly offers similar minivan tours (and day trips to Mont St. Michel for 260F), tel. 02 31 22 00 08. Taxis are another good option (figure 80F from Bayeux to Arromanches, tel. 02 31 92 92 40).

Sights—D-Day Beaches

▲▲▲Caens' Battle of Normandy Museum—Caens, the modern capital of lower Normandy, has the best World War II museum in France. Officially named "Memorial for Peace," its intent is to put the Battle of Normandy in a broader context. Your visit has four parts: the lead-up to WWII, the actual Battle of Normandy, the video presentations, and the ongoing fight for peace.

Simply put, the museum is brilliant. Begin with a downward spiral stroll tracing—almost psychoanalyzing—the path of Europe from WWI, to the rise of fascism, to WWII.

The entire lower level gives a thorough look at how WWII was fought— from General de Gaulle's London radio broadcasts, to Hitler's early missiles, to wartime fashion.

You then see a series of three powerful movies (15 minutes each, for all languages, the cycle starts every 20 minutes—a clock at the end of the lower-level exhibits lets you plan your time). Ninety percent of the incredible D-Day footage is real, with a bit taken from the movie *The Longest Day*.

The memorial then takes you beyond WWII to the Gallery of Nobel Prizes. This is a celebration of the courageous work of people like Andrei Sakharov, Elie Wiesel, and Desmond Tutu, who understand that peace is more than an absence of war.

The finale is a walk through the U.S. Armed Forces Memorial Garden. I was a bit bothered by the mindless laughing of lighthearted children unable to appreciate their blessings. Then I read on the pavement, "From the heart of our land flows the blood of our youth, given to you in the name of freedom." And their laughter made me happy.

Allow 2.5 hours, including an hour for the videos. The memorial is just off the freeway in Caen (exit: Université, follow signs to "Memorial"). By bus, take #17 from Caen's city center and station to the end of the line (every 15 minutes).

Memorial Museum entry: 63F, free for WWII veterans, 20F for other veterans, free admission and nursery for kids under 10, open daily 9:00–19:00, until 21:00 in July and August, tel. 02 31 06 06 44—as in June 6, 1944.

▲▲▲**Arromanches (Musée du Débarquement)**—In this town, the British created the first-ever prefab harbor. Churchill's brainchild, it was named Port Winston. Eighteen old ships and 115 huge cement blocks (called Mulberries) were towed across the English Channel and sunk in Arromanches bay to create a 7-mile-long breakwater and harbor for landing 54,000 vehicles and 500,000 troops in six days. You can still see remains of the temporary harbor and visit the beachfront museum where this incredible undertaking is recreated with models, maps, mementos, and two short audiovisual shows— ask for English (32F, open daily May–September 9:00–19:00, off-season 9:30–17:30, closed January, tel. 02 31 22 34 31). Walk to the top of the bluff behind the museum for a fine view and ponder how, from this makeshift harbor, began the liberation of Europe.

Longues Sur Mer—Several German bunkers, guns intact, are left guarding seaborn attacks on the city of Arromanches. Walk out to the observation post for a territorial view over the Channel (located between Arromanches and Port en Bessin, look for signs).

▲▲▲**American Cemetery at St. Laurent**—Beautifully situated on a bluff just above Omaha Beach, the 9,400 brilliant white marble crosses and Stars of David seem to glow in memory of Americans who gave their lives to free Europe on the beaches below. Notice the names and home states inscribed on the crosses. Behind the monument, surrounded by roses, are the names of 1,557 missing or unidentified soldiers. France has given the U.S.A. free permanent use of this 172-acre site. It is

immaculately maintained by the American Battle Monuments
Commission. The trail to the beach below is open 8:00–18:00,
and until 17:00 off-season.

German Military Cemetery—For an opportunity to ponder
German losses, drop by this somber, thought-provoking resting
place of 21,000 German soldiers. While the American cemetery
is the focus of American visitors, visitors here speak in hushed
German. The site is glum, with two graves per simple marker
and dark crosses that huddle together in groups of five. It's just
south of the Point du Hoc (right off the N-13 in the village of
La Cambe, 22 km west of Bayeux, follow signs to Cimitiere
Allemand).

▲▲**Point du Hoc**—During the D-Day invasion, U.S. Rangers
attempted a castle-like siege of the German-occupied cliffs by
using grappling hooks and ladders borrowed from London fire
departments. German bunkers and bomb craters remain as
they were found (20 minutes by car west of the American
cemetery in St. Laurent, just past Vierville-sur-Mer).

MONT ST. MICHEL

The distant silhouette of this Gothic island-abbey sends the
tired sightseer's spirits soaring. Mont St. Michel (moan san
mee-shell), which through the ages has been among the top
four pilgrimage sites in Christendom, is one of those rare
places that looks as enchanting in person as it does in dreams.
While it floats like a mirage on the horizon, it does show up
on film. But as you enter the fortified abbey island, tourists
trample the dreamscape. Daytime Mont St. Michel is a touristic gauntlet—worth a stop, but a short one will do. During
nonsummer nights, the island is abbey-quiet, and the illumina-
tion, beautiful.

Orientation

Mont St. Michel is an island connected by a 2-mile causeway
to the mainland. It's surrounded by a mud flat that's well on its
way to becoming a marshland. Your visit features a one-street
village that winds up to the fortified abbey. A ramble on the
ramparts offers mud-flat views and an escape from the tourist
zone. The only worthwhile entry is the abbey itself, at the
summit of the island.

The tourist tide recedes late each afternoon. Poets prefer
evenings here. And since the abbey interior is not an essential

visit (and it's open late at night as a sound-and-light show any-way), arriving late and departing early is a good option.

Tourist Information: The TI (and WC) is to your left as you enter Mont St. Michel's gates. They have handy brochures listing hotels, *chambres d'hote*, restaurants, English tour times for the abbey, bus schedules, and the tide table (*Horaires des Marées*), essential if you explore outside Mont St. Michel (daily 9:00–19:00 in summer, off-season 9:30–12:00 and 14:00–18:30, tel. 02 33 60 14 30).

The Tides: The tides here (which rise 50 feet) are the largest and most dangerous in Europe. During a flood tide, the ocean rushes in at 12 miles per hour. In medieval times it was faster, rushing in "at the speed of a galloping horse." Even today the undertow can sweep a slow horse away. High tides (*grandes marées*) lap against the tourist office door (where you'll find tide hours posted).

Parking: Remember, very high tides rise to the edge of the causeway—leaving all cars left parked well under water. Safe parking is available at the foot of Mont St. Michel; you will be instructed where to park under high-tide conditions. There's plenty of parking provided you arrive off-season, or early or late in high season.

Sights—Mont St. Michel

The Village below the Abbey—Mont St. Michel's single street of shops and hotels leads to the abbey. With only 30 full-time residents, the village lives solely for tourists. After the TI, check the tide warnings posted on the wall. Before the drawbridge, on your left, poke through the door of Restaurant Le Mere Poulard, where a virtual theater-kitchen in action shows the colorful making of the traditional omelet. Don't spend 90F for this edible tourist trap. But watch the show as old-time costumed cooks beat omelets, daddy, eight to the bar.

Passing through the old drawbridge, Mont St. Michel welcomes you with the most touristy street this side of Tijuana. You can trudge through this touristic gauntlet uphill past sev-eral gimmicky "museums" and human traffic jams to the abbey (all island hotel receptions are located on this street). Or bet-ter, to avoid the tourist deluge, climb the first steps after the drawbridge on your right, turn left at the top, then follow the ramparts all the way up and up to the abbey. Public WCs charge according to altitude: 1F at the entry to Mont St. Michel, 2F halfway up, and 3F at the abbey entrance.

▲▲**The Abbey of Mont St. Michel**—Mont St. Michel has been an important pilgrimage center since A.D. 708, when the Archangel Michael told the bishop of Avranches to "build here and build high." With impressive foresight he reassured the bishop, "If you build it . . . they will come." Today's abbey is built on the remains of a Romanesque church, which was built on the remains of a Carolingian church. Saint Michael, whose gilded statue decorates the top of the spire, was the patron saint of many French kings, making this a favored sight for French royalty through the ages. As you enter, imagine the headaches and hassles the monks ran into while building it. They had to ferry the granite from across the bay (then deeper and without the causeway) and make the same hike you just did—with more luggage.

The visit is a one-way route through fine—but barren—Gothic rooms. You'll explore the impressive church, delicate cloisters, and refectory (where the monks ate in austere silence), then climb down into the dark, damp Romanesque foundations. A highlight is the giant tread-wheel, which six workers would power (like large hamsters) to haul two-ton loads of stones and supplies from the landing below. This was used right up until the 19th century. Free (tip requested) 75-minute English language tours leave several times a day (large groups, tour times at TI). For many, they make a short story long. Those who go through on their own find no English explanations posted—but then, there's not a lot to explain. (36F, abbey open daily May 15–September 15, 9:00–17:30, off-season 9:30–11:45 and 13:45–17:00, closes one hour earlier in winter.) Buy your ticket to the abbey, then keep climbing. Tours begin at the view terrace in front of the church. Allow 20 minutes to climb at a relaxed, steady pace from the TI to the abbey. For a free near-abbey visit, hike to the ticket booth and turn right into the gift shop, where you'll find models of the abbey over the ages. From there you can enter the free abbey gardens.

▲▲**Stroll around Mont St. Michel**—To resurrect that Mont St. Michel dreamscape and evade all those tacky tourist stalls, walk out on the mud flats around the island. At low tide it's reasonably dry and a great memory. This can be extremely dangerous, so be sure to double-check the tides. Remember the scene from the Bayeux tapestry where Harold rescues Normans from the quicksand? That happened somewhere in this bay. You may notice entire school groups hiking in from the muddy horizon. Attempting this popular excursion without a local guide is reckless.

▲▲**Evening on Mont St. Michel**—After dark the island is magically floodlit. Views from the ramparts are sublime. Mont St. Michel's latest addition is a somewhat overrated nighttime, self-tour sound-and-light show, *Les Imaginaires du Mont St. Michel*, inside the abbey. For 60F, you can walk through the same rooms visitors see during the day and enjoy a well-done room-by-room audiovisual show. With fires in the fireplaces and Gregorian chant CDs, it's a medieval extravaganza (starts after dark and runs very late—ask at TI).

Sleeping on or near Mont St. Michel
(5F = about $1, postal code: 50016)

Sleeping on the island, inside the walls, is the best way to experience Mont St. Michel, though you'll pay a premium for your hotel bed. On the island, most hotels pad their profits by requiring guests to buy dinner from their restaurant. Skip their outrageously priced breakfasts. Several hotels are closed from November until Easter. To reserve by letter, addresses are simple: the hotel, 50016, Mont St. Michel, France. Because most visitors only day-trip here, you should be able to find a room, sans reservation, at almost any time of the year.

The spotless, cozy, and comfortable rooms offered by the delightful couple at the **Restaurant le St. Michel** are the best value on the island (Db-200F–300F, no dining expectations, tel. 02 33 60 08 60, or 02 33 60 14 37). The remaining hotels all offer a token few inexpensive rooms, and many high-priced ones with similar amenities and prices. The rooms at the **Vielle Auberge** are probably the best for the price in this crowd (Db-280F–480F, Tb-500F, CC:VM, tel. 02 33 60 14 34, fax 02 33 70 87 04). You can also try **Le Mouton Blanc**** (D-200F, Db-300F–500F, T-350F, Tb/Qb-450F–500F, CC:VM, tel. 02 33 60 14 08, fax 02 33 60 05 62), or the **Hôtel Croix Blanche***** (a few beautiful loft triples, a few superb-view doubles, Sb-390F, Db-430F–490F, Tb/Qb-470F–600F, CC:VM, tel. 02 33 60 14 04, fax 02 33 48 59 82). The impersonal **Hôtel du Guesclin**** offers good, clean rooms at fair prices (D-170F, Db-320F–400F, Tb/Qb-330F–440F, tel. 02 33 60 14 10, fax 02 33 60 45 80).

Rooms on the nearby mainland are a better budget bet. Among the *chambres d'hôte*, **Madame Brault's La Jacotiere**, with fine rooms and views of Mont St. Michel, is a steal (D-200F, Bf-25F, in Ardevon, postal code 50170, tel. 02 33 60 22 92). The **Hôtel de la Digue***** is good and the closest of the hotels on the approach to Mont St. Michel. Spacious, modern, and cushy rooms and a restaurant with a view of Mont St. Michel make this hard to beat for those who need to park in front of their room (Db-300F–440F, Tb-480F, Qb-500F, CC:VM, tel. 02 33 60 14 02, fax 02 33 60 37 59).

Eating on Mont St. Michel

Puffy omelets are the island's specialty. Look also for mussels and seafood platters, locally raised lamb (fed on the saltwater grass), and Muscadet wine (dry, cheap, and white). I let Patricia and Phillipe cook for me at the friendly and reasonable **Le St. Michel** (tel. 02 33 60 14 37), across from Hôtel Mouton Blanc.

Transportation Connections—Mont St. Michel

The nearest train station is in Pontorson, ten minutes away by bus (6/day). A Pontorson–MSM taxi will cost about 70F. You can rent a bike at the Pontorson train station.

To: Bayeux (3 trains/2 hrs via Pontorson), **Dinan** via Pontorson (6 trains/day, 1.5 hrs), **Amboise** (allow 8 hrs, whether by regular train with transfers in Pontorson, Caen, and Tours; or by the TGV—transfer in Pontorson, catch TGV at Rennes, catch TGV at Paris' Montparnasse station, transfer in Tours).

Paris' Gare Montparnasse: A bus/train combination is easiest; bus from Mont St. Michel to Rennes (1/day, 3.5 hrs, tel. 02 99 56 76 09), then TGV to Paris. Less convenient is the train between Pontorson and Rennes (2/day, 4.5 hrs).

Sights near Normandy—Brittany

The Couesenan River marks the border between Normandy and Brittany. It hits the sea a few hundred meters west of Mont St. Michel, leaving the island barely in Normandy. The peninsula of Brittany is rugged, with an isolated interior, a well-discovered coast, and strong Celtic ties. This region of independent-minded locals is distinctly different from Normandy.

▲▲**Dinan**—If you have time for only one stop in Brittany, do Dinan. This delightful city offers Brittany's best-preserved medieval center (one hour from Mont St. Michel).

Consider this walk: start at the TI (6 rue de l'Horloge, 9:00–18:00 with off-season lunch breaks, tel. 02 96 39 75 40, the 15F tourist magazine has more information on this self-guided tour). Inspect the nearby lookout tower, Tour de l'Horloge (10F, good view from the top), then continue down the rue de l'Horloge and turn left into Dinan's historic commercial center, the place des Merciers. The half-timbered arcaded buildings are Dinan's oldest. They date from that time when property taxes were based on the square footage of your ground floor. To provide shelter from both the taxes and the rain, owners built out their first floors. Turn right where the square ends, then rappel down rue Jerzual (*crêperies*, boutiques, and stiff knees line this street). Crossing under the medieval gate (Porte Jerzual), turn right and climb to the only accessible section of the ramparts. Enjoy the view, then double back down the ramparts. At the gate jog right and take the first left uphill to the Jardins Anglais. Survey Dinan's port and Rance valley. Then peek inside the very Breton Basilique St. Saveur (bordering the park, English explanation inside).

Dinan feels real and untouristy. It's great for an overnight. **Hôtel de la Duchesse Anne***, warmly run by Giles and Christine, is a salt-of-the-earth budget home base on a large square at the edge of the old town (Sb-170F, Db-240F, 18 place du Guesclin, tel. 02 96 39 09 43, fax 02 96 85 09 76). Even if you're not staying here, drop by the hotel bar and have Giles draw you a *bol* of *cidre*. **Hôtel Arvor**** is more expensive, more comfortable, and more central (Db-280F–360F, near the TI, 5 rue Pavie, 22100 Dinan, tel. 02 96 39 21 22, fax 02 96 39 83 09).

▲**St. Malo**—Come here to experience *the* Breton beach resort. Stroll high up on the very impressive ramparts that circle the entire old city, eat seafood, walk as far out on the beaches as the tides allow, then return to Dinan for the night. An easy day trip, St. Malo is a 45-minute drive or a one-hour bus or train ride from Mont St. Michel or Dinan.

▲**Fougères**—This very Breton city is a delightful stop for drivers traveling between the Loire châteaus and Mont St. Michel. Fougères has one of Europe's largest medieval castles, a fine city center, and a panoramic park viewpoint (from St. Leonard church in Jardin Public). Try one of the café/*crêperies* near the castle. (Crêpes are called *gallettes* in Brittany, and are the local fare.) Pick up a city map and castle description in English at the castle entrance. The interior is grass and walls.

THE LOIRE

Named for France's longest river, the Loire Valley is carpeted with fertile fields, crisscrossed by rivers, and studded with hundreds of châteaus in all shapes and sizes. The medieval castles are here because the Loire was strategically important during the Hundred Years' War. The Renaissance palaces replaced medieval castles when the Loire became fashionable among the Parisian rich and royal during that age.

The valley of a thousand châteaus is also the home to many good wines. As you travel through the Loire, look for *Dégustation* (tasting) signs. Inquire at TIs for winery tour and tasting information. Vouvray, several miles west of Amboise, and Chinon, 20 minutes west of Tours, both have many proud and hospitable family wineries.

Planning Your Time

One and a half days is sufficient to sample the best of the Loire châteaus. Amboise is the ideal springboard for a visit to the region's three most interesting ones: Chambord, Chenonceau, and Cheverny. If you have more time, tour Azay le Rideau, Villandry's gardens, and Langeais (using Chinon as a home base).

If arriving by car, try to see one château on your way in (e.g., Chambord if arriving from the north, Langeais from the west, or Azay le Rideau from the south). If arriving by train, go directly to Amboise.

Don't go overboard on château-hopping. Two châteaus, possibly three (if you're a big person), is the recommended daily dosage. Famous châteaus are least crowded early, at lunchtime, and late. Most open around 9:00 and close between 18:00 and 19:00. Off-season, many close from 12:00 to 14:00.

The lazy plan for those with low energy or no car is to catch the one Amboise–Chenonceau public bus a day (from near the TI at 10:54, giving you 90 minutes at the château and departing the château at 12:40). Spend the afternoon enjoying Amboise, its château, and Leonardo's place.

Best Day on the Loire (from Amboise by car):

9:00–11:00	Chenonceau
11:30–14:00	Cheverny (beware off-season noon cloing) and lunch
15:00–16:00	Chambord or Chaumont
17:00	Return to Amboise and tour Le Clos Luce

Getting Around the Loire Valley

By Train: Amboise is well-connected to Tours. The châteaus of Chenonceau, Langeais, Chinon, and Azay le Rideau all have train service from Tours. Check the schedules carefully, as service is sparse on some lines.

By Bike: The cycling options are endless in this region, where the only serious elevation gain is via medieval spiral staircases. From Amboise, it's 45 minutes to Chenonceau and 90 minutes to Chaumont. (Connect Chaumont and Chenonceau with a two-hour pedal.) For Chambord and Cheverny, rent your bike in Blois (allow five to six hours round-trip, bike rental info at TI, 3 avenue Laigret, tel. 02 54 74 06 49). Bike from Chinon to Langeais, Azay le Rideau, Villandry, and Ussè (see Chinon sights for details).

By Minibus Tour from Amboise: Pascal Accolay runs Acco-Dispo, a very small and personal minibus company with excellent all-day, 190F château tours from Amboise. English is the primary language. While you'll get a fun and enthusiastic running commentary on the road covering château background as well as the region's contemporary scene, you're on your own at each château covered (you pay the admission fee). Tours depart at about 9:00. Most visit three châteaus (Chenonceau, Chambord, Cheverny) and view several others, returning by 18:00. Groups range from two to eight château-hoppers (reserve by calling 02 47 57 67 13, fax 02 47 23 15 73, 61 rue Victor-Hugo in Amboise, tours go daily except Sunday in

The Loire Valley

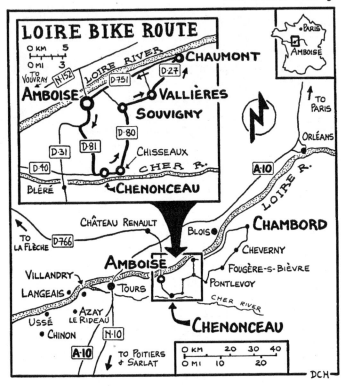

tourist season, less in winter, free hotel pickups). If this doesn't work, any Loire TI can explain your minibus options.

By Taxi: A taxi from Amboise to Chenonceau costs about 100F. Your hotel can call you one. The meter doesn't start until you do.

By Rental Car: Amboise has one car rental agency (105 route de Tours, tel. 02 47 57 17 92). The smallest Renault goes for about 250F per day (100 km free).

Cuisine Scene—Loire Valley

Here in "the garden of France," anything from the earth is bound to be good. Loire Valley rivers produce fresh trout (*truite*), salmon (*saumon*), and smelt, which is fried (*friture*). *Rilletes*, a stringy pile of whipped pork fat and liver, makes for a cheap, mouthwatering sandwich spread (use lots of mustard and add a *cornichon*—baby pickle). The area's fine goat cheeses include Crottin de Chavignol (*crottin* means horse dung, which is what this cheese, when aged, resembles), Saint-Maure Fermier (soft and creamy), and Selles-sur-Cher (mild). The best and most expensive white wines are the Sancerres and Pouilly-Fumés. Less expensive but still tasty are Tourraine Sauvignons and the sweeter Vouvrays. The better reds come from Chinon and Bourgeuil. For dessert, try a mouth-watering *tarte-tatin* (caramel apples on a pastry).

AMBOISE

Straddling the widest part of the Loire, Amboise slumbers in the shadow of its château and its most famous resident, Leonardo da Vinci. With or without a car, Amboise is the ideal small-town home base for exploring the best of château country. A castle has overlooked the Loire from Amboise since Roman times. As the royal residence of François I, the town wielded far more importance than you'd imagine from a lazy walk down the pleasant pedestrian-only commercial zone at the base of the palace.

Amboise (am-bwaz, 11,000 population) covers both sides of the Loire and an island in the middle. The station is on the north side of the river, but everything else of interest is on the south (château) side, including the information-packed TI on the riverbank.

Tourist Information: The TI is on quai du Général de Gaulle in the round building. Their Amboise city map shows restaurants, hotels, and château information, including the time and place of English-language sound-and-light shows, and information on minibus tours of the châteaus. (Open mid-June to September 9:00–20:30; Sunday 10:00–12:00 and 16:00–19:00; October to mid-June, usually open Monday–Saturday 9:00–12:30 and 15:00–18:00; Sunday 10:00–12:00, tel. 02 47 57 09 28.) The Michelin green guide to the Loire (sold for 60F—40 percent off the U.S.A. price—at all tourist shops) provides a good historical and architectural background on the region in general and each château in specific.

Bike Rental: You can rent a bike at Locacycle (70F per half day, 90F per full day, leave passport for security, open daily 9:00–19:00, near the TI at 2 rue Jean-Jacques Rousseau, tel. 02 47 57 00 28) or Cycles Peugeot (on the train station side of the river, just past the bridge at 2 rue de Nazelles, tel. 02 47 57 01 79).

Laundromat: The handy coin-op Lav'centre is a block from the TI near the fountain (22F to wash, bring four 10F coins to wash and dry a big load, figure 90 minutes; change machine, 2F detergent dispenser, open 7:00–20:00 daily, 9 allée du Sergent Turpin). The door locks at 20:00, but if you're already inside you can stay longer.

Arrival in Amboise

By Train: Amboise's train station is birds-chirping peaceful, with a small post office and the town taxi stand. From the station, walk down rue de Nazelles five minutes to the bridge that leads you over the Loire and into the center of town. Within three blocks of the station are a recommended hotel, bed and breakfast, and bike-rental shop.

By Car: Drivers simply set their sights on the flag-festooned château capping the hill above downtown Amboise. Most accommodations and restaurants listed in this book cluster just downriver of the château. Street parking near your hotel should be easy.

Sights—Amboise

▲**Château d'Amboise**—This one-time royal residence was used in the Middle Ages to greet royal pilgrims en route from Paris to Santiago de Compostela. Leonardo da Vinci is said to have designed the château's vaulted spiral staircases. Pick up the fine free English tour flier as you enter. The lacy petite chapel (first stop) is flamboyant Gothic, with two fireplaces to "comfort the king" and a plaque "evoking the final resting place" of Leonardo. Where he's actually buried no local really seems to know. After a fine town and river view, continue into and through the well-furnished château—which, while much larger in the 15th century, feels plenty big. Your last stop is the horsemen's tower, a brick ramp, climbing 40 meters in five spirals, that was designed to accommodate a mounted soldier in a hurry (34F, daily 9:00–20:00 in summer; 9:00–18:30 in May, June, September, October; closes for lunch and at 17:00 in winter, tel. 02 47 57 00 98). The château puts on a sound-and-light spectacle summer Wednesday and Saturday evenings.

▲▲**Le Clos Lucé** (luh clo loo-say)—This "House of Light" is the plush palace where Leonardo spent his last three years.

Amboise

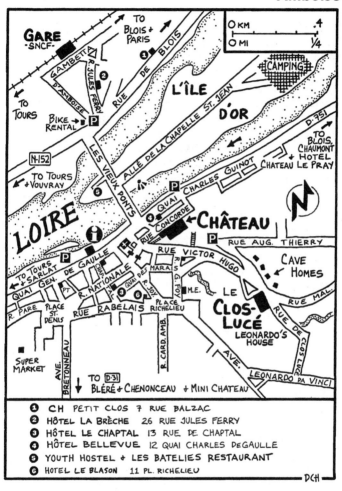

❶	CH PETIT CLOS 7 RUE BALZAC	
❷	HÔTEL LA BRÈCHE 26 RUE JULES FERRY	
❸	HÔTEL LE CHAPTAL 13 RUE DE. CHAPTAL	
❹	HÔTEL BELLEVUE 12 QUAI CHARLES DEGAULLE	
❺	YOUTH HOSTEL + LES BATELIES RESTAURANT	
❻	HOTEL LE BLASON 11 PL. RICHELIEU	

France's Renaissance king François I set Leonardo up just so he could enjoy his intellectual company. There's a touching sketch in Leonardo's bedroom of François comforting his genius pal on his deathbed. The house thoughtfully re-creates (with adequate English descriptions) the everyday atmosphere Leonardo enjoyed as he persued his passions to the very end. Of all the palaces I've seen on the Loire, I'd live here. The ground floor is filled with sketches recording the storm patterns of his brain and models of his remarkable inventions (built by IBM from his notes). It's hard to imagine that this Roman candle of creativity died nearly 500 years ago. (37F, daily 9:00–19:00 mid-March to mid-November, closed January, otherwise 9:00–18:00. Located a pleasant ten-minute walk from downtown Amboise, passing interesting troglodyte homes on your left.)

La Maison Enchantée—Your kids will love you for taking them to this automated doll museum. Push the buttons and watch them dance in 25 different settings. (25F, 12F for children, daily 10:00–19:00 in summer, other months 10:00–12:00 and 14:00–17:30 and closed Monday, 7 rue du General Foy, through the arch, tel. 02 47 23 24 50.)

Mini Château—This new 5-acre park on the edge of Amboise shows off all the Loire châteaus in 1:25 scale models, forested with 600 bonzai trees and laced together by a model TGV train (55F, kids 4 to 16 pay 37F, open daily 9:00–19:00, summer until midnight, tel. 02 47 23 44 44).

Sound-and-Light Shows—Many Loire Valley châteaus (including Amboise's) offer nighttime sound-and-light shows in the summer. They mix colored floodlights, tape-recorded history, and theater in Renaissance château courtyards. Ask if an English version is offered (they can be impressive even in French) and prepare for a late night. The local TI has up-to-date schedules.

Sleeping in Amboise
(5F = about $1, postal code: 37400)
Sleep Code: **S** = Single, **D** = Double/Twin, **T** = Triple, **Q** = Quad, **b** = bathroom, **t** = toilet only, **s** = shower only, **CC** = Credit Card (Visa, MasterCard, Amex), **SE** = Speaks English, **NSE** = No English, * = French hotel rating system (0–4 stars).

Amboise is busy in the summer, but there are lots of hotels and *chambres d'hôte* in and around the city. Many hotels require half-pension. The TI has photo albums of local hotels and CHs, and will reserve either. Except for the first hotel and the last CH, all listings are right in the old town center.

Hotels
Hôtel La Brèche** is a refuge of spotless rooms and a peaceful garden café. It's a ten-minute walk from the city center, and 100 meters from the train station. A terrific young couple runs

the hotel, and the wife speaks English. Many rooms overlook the garden. During summer, half-pension is required, which gets you a prize-winning dinner for an extra 75F per person (Sb-210F–240F, D-160F, Db-270F–310F, Tb-290F–330F, Qb-320F, huge six-bed room 360F, CC:VM, 26 rue Jules Ferry, tel. 02 47 57 00 79, fax 02 47 57 65 49).

Hôtel Le Chaptal** is cheaper and more central. While less idyllic, it's wonderfully frumpy, with birds in the lobby, comfortable rooms, and fine bathrooms but marginal beds (Db-205F–275F, Tb-255F, Qb-285F, CC:VM, 13 rue de Chaptal, tel. 02 47 57 14 46, NSE). In summer they request your dining in their cheery, inexpensive dining room.

Hôtel Belle-Vue*** overlooks the river where the bridge hits the town. It has grand public rooms and effective double-pane windows, so traffic is not a serious problem (Sb-250F, Db-280F–320F, Tb-330F, Qb-450F, CC:VM, 12 quai Charles-Guinot, tel. 02 47 57 02 26, fax 02 47 30 51 23).

Hotel Le Blason** is a half-timbered old building on a square a few blocks off the river, offering bright rooms with slick modern bathrooms under medieval timbers (Sb-270F, Db-295–330F, minibars, TV, telephones, and easy parking, CC:VM, 11 place Richelieu, tel. 02 47 23 22 41, fax 02 47 57 56 18).

Hotel de France Cheval Blanc* offers big, clean, simple rooms directly across from the TI (D-150F, Db-195F–235F, T-195F–245F, CC:VM, 6 Quai du General de Gaulle, tel. 02 47 57 02 44, fax 02 47 57 69 54). *Rue* (street) rooms have double-pane windows but some traffic noise. *Cour* (courtyard) rooms are quieter.

Bar Hotel de la Tour is a dumpy but clean little place with no stars, rickety furniture, and springy beds in a great location just under the castle entrance in the old town. For those on a tight budget, this beats the youth hostel (S-120F, D-175F, twin-190F, T-230F, only sinks in the room, 32 rue Victor-Hugo, tel. 02 47 57 25 04, NSE).

Chambres d'Hôte

The Amboise TI has a long list of private rooms. In summer, if possible, call a day in advance to reserve a room.

Maison Adam is in the old town center but rents only one room (Db-180F with breakfast, 24 rue Rabelais, tel. 02 47 57 44 07).

Le Petit Clos, 3 blocks from the station, rents three cheery cottage-type ground-floor rooms on a quiet picnic-perfect private garden with easy parking (Db-290F, family room takes up to five-500F, including big farm-fresh breakfast, a block off the river at 7 rue Balzac, tel. 02 47 57 43 52, Madam Roullet NSE).

Sleeping near Amboise

For a taste of château hotel luxury without going broke, try the cozy **Château de Pray***,** only a few minutes upriver from Amboise (toward Chaumont, same side of river as the Amboise château). Built 750 years ago, you'll feel a hint of the original medieval fortified castle behind the Renaissance elegance (Db-580F–720F, Tb/Qb-800F–870F, 37400 Amboise, tel. 02 47 57 23 67, fax 02 47 57 32 50).

If you prefer a quiet village, set up in the sleepy little Chenonceau (postal code 37150). The excellent **Hostel du Roy**** has classier rooms in the new section, spotless bargain rooms in the main building, a peaceful garden courtyard, and a wood-beamed cozy restaurant (S-120F, Sb-220F, D-125F, Db-225F–260F, T-210F, Tb/Qb-260F–310F, CC:VMA, 9 rue Dr. Bretonneau, a five-minute walk to the Chenonceau Château, tel. 02 47 23 90 17, fax 02 47 23 89 81). The nearby **Hotel du Bon Laboureur***** deserves every one of its three stars. From oak-floored, wood-beamed lounges, to its fairly priced luxury rooms (many ideal for families), to its many gardens (one surrounds a swimming pool), to its well-reputed restaurant (menus from 150F), this place is a worthy splurge (Db-220F–500F with most clustering around 350F, Tb-400F–700F, Qb-400F–800F, CC:VMA, tel. 02 47 23 90 02, fax 02 47 23 82 01).

Eating in Amboise

Local reasonable eateries abound in Amboise. **Crêperie L'Ecu** is a fine spot to sample French crêpes (open daily, indoor and outdoor tables, 7 rue Corneille, just off the pedestrian street). Their speedy three-course, 55F menu gives you a good salad, dinner crêpe, dessert crêpe, and coffee. In balmy weather, try the garden terrace at **La Brèche** (moderately priced, see Hotels for location). If you're feeling romantic, try **L'Epicerie,** (110F menu, closed Monday and Tuesday off-season, 46 place Michel DeBre, across from the château, tel. 02 47 57 08 94).

Les Bateliers offers elegant meals at fair prices on the island (7 rue Commire, tel. 02 47 30 49 49). For an after-dinner walk, cross the bridge to the island for a floodlit view of the château (the view/ambiance is good from/in **Le Shaker Bar**).

Transportation Connections—Amboise

Twelve 15-minute trains per day link Amboise to the regional train hub of St. Pierre de Corps (suburban Tours). From there you'll find reasonable connections to distant points (including the TGV to Paris–Montparnasse, about hourly, 60 minutes). The fastest way to many points, even in the south, is back through Paris.

By train to: Sarlat (2/day, 6 hrs, departures 7:38 and 14:23, transfer at St. Pierre de Corps and Bordeaux-St. Jean), **Mont St. Michel** (2/day, 8 hrs, transfer St. Pierre de Corps, Paris, Rennes, Pontorson), **Paris** (14/day, 90 minutes, via St. Pierre de Corps/Tours and TGV to Paris' Gare Montparnasse; or by regular train, 8/day, 2 hrs direct from Amboise to Paris' Gare d'Austerlitz).

The Loire's Top Châteaus

▲▲▲Chenonceau—The toast of the Loire, this 15th-century Renaissance palace arches gracefully over the Cher River. One look and you know it was designed by women: The original builder's wife designed the part of of the château that parallels the river; Diane de Poitiers, mistress of Henry II, added an arched bridge across the river. She enjoyed her lovely retreat until Henry died (pierced in a jousting tournament), and his vengeful wife, Catherine de Medici, unceremoniously kicked her out (and into the château of Chaumont). Catherine added the three-story structure on Diane's bridge. She died before completing her vision of a matching château on the far side of the river, but not before turning Chenonceau into the local aristocracy's place to see and be seen. This castle marked the border between free and Nazi France in World War II. Dramatic prisoner swaps took place here. Chenonceau is self-tourable (pick up the English translation), with piped-in classical music and glorious gardens (40F, skip the 10F Musée de Cires—wax museum, open daily March 16–September 15, 9:00–19:00, early closing off-season, tel. 02 47 23 90 07, three trains daily from Tours). To beat the crowds, arrive at 8:45. It's a 15-minute walk from the parking lot to the château. The village of Chenonceau welcomes you with a helpful TI, a handy grocery shop, and several cafés.

▲▲▲**Chambord**—More like a city than a château, this place is huge, surrounded by a lush park with wild deer and boar. First built as a simple hunting lodge for bored Blois counts, François I, using 1,800 workmen over 15 years, made a few modest additions and created this "weekend retreat." (You'll find his signature salamander everywhere.) Highlights are the huge double spiral staircase designed by Leonardo da Vinci, second-floor vaulted ceilings, enormous towers on all corners, a pincushion roof of spires and chimneys, and a 100-foot lantern supported by flying buttresses. To see what happens when you put 365 fireplaces in your house, wander through the forest of spires on the rooftop (fine views). Only 80 of its 440 rooms are open to the public—and that's plenty. With limited time or energy, skip the ground floor and second floor (rather bare rooms featuring "the hunt") and focus on the first floor, where you'll find the best royal furnishings. (36F plus 3F for the helpful English brochure, open daily April–September 9:30–17:45, until 18:45 in summer; otherwise 9:30–12:00 and 14:00–16:45, tel. 02 54 50 40 00.) Chambord's TI, next to the souvenir shops, rents bikes (25F/hour, 50F/half day, 80F/full day), and has a good list of nearby *chambres d'hôte*. To wake up with Chambord out your window, the **Hotel du Grand St-Michel**** comes with Old World, hunting-lodge charm, an elegant dining room, and a chance to roam the château grounds after all the peasants are gone (Db-300F–450F, CC:VM, 41250 Chambord, tel. 02 54 20 31 31, fax 02 54 20 36 40).

▲▲**Chaumont-sur-Loire**—Chaumont's first priority was defense—you can't even see it from the town below. As you approach the château, an interesting mix of Gothic and Renaissance architecture, veer left along the path for a better view. Originally there was another wing on the riverside, completely encircling the courtyard. Catherine de Medici force-swapped this place for Dianne de Poitier's Chenonceau, so you'll see tidbits about both ladies inside. Don't miss the *écuries*, royal horse house (they took this hobby seriously), or the Festival des Jardins (garden festival). A new display of gorgeous flowers each year makes this the Loire's best flower-garden stop. There's a guide during summer; otherwise, pick up the English brochure. (28F, open daily April through September 9:30–18:00, off-season 10:00–16:30, tel. 02 54 20 98 03.)

▲▲▲**Cheverny**—The most lavish furnishings of all the Loire châteaus decorate this very stately hunting palace. Those who complain that the Loire châteaus are stark and barren on the inside missed Cheverny. Today's château was built in 1634. It's been in the same family for nearly seven centuries. Family pride shows in its flawless preservation and intimate feel. The viscount's family still lives on the third floor—you'll see some family photos. Cheverny was spared by the French Revolution, as the owners were popular then, as today, even among the poorer farmers. Barking dogs remind visitors that the viscount still loves to hunt. The kennel (200 yards in front of the château) is especially interesting at dinnertime (17:00), when 70 hounds are fed. (The dogs—half English foxhound and half French bloodhound or Poitevin—are a hunter's dream come true.) The trophy room next door bristles with 2,000 stag antlers. (32F, pick up the English self-guided tour brochure at the château—not where you buy your ticket, open daily June–September 15, 9:15–18:30, otherwise 9:30–12:00 and 14:15–17:00, tel. 02 54 79 96 29.) Cheverny village, in front of the château, has a grocery shop and a few reasonable cafés.

▲**Azay le Rideau**—Most famous for its romantic reflecting pond setting, Azay le Rideau features glorious gardens and costly *"imaginaires"* (60F, self-touring sound-and-light show nightly at about 22:00). The château interior is nothing special. (32F, open daily 9:30–17:30, until 18:30 summer, closes from 12:00–14:00 and at 17:00 off-season, tel. 02 47 45 42 04.) If staying the night (Azay is a pleasant town), try the reasonable rooms at the Hôtel Biencourt (Ds-210F, Db-270F–330F, CC:VM, 7 rue de Balzac, postal code 37190, tel. 02 47 45 20 75, fax 02 47 45 91 73).

▲▲**Chinon**—This pleasing medieval town hides its ancient cobbles under a historic castle filled with Joan of Arc memories (25F, open 9:00–18:00). Don't underestimate this interesting château, especially if you're looking for a starker medieval contrast to those of the lavish hunting-lodge variety.

Chinon makes the best home base for seeing châteaus to the west of Tours (Azay le Rideau, Villandry, Langeais, Ussè). The TI (village center at 12 rue Voltaire, tel. 02 47 93 17 85) can tell you about bike rental, *chambres d'hôte*, and wine-tasting. Two good hotels in Chinon are the atmospheric and friendly **Hôtel Jeanne d'Arc*** (Db-180F–220F, Tb-220F, 11 rue Voltaire, postal code: 37500, tel. 02 47 93 02 85), and the almost-elegant, less warmly run **Hôtel Diderot****, with fine rooms in a centrally located 18th-century manor house (Db-300F– 400F, CC:VM, 4 rue Buffon, postal code: 37500, tel. 02 47 93 18 87, fax 02 47 93 37 10). **Les Années 30** (78 rue Voltaire) is one of many good-value restaurants in town.

▲▲**Langeais**—This epitome of a medieval castle, complete with a moat, drawbridge, lavish defenses, and turrets, is elegantly furnished and has English descriptions in each room. Langeais, which provides a good feudal contrast to the other more playful châteaus, is the area's fourth most interesting castle after Chenonceau, Chambord, and Cheverny (35F, open daily 9:00–18:30, until 21:00 in summer, closes 12:00–14:00 and at 17:00 November–March, tel. 02 47 96 72 60). Frequent train service from Tours.

▲**Villandry**—This otherwise mediocre castle has elaborate geometric gardens and a fine *Four Seasons of Villandry* slide show. Come here for the Loire's most complete gardens, skip the château interior, but don't miss the overview high above the gardens. (40F, open daily Easter–September, 9:00–18:00, until 17:00 October–Easter, tel. 02 47 50 02 09.)

Ussè—This château, famous as the "Sleeping Beauty castle," is worth a quick photo stop for its fairy-tale turrets and gardens but don't bother touring it. The best view, with reflections and a golden-slipper picnic spot, is from just across the bridge.

DORDOGNE

The Dordogne River Valley is France's version of the Rhine, with an extra splash of beauty. Hundreds of castles dot the Dordogne, a testament to its strategic importance in the Middle Ages. During the Hundred Years' War, this river marked the boundary between Britain and France. The sleepy Dordogne carries more memories now than goods. It's a profoundly French backwater filled with warm, salt-of-the-earth people.

Today Dordogne visitors enjoy rock-sculpted villages, fertile farms surrounding I-could-retire-there cottages, film-gobbling vistas, lazy canoe rides, and a local cuisine worth loosening your belt for. The Dordogne's most thrilling sights are its caves decorated with prehistoric artwork. The cave of Font-de-Gaume has the greatest ancient (15,000-year-old) cave paintings still open to the public.

To explore this beautiful river valley (in the region of Péri-gord), sleep in Beynac if you have a car and Sarlat if you don't.

Planning Your Time

You'll need at minimum a day and a half to explore this magnificent region. Your sightseeing obligations in order of priority are: the Dordogne River Valley and its villages and castles; prehistoric cave art; and the medieval town of Sarlat. The Dordogne riverfront villages offer exciting canoe-trip possibilities and an ideal break from your sightseeing. If possible, call well in advance to reserve a ticket to the cave art at Grotte de Font-de-Gaume.

A good day might be: morning and lunch in Sarlat (Wednesday and Saturday are market days); 13:00, cave tour; 15:00, two-hour canoe trip; 18:00, tour Beynac castle with river view; 19:00, walk back to the goose farm; 20:00, dine. This plan can also work well with a cave tour as the first or last stop of the day. With part or most of a second day, explore the twisting alleys in Beynac, tour the medieval castle at Castlenaud, and consider visiting Lascaux II caves.

As you drive in or out the day before or after (connecting the Dordogne with the Loire and Carcassonne), break the long drives with stops in Oradour-sur-Glane (to the north) and Cahor/Albi (to the south).

Getting Around the Dordogne

This region is a joy with a car but tough without. Rent a bike or moped, take one of the well-organized minivan tours of the region, hire all-day taxi service, or get to Beynac and toss your itinerary into the Dordogne.

By Bike or Moped: Bikers find the Dordogne scenic but hilly, with crowded roads. Consider a moped. Rent mountain bikes in Sarlat (100F per day) or mopeds (170F per day) at Peugeot Cycles (36 rue Thiers, tel. 05 53 28 51 87), or in Beynac at Quercyland Copeyre (tel. 05 53 28 95 01). A scenic Dordogne Valley loop ride is described below.

By Train: Train service in this region is limited to important cities and still is sparse. You can train from Sarlat to the caves in Les Eyzies, but service is limited, leaving you all day in Les Eyzies.

By Minivan Tour: Minivan tours of the area are offered by HEP Excursions based in Sarlat (many itineraries to choose from, half day-140F, full day-180F, four people minimum, French explanations only, no admissions included, tel. 05 53 28 10 04, fax 05 53 28 18 34). HEP prefers that you reserve through Sarlat's TI, though you can contact them directly.

By Taxi: Allo Sarlat Taxi offers 300F all-day taxi tours of the best of the Dordogne sights (tel. 05 53 59 02 43, split the cost with up to six travelers, find partners at your hotel). For taxi service from Sarlat to Beynac or La Roque-Gageac, allow 80F (120F at night); from Sarlat to Les Eyzies allow 140F, 220F at night and Sunday. Allo Taxi Bernard offers similar services, tel. 05 53 59 39 65.

By Car: You can rent a car in Sarlat chez Avis (400F per day 250 kilometers free, all insurance included, tel. 05 53 59 00 93).

Cuisine Scene—Dordogne River Valley

Gourmets flock to this area for its geese, ducks, and wild mushrooms. The geese produce (involuntarily) the region's famous *foie gras* (they're force-fed, denied exercise, and slaughtered for their livers). It tastes like butter and costs like gold. The duck specialty is *confit de canard* (duck meat preserved in its own fat—sounds terrible but tastes great). *Pommes Sarladaise* are mouthwatering thinly sliced potatoes fried in duck fat, commonly served with *confit de Canard*. Truffles are dirty wild black mushrooms that farmers traditionally locate with sniffing pigs, then charge a fortune for (3,000F per kilo, $250 per pound). Native cheeses are Cabécou (a silver-dollar-sized, pungent, nutty-flavored goat cheese) and Echourgnac (made by local Trappist monks). You'll find walnuts (*noix*) in salads, cakes, and liquers. Wines to sample are Bergerac (red and white) and Cahors (a full-bodied red). The *vin de noix* is a sweet walnut liqueur.

SARLAT

Sarlat (sar-lah) is a medieval banquet of a town scenically set amidst forested hills. The bustling old city overflows with historical monuments and, in the summer, tourists. Sarlat is just the right size: large enough to have a theater with four screens (as the locals boast) and small enough so that everything is an easy stroll from the town center. One-time capital of Périgord and current capital of *foie gras*, Sarlat has been a haven for writers and artists throughout the centuries and remains so today. Geese hate Sarlat.

Orientation

Like Siena, Sarlat is a museum city: no blockbuster sights, just a seductive tangle of cobblestone alleys peppered with medieval buildings. Rue de la République slices like an arrow through the circular old town. Sarlat's smaller half has none of the important sights but all the quiet lanes. Get lost.

Tourist Information: The helpful English-speaking TI, in the center on place de la Liberté, has free maps of the city and region, *chambres d'hôte* listings, and the helpful *Guide Practique* booklet (bus and train schedules, car, bike, and canoe

Sarlat

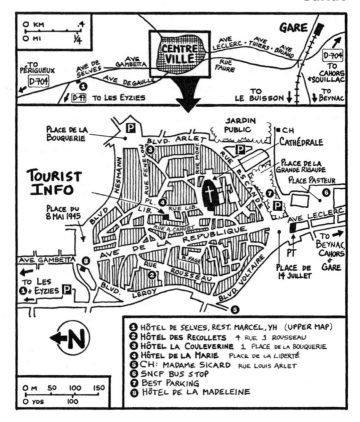

- **1** HÔTEL DE SELVES, REST. MARCEL, YH (UPPER MAP)
- **2** HÔTEL DES RECOLLETS　4 RUE J ROUSSEAU
- **3** HÔTEL LA COULEVERINE　1 PLACE DE LA BOUQUERIE
- **4** HÔTEL DE LA MARIE　PLACE DE LA LIBERTÉ
- **5** CH: MADAME SICARD　RUE LOUIS ARLET
- **6** SNCF BUS STOP
- **7** BEST PARKING
- **8** HÔTEL DE LA MADELEINE

rental, and so on). TI hours: July–September 9:00–19:00, Sunday 10:00–12:00 and 14:00–18:00; otherwise Monday–Saturday 9:00–12:00 and 14:00–18:00, tel. 05 53 59 27 67. Good English-language walking tours (24F, 60 minutes, June–September) leave from the TI (inquire about times).

Laundromats: Across from recommended Hôtel Couleverine (6:00–22:00 daily, self-serve or leave and pick up) or at 74 avenue de Selves near the recommended Hotel de Selves.

Sights—Sarlat
▲▲**Stroll through Sarlat**—Start by exploring the musty cathedral. Exit out the right transept. Snoop around through

a few quiet courtyards, then turn left, making your way toward the rear of the cathedral. Climb up the steps to that medieval space capsule called the Lanterne des Morts (Lantern of the Dead). Big shots were buried here in the Middle Ages. Exit right (with your back to the Lantern) toward my favorite house in Sarlat. Turn right and climb to the top of this lane for a good look back over Sarlat. Save time to prowl the quiet side of town (the other side of the rue de la République). If you like *Mayberry RFD*–type museums, try the Chapel of White Penitents on rue Jean-Jacques Rousseau. An automobile museum is just west of the old town (rue Thiers).

▲**Open-Air Markets**—Outdoor markets thrive on Wednesday morning and all day Saturday. Saturday's market seems to swallow the entire town.

Sleeping in Sarlat
(5F = about $1, postal code: 24200)
Sleep Code: **S** = Single, **D** = Double/Twin, **T** = Triple, **Q** = Quad, **b** = bathroom, **t** = toilet only, **s** = shower only, **CC** = Credit Card (Visa, MasterCard, Amex), **SE** = Speaks English, **NSE** = No English, ***** = French hotel rating system (0–4 stars).

Even with its miserable crowds in July and August, Sarlat is the train traveler's best home base. In July and August, many hotels require half-pension.

Hôtel des Recollets** offers modern comfort under heavy stone arches, with beautifully renovated rooms on the quiet side of the medieval city (D-200F, Db-250F–350F, Tb-320F, Qb-400F, a we-try-harder breakfast-32F, no half-pension, CC:VM, 4 rue Jean-Jacques Rousseau, tel. 05 53 59 00 49, fax 05 53 30 32 62, Christophe SE).

Hôtel La Couleverine** has a snobbish feel but plenty of medieval character. Families enjoy *la chambre famille*, the tower room (Db-260F–340F, Tb-380F, Qb-420F, CC:VMA, 1 place de la Bouquerie, tel. 05 53 59 27 80, fax 05 53 31 26 83). Half-pension (in an elegant restaurant, about 550F for two) is required at busy periods and in summer.

Hôtel de la Marie** has spacious rooms and invisible—almost eerie—management, and is as central as can be (D-170F, Ds-220F, Db-260F–290F, Ts-260F, Qb-420F, CC:VM; on place de la Liberté, tel. 05 53 59 05 71).

Hotel de la Madeleine*** is big and formal with Old World hotelesque service (Sb-295F, Db-330F–385F, no half-board requirements, elevator, CC:VMA, west edge of old town at 1 place de la Petite Rigaudie, tel. 05 53 59 10 41, fax 05 53 31 03 62).

Hotel de Selves*** is sleek and modern, with pastel French decor surrounding a swimming pool (Db-450F–570F, no half-board requirement, elevator, satellite TV and all the hotel extras, CC:VMA, five minutes' walk down Avenue Gambetta, west of the old town at 93 ave de Selves, tel. 05 53 31 50 00, fax 05 53 31 23 52).

Youth Hostel is casual, friendly, and reasonably well-located, ten minutes west of the old center (bunks-40F, small kitchen, no curfew, but call ahead for a bed, 77 rue de Selves, tel. 05 53 59 47 59).

Chambres d'hôte dot the Dordogne countryside. Several are on the fringe of old Sarlat. The **Sicards** rent two fine rooms—best budget beds in town—on the edge of the old town a five-minute walk from the TI (Sb-160F, Db-170F, Tb-190F, Le Pignol, rue Louis Arlet, tel. 05 53 59 14 28). **Mme. Feliu** rents four basic rooms without the homeyness (Db-190F–230F, where Blvd Henri hits boulevard Henri Arlet, tel. 05 53 59 03 21).

Eating in Sarlat

Sarlat is packed with moderately priced restaurants, all serving local specialties. The inexpensive **Restaurant du Commerce** is popular with locals and smack-dab in the Old City (4 rue Alberic Cahuet). Opposite the cathedral, **La Rapiere** offers wood-beam coziness and fine regional cuisine, with menus from 85F (tel. 05 53 59 03 13). The **Hôtel Marcel**'s well-respected restaurant serves a good 70F menu but is a ten-minute walk west of the center (8 rue de Selves, tel. 05 53 59 21 98).

Transportation Connections—Sarlat

The Sarlat TI has schedules for all modes of transport to and from Sarlat in its handy *Guide Practique*. From Sarlat, Bordeaux–St. Jean is the train travelers' gateway to distant points. Soulliac and Perigueux are the train hubs for points within the region. Sarlat train station tel. 05 53 59 00 21.

By train to: Bordeaux (4/day, 2.5 hrs; Bordeaux has TGV service going north, south, and east), **Amboise** (2/day, 7 hrs;

changing at Bordeaux–St. Jean and Tours), **Cahors**—catch
SNCF bus to Souillac (4/day, 45 min), then train to Cahors
(8/day, 1 hr), **Carcassonne or Albi** (5/day, 6 hrs; for Albi, transfer at Bordeaux's St. Jean station and Toulouse; for Carcassonne,
look for a direct train from Bordeaux, or transfer in Toulouse).

To Beynac: Beynac is accessible only by taxi (80F), though
the folks at Hôtel du Château and Hotel Bonnet will pick you
up at the station for no charge (see Beynac accommodations).

BEYNAC

This cliff-hanging village sees far fewer tourists than its big
brother, Sarlat, and feels more welcoming. You'll have the
Dordogne River at your doorstep and a perfectly preserved
medieval village winding like a sepia film set, from the place
where you beach your canoe to the hill-capping castle above.
The floodlit village is always open for evening strollers. The
Beynac TI ("bay-nak," open 9:00–18:30, tel. 05 53 29 43 08),
post office, and grocery shop cluster around the village riverside parking lot. Beynac's scenic cafés are on the river below
the TI and high above, near the castle entry.

Sights—Beynac

▲**Château de Beynac**—This cliff-clinging castle soars like a
trapeze artist 500 feet straight up above the Dordogne River.
During the Hundred Years' War, Beynac-et-Cazenac housed
the French, while the British headquarters was across the river
at Castelnaud. From the condition of the castles, it appears
that France won. The sparsely furnished castle is most interesting for the valley views. You have the choice of touring alone
or with a French-speaking guide; regardless, pick up the English translation. (30F, tours 10:00–18:30, usually starting on the
half-hour, in summer last visit is 18:00, lunch breaks in the off-
season, open March 15–November 15, tel. 05 53 29 50 40.)
River Cruise Trips—Boats leave regularly from Beynac's
parking lot for a mildly interesting but relaxed and scenic view
of the Dordogne (40F).

Sleeping in Beynac
(5F = about $1, postal code: 24220)

Those with a car should sleep in Beynac. With hotel pickup
services or a taxi, even those without a car may find Beynac
worth the trouble. To write any Beynac hotel, simply use the

24220 postal code. The tiny Beynac TI posts a listing of all acommodations with prices and current availability on its door.

The most central **Hôtel du Château**** is reasonable and comfortable. Patricia and Phillipe (Olivier SE) will welcome you warmly and feed you well. Rooms off the street are quieter (Db-240F–300F, Tb-360F, free Sarlat train station pickup upon request, CC:VM, tel. 05 53 29 50 13, fax 05 53 28 53 05). The adjacent **Hostellerie Malleville**** is comfortable but less homey (Db-300F, tel. 05 53 29 50 06, fax 05 53 28 28 52). For basic rooms with a great location, consider **Hôtel de la Poste***, run by Madame Montestier and her mother-in-law (NSE). No fax, no TVs, no credit cards—just simple, well-worn rooms, some with fine river views (D-170F, Db-215F–245F, Tb/ Qb-310F, 50 meters up the pedestrian street toward the castle, tel. 05 53 29 50 22). Right across from the castle atop the village (parking available, no views) hides the **Taverne des Remparts**, with four spacious yet cozy rooms and a superb restaurant (Db-230F, Tb-320F, CC:VM, tel. 05 53 29 57 76, SE).

Hotel Bonnet**, on the eastern edge of town, offers three-star, Old World comfort with two-star prices and fine river views from many rooms. Friendly Nathalie and her brother David (both SE) include a free Sarlat train station pickup service (Db-240F–290F, in summer you're requested to dine in their beautiful dining room, great firm beds, CC:VMA, tel. 05 53 29 50 01, fax 05 53 29 83 74).

Beynac and its surrounding villages have plenty of *chambres d'hôte*. In town try **M. Vaucel** (one Db-170F, a block from Hôtel du Château, tel. 05 53 29 50 26), or **M. Rubio** (tel. 05 53 29 53 32).

Sleeping near Beynac: If you need a pool, drive 2 kilometers east from Beynac to Vézac and try the modern **Relais des 5 Châteaux**** (Db-270F–300F, good restaurant, CC:VM, tel. 05 53 30 30 72, fax 05 53 31 19 39). For affordable French country luxury, stay in La Roque-Gageac at the remarkably reasonable **Hôtel Belle Étoile****, sporting classic decor, river views from most rooms, and a fine restaurant (Ds-160F–200F, Db-220F–310F, Tb-310F, Qb-350F, no half-pension requirement, postal code 24250, tel. 05 53 29 51 44, fax 05 53 29 45 63).

Eating in Beynac

You'll dine well in air-conditioned comfort at the **Hôtel du Château**. Beynac also offers the Dordogne's dreamy dinner-picnic site. Walking uphill, pass the château and continue out of the village, turning right at the cemetery. In La Roque-Gageac, the restaurant **Hôtel Belle Étoile** serves top regional cuisine in elegant surroundings (menus from 110F, reserve ahead here, tel. 05 53 29 51 44).

Sights—Dordogne Valley Region

▲▲▲**Grotte de Font-de-Gaume**—Even if you're not a connoisseur of Cro-Magnon art, you'll dig this cave. It's the last cave in Europe with prehistoric (polychrome) painting still open to the public—and its turnstyle days are numbered. On a carefully guided and controlled 100-yard walk, you'll see about 20 red and black bison—often in elegant motion—painted with an impressive sensitivity. Your guide—with a laser pointer and great reverence—will trace the faded outline of the bison and explain how, 15,000 years ago, cave dwellers used local minerals and the rock's contour to give the paintings dimension. The paintings were discovered by the village school teacher in 1901. Now, since heavy-breathing tourist hordes damage the art by raising and lowering the temperature and humidity levels, tickets are limited to 200 a day.

Visits are by appointment only. Reserve in advance by phone. Your hotel can make the call. Summertime spots are booked two weeks in advance. Even in off-season, when you can generally just show up and get in, it's smart to call ahead and get a time. Request an English tour (usually summers only). Even in French you'll find it interesting. (32F; in summer, ask for an English tour, off-season tours are French only—ask for the English translation brochure; open 9:00–12:00 and 14:00–18:00, closed Tuesday and at 17:00 November–February, tel. 05 53 06 90 80, no photography or large bags.) Drivers who can't get a spot here can try the more remote Grotte de Peche Merle, an hour east of Cahors (see below, Sights—South of the Dordogne).

Les Eyzies-de-Tayac—The touristic hub of this cluster of historic caves, castles, and rivers. Except for its interesting museum of prehistory next to the big statue of Mr. Cro-Magnon, there's little reason to stop here.

▲**Abri du Cap-Blanc**—In this prehistoric cave sculpture, early artists used the rock's natural contours to add dimension to their engraving. Look for places where the artists smoothed or

The Dordogne Region

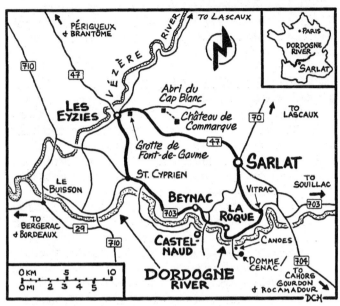

roughed the surfaces to add depth. In this single stone room, your French-speaking guide will spend 30 minutes explaining 14,000-year-old carvings. Impressive as these carvings are, their subtle majesty bypasses some. Tours (French only) leave on the half-hour. No lines. (28F, open summer 9:30–19:00, off-season 10:00–12:00 and 14:00–18:00, closed on Tuesday and November–April, tel. 05 53 29 21 74, fax 05 53 29 89 64.)

Château de Commarque and Château de Laussel—These castles' heydays passed 400 years ago with the Hundred Years' War. You can see the Château de Commarque in the distance from Abri du Cap-Blanc. But a 15-minute stroll from here down the poorly marked path takes you past Laussel Castle and right to the orange, crumbled walls of Commarque. It's not "officially" open to the public.

▲▲▲**Dordogne Valley Scenic Loop Ride or Drive**—The most scenic 10-kilometer stretch of the Dordogne lies between Carsac and Beynac. From Sarlat, follow signs toward Cahors and Carsac, then veer right to the Église de Carsac (wander into this tiny Romanesque church). From Carsac, follow the river via Montfort, La Roque-Gageac, and Beynac. The town of Domme, while impressively situated, is overrated. For bikers, the total round-trip distance from Sarlat is about 30 kilometers (18 miles). Less ambitious bikers may find the Sarlat to La Roque-Gageac to Beynac to Sarlat loop sufficient.

Foie Gras in the Making—You can witness (evenings only) the force-feeding of geese (*la gavage*), but beware: you are expected to buy. Between Sarlat and Les Eyzies-de-Tayac, you'll pass a small farm with a faded sign on the barn, a small roadside stand, and a flock of fat geese. The Lacombes, who run the place, speak only French and are as gentle with tourists as they are with their geese. Belly up to the stand and (with your mouth wide open) ask about *la gavage*. Friendlier Madame Gauthier's farm, which also offers a peek at the *gavage*, is just down the road from the Château de Beynac (park right there or walk ten minutes from the château away from the river, you'll see the signs, demonstrations 18:00–19:30, tel. 05 53 29 51 45).

▲▲**Castelnaud**—Château de Beynac's crumbling rival looks a little less mighty, but the inside packs a medieval punch. Several rooms display Hundred Years' War weaponry and artifacts. The courtyard comes with a 46-meter-deep well (drop a pebble) and an entertaining video showing the catapults, which litter the grounds, in action. The rampart views are unbeatable. The seige tools outside the walls are thought-provoking. Borrow the English explanations from the ticket lady for the room-by-room story. (35F, open May–June, 10:00–19:00, summer 9:30–20:00, otherwise 10:00–18:00, it's a steep hike through a pleasant peasant village from the car park, tel. 05 53 29 57 08). You can stop here halfway through your canoe trip or walk here along a riverside path from Beynac (45 minutes).

▲▲▲**Dordogne Canoe Trips**—For a refreshing break from the car or train, explore the riverside castles and villages of the Dordogne by rented canoe. Several outfits rent plastic two-person canoes (and one-person kayaks) upstream and pick them up where you beach them, downstream in Beynac. For 130F, two can paddle the best two-hour stretch from Cénac to Beynac (shuttle included, call ahead to arrange if you don't have a car, in summer usual pickup time in Beynac is 9:00; Dordogne Randonées, first left after crossing the bridge to Cénac, tel. 05 53 28 22 01). Or, you could float all day from Vitrac to Beynac (Safaraid, tel. 05 65 36 23 54, or ask at local TIs). While you need to be in good shape for the longer trips, complete novices are comfortable, as the only white water you'll encounter will be your partner frothing at the views. You'll get a life vest and, for a few extra francs, a watertight bucket to store whatever you want to keep dry. Simply beach your boat wherever you want to take a break. The best two stops are La Roque-Gageac village and Castelnaud. This works well for those staying at Beynac and lacking wheels. For a phone call, they'll actually pick you up.

▲**La Roque-Gageac**—La Roque (the rock), as the locals call this village, is sculpted into the cliffs rising from the Dordogne River. As you walk along the main street, look for the markers showing the water levels of three floods, and ask someone about the occasional rock avalanches from above. La Roque was once a thriving port, exporting Limousin oak to Bordeaux for making wine barrels. Find the old ramp leading down to the river. Wander up the narrow tangle of back streets that seem to disappear into the cliffs. For a splurge, have a romantic dinner; or better, sleep at **Hôtel Belle Étoile** (call to reserve, tel. 05 53 29 51 44). Popular La Roque is best early, at night, or off-season. Canoes are rentable near the small TI booth on the river.

▲▲**Lascaux**—The region's most vivid and famous cave paintings are at Lascaux. In the interest of preservation, these caves are closed to tourists. But the adjacent Lascaux II copy caves are impressive in everything but authenticity. At Lascaux II, the reindeer, horses, and bulls of Lascaux I are painstakingly reproduced by top artists using the same dyes, tools, and techniques as their predecessors did 15,000 years ago. Anyone into caveman art will appreciate the thoughtful explanations. It's worth working your schedule around English tour times. (Call ahead for English tour times, five times daily in the summer, on demand in off-season, 50F, July and August daily 9:30–19:00, otherwise 10:00–12:00, 14:00–17:30 and closed Monday, 2.5 km south of Montignac; in July and August tickets are sold only at the Montignac TI, tel. 05 53 53 44 35.)

Sights—90 Minutes East of Sarlat

Rocamadour and Gouffre de Padirac go together well. Idyllic little Carennac, a good home base, has two fine hotel values: the simple, friendly **Hotel des Touristes*** (Db-210F, tel. 05 65 10 94 31) or the more upscale **Hotel Fenelon**** (Db-300F, CC:VM, pool, tel. 05 65 10 96 46, fax 05 65 10 94 86).

▲**Rocamadour**—This would be a three-star town if its spectacular setting and medieval charm weren't trampled by daily hordes of tourists and pilgrims. Still, it's a remarkable place, worth a look if you can arrive early or late. Trains (via Brive-la-Gaillarde) will leave you 5 kilometers from the village (taxi, rent a bike from the station, hitch, or hike); a better option may be HEP Excursions' minivan tours from Sarlat (see Getting Around the Dordogne).

▲▲▲**Gouffre de Padirac**—For a fascinating natural-cave experience (lots of stalagmites but no cave art), follow the 90-minute, French-language tour through this huge system of caverns—riding elevators, hiking along a buried stream, and even taking a subterranean cruise (45F, 10 km from Rocamadour, open April–October only, 9:00–12:00 and 14:00–18:00, longer in summer, crowds and delays in summer, day trips are organized from Rocamadour, tel. 01 65 33 64 56). Trains get you to Rocamadour's train station, 10 km away.

Sights—North of the Dordogne

▲▲▲**Oradour-sur-Glane**—Located 25 kilometers west of Limoges, this is one of the most powerful sights in France. French schoolchildren know this town well. Most make a pilgrimage here. "La Ville Martyr," as it is known, was machine-gunned and burned on June 10, 1944, by Nazi troops. They were either seeking revenge for the killing of one of their officers (by French resistance fighters in a neighboring village) or simply terrorizing the populace in preparation for the upcoming Allied invasion (this was four days after D-Day). With cool German attention to detail, the Nazis methodically rounded up the entire population of 642 townspeople. The women and children were herded into the town church, where they were tear-gassed and machine-gunned. Plaques mark the place where the town's men were grouped and executed. The town was then set on fire, its victims left under a blanket of ashes.

Today the ghost town, left untouched for 50 years, greets every pilgrim who enters with only one English word: Remember. Hushed visitors walk the length of Oradour's main street past gutted, charred buildings in the shade of lush strong trees to the underground memorial on the market square (rusted toys, broken crucifixes, town mementos under glass). Visit the cemetery where most lives ended on June 10, 1944, and finish with the church with its bullet-pocked altar (free, 10F English brochure in the shop by the church, daily, long hours).

Seven daily buses connect Limoges' train station with Oradour in 20 minutes. By car, try a picnic in the sleepy, untouristed village of Mortemart (walk behind the Duc's residence, 15 minutes northwest of Oradour on D-675).

Sights—South of the Dordogne

Lot River and Cahors—Were it not for the Dordogne, the Lot River Valley might be considered France's most beautiful. The prehistoric cave paintings at the Grotte de Peche Merle, the medieval bridge at Cahors (Pont Valentré), and the rock-top village of St. Cirq Lapopie are each remarkable sights, within a half-hour of each other and within a 1.5-hour drive of Sarlat. These sights are worthwhile for drivers connecting the Dordogne (Sarlat) with Albi or Carcassonne or as a long day trip from Sarlat. Without a car, skip 'em.

▲▲**Pont Valentré at Cahors**—One of Europe's finest medieval monuments, this three-towered, fortified bridge was built in 1308 to keep the English out of Cahors. It worked. Poke around and learn the reason for the devil on the center tower. The steep trail on the non-city side leads up to great views (keep climbing, avoid branch trails, and be careful if trail is wet). Just past the city-side end of the bridge is. a friendly wine shop/café/souvenir stand, where you can taste Cahors' well-respected black wine and *foie gras*. The duck is cheaper than the goose and just as tasty.

▲▲**Grotte de Peche Merle**—About 30 minutes east of Cahors (by car) lies this relatively obscure cave with prehistoric paintings to rival the better-known ones at the Grotte de Font-de-Gaume. The cave is filled with stalactites and stalagmites, and you can even see a Cro-Magnon footprint preserved by the subterranean mud. (42F, open daily Easter–October, 9:30–12:00 and 14:00–18:00, closes earlier off-season, tel. 05 65 31 27 05, fax 05 65 31 20 47.)

▲**St. Cirq Lapopie**—Another of southern France's delightful hill towns, this one offers a Lot River–view bonus. Wander the rambling footpaths and stay for lunch. You'll find ideal picnic perches and several reasonable restaurants. Sleep at the **Auberge du Sombral**** (Db-275F–375F, CC:VM, tel. 05 65 31 26 08, fax 05 65 30 26 37).

LANGUEDOC

From the tenth to the 13th century, this powerful, open-minded, and independent region ruled an area reaching from the Rhône River to the Pyrénées. The Albigensian (Cathar) Crusades started here in 1208, which ultimately led to Languedoc's demise and incorporation into the state of France. The word *languedoc* comes from the language its people spoke at that time: *Langue d'oc* ("language of Oc," *Oc* for the way they said "yes") was the dialect of southern France, as opposed to *langue d'oil*, the dialect of northern France (where *oil*, later to become *oui*, was the way of saying "yes"). As Languedoc's power faded, so did its language.

The Moors, Charlemagne, and the Spanish called this home at various times. You'll see, hear, and feel the strong Spanish influence on this dry, hilly region. We're lumping Albi in with the Languedoc region, though it's no longer really a part of what locals think of as true Languedoc.

Planning Your Time

Key sights in Languedoc are Albi, Carcassonne, Minerve, Cathar castle ruins, and Collioure. Albi makes a good day- or overnight stop between the Dordogne region and Carcassonne. Plan your arrival at Carcassonne carefully: arrive late in the afternoon, spend the night, and leave by noon the next day, and you'll miss 90 percent of the day-trippers. Collioure is your Mediterranean beach town vacation-from-your-vacation. You'll need wheels of your own and a good map to find the Cathar

Languedoc

castle ruins and Minerve. If driving, the most exciting Cathar
castles, Peyrepertuse and Queribus, work well as a stop between
Carcassonne and Collioure. No matter what transport you use,
Languedoc is a logical stop between the Dordogne and
Provence, or on the way to Barcelona, just over the border.

Getting Around Languedoc

Albi, Carcassonne, and Collioure are a snap by train, but a car
is essential for seeing the remote sights in this area. You can
rent a car near the train stations in Albi or Carcassonne or in
downtown Collioure. Buy the local Michelin map #83. The
roads can be tiny and the traffic very slow.

Cuisine Scene—Languedoc

Hearty peasant cooking and full-bodied red wines are Languedoc's tasty trademarks. Be adventurous. *Cassoulet*, an old

Roman concoction of goose, duck, pork, mutton, sausage, and white beans, is *the* main course specialty. You'll also see *cargolade*, a stew of snail, lamb, and sausage. Local cheeses are Roquefort and Pelardon (a nutty-tasting goat cheese). Corbières, Minervois, and Côtes du Roussillon are the area's good-value red wines. The locals distill a fine brandy, Armagnac, that tastes just like cognac and costs less.

The Cathars

The Cathars, a heretical group of Christians based in the Languedoc from the 11th through the 13th centuries, saw life as a battle between good (the spiritual) and bad (the material). They considered material things evil and of the devil. While others called them "Cathars" (from the Greek word for "pure") or "Albigenses" (for their main city, Albi), they called themselves simply "friends of God."

Cathars focused on the teachings of St. John and recognized only baptism as a sacrament. Because they believed in reincarnation, they were vegetarians.

Travelers encounter the Cathars in their Languedoc sightseeing because of the Albigensian Crusades (1209–1240s). Both the king of France (who wanted to consolidate his grip on southern France) and the Pope (who needed to make a strong point that the only acceptable Christianity was Roman-style) found self-serving reasons to wage a genocidal war against these people—who never amounted to more than 10 percent of the local population and who coexisted happily with their non-Cathar neighbors. After a terrible generation of torture and mass burnings, the Cathars were wiped out. The last Cathar was burnt in 1321.

Today tourists find haunting castle ruins high in the Pyrénées (Cathar strongholds) and eat hearty *salade Cathar*.

ALBI

Those coming to see the cathedral and the Toulouse-Lautrec museum will be pleasantly surprised by Albi's enchanting city center. The Albigensian Crusades were born here, as was Toulouse-(better named Albi-)Lautrec. The visitor's Albi (TI, Toulouse-Lautrec museum, and cobbled pedestrian zone) clumps together around its fortress cathedral.

Tourist Information: Albi's information-packed TI is between the cathedral and the Toulouse-Lautrec museum

(open July–August 9:00–18:30, Sunday 10:30–13:00 and
15:30–18:30, otherwise Monday–Saturday 9:00–12:00 and
14:00–18:00, Sunday 10:30–12:30 and 15:30–17:30, tel. 05 63
49 48 80).

Arrival in Albi

By Train: Take a left onto avenue Marechal Joffre, then
another left on avenue General de Gaulle, then follow signs to
cathédrale to Albi's old city.

By Car: Follow signs to *centre-ville* and *cathédrale* and park
in front of the cathedral.

Sights—Albi

Pick up a map of the center city at the TI (get the purple *circuit
poupre* walking tour in English) and follow its suggested walking tour, reading the English information posted at key points
along the way. On this walk you'll see:

▲▲▲**Basilique Ste. Cécile**—This 13th-century fortress/
basilica was the nail in the Albigensian coffin. Both the
imposing exterior and the stunning interior drive home the
message of the Catholic (read "universal") church. The
extravagant porch seems like an afterthought. Inside, be
prepared for an explosion of colors and geometric shapes
and a vivid *Last Judgment*. Even with the gaping hole that
was cut from it to make room for a newer pipe organ, the
graphic *Last Judgment* makes its point in a way that would
stick with any medieval worshiper. (Open all day in summer, otherwise closes 11:45–14:00; the choir is worth the
small admission.)

▲▲**Musée Toulouse-Lautrec**—The Palais de la Berbie
(once the fortified home of the archbishop) has the world's
best collection of Lautrec's paintings, posters, and sketches.
The artist, crippled from youth and therefore on the fringe
of society, had an affinity for people who didn't quite fit in.
He painted the dregs of Parisian society because that was
his world. His famous Parisian nightlife posters are here.
The top floor houses a mediocre collection of contemporary
art (20F, open June–September daily 9:00–12:00 and 14:00–
18:00; October–March 10:00–12:00, 14:00–17:00 and closed
Tuesday; April–May daily 10:00–12:00, 14:00–18:00, tel. 05
63 49 48 70). Even if you decide against this museum, walk
underneath it to the palace's gardens for the great views.

Église St. Salvy and Cloître—This is an OK church with fine cloisters. Delicate arches surround an enclosed courtyard, providing a peaceful interlude from the maniacal shoppers that fill the pedestrian streets (open all day).

Market Hall—This Art Nouveau market is ideal for picnic-gathering and people-watching (two blocks from the cathedral; open daily, except Monday, until 13:00).

Sleeping and Eating in Albi
(5F = about $1)

Hôtel St. Clair**, offering steep stairs and elegant rooms, is decorated with a loving touch, 2 blocks from the cathedral in the pedestrian zone on rue St. Clair (Db-220F–300F, Tb-420F, CC:VM, 20-minute walk from the station, tel. 05 63 54 25 66). Albi's **youth hostel** is cheap, clean, and basic (13 rue de la République, hostel card mandatory, check-in from 18:00–21:00, tel. 05 65 54 53 56). Albi is full of inexpensive restaurants. For exceptional couscous in a "Little Morocco," try **Le Marrakesh**, two blocks down from the Hôtel St. Clair at 11 rue Toulouse-Lautrec (hearty, even splittable 50F menu, closed Monday).

Transportation Connections—Albi
By train to: Toulouse (18/day, 1 hr; no trains between 14:00–17:00 from Toulouse, and from 18:45–21:00 from Albi), **Carcassonne** (18/day, 2.5 hours, transfer in Toulouse—see above, Trains to Toulouse).

CARCASSONNE
Medieval Carcassonne (car-cass-sohn) is a 13th-century world of towers, turrets, and cobblestone alleys. It's Camelot's castle and a walled city rolled into one, frosted with too many day-tripping tourists. But an empty Carcassonne rattles in the early morning or late-afternoon breeze. At 10:00 the salespeople stand at the doors of their main-street shops, their gauntlet of tacky temptations poised and ready for their daily ration of customers. Enjoy the town early or late.

Twelve hundred years ago, Charlemagne stood before this fortress/town with his troops, besieging it for several years. A cunning townsperson, Madame Carcas, saved the Cité. Just as food was running out, she fed the last bits of grain to the last pig and tossed him over the wall. Splat. Charlemagne's bored and frustrated forces, amazed that the town still had enough food to throw fat party pigs over the wall, decided they would never succeed in starving the people out. They ended the siege, and the city was saved. Madame Carcas "*sonned*" (sounded) the long-awaited victory bells, and the Cité had a name, "Carcas-sonne." Most tourists lay siege to Carcassonne 11:00–17:00 as a day trip from nearby resorts. Avoid them by staying the night.

From Rick's journal on his first visit to Carcassonne: "Before me lives Carcassonne, the perfect medieval city. Like a fish that everyone thought was extinct, somehow Europe's greatest Romanesque fortress city has survived the centuries. I was supposed to be gone yesterday, but here I sit imprisoned by choice—curled in a cranny on top of the wall. The wind blows away the sounds of today, and my imagination 'medievals' me. The moat is one foot over and 100 feet down. Small plants and moss upholster my throne."

Orientation

There are two TIs, one in the *ville basse* and one in the Cité. The Cité TI is just to your right as you enter the main (Narbonnaise) gate (daily 9:00–13:00, 14:00–18:00). The *ville basse* TI is on the place Gambetta, near the huge French flags, at 15 boulevard Camille Pelletan (9:00–12:15, 14:00–18:30, closed Sunday, tel. 04 68 25 07 04 and 04 68 25 68 81).

Arrival in Carcassonne

Contemporary Carcassonne is neatly divided into two cities: the magnificent Cité (medieval city) and the forgettable *ville basse* (new downtown below). The train station is located in the *ville basse*.

By Train: Bus #4 connects the station with La Cité (2/hr, 6F, pay driver), or you can walk across the Canal du Midi, across the traffic circle, and up the pedestrian street to the heart of the *ville basse*. From there, a left on the rue de Verdun takes you to the place Gambetta and across the Pont Vieux to La Cité. Figure 50F for a taxi to La Cité from the train station.

By Car: Following signs to La Cité, you'll come to a large parking lot (20F) and a drawbridge (the Porte Narbonnaise) at the entrance to the walled city. If staying inside the walls, show your reservation and you can park free in the outside lot and drive into the city after 18:00. Theft is a big problem—leave nothing in your car.

Carcassonne

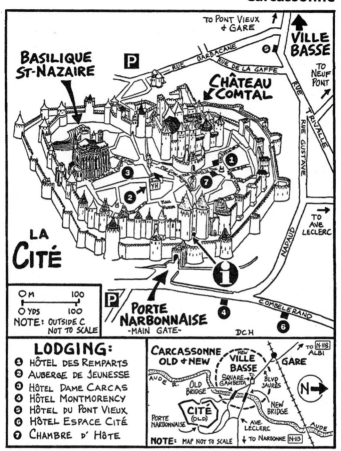

LODGING:
1. HÔTEL DES REMPARTS
2. AUBERGE DE JEUNESSE
3. HÔTEL DAME CARCAS
4. HÔTEL MONTMORENCY
5. HÔTEL DU PONT VIEUX
6. HÔTEL ESPACE CITÉ
7. CHAMBRE D' HÔTE

Sights—Carcassonne

▲▲▲**Medieval Wall Walk**—La Cité is a medieval fortress first constructed during the Roman Empire. It was completely reconstructed in 1844 as part of a program to restore France's important monuments. Walk the entire outer wall (no charge, in town, follow signs to *lices*). The higher, inner walls are mostly inaccessible, except for those in Château Comtal. Savor every step and view.

▲**Cité en Scenes**—A busy medieval fair fills the calendar with events during the first half of August. Don't miss the jousting tournament (*spectacle équestre*), usually at 18:00.

▲▲▲**Walk to Pont Vieux**—For the best view back onto the floodlit Cité, hike down to the old bridge. As you exit the Narbonne Gate, go left on rue Nadaud to rue Gustave, then turn left onto rue Trivalle. Ask, *"Où est le Pont Vieux?"* (oo ay la pohn vee-uh). Return up the back door entry to La Cité near the Basilique St. Nazaire.

▲**Basilique St. Nazaire**—Enter this church and slowly walk down the aisle to enjoy the colors of the 14th-century stained glass sparkling all around you and find the delicately vaulted Gothic ceiling behind the altar. This is one of the best examples of Gothic architecture in southern France.

Château Comtal—Carcassonne's third layer of defense was originally constructed in 1125 but completely redesigned in later reconstructions. Peek into the inner courtyard and admire the towers but skip the French tour (no English translation), unless you've just got to see the interior. Ask about English tours, usually three to four daily June–September (28F, open daily June–September 9:00–19:00, off-season 9:30–12:30 and 14:00–17:30).

Exposition Torture—You'll have even more sympathy for the Cathars after touring Carcassonne's torture chamber, worth a look only if you've got the time and money to burn (30F, open daily June–November 10:00–20:00, 9 rue St. Jean, to the right of the main drag as you enter La Cité).

"The Middle Ages in La Cité"—This is another entrepreneurial "museum," with five rooms of costumes trying to re-create life in old Carcassonne (15F, 5F for kids, daily 10:00– 18:00, decent English explanations). It's worthwhile only for kids.

Canal du Midi—Completed in 1681, this sleepy, 150-mile canal connects France's Mediterranean and Atlantic coasts. Before railways, the Canal du Midi was jammed with commercial traffic. Today it's busy with pleasure craft. Look for the slow-moving hotel barges strewn with tanned, well-fed, and well-watered vacationers. The towpath that spans the length of the canal makes for ideal biking. The canal runs right in front of the train station in Carcassonne.

Sleeping in Carcassonne's La Cité
(5F = about $1, postal code: 11000)
Sleep Code: **S** = Single, **D** = Double/Twin, **T** = Triple, **Q** = Quad, **b** = bathroom, **t** = toilet only, **s** = shower only,

CC = Credit Card (**V**isa, **M**asterCard, **A**mex), **SE** = Speaks English, **NSE** = No English, * = French hotel rating system (0–4 stars).

Ideally, sleep in the Cité. Four hotels (one a four-star budget-breaker, **Hôtel de la Cité**) and a great youth hostel offer rooms inside the walls. These listings are in or very near the Cité. The obligatory half-pension doesn't seem to exist in Carcassonne, and except for the mid-July to mid-August peak of high season, there are plenty of rooms.

Hôtel des Remparts**, right up by the castle, has a 12th-century staircase leading to modern comfortable rooms and an owner with a fetish for cleanliness (Db-300F–330F, Tb-480F, parking-20F, CC:VM, 5 place de Grands-Puits, tel. 04 68 71 27 72, fax 04 68 72 73 26, Christian SE, Jeanine NSE).

The *chambre d'hôte* across from the Hôtel des Remparts (inquire in the Brocante shop) rents two huge apartment-like rooms that could sleep five, with kitchenette and private *terasse* (Db or Tb-290F, family deals, stocked fridge and self-serve breakfast included, tel. 04 68 25 16 67).

The **Auberge de Jeunesse** (youth hostel) is clean and well-run, with an outdoor garden courtyard, self-service kitchen, TV room, and lots of video games. If you ever wanted to bunk down in a youth hostel, do it here. Only July is tight. Nonmembers pay 19F extra (69F per bed with breakfast, two doubles, a few quads, otherwise six to a room, rue de Vicomte Trencavel, generally closed 13:00 to 17:00 and after 01:00, tel. 04 68 25 23 16, fax 04 68 71 14 84).

Hôtel Dame Carcas*** is best for a splurge (Sb-400F– 670F, Db-500F–750F, 150F per extra person, CC:VMA, 15 rue St. Louis, tel. 04 68 71 37 37, fax 04 68 71 50 15). It is a beautifully restored building with classy attire, period furniture, and inviting sitting rooms. Room 224 is royal, with a canopy bed and old-time tub.

Hôtel Montmorency**, 100 yards outside the Cité's draw-bridge, is a Santa Fe–style place sporting a pool from which to gaze at the fortress in cool comfort. Rooms for three or four persons are very spacious (Sb-220F, Db with shower-260F–300F, Db with tub-350F–400F, Tb-450F, Qb-500F, free parking, CC:VMA, 2 rue Camille St. Saens, tel. 04 68 25 19 92, fax 04 68 25 43 15, SE).

Hôtel du Pont Vieux** is a ten-minute walk to the Cité. This Old World hotel offers a pleasant garden courtyard, 30F garage parking, and a third-floor three-person suite that opens out onto a private terrace with a five-star view up to the Cité (Db-250F–320F, Tb-360F, Qb-400F, CC:VM, 32 rue Trivalle, tel. 04 68 25 24 99, fax 04 68 47 62 71).

Train travelers will appreciate the spotless, dirt cheap **Hôtel Astoria*** (S-100F, D-120F, Ds-155F, Ts-170F–190F, Qs-230F, 18 rue Tourtel, tel. 04 68 25 31 38, fax 04 68 71 34 14, SE). The new **Hôtel Espace Cité****, 200 yards downhill from the main entry to La Cité, is a clean, modern and efficient place with easy parking (Db-300F, Tb-350F, Qb-400F, small rooms, CC:VM, 132 rue Trivalle, tel. 04 68 25 24 24, fax 04 68 25 17 17).

Eating in La Cité

Other than the touristy joints lining the main drag, prices and quality seem about the same everywhere. For good *cassoulet*, try **La Table Ronde** (moderately priced, 30 rue du Plô, tel. 04 68 47 38 21). For a bit more, enjoy the fine regional cuisine in an elegant setting at **l'Ecu d'Or** (menus from 110F, tel. 04 68 25 49 03), across from the Hôtel Donjon. True gourmets enjoy a splurge at the country-posh **Auberge du Pont Levi** (off the main parking lot just outside the walls, tel. 04 68 25 55 23).

Lighter meals (decent salads) and a lively bar ambiance can be found across from the Château Comtal at the **Bar Senechal**. For quiet refreshments and a pleasant escape, try **Bar à Vin**'s grassy courtyard (100 meters up rue du Plô from place Marcou). **La Ostal** is the place to eat if you want gypsy music (near Hôtel des Remparts). For mellow jazz rather than castanets, dine with Jacques Brel at **L'Auberge du Grand Puits** (70F for a hearty *salade Cathar* and a good *cassoulet* with dessert, next to Hôtel des Remparts, tel. 04 68 71 27 88).

Picnics can be gathered at the small *alimentation* on the main drag (generally open until 20:30). For your beggar's banquet, picnic on the city walls. For fast, cheap, hot food, look for places on the main drag with quiche and pizza to go.

Transportation Connections—Carcassonne

By train to: Sarlat (5/day, 6 hrs, transfer at Bordeaux's St. Jean station), **Arles** (8/day, 3 hrs, a few are direct, but most require a transfer in Narbonne), **Nice** (6.5 hrs, several direct, or transfer in Narbonne and Marseille), **Paris**' Gare Montparnasse (6.5 hrs by TGV via Toulouse; additional transfer possible in Bordeaux), **Toulouse** (hrly, 60 min), **Barcelona** (3/day, 5 hrs, transfer in Narbonne and Port Bou, the border town).

COLLIOURE

Blessed with an ideal climate and a romantic setting but surrounded by unappealing resorts, Collioure is like a pearl lost in the sea. By Mediterranean standards, this seaside village should be overrun—it has everything: sandy beaches, a charming old city in which to meander, a few interesting vestiges of its 2,000-year past to visit, and the Pyrénées as a backdrop. Come here to unwind and do nothing. Even with its crowds of French vacationers in peak season, Collioure is what many are looking for when heading to the Riviera—a sunny, peaceful vacation from their vacation.

Tourist Information: The TI is at place du 18 Juin (open weekdays 9:30–12:00 and 14:00–18:00, in summer daily 9:00–20:00, tel. 04 68 82 15 47).

Car Rental: The Garage Renault rents cars (tel. 04 68 82 08 34).

Sights—Collioure

Ambition is a four-letter word here. Slow down, enjoy a slow coffee at a beachfront café, snuggle into the sand, and lose yourself in the old city's narrow, hilly streets. The 800-year-old **Château Royal** (great ramparts, fine views, and a mildly interesting exhibit on the local history) and waterfront church **Notre Dame des Anges** are worth a look. Consider a **Promenade sur Mer** motorboat excursion (one or three hours, the longer trip is better, boats depart from the breakwater near the château).

Sleeping in Collioure
(5 F = about $1, postal code: 66190)

Stay in the old city, tucked behind the castle. You'll find several *chambres d'hôte* (the TI has a list), the best of which must be the clean and spacious rooms at Monsieur et Madame Peroneille's **Chambres** (Db-250F, Tb-350F, Qb-400F, 20 rue Pasteur, tel. 04 68 82 15 31). The Spanish-feeling **Hôtel Templiers** rents thoughtfully appointed rooms (some with views) with wall-to-wall art and an easygoing staff (Db-300F–400F, 12 avenue l'Amiraute, tel. 04 68 98 31 10, fax 04 68 98

01 24). The **Hôtel Triton**, just off the main drag across from the old city but still on the bay, offers just-remodeled rooms at fair rates (Ds-180F, Db-290F, rue Jean Bart, tel. 04 68 82 06 52, fax 04 68 82 11 32).

Transportation Connections—Collioure
By train to: Carcassonne (10/day, 2 hrs, via Narbonne), **Paris** (1/day direct to Gare d'Austerlitz, 10 hrs; or even better, transfer at Narbonne and Toulouse to TGV and zip into Gare Montparnasse), **Barcelona** (5/day, 3 hrs), **Avignon/Arles** (12/day, 3 hrs, transfer in Perpignan).

Sights—Languedoc
These sights are worth a visit only if you're driving.

▲▲▲**Châteaus of Hautes Corbières**—Ninety minutes south of Carcassonne, toward the boring little country of Andorra, in the scenic foothills of the Pyrénées, lies a series of surreal, mountain-capping castle ruins. The Maginot Line of the 13th century, these sky-high castles were strategically located between France and the Spanish kingdom of Roussillon. As you can see by flipping through the picture books in Carcassonne tourist shops, these castles' crumpled ruins are an impressive contrast to the restored walls of Carcassonne. Bring a good map and sturdy walking shoes.

The most spectacular is the château of **Peyrepertuse.** The ruins seem to grow right out of a narrow splinter of cliff. The views are sensational—you can almost reach out and touch Spain. Let your imagination soar, but watch your step as you try to reconstruct this eagle's nest (12F, open all year from 10:00–sunset, tel. 04 68 45 40 55).

Nearby **Queribus** is also impressive and is famous as the last Cathar castle to fall. It was left useless when the border between France and Spain was moved (in 1659) farther south into the high Pyrénées.

▲**Châteaus of Lastours**—Ten miles north of Carcassonne (forget public transportation), these five side-by-side ruined hilltop castles offer the most accessible look at the region's Cathar castles and an ideal picnic site. From Carcassonne, follow signs to Conques, then Lastours. In Lastours, follow signs to the Bellevedere for a panorama overlooking the five castles. The small fee also allows you to hike up to the castles (park back down the hill). It's steep but worthwhile if it's not too hot.

▲**Minerve**—A one-time Cathar hideout, Minerve is remarkably situated in the middle of a deep canyon that provided a natural defense. Strong as it was, it didn't keep out the pope's army. The entire village was destroyed and all residents killed during the Albigensian Crusades. An interesting path leads down to the river and around the village. There are two pleasant cafés—and not much more—in Minerve.

Minerve, between Carcassonne and Beziers, is 15 km east of Olonzac (40 minutes by car from Carcassonne). It makes an ideal stop between Provence and Carcassonne. In the mood for wine-tasting? The friendly (and French-only) Remaurys offer an excellent selection and a beautiful setting in which to sample the local product. Just over the hill from Minerve, toward Carcassonne and past Azillanet, you'll see the signs to the **Domaine de Pech d'Andre** (tel. 04 68 91 22 66).

Sleeping and eating in Minerve: If you're tired of competing with tourists, stay here and melt into southern France. Sleep and eat at the cozy **Relais Chantovent** (Db-220F–250F, ask for the new rooms, postal code 34210, tel. 04 68 91 14 18, fax 04 68 91 81 99). People travel great distances to dine here (moderately priced), so reserve early.

PROVENCE

This magnificent region is shaped like a wedge of quiche. From its sunburnt crust that fans out along the Mediterranean coast from Nîmes to Nice, it stretches north along the Rhône Valley to Orange. The Romans were here in force and left many ruins—some of the best anywhere. Seven popes, great artists like van Gogh, Cézanne, and Picasso, and author Peter Mayle all enjoyed their years in Provence. Provence offers a splendid recipe of arid climate (but brutal winds known as the mistral), captivating cities, exciting hill towns, and remarkably varied landscapes.

Wander through the ghost town of ancient Les Baux and under France's greatest Roman ruin, the Pont du Gard. Spend your starry, starry nights where van Gogh did, in Arles. Explore its Roman past, then find the linger-longer squares and café corners that inspired Vincent. Some may prefer Avignon's more elegant feel and softer edge as a home base. Just north of Arles, stately Avignon bustles in the shadow of its brooding popes' palace. It's a short hop from Arles and Avignon into the splendid scenery and hill towns of the Luberon that make Provence so popular today.

Planning Your Time

Make Arles or Avignon your base (Italophiles prefer Arles, while poodles pick Avignon) and, if driving, consider basing in Isle sur la Sorgue. Avignon (well-connected to Arles by train) is the regional transportation hub for destinations north of Arles (Pont du Gard, Uzès, Orange, and Isle sur la Sorgue). You'll want a

Provence

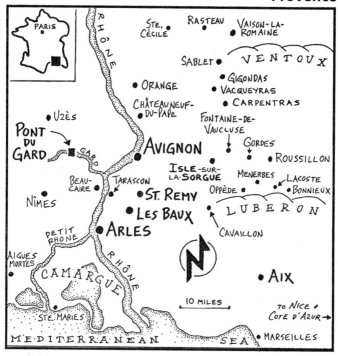

full day for Arles sightseeing (ideally on a Wednesday or Saturday, when the morning market rages), a half day for Avignon, and a day or two for the villages and sights in the countryside. To best feel the endearing pulse of Provence, get out of the city and spend a night in a Provençale village (as described below).

Getting Around Provence

The yellow Michelin map to this region is essential for drivers. Public transit is good: frequent trains link Avignon, Arles, and Nîmes; Les Baux is accessible by bus from Arles; and the Pont du Gard and Uzès are accessible by bus from Avignon. While a tour of the villages of Luberon is worthwhile only by car, Isle sur la Sorgue is an easy hop by train from Avignon.

Cuisine Scene—Provence

The almost extravagant use of garlic, olive oil, herbs, and tomatoes makes Provence's cuisine France's liveliest. To sample it, order anything *à la Provençale*. Among the area's spicy specialties are *ratatouille* (a thick mixture of vegetables in an herb-flavored tomato sauce), *brandade* (a salt cod, garlic, and cream mousse), *aïoli* (a garlicky mayonnaise often served atop fresh vegetables), *tapenade* (a sauce of puréed olives, anchovies, tuna, and herbs), *soupe au pistou* (vegetable soup with basil, garlic, and cheese), and *soupe à l'ail* (garlic soup). Look also for *riz Camarguaise* (rice from the Camargue) and *taureau* (bull meat). Banon (wrapped in chestnut leaves) and Picodon (nutty taste) are the native cheeses. Provence also produces some of France's great wines at relatively reasonable prices. Look for Gigondas, Sablet, Côte du Rhône, and Côte de Provence. If you like rosé, try the Tavel. This is the place to splurge for a bottle of Châteauneuf-du-Pape.

ARLES

By helping Julius Caesar defeat Marseille, Arles earned the imperial nod and was made an important port city. With the first bridge over the Rhône, Arles was a key stop on the Roman road from Italy to Spain. After reigning as a political center of the early Christian church (the seat of an archbishop for centuries) and a thriving trading city on and off until the 18th century, Arles all but disappeared from the map. Van Gogh settled here a hundred years ago but left only memories. After taking a beating from American bombers in World War II, Arles thrives again. Today this compact city is alive with great Roman ruins, some fine early Christian art, an eclectic assortment of museums, made-for-ice-cream pedestrian zones, squares that play hide-and-seek with visitors, and too many cars. Arles is a fine springboard for Provence explorations.

Tourist Information: Arles has two TIs. The one at the train station is relaxed and easy by car. (Open 9:00–13:00 and 14:00–18:00, Sunday 10:00–14:00; closed off-season Sundays.) The main TI on esplanade Charles de Gaulle is a high-powered mega-information site. (Open 9:00–19:00, Sunday 9:00–13:00, off-season closing at 18:00, tel. 04 90 18 41 20.) Pick up the free handy *Guide Touristique 1997* and ask about bullfights.

Laundry: The laundromat (6 rue Cavalarie near place Voltaire, daily 7:00–21:00, later once you're in) has a confusing central command panel: 20F for wash—push machine number on top row, 10F for 25 minutes of dryer—push dryer number on third row five times slowly, 2F for flakes—button #11 (recommended Saveurs Provençales restaurant 1 block away to dine while you clean).

Supermarket: Place Lamartine has a big handy Monoprix supermarket/department store (8:30–19:25, closed Sunday).

Banks: Several banks change money on the place de la République, across from St. Trophime.

Arrival in Arles

By Train and Bus: Both stations sit side by side on the river, a ten-minute walk from the city center. To reach the old town, walk to the river and turn left.

By Car: Follow signs to *centre-ville*, then be on the lookout for signs to the *gare SNCF* (the train station; go there for the TI). You'll come to a huge roundabout, place Lamartine, with a Monoprix to the right. There is parking on the left, along the base of the wall. Pay attention to no-parking signs on Wednesday and Saturday until 13:00—they mean it. Theft is a problem; park at your hotel if possible. Take everything out of your car for safety. From place Lamartine, walk into the city through the two stumpy towers.

Getting Around Arles

Arles faces the Mediterranean more than Paris. Its spaghetti streetplan disorients the first-time visitor. Landmarks hide in the medieval tangle of narrow, winding streets. Everything is deceptively close. While Arles sits on the Rhône, it completely ignores the river. The elevated riverside walk does provide a direct—if lonesome—return to the station. Hotels have free city maps, but Arles works best if you simply follow the numerous streetcorner signs pointing you toward the sights and hotels of the town center. Racing cars seem to enjoy Arles' medieval lanes, turning sidewalks into tightropes and pedestrians into leaping targets.

By Minibus: The free "Starlette" shuttle minibus, which circles the town's major sights twice an hour (just wave at the driver and hop in, 7:30–19:30, not Sunday), is worthwhile only to get to or from the distant ancient history museum.

By Bike and Car: The Peugeot store rents bikes (#15 rue du Pont, tel. 04 90 96 03 77). Avis (at the train station, tel. 04 90 96 82 42) and Europcar (downtown at 15 boulevard Victor Hugo, tel. 04 90 93 23 24) rent cars.

By Taxi: Arles' taxis charge a minimum flat 50F fee. Nothing in town is worth a taxi ride.

Sights—Arles

Arles' *global billet* covers all the sights (55F, sold at each sight). Otherwise, it's 15F per sight and museum (35F for the ancient history museum). While any sight is worth a few minutes of your time, many aren't worth the individual admission. For the small price of a *global billet*, the city is yours. Except for the Musées Réattu and Arlaten, all sights are open April–September 9:00–19:00, otherwise 10:00–16:30.

▲▲**Place du Forum**—This café-crammed square, while always lively, is best at night. Named for the Roman Forum that stood here, only two columns from a second-century temple survive. They are incorporated into the wall of the Hotel Nord Pinus. (After a few drinks at the Café van Gogh, the corner of that hotel actually starts to look phallic.) Van Gogh hung out here under these same plane trees. In fact, his *Starry Starry Night* was painted from this square. The bistros on the square, while no place for a fine dinner, put together a good salad, and when you sprinkle in the ambiance, that's 45F well spent. The guy on the pedestal is Frederic Mistral who, in 1904, received the Nobel Prize for literature. He used his prize money to preserve and display the folk identity of Provence at a time when France was rapidly centralizing. (He founded the Arlatan museum—see below.)

▲▲**Wednesday and Saturday Market**—On these days until around noon, Arles' ring road (blvd. Emile Combes on Wednesday, blvd. Lices on Saturday) erupts into an outdoor market of fish, flowers, produce, and you-name-it. Join in, buy flowers, try the olives, sample some wine, and slap a pickpocket. On the first Wednesday of the month, it's a grand flea market.

▲▲▲**Ancient History Museum (Musée de L'Arles Antique)**—The sights of Roman Arles make maximum sense if you start your visit in this slick new museum. Models and original sculpture (with the help of the free English handout) re-create the Roman city of Arles, making workaday life and culture easier to imagine. Models of Arles' arena even illustrate the moveable stadium cover, good for shade and rain. While virtually nothing is left of Arles' chariot racecourse, the model shows how it must have rivaled Rome's Circus Max-

Arles

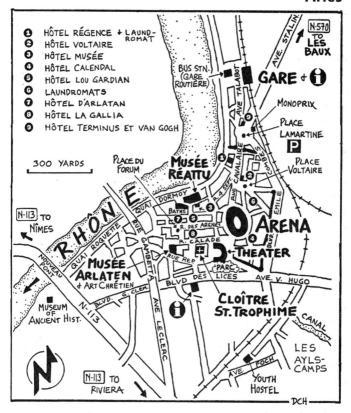

Hôtels

❶ HÔTEL RÉGENCE ♦ LAUNDROMAT
❷ HÔTEL VOLTAIRE
❸ HÔTEL MUSÉE
❹ HÔTEL CALENDAL
❺ HÔTEL LOU GARDIAN
❻ LAUNDROMATS
❼ HÔTEL D'ARLATAN
❽ HÔTEL LA GALLIA
❾ HÔTEL TERMINUS ET VAN GOGH

300 YARDS

DCH

imus. Jewelry, fine metal and glass artifacts, and fine mosaic floors make it clear, Roman Arles was a city of art and culture. The finale is an impressive row of pagan and early Christian sarcophagi (second to fifth centuries). In the early days of the Church, Jesus was often portrayed beardless and as the good shepherd—with a lamb over his shoulder.

Built at the site of the chariot racecourse, this museum is a 15-minute walk from Arles along the river. Turn left at the river and follow it to the big modern building just past the new bridge—or ride the free Starlette shuttle bus. (35F, 9:00–19:00 April–September, 10:00–18:00 off-season, tel. 04 90 18 88 88.)

▲▲**Roman Arena (Amphithéàtre)**—1,900 years ago, gladiators fought wild animals here to the delight of 20,000 screaming fans—cruel. Today matadors fight wild bulls to the delight of local fans—still cruel. While the ancient third row of arches is long gone, three towers survive from medieval times, when the arena was used as a fortress. In the 1800s it corralled 200 humble homes and functioned as a town within the town. Today modern gladiators fight bulls, and if you don't mind the gore, it's an exciting show. Climb the tower. Walk through the inner corridors of this 440' x 350' oval and notice the similarity to 20th-century stadium floor plans.

▲▲**Bullfights (Courses Camarguaise)**—Occupy the same seats fans have been sitting in for nearly 2,000 years and take in one of Arles' most memorable treats—a bullfight *à la* Provençale. Three classes of bullfights take place here. The *course protection* is for aspiring matadors; it's a daring dodge-bull game of scraping hair off the angry bull's nose for prize money offered by local businesses (no blood). The *trophée de l'avenir* is the next class, with amateur matadors. The *trophée des as excellence* is the real thing *à la* Spain: outfits, swords, spikes, and the whole gory shebang. (In Arles, Saturday, Sunday, and holidays from April through early October. Skip their "rodeo" spectacle. Tickets 30F–50F, tel. 04 90 96 03 70 or TI.) There are nearby village bullfights in small wooden bullrings nearly every weekend (TI has schedule).

Classical Theater (Théâtre Antique)—Precious little survives from this Roman theater, which served as a handy town quarry throughout the Middle Ages. Two lonely Corinthian columns look from the stage out over the audience. The 10,000 now mostly modern seats are still used for local concerts and festivals. Take a stroll backstage through broken bits of Rome. Sit in a seat and contemplate a society that enjoyed Greek dramas one night and gladiator battles the next.

▲▲**St. Trophime Cloisters and Church**—This church, named after a third-century bishop of Arles, sports the finest Romanesque west portal (main doorway) I've seen anywhere.

But first enjoy the place de la République. Sit on the steps opposite the church. The Egyptian obelisk used to be the centerpiece of Arles' Roman Circus. Watch the peasants—pilgrims, locals, buskers—nothing new about this scene. Like a Roman triumphal arch, the church trumpets the promise of Judgment Day. The tympanum is filled with Christian symbolism. Christ sits in majesty surrounded by symbols of the four evangelists (Matthew—the winged man, Mark—the winged

lion, Luke—the ox, and John—the eagle). The 12 apostles are
lined up below Jesus. Move up closer. This is it. Some are
saved and others aren't. Notice the condemned—a chain gang
on the right bunny-hopping over the fires of hell. For them the
tune trumpeted by the three angels on the very top isn't a
happy one. Ride the exquisite detail back to a simpler age. In
an illiterate medieval world long before the vivid images of our
technicolor age, this message was a neon billboard over this
town's everything square. A chart just inside the church (on the
right) helps explain the carvings. On the right side of the nave,
a fourth-century early Christian sarcophagus is used as an altar.

The adjacent cloisters are the best in Provence (15F, enter
from the square, 20 meters to the right of the church). Enjoy
the sculpted capitals of the rounded Romanesque columns
(12th century) and the pointed Gothic columns (14th century).
The second floor offers only a view of the cloisters from above.
Musée Réattu—Highlights of this mildly interesting museum
are a fun collection of 70 Picasso drawings (some two-sided,
and all done in a flurry of creativity) and a room of Henri
Rousseau's Camargue watercolors. (Open April–September
9:00–12:00 and 14:00–19:00, otherwise 10:00–12:00 and
14:00–16:30.)
▲**Musée Arlaten**—This cluttered folklore museum, given to
Arles by Monsieur Mistral, is filled with interesting odds and
ends of Provence life. The employees wear the native costumes. Like a failed turn-of-the-century garage sale, you'll
find shoes, hats, wigs, old photos, bread cupboards, and the
beetle-dragon monster. If you're into folklore, this is better
than sitting on a wet bench in the rain. (Open 9:00–12:00 and
14:00– 18:30, closes at 19:00 in summer, at 17:00 November–
March, and on Monday October–June.)

Sleeping in Arles
(5F = about $1, postal code: 13200)
Sleep Code: **S** = Single, **D** = Double/Twin, **T** = Triple,
Q = Quad, **b** = bathroom, **t** = toilet only, **s** = shower only,
CC = Credit Card (Visa, MasterCard, Amex), **SE** = Speaks
English, **NSE** = No English, ***** = French hotel rating system
(0–4 stars).

Hôtel Régence** is immaculate, comfortable, and homey,
with good beds. Helpful and friendly Sylvie speaks English
(one D-140F, Ds-170F, Db-190F–275F, Tb-245F–325F,

Qb-320F, choose river view or quiet courtyard rooms, safe, free parking in courtyard, CC:VM, 5 rue Marius Jouveau; from place Lamartine turn right immediately after passing through the towers, tel. 04 90 96 39 85, fax 04 90 96 67 64).

Hôtel du Musée** is a quiet, delightful manor house hideaway with spacious rooms and a terrific courtyard terrace. Its friendly owners, M. and Mme. Dubreuil, speak some English (Sb-180F, Db-220F–300F, Tb-330F–380F, Qb-420F, parking-40F, mostly air-con rooms, CC:VMA, 11 rue de la Grande Prieure, follow signs to Musée Réattu, tel. 04 90 93 88 88, fax 04 90 49 98 15).

The **Hôtel Calendal**** is trés Provençal, with a peaceful outdoor garden, thoughtfully decorated rooms, and three-star ambiance for the price of two (Db-250F–350F, Tb-320F–400F, Qb-420F, garage 50F, air-con rooms with strong beds and modern bathrooms, CC:VMA, located above the arena at 22 place Pomme, tel. 04 90 96 11 89, fax 04 90 96 05 84, Cecile and Catherine SE).

Hôtel d'Arlatan***, one of France's more affordable classy hotels, comes with a beautiful lobby, courtyard terrace, and air-con, antique-filled rooms. In the lobby of this 15th-century building, a glass floor looks down into Roman ruins (Db-450F–795F, garage 60F, elevator, very central, CC:VMA, a block off the place du Forum at 26 rue du Sauvage, tel. 04 90 93 56 66; fax 04 90 49 68 45, SE).

Hotel Terminus et Van Gogh*, a block from the train station facing a busy square at the gate of the old town, has spacious, bright rooms. Joelle (SE) proudly posts photos and pictures of how her building is in the painting of van Gogh's house, which was bombed in WWII (D-145 with no shower available, Ds-180F, Db-200F, 5 place Lamartine, tel and fax 04 90 96 12 32).

Hôtel Lou Gardian** is well-located with steep stairs and decent rooms (Db-230F, Tb-310F, Qb-390F, CC:VMA, located near the Musée Réattu, 68 rue du 4 Septembre, tel. 04 90 96 76 15, fax 04 90 49 80 77).

Starving artists can afford these clean but spartan places: **Hôtel Voltaire*** rents 12 dumpy rooms with great balconies overlooking a caffeine-stained square a block below the arena (D-120F–130F, Ds-140F add 40F per person for three or four, CC:VM, place Voltaire, tel. 04 90 96 13 58). **Hotel Lamartine*** is a pay-in-advance kind of place, featuring industrial simplicity. It's well-located and handier than a youth hostel (D-120F, Ds-150F, Ts-200F, beds of variable quality—worth checking, just inside the place Lamartine gate at 2 rue Cavalerie, tel. 04 90 96 13 83, fax 04 90 96 08 84). **Hôtel La Gallia** is another sleepable cheapie (D-120F, Dt-140F, above a friendly café, 22 rue de l'Hôtel de Ville, tel. 04 90 96 00 63).

Eating in Arles

The restaurants and cafés, such as **Le Bistro Arlesien** (good 45F *salade niçoise*) and **L'Estaminet**, on place du Forum, serve basic food with great atmosphere. The well-respected **Les Saveurs Provençales** serves fine regional specialties at moderate prices (105F menu, closed Monday, a block below the arena, 65 rue Amédée Pichot, tel. 04 90 96 13 32). For local cuisine at bargain prices, **La Côte d'Adam** (just off the place du Forum on 12 rue de la Liberté) and the **Hotel Lou Gardin**'s restaurant (68 rue 4 Septembre) each have 70F menus. **La Vitamine** (below place du Forum on rue Dr. Fanton) pleases local vegetarians. The riverfront walk is a good spot for a picnic dinner.

Transportation Connections—Arles

By bus to: Les Baux (4/day, 30 min; departs Arles' bus station and #16 boulevard Clemenceau in downtown Arles). Service is reduced November–March, and on Sunday and holidays (tel. 04 90 49 38 01).

By train to: Avignon (8/day, 20 min, check for afternoon gaps), **Carcassonne** (8/day, 3 hrs, usually with painless transfer in Narbonne), **Beaune** (3/day, 5 hrs, transfer in Lyon), **Nice** (8/day, 3 hrs, likely transfer in Marseille), **Barcelona** (3/day, 7 hrs, at least one transfer), **Italy** (3/day, via Marseille and Nice; from Arles, it's 5 hrs to Ventimiglia on the border, 9 hrs to the Cinque Terre, 9 hrs to Milan, 11 hrs to Florence, 13 hrs to Venice or Rome). Train information tel. 04 90 96 43 94.

AVIGNON

Famous for its nursery rhyme, medieval bridge, and brooding Palace of the Popes, contemporary Avignon (a-veen-yohn) bustles and prospers behind its walls. During the 68 years (1309–1377) that Avignon played Franco Vaticano, it grew from an irrelevant speck on the map to the thriving city that it still is. Today this city combines a young, hip student population with

a white-collar, sophisticated city feel. Street mimes play to
crowds enjoying Avignon's slick cafés and chic boutiques. If
you're here in July, save evening time for Avignon's rollicking
theater festival and reserve your hotel early. The streets throng
with jugglers, skits, and singing, as visitors from around the
world converge on Avignon.

The cours Jean Jaurés (which turns into the rue de la
République) leads from the train station to place de l'Horloge
and the Palace of the Popes, forming Avignon's spine. Climb
to the parc de Rochers des Doms for a fine view, enjoy the
people scene on place de l'Horloge, and meander the back
streets. Avignon's shopping district fills the pedestrian streets
where the rue de la République meets the place de l'Horloge.
Walk across the Pont Daladier (bridge) for a great view back
on Avignon and the Rhône River.

Tourist Information: The main TI is between the train
station and the old town at 41 cours Jean Juarés (open Monday–Friday 9:00–18:00, Saturday 9:00–12:00 and 14:00–18:00,
tel. 04 90 82 65 11), while a smaller branch is on the Rhône
river at the Pont St. Bénezet. They have regional bus and train
schedules and information on Isle sur la Sorgue and the wine
villages north of Avignon and the Luberon.

Arrival in Avignon
By Train: In front of the bus or train station, the main drag—
the cours Jean Juarés that becomes rue de la République—leads
into the old city center (20 minute walk, TI on right in a few
blocks).

By Car: Drivers enter Avignon following *centre-ville* signs.
Park along the wall close to the Pont St. Bénezet (ruined old
bridge) and use that TI. Hotels have advice for smart overnight
parking.

Sights—Avignon
▲**Palace of the Popes (Palais des Papes)**—In 1309, a French
pope was elected (Pope Clement V). At the urging of the
French king, His Holiness decided he'd had enough of unholy
Italy. So he loaded up his carts and moved out of the chaos
north to Avignon for a steady rule under a friendly, supportive
king. The Catholic Church literally bought Avignon, then a
two-bit town, and popes resided here until 1403. From 1378
on, there were twin popes, one in Rome and one in Avignon,

causing a split in the Catholic Church that wasn't fully resolved until 1417.

The pope's palace is two distinct buildings, one old and one older. Along with lots of big, barren rooms, you'll see brilliant frescoes, enormous tapestries, and remarkable floor tiles. While scheduling your day around the English tour times can be a hassle, guided tours can be worthwhile. (33F, 10F more for the guided tour, occasional supplements for special exhibits, open daily April–November 1, 9:00–18:00, until 20:00 summer, off-season 9:00–12:45 and 14:00–18:00, tours in English twice daily, about 10:00 and 15:00, roughly March–October, but call 04 90 27 50 74 to confirm.)

▲**Petit Palais**—This palace superbly displays collections of early Italian (14th- and 15th-century) painting and sculpture. Since the Catholic Church was the patron of the arts in those days, all 350 paintings deal with Christian themes. Visiting this museum before going to the Palace of the Popes gives you a sense of art and life during the Avignon papacy. Notice the improvement in perspective in the later paintings. (20F, open 9:00–12:00 and 14:00–18:00, closed Tuesday.)

▲**Parc de Rochers des Doms and Pont St. Bénezet**—Hike above the Pope's Palace for a panoramic view over Avignon and the Rhône valley. At the far end drop down a few steps for a good view of the Pont St. Bénezet. This is the famous "sur le Pont d'Avignon," whose construction and location were inspired by a shepherd's religious vision. Imagine a 22-arch, 3,000-foot-long bridge extending across two rivers to that lonely Tower of Philippe the Fair (the bridge's former tollgate on the distant side). The island the bridge spanned is now filled with campgrounds. You can pay 10F to walk along a section of the ramparts and do your own jig on the bridge, but it's best appreciated from where you are. The castle on the right, the St. André Fortress, was once another island in the Rhône. Cross Daladier Bridge for the best view of the old bridge and Avignon's skyline.

Sleeping in Avignon
(5F = about $1, postal code: 84000)
The cozy and almost elegant **Hôtel Blauvac**** is in the pedestrian zone on 11 rue de La Bancasse (Db-310F–410F, Tb-380F–460F, Qb-500F, CC:VMA, tel. 04 90 86 34 11, fax 04 90 86 27 41). Right off the rue de la République, the bright and cheery

Hotel Danelli** offers modern and comfortable rooms in shiny surroundings (Db-400F, Tb-450F, CC:VM, tel. 04 90 86 46 82, fax 04 90 27 09 24). The compact **Hôtel Mignon*** is simpler (but a good value), friendly, and clean (Ss-150F, Ds-175F, Db-250F, 12 rue Joseph Vernet, tel. 04 90 82 17 30, fax 04 90 85 78 46). **Hôtel Splendid*** rents firm beds in pleasant rooms near the station, on the small park near the TI (Ss-120F– 160F, Ds-210F, 17 rue Agricole Perdiguier, tel. 04 90 86 14 46). Across the street at #17, **Hotel du Parc*** is another good value (Ds-170F, tel. 04 90 82 71 55, fax 04 90 85 64 86).

Transportation Connections—Avignon
By train to: Arles (8/day, 20 min), **Orange** (hrly, 15 min), **Nîmes** (hrly, 21 min), **Nice** (10/day, 4 hrs, a few direct, but most require transfer in Marseille), **Carcassonne** (10/day, 3 hrs, possible transfer in Narbonne), **Paris'** Gare de Lyon (10 TGVs/day, 4 hrs), **Barcelona** (2/day, 5 hrs, possible transfer in Narbonne; direct night train is convenient).

Bus service to: Pont du Gard and **Uzès** (3/day, 1 hr) can leave you stranded for hours. Consider visiting the Pont du Gard, then continuing on to Uzès or Nîmes (both merit exploration) and returning to Avignon from there. Make sure you're waiting for the bus on the right side of the road at the Pont du Gard (ask at the small inn: "Nîmes? Uzès? Avignon? *Par ici*?"). The Avignon TI has all schedules. Note reduced or no service on Sunday and holidays. The bus station (tel. 04 90 82 07 35) is adjacent to the train station.

Sights—Provence
▲▲▲**Les Baux**—This rock-top ghost town is worth visiting for the lunar landscape alone. Arrive by 9:00 or after 17:00 to avoid the crowds. A 12th-century regional powerhouse with 6,000 fierce residents, Les Baux was razed in 1632 by a paranoid Louis XIII, afraid of these trouble-making upstarts. What remains are a reconstructed "live city" of tourist shops and snack stands, and the "dead city" ruins carved into, out of, and on top of a 600-foot-high rock. Spend most of your time in the dead city—it's most dramatic and enjoyable in the morning or early evening light. Don't miss the slide show on van Gogh, Gaugin, and Cézanne in the small chapel near the entry. Spend some time in the small museum as you enter (good exhibits) and pick up the English explanations before exploring the dead

city. In the tourist-trampled live city, you'll find artsy shops, several interesting Renaissance homes, and a fine exhibit of paintings by Yves Brayer (20F), who spent his final years here. (The dead city is open Easter–October 8:30–dusk, otherwise 19:00–20:00 and 9:30–17:30, 33F, tickets include entry to all the town's sights, TI tel. 04 90 54 34 39.)

If tempted to sleep and eat here, I like the **Hotel Reine Jeanne****, 50 yards on your right after the main entry (Db-270F–330F, menus from 100F, CC:VM, 13520 Les Baux, tel. 04 90 54 32 06, fax 04 90 54 32 33).

Four daily buses serve Les Baux from Arles' train station, and two daily buses (summers only) leave from Avignon. Les Baux is 15 kilometers northeast of Arles, just past Fontvielle.
St. Rémy—This trés Provençale town with a pleasant center is a scenic ride just over the hill from Les Baux. Here you'll find the crumbled ruins of Glanum, a once-thriving Roman city located at the crossroads of two ancient trade routes between Italy and Spain, and the mental ward where Vincent van Gogh was sent after cutting off his ear. Glanum is just outside St. Rémy, on the road to Les Baux (D-5). Walk to the gate and peek in to get a feel for its scale. The ruins are worth the effort if you have the time and haven't been to Pompeii or Ephesus (26F, open daily 9:00–12:00 and 14:00–18:00, closes at 17:00 October–April). Across the street, opposite the entry, is a free Roman arch and tower. The arch marked the entry into Glanum. The tower is a memorial to the grandsons of Emperor Augustus, located there to remind folks of them when entering or leaving Glanum.

Across the street from Glanum is the still-functioning mental hospital that housed van Gogh (Clinique St. Paul). Wander into the small chapel and peaceful cloisters. Vincent's favorite walks outside the hospital are clearly signposted. If St. Rémy tempts you to stay longer, sleep at **Canto Cigalo** (chemin Canto Cigalo, tel. 04 90 92 14 28, fax 04 90 92 18 56). Wednesday is market day in St. Rémy.
▲▲▲**Pont du Gard**—One of Europe's great treats, this remarkably well-preserved Roman aqueduct was built before the time of Christ. It was the missing link of a 35-mile canal that, by dropping one foot for every 300, supplied 44 million gallons of water to Nîmes daily. While the top is now closed to daredevils, just walking under it is a marvel. Study it up close— no mortar, just expertly cut stones. Signs direct you to

"panaromas" above the bridge on either side. The best view of the aqueduct is from the cool of the river below, floating flat on your back—bring a swimsuit (always open and free). Buses run from Nîmes, Uzès, or Avignon. Combine Uzès and the Pont du Gard for an ideal day excursion from Avignon. By car, the Pont du Gard is an easy 30-minute drive due west of Avignon (follow Nîmes) and 45 minutes northwest of Arles (via Tarascon). Park on the *rive gauche* side (you'll see signs).

Uzès—A pleasant, less-trampled town near the Pont du Gard, Uzès is best seen slowly on foot, with a long coffee break in its mellow main square, the place aux Herbes. (Not so mellow during the colorful Sunday morning market.) Check out the Tour Fenestrelle and the Duché de Uzès. Uzès is a short hop west (by bus) of the Pont du Gard and is well-served from Nîmes (9/day) and Avignon (3/day).

The Camargue—One of the few truly "wild areas" of France, where pink flamingos, wild bulls, and the famous white horses wander freely amid rice fields and lagoons. Even so, skip it. The Camargue's biggest town is Aigue Mortes. That means "dead town," and it should stay that way.

▲▲Orange—This most northern town in Provence is notable for its Roman arch and theater. Its 60-foot-tall Roman Arch (from 25 B.C.) shows off Julius Caesar's defeat of the Gauls in 49 B.C. Its best-preserved Roman theater in existence still seats 10,000. Of particular interest is its 120-foot-high stage wall, which you'll see nowhere else. (25F, open daily April–early October 9:00–18:30, winter 9:00–12:00, 13:30–17:00, ticket includes entrance to the city museum across the street with more Roman art. Orange TI tel. 04 90 34 70 88, trains to Avignon hourly, 15-minute ride, bus #2 takes you the mile from the station to the old town center.) From Orange, drivers can tour the adjacent wine region, described below.

Loop Trip for Wine Lovers—If you have a car (or a bike, best rented in Vaison la Romaine—ideal riding from here) and a fondness for fine wine, take a loop trip of Provence's wine country. From Avignon, head to Carpentras (a great city itself), then connect the Cote du Rhône wine villages of Vaqueryas, Gigondas, Rasteau, Sablet, and adorable, if overrestored, Seguret (figure 100-km round-trip from Avignon). This is a hospitable and relaxed wine-tasting region, with generous samples and little pressure to buy. Near Rasteau village, at Le Domaine des Girasols, a friendly couple and their American son-in-law (John) will take your palate on a tour of some of the area's best wine. It's well-marked and worth a stop, and while you aren't pressured to buy, it is a great value. Ideally, have lunch in Gigondas at the outdoor restaurant on the small town square and consider sleeping here at the very comfortable **Hostellerie les Florets***** (Db-350F, excellent restaurant, 84190 Gigondas, tel. 04 90 65 85 01, fax 04 90 65 83 80). The nearby wine village of Sablet, which makes a good base for budget travelers, is chock-full of *chambres d'hôte* (try **Madame Fert's** *chambres*, Db-290F, breakfast included, follow the signs, tel. 04 90 46 94 77).

NOT QUITE A YEAR IN PROVENCE—THE HILL TOWNS OF LUBERON

The Luberon region, stretching 30 miles along a ridge of rugged hills east of Avignon, hides some of France's most appealing hill towns. Bonnieux, Lacoste, Oppède le Vieux, Roussillon, and the very-discovered (and overpriced) Gordes, to mention a few, are quintessential Provençal hill towns.

Those intrigued by Peter Mayle's *A Year in Provence* will enjoy a day joyriding through the region. Mayle's best-selling book describes the ruddy local culture from an Englishman's perspective, as he buys an old home, fixes it up, and adopts the region as his new home.

The Luberon terrain in general (much of which is a French regional natural park) is as appealing as its hill towns. Gnarled vineyards and wind-sculpted trees separate tidy stone structures from abandoned buildings—little more than rock piles—that seem to challenge city slickers to fix them up.

The wind is an integral part of life here. The infamous mistral, finishing its long ride in from Siberia, hits like a hammer—hard enough, it's said, to blow the ears off a donkey. Throughout the region, you'll see houses designed with windowless walls facing the mistral (but no donkey ears). Walking from village to village is a popular pastime here—local TIs have trail information.

Planning Your Time

To enjoy the windblown ambiance of the Luberon, plan a leisurely day trip visiting three or four of the characteristic towns. While the area isn't worth the trouble without a car, Isle sur la Sorgue, which offers a fine introduction to this sunny slice of France, is handy to Avignon by train. An overnight here gives a fine taste of the region's appeal. By car, town-hop for a day side-tripping from Arles or as a detour en route to the French Riviera. Of course, tumbling in for an hour from the car park, you'll be just another splash-in-the-pan camera-toting Provence fan. Spend a night and you'll feel more a part of the scene. By car, get on the N-100 toward Apt, east of Avignon. Veer left onto the D-2, where you'll see signs to Gordes. Roussillon is signed from Gordes.

Isle sur la Sorgue

This sturdy market town, literally "island on the Sorgue river," sits within a split in its happy little river. The town erupts into a market frenzy with hearty crafts and local produce each Sunday and Thursday. With clear water babbling under flower box–decorated pedestrian bridges and its old-time carousel always spinning, Isle sur la Sorge invites exploration. Navigate by mossy water wheels which, while still turning, power only memories of the town's wool and silk industries. The 12th-century church with a festive Baroque interior seems too big for its town. Next to it is the antique green Café de France—the place to sip a *pastis* with locals and ponder the action on place de la Liberté. The shady riverside park 1 kilometer upstream is popular in the summer.

The TI (9:00–12:30, 14:00–18:00, closed Sunday afternoon and Monday, tel. 04 90 38 04 78), has a line on rooms in private homes and information on handy Avignon train connections (8/day, 20 min). **Hotel Bar Restaurant Grill Le Bassin***, overlooking the river on the upstream tip of the "island," provides a cheery blue and pink home (Ds-180F, Db-230F, Tb-280F, CC:VM, avenue du General de Gaulle, postal code: 84800, tel. 04 90 38 03 16). The tiny **La Saladelle** offers rooms for a three-day minimum, or one night if reserved the day of arrival. It's half-pension only but a good value at 170F per person (33 rue Carnot, tel. 04 90 20 68 59). Those in need of more comfort will appreciate the **Mas de Cure Bourse*****, just outside town at the intersection of the roads D-31 and D-938 (Db-400–520F, CC:VM, route de Caumont, postal code: 84800, tel. 04 90 38 16 58, fax 04 90 38 52 31).

Gordes

This is the most touristy and trendy town in the Luberon. Parisian big shots love it. Once a virtual ghost town of derelict buildings, it's now completely fixed up and filled by people who live in a world without callouses. See it from a distance.

Rousillon

With all the trendy charm of Santa Fe on a hilltop, a stop here will cost you at least a roll of film. Climb ten minutes from your car park, past the picture-perfect square and under the church, to the summit of the town (signs to *castum*), where a dramatic view complete with a howling mistral and an interesting *table d'orientation* await. Then, back under the church, see how local (or artsy) you can look over a cup of coffee on what must be the most scenic village square in the Luberon. On the far end of town, beyond the parking lot, a brilliant ochre canyon (10F)—formerly a quarry—stands ready for those who wish they were in Bryce Canyon. You could paint the entire town without ever leaving the red and orange corner of your palette—many do.

Sleeping in Rousillon (postal code 84220): A short walk below the charm on the road into town from Gordes is the comfortable **Hôtel Residence des Ocres**** (Db-295F–380F, Tb-380F, Qb-400F, air-con, CC:VM, tel. 04 90 05 60 50, fax 04 90 05 79 74). At the house or restaurant of **Madame Cheryl** you can rent spotless rooms with firm mattresses (D-180F, 70 yards north of the PTT below the village, tel. 04 90 05 68 47). She speaks English, is a wealth of regional travel tips, and rents mountain bikes (100F/day). The **Mas Garrigon***** takes elaborate care of upscale travelers in a beautiful setting with a pool, exquisite rooms, and an elegant restaurant (Db-600–800F, they kindly request that guests take dinner in their restaurant, CC:VMA, 1 mile below Roussillon, tel. 04 90 05 63 22, fax 04 90 05 70 10). If all else fails, the TI posts a listing of accommodation options in the area.

Oppède le Vieux

This is a windy barnacle of a town, with a few boutiques and a dusty main square at the base of a short, ankle-twisting climb to an evocative ruined church and castle. The Luberon views justify the effort. This way-off-the-beaten path, fixer-upper of a village must be how Gordes looked before it became chic. It's ideal for those looking to vanish in Provence. The cozy **Restaurant L'Oppidum** rents two classy rooms (Db-300F, place de la Croix, tel. 04 90 76 84 15, NSE).

THE FRENCH RIVIERA

A hundred years ago, celebrities from London to Moscow flocked here to escape the drab, dreary weather at home. The *belle époque* is now the tourist *époque*, as this most sought after fun-in-the-sun destination now caters to more than Europe's aristocracy. Some of the Continent's most stunning scenery and superb museums lie along this strip of land—and so do millions of sun-worshiping tourists.

Nice is this region's capital and your best home base. Nearby Antibes has a cozy old town center and fine beaches, Monte Carlo welcomes all with open cash registers, and the hill towns offer a breezy and photogenic alternative to the beach scene. Evenings on the Riviera, a.k.a. the Côte d'Azur, were made for the promenade.

Planning Your Time

Nice is the logical base of operation for most, with excellent public transportation to most regional sights, world-class museums, plenty of hotels in all price ranges, and a marvelous beachfront promenade. But Antibes or Villefranche offer sandy beaches and a small-town warmth that lures many their way. I've focused my accommodations listings on these three cities. If you choose Nice, remember that it's France's fifth-biggest city. While likeable, it's a big city nevertheless.

Once situated, spend a full day in Nice, then consider half-day trips to Monaco, Antibes, and St. Paul/Vence—in that order.

The French Riviera

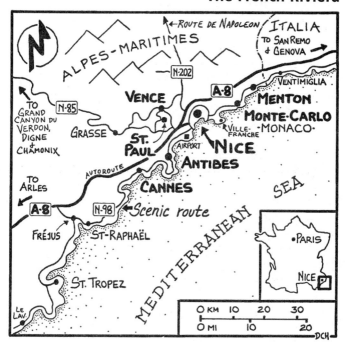

Getting Around the Riviera

Getting around the Côte d'Azur by train or bus is easy. Nice is perfectly located for exploring the Riviera. Like prostitutes on bar stools, the resort towns of the Riviera await your visit. Monaco, Eze, Villefranche on the left, and Antibes and Cannes on the right—each are a 15- to 60-minute bus or train ride apart.

While rail travelers have a tough time breaking away from the tracks, bus service can be cheaper and more frequent and scenic—plus it often drops you closer to where you want to be. At Nice's efficient bus station (*gare routière*, on boulevard J. Jaures—see map of Nice), competing companies vie for your business, offering free return trips. Get schedules and prices at the helpful information desk in the bus station (sample fares: to Villefranche-8F, Antibes-25F, departures 3/hr; tel. 04 93 85 61 81).

Cuisine Scene—Côte d'Azur

The Côte d'Azur (technically a part of Provence) gives Provence's cuisine a Mediterranean flair. *Bouillabaisse* (the spicy seafood stew-soup seems worth the cost only for those with a seafood fetish), *bourride* (a creamy fish soup thickened with *aïoli*), and *salade niçoise* (nee-swaz: a tasty tomato, potato, olive, anchovy, and tuna salad) are the local specialties. You'll also find these tasty bread treats: *pissaladière* (bread dough topped with onions, olives, and anchovies), *fougasse* (a spindly, lacelike bread), *socca* (a thin chickpea crêpe), and *pan bagna* (a bread shell stuffed with tomatoes, anchovies, olives, onions, and tuna). Bellet is the local wine, both red and white, served chilled.

NICE

Nice is a melting pot of thousands of tanning tourists and 340,000 already-tanned residents. Here you'll see the chicest of the chic, the cheapest of the cheap, and everyone else in this strange scramble to be where the European land hits the water. Nice's superb mountain-to-Mediterranean scenery, its thriving Old City, eternally entertaining seafront promenade, and superb museums make settling into this town a joy. Nice is nice—but hot and jammed in July and August.

Take only a piece of Nice and leave the rest to the residents. Outside of a few museums, everything you want is within a small area—near the Old City and along the seafront.

Orientation

Tourist Information: Nice has three TIs (at the train station, on the RN-7 as you drive into town on the right just after the airport, and downtown at 2 rue Masséna facing the beach). All are open daily 8:00–19:00, until 20:00 in summer (tel. 04 93 87 07 07 or 04 93 87 60 60). Pick up the excellent free Nice map (which lists all the sights and hours), the museums booklet, and the extensive "Practical Guide to Nice." TIs make hotel reservations for a small fee.

Arrival in Nice

By Train: Nice has one main station (Nice-Ville) where all trains stop and you get off. Avoid the suburban station (Gare Riquier). To reach my recommended hotels, turn left out of the station, then right on avenue Jean Médecin. From the station, bus #5 goes to the old town and bus station, and bus #15 takes you to the beach and the promenade des Anglais (catch it across the street from the station).

By Car: For some of the Riviera's best scenery, follow the coast road between Cannes and Fréjus. Use the roadside TI just past the airport and park at the lot at Nice Étoile on avenue Jean Médecin. Most Nice street parking is metered.

By Plane: Nice's mellow and user-friendly airport (tel. 04 93 21 30 30) is right on the Mediterranean, a quick 20–30 minutes from the city center by bus (3/hr to the bus station, 20F) or taxi (150F). International flights use terminal 1; domestic flights use terminal 2.

Helpful Hints

Self-serve laundromats abound in Nice; ask your hotelier and guard your load (the one at 12 rue des Suisses, 2 blocks west of avenue Jean Médecin, next to the cathedral, is user-friendly). The American Express office faces the beach at 11 promenade des Anglais (tel. 04 93 16 53 53), and new and used English language books and guidebooks are available at The Cat's Whiskers (26 rue Lamartine, near the Hôtel Star, closed Sunday). Cycles Arnaud rents bikes (4 place Grimaldi, just off the rue Jean Médecin, tel. 04 93 87 88 55). Cars rent for 260F (100 free km) to 400F (250 free km) per day.

Sights—Nice

▲▲Promenade des Anglais and the Beaches of Nice— There's something for everyone along this seafront circus. Watch the Europeans at play, admire the azure Mediterranean, anchor yourself in a blue chair, and prop your feet up on the made-to-order guardrail. Join the evening parade of tans along the promenade. Start at the pink-domed Hotel Negresco and, like the *belle époque* English aristocrats for whom the promenade was built, stroll to the Old City and Castle Hill.

Hotel Negresco, Nice's finest hotel and a historic monument, offers the city's most costly beds and a free "museum" interior. March through the lobby into the exquisite Salon Royal. The tsar's chandelier hangs from an Eiffel-built dome. Read the explanation, stroll the circle, and on your way out, pop into the Salon Louis XIV.

The next block toward the castle is filled with a lush public park and the Masséna Museum. The TI is just beyond that. But get down on the beach.

Nice

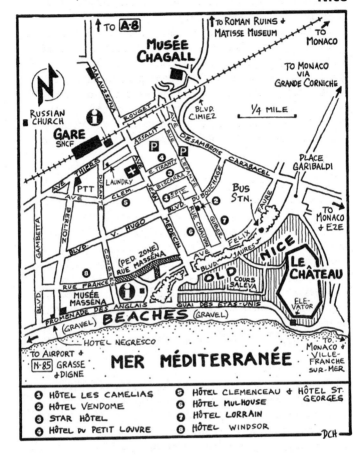

TO A·8
MUSÉE CHAGALL
TO ROMAN RUINS & MATISSE MUSEUM
TO MONACO
TO MONACO VIA GRANDE CORNICHE
RUSSIAN CHURCH
GARE SNCF
BLVD. CIMIEZ
¼ MILE
MALAUSSENA
ROUGET
AVE. DESAMBROIS
PLACE GARIBALDI
ASSALIT
RUE LEPANTE
CARABACEL
AVE. THIERS
E. TIRANTY
DURANTE
LAUNDRY
PTT
BISCARRA
CLEM.
RUE DU BOUCHAGE
BUS STN.
GAMBETTA
AVE. BERLIOZ
J. GUBERNATIS
BLVD. DUBOUCHAGE
RUE CHAUVIN
GUBEL
FAURE
BLVD. V. HUGO
RUE MEDECIN
FELIX
AVE. JAURES
TO MONACO & EZE
OLD NICE
LE CHÂTEAU
(PED ZONE) RUE MASSENA
RUE FRANCE
BLVD.
COURS SALEYA
ELEVATOR
MUSÉE MASSENA
PROMENADE DES ANGLAIS
QUAI DES ETATS-UNIS
(GRAVEL) BEACHES (GRAVEL)
HÔTEL NEGRESCO
TO AIRPORT & N-85 GRASSE & DIGNE
MER MÉDITERRANÉE
TO MONACO & VILLEFRANCHE-SUR-MER

❶ HÔTEL LES CAMELIAS	❺ HÔTEL CLEMENCEAU & HÔTEL ST. GEORGES
❷ HÔTEL VENDOME	❻ HÔTEL MULHOUSE
❸ STAR HÔTEL	❼ HÔTEL LORRAIN
❹ HÔTEL DU PETIT LOUVRE	❽ HÔTEL WINDSOR

DCH

The beaches of Nice are where the jet set lays on rocks. After settling into the smooth pebbles, you can play beach volleyball, ping-pong, or *boules*; rent paddle boats, Jet Skis, or windsurfers; explore ways to use your zoom lens as a telescope; or snooze on comfy beach beds with end tables. Before you head off in search of sandy beaches, try it on the rocks.

▲▲**Old City (Vieux Nice)**—This thriving Old City is characteristic Nice in the buff. Here Italian and French flavors mix to create a spicy Mediterranean dressing. The 20th century has driven old Nice into a triangle of spindly streets filling a corner between the castle hill and beach. A broad park-lined boulevard seals it off. The streets, while straight, are anything but predictable. Stealth pigeons fly under tall pastel domestic cliffs, while tattoo shops show off their work. Laundry flaps and tattered squares say "sit." Cours Saleya, a long broad square, collects people and produce like a trough between all this and the sea. Restaurant tables tangle with market stalls here. The daily flower and fish market becomes a flea market on Monday.

Castle Hill—Providing a saddle horn for an otherwise flat city center, climb this only for exercise or the view. Walk up rue Rossetti or catch the elevator from the beach side. The 360-degree view of Nice, the Alps foothills, and the Mediterranean is a decent reward. There are a waterfall, tacky souvenirs, playground, and cemetery, but no castle on Castle Hill.

Shopping Streets—The pedestrian street rue Masséna is packed with tourists, run-of-the-mill cafés, and boutiques. Window-shop the expensive boutiques and sift through the international crowds.

▲▲▲**Musée National Marc Chagall**—Even if you're suspicious of modern art, this museum—with the largest collection of Chagall's work anywhere—is a delight. After WWII, Chagall returned from the U.S.A. to settle in Vence, a hill town above Nice. Between 1954 and 1967, he painted a cycle of 17 large murals designed for and donated to this museum. These paintings, inspired by the books of Genesis, Exodus, and the Song of Songs, make up the "nave," or core, of what Chagall called the "House of Brotherhood."

Each painting is a lighter-than-air collage of images drawing from Chagall's Russian-folk-village youth, his Jewish heritage, Biblical themes, and his feeling that he existed somewhere between heaven and earth. He felt the Bible was a synonym for nature, and color and Biblical themes were key ingredients for understanding God's love for His creation. Chagall's brilliant blues and reds celebrate nature, as do his spiritual and folk themes. Notice the focus on couples. To Chagall, humans loving each other mirrored God's love of creation.

Don't miss the stained-glass windows of the auditorium, early family photos of the artist, and a room full of Chagall lithographs. The small 10F-guidebook begins with a philosophical introduction by Chagall himself. (28F, open July–September 10:00–18:00, off-season 10:00–17:00, closed Tuesday, 24F English tours often available on request, tel. 04

93 53 87 20.) From the train station, turn left along avenue Thiers and walk about 8 blocks (the museum is signposted) or take bus #15 (to "Chagall"). There's a taxi rank at the museum (50F to the beach).

Nice City Museum (Musée Masséna)—The city-history museum, housed in a beautiful mansion, is packed with historical—but forgettable—paraphernalia (25F, daily except Monday, May–September 10:00–12:00, 15:00–18:00; off-season 10:00–12:00, 14:00–17:00, in a fine garden facing the beach next to the Hotel Negresco at 65 rue de France, tel. 04 93 88 11 34).

Modern Art Museum—This ultramodern museum features a fine collection of art from the 1960s and 1970s (25F, open 11:00–18:00, Friday evening until 22:00, closed Tuesday, on the promenade des Arts near the bus station).

▲**Russian Cathedral**—Even if you've been to Russia, this Russian Orthodox church, which claims to be the finest outside Russia, is interesting. Its one-room interior is filled with icons and candles. Tsar Nicholas II gave his aristocratic country-folk—who wintered on the Riviera—this church in 1912. (A few years later, Russian comrades who didn't winter on the Riviera shot him.) Here in the land of olives and anchovies, these proud onion domes seem odd. But so, I imagine, did those old Russians. (12F, open daily 9:00–12:00 and 14:30–18:00, services Saturday at 18:00, Sunday at 10:00, no shorts, ten-minute walk behind the station at 17 boulevard du Tsarevitch, tel. 04 93 96 88 02.)

▲**Matisse Museum**—A three-star sight for his fans, the art is beautifully displayed in this newly renovated showpiece, representing the largest collection of Matisse paintings. Personally, I don't get Matisse. (25F, open April–September 11:00–19:00, otherwise 10:00–17:00, closed Tuesday. Take bus #15, #17, #22 to the Arènes stop, or hike 45 minutes to 164 avenue des Arènes de Cimiez, tel. 04 93 81 08 08.)

Nightlife—Nice's bars play host to a lively late-night scene with jazz and rock 'n' roll. Most activity focuses on Old Nice, near the place Rossetti. If you're out very late, avoid walking alone. Plan on a cover charge or expensive drinks.

Sleeping in Nice
(5F = about $1, postal code: 06000)
Sleep Code: **S** = Single, **D** = Double/Twin, **T** = Triple, **Q** = Quad, **b** = bathroom, **t** = toilet only, **s** = shower only,

CC = Credit Card (Visa, MasterCard, Amex), **SE** = Speaks English, **NSE** = No English, * = Hotel rating (0–4 stars).

Don't look for charm in Nice. Go for modern and clean with a central location. Reserve early for summer visits. Prices go down from October to April. There are very few hotels in the Old City, and the hotels near the station are overrun, over-priced, and loud. I sleep halfway between the Old City (Vieux Nice) and the train station, near avenue Jean Médecin. From the train station, turn left out of the station onto avenue Thiers, then right onto avenue Jean Médecin. Drivers can park under the Nice Étoile shopping center (at avenue J. Médecin and boulevard Dubouchage/Victor Hugo). This handy location feels safe and relatively peaceful, and is midway between the Old City, train station, bus station, and seafront.

Hôtel Star** is immaculate in every way, very comfort-able, and a great value. It's ideally located a few blocks east of avenue Jean Médecin, and warmly run by Françoise and Georges, who practically trip over themselves trying to be helpful (Sb-180F–200F, Db-250F–320F, Tb-320F–390F, fine beds, no elevator, CC:VMA, 14 rue Biscarra, tel. 04 93 85 19 03, fax 04 93 13 04 23, SE).

Hôtel du Petit Louvre* has art-festooned walls, light-hearted owners, and almost clean rooms (Ds-190F, Db-220F, Tb-240F–275F, elevator, CC:VM, 10 rue Emma Tiranty, tel. 04 93 80 15 54, fax 04 93 62 45 08).

Hôtel Lorrain* rents cheap rooms with kitchenettes (S-150F, Ds-170F, Db-200F–250F, Tb-270F, CC:VM, 6 rue Gubernatis, tel. 04 93 85 42 90, fax 04 90 85 55 54). This clean, simple hotel may request longer stays in the high sea-son and a two-night minimum off-season. Friendly Patricia Scoffier tries her best to speak English.

Hôtel Clemenceau** comes with spacious, comfortable yet simple rooms and a friendly owner, Mme. Lasserre (D-150F, Db-200F–300F, Tb-250F–350F, Qb-400F–500F, plus 50F for a kitchenette, CC:VM, 1 block west of avenue Jean Médecin, 3 avenue Clemenceau, tel. 04 93 88 61 19, fax 04 93 88 03 23).

Hotel St. Georges**, a block away, is big and modern (Db-300F, Tb-400F, pleasant outdoor garden, CC:VM, 7 avenue Clemenceau, tel. 04 93 88 79 21, fax 04 93 16 22 85).

For a taste of la *belle époque* and faded three-star elegance, waltz into the unusual **Hotel Vendome*****, well-located in an old manor house with off-street parking. The best rooms have balconies—request *avec balcon*—ideally rooms 105, 102 or any on the fifth floor (Db-500F–650F, Tb-650F, Qb-750F in loft room, 26 rue Pastorelli, tel. 04 93 62 00 77, fax 04 93 13 40 78).

Hôtel Windsor*** is a pleasant garden retreat with art-fully designed rooms and a swimming pool (Sb-400F–500F, Db-500F–650F, elevator, sauna-60F, free gym, rooms over the garden are worth the higher price, CC:VMA, 1 block east of the Musée Masséna and 5 blocks from the sea, 11 rue Dalpozzo, tel. 04 93 88 59 35, fax 04 93 88 94 57).

Hôtel les Camelias** reminds me of the Old World places I stayed in as a kid traveling with my parents. An ideally located dark and floral place burrowed in a garden, it has simple rooms and a loyal clientele who give the TV lounge a retirement-home-after-dinner feeling. Some basic rooms have balconies—*chambre avec balcon* (S-150F, Ss-180F, Sb-220F, Db-320F–350F, Tb-400F, prices include breakfast, parking-20F, elevator, CC:VM, 3 rue Spitaleri, tel. 04 93 62 15 54, Mme. Vimont and her son Jean Claude SE). Guests here will enjoy their 65F four-course dinner—simple, hearty, and stressless.

The Hôtel Mulhouse** is close to Old Nice, and rather plain but comfortable (Sb-235F, Db-290F–320F, Tb-300F–400F, Qb-400F–480F, elevator, CC:VMA, 9 rue de Chauvain, tel. 04 93 92 36 39, fax 04 93 13 96 80).

Sleeping near Nice in Villefranche-sur-Mer
(5F = about $1, postal code: 06230)

For small-town atmosphere, nearby Villefranche-sur-Mer is a mini-Nice. Villefranche (between Nice and Monte Carlo, with frequent 15-minute bus and train service to both), is classier, quieter, and more exotic. Even if you're sleeping elsewhere, consider a beachfront dinner or an ice-cream-licking village stroll. The first two hotels listed are the fanciest in this entire chapter. Beyond the requisite castle, yachts, and boutiques, Villefranche has the unique rue Obscure. The TI is in the small park (Jardin François Binon, just below the main inter-section on boulevard Princess Grace, daily 8:00–20:00 in sum-mer, closed earlier and on Sundays off-season, tel. 04 93 01 73 68). The bus stops at the TI, near all listed hotels. The train station is a 20-minute walk or 40F taxi ride away.

If your idea of sightseeing is to enjoy the view from your hotel's dining room or pool, stay at the friendly and family run **Hôtel La Flore***** (Db-400F–660F, Tb-790F, Qb-890F, less November–March, no half-pension required but a fine restaurant, smartly designed family rooms, elevator, private pool, high above the harbor with great views, CC:VMA, a block from the TI on boulevard Princess Grace de Monaco, tel. 04 93 76 30 30, fax 04 93 76 99 99, SE). Sea views and balconies are worth the extra cost.

Hotel Welcome*** is buried in the heart of the old town, right on the water, with most rooms overlooking the harbor. You'll pay top dollar for all the comforts in a formal hotel that seems to do everything right and couldn't be better located (Db-630F–890F, breakfast included, quai Courbet, tel. 04 93 76 76 93, fax 04 93 01 88 81, E-mail welcome@riviera.fr, SE). The rooms at both Hôtel La Flore and Hotel Welcome, while hugely different in cost, are about the same in comfort. One's on a road; the other's on the harbor.

The tight and hotelesque **Hôtel Provençal**** offers fine views from well-worn rooms and impersonal service, with a pool and a costly mandatory half-pension in July and August (Db-300F–460F, Tb-480F–550F, Qb-550F–640F, CC:VMA, a block below the TI at 4 avenue Maréchal Joffre, tel. 04 93 01 71 42, fax 04 93 76 96 00).

Hôtel la Darse** is tucked behind the castle, right on the water in Villefranche's Port de la Darse. Simple but sleepable rooms and beds of variable quality; ask for a bay-side room with a balcony (Db-280F–320F, extra person-60F, 40F less without view, no half-board requirements, tel. 04 93 01 72 54, fax 04 93 01 84 37).

Le Home, easily the best budget beds in town, rents ten simple rooms in a cheery and simple garden with a welcoming terrace, 2 blocks up the hill from the TI and bus stop (Db-180F, avenue de Grande Bretagne, tel. 04 93 76 79 88).

Eating in Nice

Nice's Old City overflows with cheap, moderate, and expensive restaurants, pizza stands, and taverns.

Charcuterie Julien is a good deli that sells an impressive array of local dishes by the weight. Buy 200 grams (dew-sahn grahm) plopped into a plastic carton to go (open 11:00–19:30, closed Wednesday, rue de la Poissonnerie, at the Castle Hill end of cours Saleya). The **Nissa Socca** café (a block off the place Rossini on the rue Reparate), offers the best cheap Italian cuisine in town in a lively atmosphere. Come early.

Rue Droite has Nice's best concentration of pizza stands and local eateries. Check out **Acchiardo's** (#37) for the fish soup. Stop by **Le four à bois** bakery (#38) and watch them make *fougasse*. For more traditional, more atmospheric, and more expensive dining, try the locally popular **La Cambuse** on the cours Saleya, or the excellent **Lou Nissart** (moderate, across the place Masséna, at 1 rue de l'Opéra, tel. 04 93 85 34 49).

Near most hotels recommended in this book: **L'Ange Gourmand** serves a delicious 70F-menu with a homey and caring touch (closed Sunday, no-smoking section, 47 rue Lamartine, tel. 04 93 13 99 11); and **L'Authentic** offers fine pastas and seafood in a relaxed setting, from 50F for the plate of the day to 75F *menus* (18 rue Biscarra, tel. 04 93 62 48 88).

Transportation Connections—Nice
By train to: Arles (10/day, 3 hrs, transfer in Marseille), **Dijon** (8/day, 8 hrs, most are direct), **Chamonix** (there is a direct night train around 20:30 and also a very scenic train via **Digne** that runs due north through canyons and along white-water rivers—5/day, 3 hrs, Chemins de Fer de Provence), **Florence** (2/day, 8 hrs, transfer in Pisa and/or Genoa, morning departures), **Paris'** Gare de Lyon (7 TGVs/day, 7 hrs, night train available), **Barcelona** (4/day, 10 hrs, direct night train or day trips with at least one transfer).

ANTIBES
For sandy beaches, an interesting old town, and a fine Picasso collection, visit Antibes. Just 20 minutes from Nice by train, Antibes' glamorous port glistens below its fortifications with luxurious yachts and colorful fishing boats. Boat lovers are welcome to browse. This compact town's attractions lie near the port within the Old City walls (and atop the ruins of the fourth-century B.C. Greek city of Antipolis). The festive Old City is charming in a sandy-sophisticated way. The daily market (*Marché Provençal*), in an easy-to-digest light under a 19th-century canopy, brings out the locals (behind the Picasso museum on cours Masséna, daily until 13:00 except on off-season Mondays). Place Audiberti becomes a flea market on Thursday and Saturday (7:00–18:00).

Tourist Information: The sultry Maison de Tourisme has an interesting "Discovering Old Antibes" brochure (downtown at 11 place de Gaulle, 9:00–20:00, 9:00–13:00 Sunday, off-season lunch breaks, tel. 04 92 90 53 00). The Nice TI has Antibes maps; plan ahead.

Arrival in Antibes

By Train: From the train station, the port is straight ahead, and the Old City center (and TI) is five minutes to the right down avenue Soleau. The Nice–Antibes train (15 minutes, 21F) beats the Nice–Antibes bus (60 minutes, 25F). Train info: 04 93 99 50 50.

By Bus: The bus station is a block from the TI on place Guynemer.

By Car: Park near the Old City walls on the port.

Sights—Antibes

▲▲**Musée Picasso** sits serenely where the Old City meets the sea (look for signs from the Old City) in the Château Grimaldi and offers a remarkable collection of this artist's work—paintings, sketches, and ceramics. Picasso, who lived and worked here in 1946, said if you want to see work from his "Antibes period," you'll need to do it in Antibes. You'll understand why Picasso liked working here. Several photos of the artist make this already intimate museum more so. In his famous *Joie de Vivre* painting (the museum's highlight), there's a new love in Picasso's life, and he's feelin' groovy (20F, open 10:00–18:00, closed Monday and off-season from 12:00–14:00, tel. 04 92 90 54 20).

Beaches—The best beaches stretch between Antibes' port and the Cap d'Antibes, offering long stretches of fine sand. The main beaches (near the Cap d'Antibes) are jammed only in the summer, though the smaller *plage* (beach) *de la Gravette* at the port remains relatively calm in any season.

Sleeping in Antibes
(5F = about $1, postal code: 06600)

Relais du Postillon** offers pleasant, comfortable rooms on a central square, and helpful owners (Db-250F–400F, extra bed-30F–50F, elevator, CC:VMA, 8 rue Championnet, tel. 04 93 34 20 77, fax 04 93 34 61 24).

Hotel Le Cameo** is a big rambling, pleasantly unaggressive old place. It faces a characteristic square above a bar filled with smoke and locals. The public areas are dark and disorienting, but its nine *bon petit* rooms are almost huggable (Ds-220F, Db-280F, Ts-300F, Tb-360F, place Nationale, tel. 04 93 34 24 17, fax 04 93 34 35 80, NSE).

Auberge Provençale*, on the same square, has seven pleasant rooms, a hard-to-find reception, and an inattentive management (S-150F, D-200F, Db-250F–400F, Tb-320F–450F, Qb-500F, CC:VMA, 61 place Nationale, tel. 04 93 34 13 24, fax 04 93 34 89 88). Rooms come with "Mini-tel," the French computer-telephone info service. Their loft room, named Celine, is huge, with a royal canopy bed, a dramatic open-timbered ceiling, and—if available—costs no more.

Hôtel Ponteil** has bungalow-style rooms in and around a breezy manor house, with free and safe private parking, a garden terrace, quick beach access, and a friendly family feel (S-250F, D-310F, Db-420F, bunky family deals, breakfast is included in room prices, and a costly half-pension is required from June 15 through September 15, CC:VM, 11 impasse Jean-Mesnier, tel. 04 93 34 67 92, fax 04 93 34 49 47). A long walk from the train station near the beach on the far side of town, this hotel is best for drivers.

MONACO

Still dazzling despite overdevelopment and crass commercialization, Monaco will disappoint those who look for something below the surface. This 2-square-kilometer country is a tax haven for its tiny full-time population. The TI is near the casino (2 boulevard des Moulins, tel. 04 92 16 61 66). Small buses effortlessly shuttle tourists and locals through Monaco.

Monaco (the principality) is best understood when separated into its two key areas: Monaco Ville, the old city housing Prince Rainier's palace; and Monte Carlo, the area around the casino. The harbor divides the two. A short bus ride (every ten minutes, 8.5F, 19F for four tickets), or a 30-minute uphill walk, links each area to the bus and train stations. Frequent buses also connect Monaco Ville and the casino. Start with a look at Monaco Ville for a *magnifique* view (particularly at night) over the harbor and the casino. If you arrive in the morning, you can watch the uninspiring changing of the guard (11:55), wander over to the beautiful Cathédrale de Monaco, where Princess Grace is buried, and picnic in the immaculate and scenic gardens overlooking the blue Mediterranean. (Pick up a *pan bagna* sandwich in the old city.)

The nearby and costly (60F, CC:VM) Musée de l'Océanographique (Cousteau Aquarium) is the largest of its kind. It can be jammed and disappoints some, though aquarium lovers leave impressed. The *Monte Carlo Story* film gives an interesting account in English of this city's history, mostly about Prince Rainier's family (40F, in the parking garage next to the aquarium, take the escalator down to the elevator, then another escalator down one more level).

Leave Monaco Ville and ride the shuttle bus or stroll the harborfront up to the casino. Count the counts and Rolls Royces in front of the Hôtel de Paris. Strut inside the lavish casino (opens at 12:00)—anyone can get as far as the one-armed bandits, but only adults (21 and older) can pay the 50F- or 100F-charge to enter the private game rooms and rub shoulders with high rollers (some rooms open at 15:00, others at 21:00). Entrance is free to all games in the new, plebeian American–style Loews Casino, adjacent to the main casino. If you must spend the night, try the Hôtel de France (moderately priced, 6 rue de la Turbie, near the train station, tel. 04 93 30 24 64).

You can get to Monaco by train or bus. From Nice, it's 20 minutes by train or slower and cheaper by bus (18F, round-trip with same company). Tell the driver you want the place d'Armes stop—Monaco's old city and palace.

MORE FRENCH RIVIERA TOWNS

Menton—Just a few minutes by train (8/day) from Monte Carlo or 40 minutes from Nice, beautiful Menton is a relatively quiet and relaxing spa/beach town (TI tel. 04 93 57 57 00).
Cannes—Its sister city is Beverly Hills, but its beaches and the beachfront promenade are beautiful.
St. Paul-de-Vence and Vence—If you prefer hill towns to beaches, head for St. Paul and Vence (the same bus from Nice's bus station serves both towns, 45 minutes, 20F one way, every 30 minutes). Unless you go early, you'll escape only some of the heat and none of the crowds. **St. Paul** is part cozy medieval hill town and part local artist shopping mall. It's pleasantly artsy but gets swamped with tour buses. Meander into St. Paul's quieter streets and wander far to enjoy the panoramic views (TI tel. 04 93 32 86 95).

The prestigious, far-out, and high-priced **Fondation Maeght** art gallery is a steep, uphill, ten-minute walk from St. Paul. If ever modern art could appeal to you, it would be in this place. Its world-class contemporary art collection is arranged between pleasant gardens and well-lit rooms. (45F, open daily July–September 10:00–19:00, October–June 10:00–12:30 and 14:30–18:00, tel. 04 93 32 81 63.)

The enjoyable hill town of Vence (ten minutes from St. Paul by bus) disperses St. Paul's crowds over a larger and more interesting city. Vence bubbles with workaday and tourist activity. Catch the daily market (ends at 12:30), and don't miss the small church with its Chagall mosaic and moving Chapelle St. Sacrament. The Vence TI is on place du Grand Jardin (tel. 04 93 58 06 38). Matisse's much-raved-about **Chapelle du Rosaire** (1 mile from Vence toward St. Jeannet, taxi or walk) may disappoint all but Matisse fans, for whom this is a necessary pilgrimage: the yellow-, blue-, and green-filtered sunlight does a cheery dance in stark contrast to the gloomy tile sketches (donation, open only Tuesday and Thursday 10:00–11:30, 14:30–17:30; during the summer the chapel is also open on Wednesday and Friday afternoon and on Saturday from 10:00–11:30 and 14:30–17:30; closed November–December 15; tel. 04 93 58 03 26).

Route Tips for Drivers—La Route de Napoleon

When driving between the Riviera and the Alps, take the route Napoleon followed when returning from exile (from Nice, follow signs to Digne and the N-75 via Sisteron and Grenoble).

After getting bored in his toy Elba empire, Napoleon gathered his entourage, landed on the Riviera, bared his breast, and told his fellow Frenchmen, "Strike me down or follow me." France followed. But just in case, he took the high road, returning to Paris along the route today's holiday-goers call "La Route de Napoleon." (Waterloo followed shortly afterward.)

This scenic road passes two worth-a-stop villages. Entrevaux feels forgotten and still stuck in its medieval shell. Cross the bridge and meet a local. Sisteron's Romanesque church alone makes it worth a quick leg stretch. Farther north, near the tiny hamlet of Clelles, is **Hôtel Ferrat****. This family run mountain hacienda at the base of Mont Aiguille (which Gibraltar was modeled after) is the place to break this long drive. Enjoy your own *boules* court, a swimming pool, lovely rooms, a fine restaurant, and a very warm welcome (Db-280F, postal code 38930, tel. 04 76 34 42 70, fax 04 76 34 47 47).

After Clelles, the route traverses a Kashmir-type Alpine valley. Skirt Grenoble (the biggest city within Europe's Alps), and follow the signs to Geneva, Annecy, then Chamonix.

THE FRENCH ALPS (ALPES-SAVOIE)

Savoie is the northern and highest tier of the French Alps (the Alpes-Dauphiné lie to the south). In the 11th century, Savoie was a powerful region with borders stretching down to the Riviera and out to the Rhône. Today it is France's mountain sports capital, with Europe's highest point, Mont Blanc, as its centerpiece. Savoie didn't become part of France until 1860. Today it feels more Swiss than French.

The scenery is spectacular. It's just you and Madame Nature—there's not a museum or important building in sight. If the weather's right, take Europe's ultimate cable-car ride to the 12,600-foot Aiguille du Midi in Chamonix.

Planning Your Time

Annecy is charmingly elegant. But if you've got Alps on your mind, go directly to Chamonix. In Chamonix you can hike thrillingly high Alpine trails or stroll tranquil Arve river valley paths. You can zip down the mountain on a wheeled bobsled or rent a mountain bike. Ride the gondolas early (the crowds and the clouds both roll in later in the morning), and save your afternoons for lower altitudes. Two nights and one day in Chamonix is the minimum dose. (Note: If you're driving from here to the Riviera, see the Route de Napoleon tips on the previous page.)

Cuisine Scene—Savoie

This is mountain country cuisine. Robust and hearty, it shares much with the Swiss. *Fondue savoyarde* (melted Beaufort and

Comté cheese and local white wine, sometimes with a dash of cognac), *raclette* (chunks of semimelted cheese served with potatoes, pickles, sausage, and bread), *poulet de Bresse* (the best chicken in France), *morteau* (smoked pork sausage), *gratin savoyarde* (a potato dish using cream, cheese, and garlic), and freshly caught fish are the specialties. Local cheeses are Morbier (look for a charcoal streak down the middle), Comté (like Gruyère), Beaufort (aged for two years, hard and strong), Reblochon (mild and creamy), and Tomme de Savoie (semihard and mild). Evian water comes from Savoie, as does Chartreuse liqueur. Aprémont and Crépy are two of the area's surprisingly good white wines.

ANNECY

There's something for everyone in this lakefront city: mountain views, a cobbled old town, canals, flowers, a château, and swimming or boating in the lake. Annecy (ahn-see) is France's answer to Switzerland's Lucerne. You may not have the mountains in your lap as in nearby Chamonix, but the distant peaks make a beautiful picture with Annecy's lakefront setting.

Tourist Information: The TI is a few blocks from the old center in the modern Bonlieu shopping center (open daily 9:00–12:00 and 13:45–18:30, no summer lunch closing, 1 rue Jean Jaures, tel. 04 50 45 00 33).

Sights—Annecy

Strolling—Amble along the canals and arcaded streets of the delightful old city. Wander by the Palais de l'Île (where you'll find the Museum of Annecy, 30F) and under Annecy's famous arcaded overhangs. The views from the château alone make it worth the entry price.

Boating—Rent a paddle boat (50F/hour) and cruise the lake at your own speed. Also consider a one-way cruise to Talloires (return by bus). Schedules and prices at the TI; skip the longer, more costly cruises.

Open-Air Market—A thriving outdoor market occupies most of the old city center on Tuesday, Friday, and Sunday mornings.

Sleeping in Annecy

Try the spotless rooms at the **Hôtel du Château*** and enjoy its view terrace (Ds-220F, Db-260F–300F, Tb-310F, 16 rampe du Château, reserve early in the summer, tel. 04 50 45 27 66).

For more comfort, the very cozy **Hôtel de Savoie**** has some view rooms overlooking the canal (S-140F, D-200F, Db-280F–350F, Tb-390F–420F, Qb-480F, CC:VM, place St. François, tel. 04 50 45 15 45, fax 04 50 45 11 99).

Transportation Connections—Annecy
By train to: Chamonix (nearly hrly, 2.5 hrs, transfer in St. Gervais), **Beaune** (6/day, 6.5 hrs, transfer in Lyon), **Nice** (8/day, 10 hrs, transfer in Lyon), **Paris'** Gare de Lyon (6 TGVs/day, 4 hrs).

CHAMONIX
Hemmed in by snow-capped peaks, churning with mountain lifts, and criss-crossed with hikes of all levels of difficulty, the resort of Chamonix (sham-oh-nee) is France's best base for Alpine exploration. Chamonix is the largest of several villages at the base of Mt. Blanc and is the best-served by mountain lifts. Chamonix's purpose in life has always been to accommo- date those coming here for some of Europe's top Alpine thrills. The small pedestrian zone is the center, though you'll find most activity along the rue du Docteur Paccard. To the east is the Mont Blanc range; to the west, the Aiguilles Rouges chain.

Planning Your Time
If you have one sunny day, spend it this way: Start with the Aiguille du Midi lift (go as early as you can), take it all the way to Hellbronner (hang around the needle longer if you can't get to Hellbronner), then double back to the Plan de l'Aiguille and hike to Montenvers (Mer de Glace—snow level–permitting), and train (or hike) down from there. If the weather disappoints or the snow line's too low, hike the Petit Balcon Sud trail (near the Le Brévent lift), go to Les Praz, then return through the valley along the Arve river.

Orientation
Tourist Information: The TI provides hotel and hiking hut reservations, a map of the town and valley listing restaurants and hotels, and an essential 20F hiking mountain map called "Carte des Sentiers." It's located one block west of rue du Doc- teur Paccard and the pedestrian area, on the place de l'Église (daily July and August 8:30–19:30, October–June 8:30–12:30 and 14:00–19:00, tel. 04 50 53 00 24 for the weather forecast).

Chamonix Town

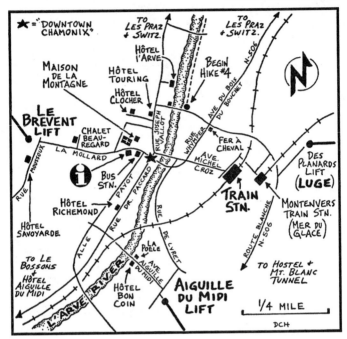

Chamonix Quick History

1786—Mssrs. Balmot and Paccard are the first to climb Mont
Blanc
1818—First ascent of Aiguille du Midi
1924—First winter Olympics held in Chamonix
1955—Aiguille du Midi *téléphérique* open to tourists
1997—Your visit

Arrival in Chamonix

By Train: Walk straight out of the station and up avenue
Michel Croz. In 3 blocks you'll hit the center and TI.

   By Car: Take the second Chamonix turnoff (coming from
Annecy direction) and park at the huge lot adjacent to the large
traffic circle near the Hôtel Alpina.

Getting Around Chamonix

By Lifts: Gondolas (*téléphériques*) climb mountains all along
the valley, but the best two leave from Chamonix (explained

below). Sightseeing is optimal from the Aiguille du Midi gondola, but hiking is better from the Le Brévent gondola. Those buying tickets at the hostel, or over 59, get a 20 percent reduction on the area's lifts. Kids 4 to 12 ride for half price. While the lift to Aiguille du Midi stays open year-round, the *télécabines* to Hellbronner (Italy) close from late October to early May (call the TI to confirm). Other area lifts close around mid-April through June, and in late October through December.

By Hiking: For all your options, visit the Office de Haute Montagne (Office of the High Mountains, a block uphill from the TI on the third floor of the building marked "Maison de la Montagne"). Get opinions on the best hikes and up-to-date weather and trail-condition reports (8:30–12:30 and 14:30–18:00, tel. 04 50 23 22 08). Review your hiking plans at this office, and remember to bring rain gear, warm clothes, water, sunglasses, good shoes, and picnic food on your hike.

By Bike: Mountain bikes are rented by the hour and day at several downtown spots. The TI has a brochure proposing the best bike rides. The river valley trail is ideal for bikes and pedestrians.

By Bus or Train: One road and one rail line lace together the towns and lifts of the valley. Local buses go twice an hour (from in front of the TI for local destinations).

Sights—Chamonix

▲▲▲**Aiguille du Midi**—This is easily the valley's (and arguably, Europe's) most spectacular and popular lift. If the weather's clear, the price doesn't matter. Pile into the *téléphérique* (gondola) and fly to the tip of a rock needle 12,600 feet above sea level. Chamonix shrinks as trees fly by, soon replaced by whizzing rocks, ice, and snow until you reach the top. No matter how sunny it is, it's cold. The air is thin. People are giddy. Fun things can happen at Aiguille du Midi if you're not too winded to join the locals in the halfway-to-heaven tango.

From the top of the lift, cross the bridge and ride the elevator through the rock to the summit of this pinnacle. Missing the elevator is a kind of Alpus-Interruptus I'd rather not experience. The Alps spread before you. In the distance is the bent little Matterhorn (a tall shady pyramid behind a broader mountain, listed on the observation table in French as "Cervin—4,505 meters"). And looming just over there is Mont Blanc, at 15,781

Chamonix Valley

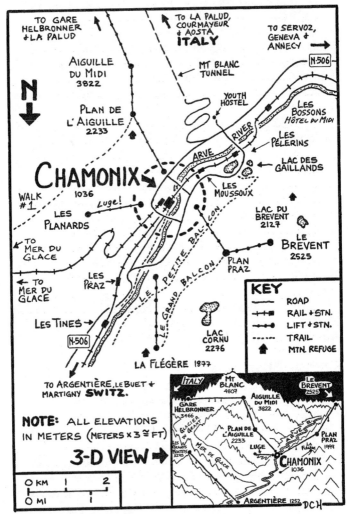

feet, Europe's highest point. Use the free telescope to spot mountain climbers. Dial English and let the info box take you on a visual tour. Check the temperature next to the elevator.

Explore Europe's tallest lift station. One hundred-fifty meters of tunnels lead to a cafeteria, restaurant, gift shop, and the icicle-covered gateway to the glacial world. This "ice tunnel" is where summer skiers and mountain climbers depart. Just observing is exhilarating. Peek down the icy cliff and ponder the value of an ice axe.

Next, for your own private glacial dream world, get into the little red *télécabine* and head south to Hellbronner Point, the Italian border station. This line stretches 5 kilometers with no solid pylon. (It's propped by a "suspended pylon," a line stretched between two peaks 400 meters from the Italian end.) In a gondola for four, you'll dangle silently for 40 minutes as you glide over the glacier to Italy. Hang your head out the window; explore every corner of your view. You can continue into Italy (see Connections, below), but there's really no point unless you're traveling that way.

From Aiguille du Midi, you can ride all the way back to Chamonix or get off halfway down (Plan des Aiguille) and hike from 7,500 feet to the valley floor at 3,400 feet. Or better yet, hike the scenic, undulating two-hour trail to Montenvers (the Mer de Glace, 6,000 feet). From there you can hike or ride the train (48F) back into Chamonix.

To beat the clouds and crowds, ride the lifts (up and down) as early as you can. To beat major delays in August, leave by 7:00. If the weather's good, don't dilly-dally. The lift runs daily 7:00–17:00 in summer; 8:00–16:45 in May, June, and September; 8:00–15:45 in winter, with the last one to Hellbronner at around 14:00.

Approximate ticket costs for summer (slightly less in off-season): Chamonix to Plan des Aiguille—76F round-trip (60F one way); to Aiguille du Midi—184F round-trip (144F one way, not including parachute); all the way to Hellbronner—270F round-trip (198F one way). Aiguille du Midi–Hellbronner tickets (74F, or 46F one way) are sold at the base or on top. It's about 33,000 lire ($18, sold there, many currencies accepted) to drop down into Italy. Time to allow: to Aiguille du Midi—20 minutes, 2 hours round-trip, 3–4 hours in peak season; Chamonix to Hellbronner: 1.5 hours one way, 3–4 hours round-trip, longer in peak season). Plan on 32 degrees F even on a sunny day. Sunglasses are essential. On busy days, get your return lift time upon arrival at the top. Tel. 04 50 53 30 80.

Mer de Glace—From the little station over the tracks from Chamonix's main train station (look for the red trains), a two-car cogwheel train toots you up to a rapidly moving and very dirty glacier called the Mer de Glace, or Sea of Ice. The glacier

Over the Alps—France to Italy

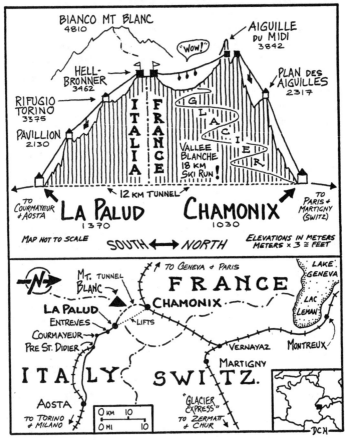

is interesting, as are its funky ice caves filled with ice sculpture (take the small lift-10F, or the short hike). The view is glorious, but if you've already seen a glacier up close, you could skip this one. One good option is to go one way and take the two-hour uphill hike to the Plan des Aiguille, catching the lift or continuing to hike down from there (63F round-trip, 48F one way).

▲**Luge**—Here's something new for the thrill-seeker in you. You can ride a chair lift up and scream down the mountain's windy, banked concrete slalom course on a wheeled sled. Chamonix has two roughly parallel luge courses. While each course is a kilometer long and about the same speed, one is marked for slower bobsledders and the other for the speed demons. Young or old, hare or tortoise, any fit person can manage a luge. Don't take your hands off your stick. The course is fast and slippery. (31F/one ride, 132F/five rides, 235F/ten rides, splittable with companions, open daily 10:00–19:30 in July and August, 13:30 until about 18:00 in June and September, April and May weekends and holidays only 13:30–17:30, ten-minute walk from the center, just beyond the train station.)

▲▲▲The *Téléphérique* to Le Brévent—While the Aiguille de Midi offers a more spectacular ride, hiking options are better on this lower side of the valley, with views of the Mont Blanc range to the east and the Aiguilles Rouges peaks to the west.

From Chamonix, walk up the road past the TI and keep going to the Le Brévent station. Take the *téléphérique* to Planpraz (good views and hiking, particularly the two-hour hike along the Grand Balcon Sud to La Flégère lift, see Hikes, below; 52F round-trip, 43F one way), then catch the *téléphérique* up to Brévent (great views and hikes, 76F round-trip, 52F one way from Chamonix, open 8:00–18:00, closed April to mid-June and November).

Chamonix Area Hikes

Four fine hikes give nature lovers of almost any ability in just about any weather a good opportunity to enjoy the valley. You'll find the region's hiking map extremely helpful; pick it up at the TI (20F).

Hike #1: Plan des Aiguille to Montenvers: This is the easiest way to incorporate a two-hour high-country walk into your ride down from the valley's greatest lift and check out a glacier to boot. From Aiguille du Midi, get off halfway down (Plan des Aiguille) and hike the scenic up-and-down two-hour trail to Montenvers and the Mer de Glace. From there, hike or ride the train (48F) into Chamonix.

Hike #2: Grand Balcon Sud: For a moderately easy and scenic high-country hike, walk 40 minutes along the Arve river or take the Chamonix bus (five-minute ride, every 30 minutes from the TI) to the tiny village of Les Praz. Ride the lift from Les Praz to La Flégère (40F one way, 52F round-trip), then hike the scenic Grand Balcon Sud two hours back to Chamonix, taking the lift down to Chamonix at Plan Praz (43F one way, 52F-round-trip) or hiking down a very steep trail. Of course, this can be reversed by hiking from Chamonix, taking the Le Brévent lift to Plan Praz, and hiking the Grand Balcon Sud to Les Praz.

Hike #3: Petit Balcon Sud: This hike parallels the Grand Balcon Sud at a lower elevation, and is ideal when snow or poor weather make the Grand Balcon Sud inaccessible. No lifts are required. From Chamonix, walk up to the Le Brévent lift station, walk behind it, and find the path up to the Petit Balcon Sud trail. Head toward Les Praz. You can walk all the way there (two hours) and return by Chamonix bus or by walking the level Arve river trail (40 minutes); or walk only as far as your legs take you and turn around. This hike works just as well in reverse.

Hike #4: Arve riverbank stroll: For an easy forested valley stroll, follow the sleepy Arve river out of Chamonix toward Les Praz (the path starts across the river from Chamonix's Alpina Hôtel). Les Praz makes a pleasant destination. Several cafés, restaurants, and a charming village green lend a tranquil air to this Alpine hamlet.

Sleeping in Chamonix
(5F = about $1, postal code: 74400)
Sleep Code: **S** = Single, **D** = Double/Twin, **T** = Triple, **Q** = Quad, **b** = bathroom, **t** = toilet only, **s** = shower only, **CC** = Credit Card (**V**isa, **M**asterCard, **A**mex), **SE** = Speaks English, **NSE** = No English, ***** = French hotel rating system (0–4 stars).

Reasonable hotels and dormlike chalets abound. With the helpful TI, you can find budget accommodations anytime. July 20–August 16 is most difficult. Prices tumble off-season. There's a laundromat at 174 avenue du Aiguille du Midi (daily, 9:00–20:00).

Hotels
Hôtel de l'Arve** has a slick modern Alpine feel, with fine view rooms right on the Arve river overlooking Mont Blanc, or cheaper rooms sans the view (Sb-160F–200F, Db-250F–440F, extra bed-60F, elevator, across the river from the Olympic complex, CC:VMA, tel. 04 50 53 02 31, fax 04 50 53 56 92, friendly Isabelle and Bertrice SE).

Hotel Savoyarde***, with fine views from the outdoor café tables, elegant chalet ambiance, and the owner's attention to detail, is a worthwhile splurge (Db-580F, CC:VMA, a ten-minute walk above the TI overlooking Chamonix at 28 rue des Moussoux, tel. 04 50 53 00 77, fax 04 50 55 86 82).

Hôtel de Clocher** is a tidy family-run little place offering eight cozy rooms, private parking, a quiet garden, and a smokers' lobby (Sb-255F–285F, Db-274F–324F, extra beds-50F, CC:VMA, a block to the right of the church as you face it on l'Impasse de l'Androsace, tel. 04 50 53 30 27, fax 04 50 53 73 19).

Hôtel Au Bon Coin** has great views and a balcony for each room (D-220F, Db-324F–344F, Tb-370F, Qb-420F, closed mid-April to June 30, and October to mid-December, 80 avenue L'Aiguille du Midi, tel. 04 50 53 15 67, fax 04 50 53 51 51).

Hôtel Touring**, with large and well-worn rooms (many with four beds), is ideal for families. It's English-run by Dolly and Nick, so you'll have no trouble communicating (Ds-215F– 275F, Db-285F–350F, add 60F for three and 40F more for four, rue Joseph Vallot, tel. 04 50 53 59 18, fax 04 50 53 67 25).

Chamonix's best *chambre d'hôte*, the **Chalet Beauregard**, is friendly and peaceful with a private garden. Five of its seven comfortable rooms come with a glorious view balcony (Sb-190F, Db-250F–360F, Tb-330F, breakfast included, free parking, three-minute walk above the TI toward Le Brévent lift, 182 montée La Mollard, tel. and fax 04 50 55 86 30, SE).

Hôtel le Chamonix** is tall, old, and skinny with no elevator. Its rooms are clean and simple (some with balconies), above a café, and across from the TI (Db-300F–420F, Tb/Qb-400F–450F, CC:VM, tel. 04 50 53 11 07).

Richemond Hôtel** offers Alpine elegance, spacious lobbies, overstuffed chairs, serious management, and extraordinary rooms (Sb-280F, Db-360F–430F, Tb-505F, Qb-560F, CC:VMA, 228 rue du Docteur Paccard, tel. 04 50 53 08 85, fax 04 50 55 91 69). They're unaccustomed to drop-in guests, so be patient. Avoid this place in the summer, when half-pension is required.

Sleeping near Chamonix

If nature calls (or summer crowds heckle), spend the night in one of the valley's peaceful, lower-profile villages. The pleasant village of Les Praz, while just up the valley from Chamonix, is a world away (five minutes by car, 40 minutes on foot). The town surrounds a pretty village green and is home to the Flégère lift, which allows access to the recommended le Grand Balcon Sud hike.

Hotel Rhodendron** (Db-260F, half-pension required in summer, tel. 04 50 53 06 39, fax 04 50 53 55 76) and **Hotel Eden**** (Db-300F–350F, tel. 04 50 53 18 43, fax 04 50 53 51 50) offer comfortable lodgings in scenic settings.

Three miles away down the valley (toward Annecy), in the village of Les Bossons, is the almost luxurious **Hôtel l'Aiguille du Midi****. The friendly owner offers polished service, gorgeous gardens, swimming pool, tennis courts, comfortable rooms, and a restaurant where Chamonix locals go for their Sunday meal (Db-300F–500F, add 30 percent each for three and four persons, half-pension required in summer, Les Bossons, tel. 04 50 53 00 65, fax 04 50 55 93 69).

Dorms

For cheaper dormlike accommodations in a quiet neighborhood a ten-minute walk to Chamonix, try **Les Grands Charmoz**. Seventy-two francs buys a bunk and sheet, showers, and a kitchen (184F buys a double room). They also have a few clean doubles with kitchen privileges, as well as apartments upstairs (468 chemin des Cristalliers; turn right out of the station, walk under the bridge and into the Hotel Albert's driveway, veer right, cross the tracks, then turn left, tel./fax 04 50 53 45 57). The **Chalet Ski Station** also has bunks but no doubles (60F for a bed, reductions on area lifts for clients, next to the Brévent *téléphérique*, a ten-minute hike up from the TI, tel. 04 50 53 20 25).

Chamonix's classy **youth hostel** was formerly the barracks for the diggers of the Mont Blanc tunnel. Well-run, cheap, and almost luxurious, it sells substantially discounted lift tickets for the most expensive lifts in the valley. Hostel members are welcome to drop in and buy these discounted tickets, even if they sleep elsewhere (72F dorm bed, S-130F, D-200F, 15-minute walk from the base of the Aiguille du Midi lift or a ten-minute walk from the Les Pèlerins Station, 2 kilometers below Chamonix in Les Pèlerins, open 8:00–12:00 and 14:00–22:00, tel. 04 50 53 14 52).

Refuges

The French have the perfect answer for hikers who don't want to pack tents, sleeping bags, stoves, and food: refuges.

For about 60F, you can sleep on bunks high in the peaceful mountains. Bring your own food or let the guardian cook your dinner and breakfast (around 80F for dinner, 35F for breakfast). The Office de Haute Montagne in Chamonix can explain your options and reserve. Some refuges are located an easy walk from a lift station, and most are open from mid-June to mid-September. Comfort ranges from very basic to downright luxurious. Try **La Pierre à Berard** refuge, a beautiful hike from Le Buet (45F per bed, 145F half-pension, tel. 04 50 54 62 08).

Eating in Chamonix

While Chamonix, like any mountain resort, has its share of bad food and bad-price restaurants, there are several good values to be found.

Bistrot des Sports is a rare souvenir of old Chamonix, with wood tables, old photos, and fine food (50F–100F, 182 rue J. Vallot, tel. 04 50 53 00 46). **Le Fer à Cheval** is famous as the place for fondue and *raclette* in Chamonix (moderate, on rue Whymper near place Mont Blanc). **La Poele** is popular with the locals (50F–100F, 79 avenue Aiguille du Midi, tel. 04 50 55 96 13) and combines more than 100 filling omelets, fine *raclette*, and many other Savoyarde specialties. **La Boccolatte**, next to La Poele, is also worth considering.

Le National offers regional specialities in a cozy setting, next to the post office, dead-center in Chamonix (85F menu, 3 rue Paccard, tel. 04 50 53 02 23).

If dipping bread into hot gurgling cheese isn't your idea of haute cuisine, try **Le Sabot** (above the intersection of avenue Aguille du Midi and rue du Docteur Paccard) for crêpes and Italian food on allée Recteur Payot. **La Caboulé**, next to the Brévent *téléphérique*, is a funky eatery with great omelets and an unbeatable view from its outdoor tables. **L'Impossible** is a characteristic place a five-minute walk beyond the Aiguille du Midi lift, named for a local ski champ who could do *"l'impossible"* (100F menus, daily in summer, route des Pelerins, tel. 04 50 53 20 36).

A fine place for a coffee, pastry, and view (from back deck) is **Café des Arcades** (17 rue du Docteur Paccard). Hang with the local hikers after hours at the **Bar Choucas** (206 rue du Docteur Paccard) or the **Bistrot des Sports** (182 rue J. Vallot).

Picnic assembly: A good *boulangerie* and a vegetable market are adjacent to the TI. The best grocery is the Codec, below Hôtel Alpina. There's also a supermarket on rue Vallot (open even Sunday morning) and a long-hours place a block in front of the train station. The park next to the church is picnic-pretty.

Transportation Connections—Chamonix

Bus and train service to Chamonix are surprisingly good. Both the bus and train stations (on the same square) have helpful information desks.

By train to: Annecy (5/day, 2.5 hrs, transfer in St. Gervais), **Beaune** and **Dijon** (3/day, 8 hrs, transfers in St. Gervais and Lyon), **Nice** (5/day, 10 hrs, with a transfer in St. Gervais and Lyon, night train possible), **Arles** (5/day, 8 hrs, transfer in St. Gervais and Lyon), **Paris'** Gare de Lyon (4/day, 7 hrs, longer at night, transfers in St. Gervais and Annecy; take the handy night train), **Martigny, Switzerland** (2 hrs, a very scenic trip), **Geneva** (3/day, 2.5 hrs, quick transfers in St. Gervais, La Roche-sur-Foron, and Annemasse).

By bus: Buses provide service to destinations not served by train and also to some cities that are served by train, but at a lower cost and higher speed. Get information at the bus station (*gare routière*) in the SNCF station (tel. 04 50 53 01 15).

By bus to: Aosta, Italy (5/day, 90 min; Aosta connects you with the Italian rail system).

Itinerary Options

A Day in French-Speaking Switzerland

There are plenty of tempting Alpine and cultural thrills just an hour or two away in Switzerland. A road and train line sneak you scenically from Chamonix to the Swiss town of Martigny. Remember, while train travelers cross without formalities, drivers are charged the $32 Swiss annual highway tax just to cross the border.

A Little Italy?

The remote Valle d'Aosta and its historic capital city of Aosta are a short but costly drive east of Chamonix through the Mont Blanc tunnel, or a spectacular gondola ride over the Mont Blanc range. The side trip is worthwhile if you'd like to taste Italy (spaghetti, gelati, and cappuccino), enjoy the town's great evening ambiance, or look at the ruins of Aosta, often called "the Rome of the North."

From Hellbronner (see Aiguille du Midi lift), catch the 33,000-lire lift down to Entreves and take the bus to Aosta (hrly, change in Courmayeur). Those with exceptional social skills can probably talk a gondola mate with a car in Entreves into a ride down the valley. From Aosta, trains or buses will take you to Milan and the rest of Italy, or you can take a bus back to Chamonix under Mont Blanc (5/day, 90 min).

Sleeping in Aosta, Italy
(tel. code 0165, L1,500 = $1)

Hotel Ponte Romano, on the Roman bridge, with a warm woody interior, is one of Aosta's finest local hotels (Sb-L85,000, Db-L120,000, Via Ponte Romano 27, tel. 45262, fax 31736). **La Belle Epoque** (Sb-L40,000–55,000, Db-L60,000–75,000, Via D'Avise 18, off Via E. Aubert, tel. 262276) offers clean and simple rooms and a grumpy staff. Cheaper beds are found in a less charming, more industrial area at the **Barrano family** (S-L30,000, D-L60,000, Via Voison 9, tel. 43224) and Sra. Mancuso's **Albergo Mancuso** (Sb-L45,000, Db-L55,000, Via Voison 32, tel. 34526).

BURGUNDY

Burgundy has what the rest of France wants: superior wine and cuisine, lovely countryside, and quick access east to the Alps and south to Provence. Only a small part of Burgundy's land is covered by vineyards, but wine-making is what they do best here. The white cows you see everywhere are Charolais. They make France's best beef and end up in *boeuf bourguignon*. The Romanesque churches dotting the countryside owe their origin to the once-powerful influence of the Abbey of Cluny in southern Burgundy.

Planning Your Time

Dijon, the capital of Burgundy, is worth a close look but set up camp in Beaune. It's better located for touring the vineyards and lovely countryside. You'll want two days here, a half day for Dijon, and one day in Beaune and its environs. Trains link Beaune and Dijon with ease; bikes, buses, and minivan tours will get nondrivers into the countryside.

Cuisine Scene—Burgundy

Your tastebuds are going to thank you for bringing them here. Considered by many to be France's best, Burgundian cuisine is peasant cooking elevated to an art. Burgundy is home to several classic dishes, such as *escargots bourguignonne* (snails served sizzling hot in garlic butter), *boeuf bourguignon* (beef simmered for hours in red wine with onions and mushrooms), *coq au vin* (chicken stewed in red wine), and the

Beaune Region

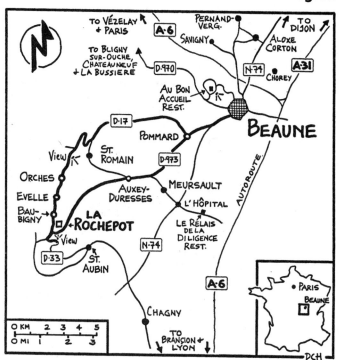

famous Dijon mustards. Look also for *jambon persillé* (cold ham layered in a garlic-parsley gelatin), *pain d'épices* (spice bread), and *gougère* (light, puffy cheese pastries). Native cheeses are Epoisses and Langres (both mushy and great), and my favorite, Montrachet (a tasty goat cheese). Crème de cassis (a black currant liqueur) is another Burgundian specialty; look for it in desserts and snazzy drinks (try a kir).

Along with Bordeaux, Burgundy is why France is famous for wine. You'll find it all here—great reds, whites, and rosés. The key grapes are Chardonnay (producing dry white wines) and Pinot Noir (producing medium-bodied red wines). Every village produces its own distinctive wine (usually named after the village—like Chablis and Meursault). Look for the *Dégustation Gratuite* (free tasting) signs and prepare for serious tasting and steep prices if you're not careful. The least expensive (but still excellent) wines are the Bourgogne Aligote (white), Bourgogne

Ordinaire and Passetoutgrain (both red), and those from the Macon, Chalon, and Beaujolais areas. If you like rosé, try the Marsannay, considered the best rosé in France.

BEAUNE

You'll feel comfortable right away in this hardworking but fun-loving wine capital. Here, life centers around the production and consumption of the prestigious, expensive Côte d'Or wines. "Côte d'Or" means "golden hillsides," and they are a spectacle to enjoy in late October, as the leaves of the vineyards turn colors.

Beaune (bone) is a compact, thriving little city with vineyards on its doorstep. Limit your Beaune ramblings to the town center, contained within its medieval walls and circled by a one-way ring road. All roads and activities converge on the perfectly French place Carnot.

Tourist Information: The TI, across the street from the Hôtel Dieu (Hospice de Beaune) on the place de la Halle (from place Carnot, walk toward the thin spire), has city maps, brochures on Beaune hotels and restaurants, a room-finding service, *chambre d'hôte* pamphlets, advice on special events, and minibus wine-tasting tours. (Open daily April–October 9:00–20:00, otherwise 9:00–19:00, tel. 03 80 26 21 30.)

Arrival in Beaune

By Train: To reach the city center, walk straight out of the train station up avenue du Huit Septembre, cross the busy ring road, and continue up the rue du Château.

By Car: Follow *centre-ville* signs to the ring road. Once on the ring road, turn right at the first signal after the new post office and park (free) in the place Madeleine.

Sights—Beaune

▲▲▲**Hôtel Dieu**—The Hundred Years' War and the Black Death devastated Beaune, leaving more than 90 percent of its population destitute. Nicholas Rolin, Chancellor of Burgundy and a peasant by birth, had to do something for "his people." So, in 1443, he paid to build this flamboyant Flemish/Gothic charity hospital. It was completed in only eight years. Tour it on your own; you'll find (for once) good English explanations (pick up description at ticket desk). How about those medical instruments? Yeow! The pharmacy once provided slug-slime

Beaune

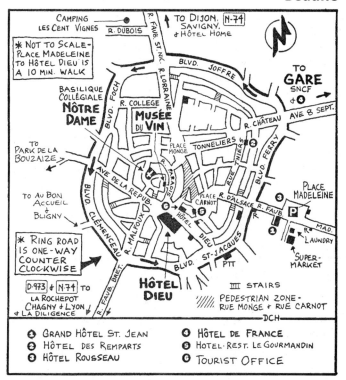

CAMPING — ● TO DIJON, [N-74]
LES CENT VIGNES   R. DUBOIS   SAVIGNY,
& HÔTEL HOME

✳ NOT TO SCALE-
PLACE MADELEINE
TO HÔTEL DIEU IS
A 10 MIN. WALK

BLVD. JOFFRE

TO
GARE
SNCF
& ●

BASILIQUE
COLLÉGIALE
**NÔTRE
DAME**

R. COLLEGE

**MUSÉE
DU VIN**

AVE 8 SEPT.

R. CHÂTEAU

TO
PARK DE LA
BOUZAIZE →

PLACE
MONGE   TONNELIERS

TO AU BON
ACCUEIL
&
BLIGNY

AVE DE LA REPUB.

PLACE
CARNOT   R. D'ALSACE   R. FAUB.

PLACE
MADELEINE

P

R. MAD.

LAUNDRY

✳ RING ROAD
IS ONE-WAY
COUNTER
CLOCKWISE →

SUPER-
MARKET

[D-973] & [N-74] TO
LA ROCHEPOT
CHAGNY & LYON
& LA DILIGENCE

**HÔTEL
DIEU**

▦ STAIRS

///// PEDESTRIAN ZONE-
RUE MONGE & RUE CARNOT

——DCH——

❶ GRAND HÔTEL ST. JEAN   ❹ HÔTEL DE FRANCE
❷ HÔTEL DES REMPARTS   ❺ HOTEL·REST. LE GOURMANDIN
❸ HÔTEL ROUSSEAU   ❻ TOURIST OFFICE

cures for sore throats and cockroach powders for constipa-
tion. Next, shuffle into a dark room to admire Van der Weyden's dramatic *The Last Judgment* polyptych, commissioned
by Rolin to give the dying something to ponder. Your visit
ends after the magnifying glass demonstration (ask the attendant)
with a look at Flemish tapestries. In the St. Louis room, *The Story
of Jacob*, woven by one person in 17 years, is magnificent (29F,
open daily 9:00–18:30 April–November, otherwise 9:00–11:30
and 14:00–17:30).

▲**Collégiale Notre Dame**—Built in the 12th and 13th centuries, this is a good example of Cluny-style architecture. Enter
to see the 15th-century tapestries (behind the altar, drop in a
franc for lights), a variety of stained glass, and what's left of
frescoes depicting the life of Lazarus (open daily 8:30–19:00).
Walk one block straight out of the cathedral, turn left down a

cobbled alley, and enter the courtyard of the Musée du Vin, located in the old residence of the Dukes of Burgundy.

Musée du Vin—You don't have to like wine to appreciate this folk-wine museum. The history and culture of Burgundy and wine were fermented in the same bottle. Even if you opt against the museum, wander into the courtyard for a look at the Duke's Palace, antique wine presses (in the barn), and a nifty model of 15th-century Beaune. Inside the museum you'll find tools, costumes, and scenes of Burgundian wine history, but no tasting. There's a fine model of the wine region. If you wondered how the wine bottle got its shape, you'll enjoy the last room. Buy the 3F English explanation (25F, ticket good for other Beaune museums, open 9:30–17:30, closed Tuesday).

Parc de la Bouzaise—Just outside the city walls, on avenue de la République, this is a good place to relax and do some people-watching. From here, take a stroll into the vineyards.

Wine-Tasting in Beaune

Countless opportunities exist (for a price) to allow you to become knowledgeable of the local product. Small wineries in the countryside expect you to buy, while those in Beaune simply charge an entry fee and allow you to taste from a variety of wines. Most offer some form of introduction or self-guided tours and are open daily from 9:30–11:30 and 14:00–17:30.

▲▲▲**Marché aux Vins**—This is Burgundy's wine smorgasbord and the best way to sample its impressive wines. You pay 50F for a traditional wine-tasting cup (you keep it) and get 45 minutes to sip away at Burgundy's beloved. Plunge into the labyrinth of candlelit caves dotted with 20 wine-barrel tables, each offering a new tasting experience. You're on your own. Relax; this is world-class stuff. The $70 reds are upstairs in the chapel, at the end of the tasting. (Hint: Taste better by sneaking in crackers.) If you grab an empty wine carton at the beginning and at least pretend you're going to buy, the occasional time checker will leave you alone. (Open daily 9:00–12:00, 14:30–18:30, last entry at 18:00, closes at 17:00 in winter, tel. 03 80 22 27 69.)

More Self-Guided Tours—While the Marché aux Vins is the ultimate wine-tasting experience, it can overwhelm some. If you have less time for wine, the **Caves des Cordeliers** offers good self-guided tours of its convent premises (with English explanations) and five wines to taste for just 20F (6 rue de l'Hôtel Dieu, tel. 03 80 22 14 25). **Maison Patriache Père et Fils** also has self-guided tours and Beaune's largest underground cellars, with a selection of 13 different wines to sample (50F, tasting cup included, 7 rue du Collège, tel. 03 80 24 53 78).

Sleeping in Beaune
(5F = about $1, postal code: 21200)
Sleep Code: **S** = Single, **D** = Double/Twin, **T** = Triple, **Q** = Quad, **b** = bathroom, **t** = toilet only, **s** = shower only, **CC** = Credit Card (Visa, MasterCard, Amex), **SE** = Speaks English, **NSE** = No English, ***** = French hotel rating system (0–4 stars).

The **Hôtel des Remparts***** offers affordable luxury, with fine rooms in a recently restored manor house complete with beamed ceilings, period furniture, a quiet courtyard, and great rooms for families (Db-300F–450F, Tb-490F–520F, Qb-520F–690F, parking garage-35F, no elevator, toward the train station from the center but inside the center city, the attic rooms are beyond cozy, CC:VM, 48 rue Thiers, tel. 03 80 24 94 94, fax 03 80 24 97 08, SE).

The three nifty but spacious and comfortable rooms at the restaurant **Le Gourmandin** are as central as you can get and perfect for those who need to stretch out (Db-330F, many stairs, 8 place Carnot, tel. 03 80 24 07 88, fax 03 80 22 27 42).

Hôtel Le Home** is an old vine-covered mansion and Beaune's most elegant and most expensive two-star hotel value. It's a half-mile out of town on the N-74 toward Dijon (Db-340F–470F, Tb/Qb-520F, CC:VM, on your right at 138 route de Dijon, tel. 03 80 22 16 43, fax 03 80 24 90 74). Call ahead—it's popular.

What **Hôtel au Grand St. Jean**** lacks in character, it makes up for with value and location (Db-220F, Tb/Qb-280F, CC:VM, on place Madeleine, tel. 03 80 24 12 22, fax 03 80 24 15 43). Its helpful owner, M. Neaux, speaks English. Color-blind travelers will love the TV lounge.

Hôtel Rousseau is good for those traveling on a budget, though the rooms with showers are overpriced and maintenance is spotty. It will make you smile, with cheap, basic rooms, pet birds, and a pleasant enclosed garden (S-125F, Ss-170F, D-170F, Db-300F, T-245F, Tb-330F, Q-290F, Qb-350F, prices include breakfast, 20F showers down the hall, private parking, 11 place Madeleine, tel. 03 80 22 13 59).

The **Hotel Athanor***** mixes modern comfort with a touch of old Beaune and is very central (Db-375F– 540F, elevator, CC:VMA, 9 avenue de la République, tel. 03 80 24 09 20, fax 03 80 24 09 15, SE).

Train travelers will appreciate the **Hôtel de France**** (Sb-200F, Db-260F–400F, Tb/Qb-350F–420F, across from the station, 35 avenue du 8 Septembre, tel. 03 80 24 10 34, fax 03 80 24 96 78).

Drivers in search of reliable plumbing can park below their window at the simple, sterile, but great value **Villages Hotel** (Db-or Tb-140F, CC:VM, on the way into Beaune from the autoroute, rue Burgalat la Charteuese, tel. 03 80 24 14 50, fax 03 80 24 14 45); or at the more central, comfortable, and costly **Hotel Bleu Marine***** (Db-520F, Tb-605F, on Beaune's ring road at 10 boulevard Marechal Foch, tel. 03 80 24 01 01, fax 03 80 24 09 90).

Chambres d'Hôte near Beaune

The Côte d'Or has many *chambres d'hôte*; get a pamphlet at the TI. Most can be found only in small wine villages, and many are only a short drive from Beaune. I particularly like one in Magny-les-Villers. From Beaune, go north on the N-74, then west at Ladoix. The friendly **Dumays** have two attached rooms in a restored farmhouse; great for three or more (Ss-180F, Db-220F, Tb-280F, Qb-340F, behind the church, tel. 03 80 62 91 16). In the cliff-dwelling village of Orches, near La Rochepot, is **M. Rocault**'s friendly home, with five comfortable rooms (Db-250F, tel. 03 80 21 78 72, fax 03 80 21 85 95).

Château Hotels in the Burgundian Countryside
(postal code: 21320)

To stay in or near a château, leave Beaune (car only) for these exceptional hotels. Each is located ten minutes from the A-6 autoroute (toward Paris) exit at Pouilly en Auxois, about 30 miuntes from Beaune by car. The **Hostellerie du Château**, in Châteauneuf-en-Auxois, is a good value if you get a room in the main building. Many of the half-timbered rooms have views over the château next door. The elegant restaurant is a little pricey but a fair value (Db-280F–380F, tel. 03 80 49 22 00, fax 03 80 49 21 27). For driving directions to Châteauneuf, see Sights—Beaune Region, below.

The nearby **Hostellerie du Château de Sainte Sabine** is a recently renovated château/hotel with a pool and fair prices, for a château. It's located in the tiny village of Sainte Sabine. Skip their overpriced restaurant (Db-330F–740F, one room with five beds-900F, tel. 03 80 49 22 01, fax 03 80 49 20 01).

Eating in Beaune

Several good restaurants line the rue d'Alsace near the place Madeleine. I like **Le Picboeuf,** where rue d'Alsace meets the ring road, for good steaks and salads, closed Thursday. **Le Gourmandin** (8 place Carnot) is a good, reasonable, and cozy place (75F menus, closed Wednesday). For traditional Burgundian cuisine, I go to the elegant **La Grilladine** (72F, 100F, and 129F menus, exquisite *escargots*, hot goat cheese salad, and *oeufs en Meurette*, closed Monday, 17 rue Maufoux, tel. 03 80 22 22 36). A good budget restaurant is the **Relais de la Madeleine** (44 place Madeleine, tel. 03 80 22 07 47).

In Beaune, gather picnics at the charcuterie on rue Monge and pick up a slice of the *jambon persillé* (zham-bone pehr-sill-ay). Get your cheese at **Taste Fromage,** across the street on rue Carnot. How about that for a French stench? Gather the rest of your needs at any grocery (*épicerie*). There's a Casino supermarket just off place Madeleine, through the archway.

If you've had enough wine, drop by the **Café Hallebarde** for a fine selection of draft beer (24 rue d'Alsace); and if you're tired of speaking French, pop into the late-night lively **Pickwicks Pub** (behind the church, 2 rue Notre Dame).

Eating near Beaune

Sans question, the best restaurants are outside Beaune. For fine dining near Beaune, try **Le Relais de la Diligence.** There you can surround yourself with vineyards and taste the area's best budget Burgundian cuisine with many menu options (inexpensive/moderate, take the N-74 toward Chagny/Chalon and make a left at L'Hôpital Meursault on the D-23, closed Tuesday evening and Wednesday, tel. 03 80 21 21 32). **Au Bon Accueil** is my favorite; on a hill overlooking Beaune (Montagne de Beaune), it has the friendliest waitress (Gina) and waiter (Christophe) I've met in France. Try the *coq au vin.* To get there, leave Beaune's ring road and take the Bligny-sur-Ouche turnoff. A few minutes outside Beaune, you'll see signs to Au Bon Accueil (tel. 03 80 22 08 80, closed Monday, Tuesday, and Wednesday). If you're willing to drive 45 minutes, consider a late afternoon and evening in Châteauneuf-en-Auxois. Four reasonable restaurants line the little main drag of this sky-high hill town. For more information, read about Châteauneuf under Sights—Beaune Region, below.

Transportation Connections—Beaune

By train to: Dijon (9/day, 30 min), **Colmar** (5/day, 4.5 hrs, transfers in Dijon and Belfort), **Arles** (7/day, 5 hrs, transfer in Lyon), **Nice** (7/day, 8 hrs, transfer in Lyon), **Chamonix** (3/day, 8.5 hrs, transfers in Lyon and St. Gervais), **Paris'** Gare de Lyon (3 TGVs/day, 2 hrs; otherwise transfer to the TGV in Dijon, 3 hrs).

Getting Around the Beaune Region

By Bus: Transco buses run from Beaune through the vineyards and villages north to Dijon, south to Chalon-sur-Saône, and west to La Rochepot. Ask at the TI for schedules and stop locations or call for bus information (tel. 03 80 42 11 00).

    By Tour: Minibus wine-tasting tours (5/day from the TI for about 180F) are well-run, English-speaking, and will get you through the countryside and to the wineries you couldn't get into otherwise.

    By Bike: The well-organized, English-speaking, and very helpful Bourgogne Randonnées has excellent bikes, maps, and good itineraries through the countryside (bike rental 20F/hour, 90F/full day, open 9:00–12:00 and 13:30–19:00, located near the train station at 7 avenue Huit September, tel. 03 80 22 06 03).

Sights—Beaune Region

Bike routes—Get the local Michelin map and suggestions from Bourgogne Randonnées, then consider the long (all-day, 20-mile round-trip), scenic loop ride through vineyards and over hills to La Rochepot, St. Aubin, the tiny road from Gamay to Puligny, Montrachet, and Meursault, then back to Beaune. To give your legs a break, ride instead along the D-18 to Savigny-les-Beaune and Pernand Vergelesses. (Check out Savigny's unusual château.)

▲▲**Château La Rochepot**—Eight miles from Beaune, accessible by car, bike (hilly), or infrequent bus, you'll find this very Burgundian castle rising above the trees. The sign across the drawbridge asks you to knock three times with the ancient knocker, then push the doorbell. (English tours are occasionally available.) This castle is splendid inside and out. The kitchen will bowl you over. Look for the 15th-century highchair in the dining room. Don't leave the castle without climbing the tower and seeing the Chinese room, singing chants in the resonant chapel, and making ripples in the well. (Can you spit a bull's-eye? It's 72 meters down!) And don't leave La

Rochepot without driving, walking, or pedaling up the D-33 a few hundred meters toward St. Aubin (behind the Hôtel Relais du Château) for a romantic view of this classically Burgundian castle. (30F, open June–August 10:00–11:30 and 14:00–17:30, shoulder season 10:00–11:30 and 14:30–16:00, closed Tuesday, closes at 16:30 in winter, tel. 03 80 21 71 37.)

▲**Châteauneuf-en-Auxois and Abbey of La Bussière**—This half-day loop trip takes you through pastoral landscapes, along the Burgundy canal, past abbeys, medieval villages, and vineyards. It requires a car and the local Michelin map. From Beaune's ring road, take the Bligny-sur-Ouche turnoff. In Bligny-sur-Ouche, head for Pont de Pany. At Pont d'Ouche, turn left and follow the canal. In about ten minutes you'll see a stunning view of Châteauneuf's brooding castle; follow the signs.

Châteauneuf's medieval château towers over the valleys below. The village huddles securely in the shadow of the castle's protection and merits close inspection. Park at the lot in the upper end of the village and stroll down into the village. Don't miss the panoramic viewpoint near the parking lot or the small church at the opposite end of town. Walk into the château's courtyard but skip the interior and relax at the Café au Marroniers on the small square. Four small restaurants offer fine Burgundian cuisine at fair prices in Châteauneuf: the *coq au vin* at **Au Marroniers** (tel. 03 80 49 21 91) is mouthwatering; and the steak at **La Grill du Castel** (tel. 03 80 49 26 82) justifies the trip. You can sleep in Châteauneuf's one hotel (see my listings under Château Hotels, above).

Follow signs leading behind Châteauneuf and tiny roads to La Bussière and wander into its abbey grounds. La Bussière's abbey was founded in the 1200s by Cistercian monks but goes largely unnoticed by most tourists today. Stroll the lovely gardens, then check out the refectory (look for the door in the rear of the main building marked "*accueil*" and enter here). Ask for the key to the *vieux pressoir* (old press).

To return to Beaune, go back to Pont d'Ouche (direction: Bligny-sur-Ouche), turn left, and follow signs home to Beaune.

▲▲**Brancion and Chapaize**—An hour south of Beaune by car (20 km west of Tournus on the D-14) are two must-see churches that owe their existence and architectural design to the nearby, once-powerful Cluny Abbey. Brancion's nine-building hamlet floats on a hill above Chapaize and offers the purest example of Romanesque architecture I've seen—a 12th-century church (with faint frescoes inside), a cute château (climb the tower for views), and a 15th-century market hall. The benches in front of the church are picnic-perfect (though officially off-limits to picnickers), and the Auberge du Vieux Brancion offers fine Burgundian cuisine at fair prices. For a wonderfully peaceful break, spend a night in one of the Auberge's cozy, inexpensive rooms (if you do, call ahead and François family will treat you right, tel. 03 85 51 03 83). If you're really on vacation and can spend the time, a night here is a must. One mile downhill from Brancion, Chapaize's beautifully restored church is famous for its 11th-century belfry and its listing interior. Wander around the back for a great view of the belfry. Contrast it with the simplicity of Brancion's church.

Cluny and Taizé—Twenty kilometers southwest of Brancion lies the historic town of Cluny (cloo-nee). The center of a rich and powerful monastic movement in the Middle Ages is today a pleasant town with very sparse and crumbled remains of its once-powerful abbey. For a new trend in monasticism, consider visiting the booming Christian community of Taizé (teh-zay), just north of Cluny. Brother Roger and his community welcome visitors who'd like to spend a few days getting close to God through meditation, singing, and simple living. Call or write first if you plan to stay overnight; dorm beds only. (Taizé Community, 71250 Cluny, tel. 03 85 50 14 14.)

DIJON

Beaune may be Burgundy's wine capital, but prosperous and sprawling Dijon is its undisputed economic powerhouse and cultural capital. This is one of France's finest midsized cities (pop. 150,000), offering a main course of half-timbered houses, busy pedestrian streets, and interesting churches. It's easily worth a half day on your schedule.

Tourist Information: Dijon has two helpful TIs—one between the train station and the center city (open daily May–October 9:00–21:00, otherwise 9:00–13:00 and 14:00–19:00, place Darcy) and another in the pedestrian street thick of things (open weekdays 9:00–12:00 and 13:00–18:00, 34 rue des Forges, tel. 03 80 44 11 44). Pick up a free English map illustrating a walking tour through the nicely restored old town center, and consider the Dijon museum package deal with a self-guided Walkman tour of Dijon (45F, worthwhile only if you have at least a full day for Dijon).

Arrival in Dijon

By Train: Walk straight out of the station and up avenue Marechal Foch, stopping at the main TI, then continue to the arch to enter Dijon's center.

By Car: Enter Dijon following signs to *centre-ville*, then follow the blue "P" (parking) for place Darcy and park at the reasonable underground structure.

Sights—Dijon

▲▲**Dijon Walking Tour**—You can use the TI's maps and English explanations and follow an extensive walking tour of old Dijon, or save time and focus on the heart of Dijon and follow this walking tour (still using the TI map and explanations). From the TI (on place Darcy), walk through the arch at the other end of place Darcy and down rue de la Liberté (passing the famous Grey Poupon store at #32), to place Rude, ground zero in Dijon. Veer left down rue François Rude to the market hall (open Tuesday and Friday mornings and all day Saturday). Explore this famous market hall (picnic today?), then return to the rue Musette and walk toward the Venetianlike facade of the Église Notre Dame (see description below).

From Notre Dame, find the rue de Chouette that follows the north side of the church, then stop to rub the tiny stone owl for good luck (down about 50 yards on your right). Continue to the rue Verrerie, take a left, and admire the antiques. A right on rue Chaudronnerie, another right on rue Lamonnoye, and a left on rue Vaillant lead to the Église St. Michel. Admire the jumble of 16th-century Gothic and Renaissance styles and don't miss the free Musée Rude (next to the church) for a great look at Napoleonic (neoclassical) sculpture (you'll come face-to-face with an overpowering study for the Arc de Triomphe). Then double back on the rue Vaillant to the Musée des Beaux Arts (entrance is through a courtyard opposite the BNP bank, description below) and peek into the Duke's five-chimneyed kitchen in the museum courtyard. The Musée des Beaux Arts occupies part of what was once the Palace of the Dukes of Burgundy. The only interesting vestige that remains is the Tour (tower) Phillipe Bon that you can climb for fine views over Dijon (escorted departures up the tower leave every 30 minutes from 9:00 to 17:30, 15F for 320 steps). To find the tower, leave the Musée des Beaux Arts courtyard, passing under the arch guarded by two strange stone soldiers into a large courtyard, then walk into the doorway under the French flag. Leave the tower (and the Duke's palace) through the doorway leading into the small park. A left on the rue des Forges leads to a pleasant pedestrian street with many fine houses (wander into the surprise courtyard at #34) to the place Rude and the end of this tour. Celebrate with a refreshment at the Café des Moulin à Vent.

▲Église de Notre Dame—Gushing with three tiers of gargoyles (stare straight up before entering), this is a fine example of 13th-century Burgundian design. Notice the clock Jacquemart above the right tower; for 600 years it has rung out the time in three-part harmony. Inside you'll find beautiful 13th-century stained glass and a curious, almost haunting, 11th-century *Vierge noir* (black virgin), whose hands and feet were sawed off during the revolution.

▲▲Musée des Beaux Arts—This excellent museum occupies one wing of the once-powerful Palace of the Dukes of Burgundy and has a little something for everyone. Besides its fine collection of European paintings from all periods are the Salle des Gardes (home to two incredibly ornate tombs, climb the stairs to the balcony for the best angle), the sculptures of Carpeaux and Rude near the Salles des Gardes, a 3-D modern art room, and the huge model of the Palais des Ducs de Bourgogne (18F, free on Sunday, open 10:00–18:00, Sunday 10:00–12:30 and 14:00–18:00, closed Tuesday).

Sleeping in Dijon

Stay at the ideally located and very reasonable **Hotel le Jaquemart** (D-170F, Db-290F–320F, 32 rue Verrerie, Dijon 21000, tel. 03 80 73 39 74, fax 03 80 73 20 99).

Transportation Connections—Dijon

Dijon is Burgundy's hub, with excellent bus and rail service. **By train to: Colmar** (5/day, 4 hrs, transfer in Belfort), **Beaune** (9/day, 30 min), **Paris'** Gare de Lyon (10 TGVs/day, 95 min), **Arles** (5/day, 5 hrs; other departures possible with a transfer in Lyon), **Nice** (8/day, 8 hrs, most are direct), **Chamonix** (3/day, 8 hrs, transfer in Lyon and St. Gervais).

    By bus: Buses leave from the train station for villages along the wine route and many Burgundian cities (tel. 03 80 42 11 00).

ALSACE AND NORTHERN FRANCE

The French province of Alsace stands like a flower-child referee between Germany and France. Bounded by the Rhine on the east and the softly rolling Vosges Mountains on the west, this is a lush land of villages, vineyards, ruined castles, and almost naive cheeriness. Wine is the primary industry, topic of conversation, dominant mouthwash, and perfect excuse for countless festivals.

Because of its location, natural wealth, naked vulnerability, and the fact that Germany thinks the mountains are the natural border while France thinks the Rhine is, Alsace has changed hands several times. Having been a political pawn between Germany and France for 1,000 years, Alsace has a hybrid culture—locals who swear do so bilingually, and the local cuisine features sauerkraut and fine wine.

The humbling battlefields of Verdun and the bubbly vigor of Reims in northern France are closer to Paris than the Alsace, and follow logically only if your next destination is Paris.

Planning Your Time
Set up in Colmar. You can then explore Alsace's Route du Vin (wine road). Allow most of a day for Colmar, and at least a half day for the Route du Vin. Ideally, you'd wander Colmar's sights until after lunch, then set out for the Route du Vin. Ideally, see Strasbourg on your way to or from the Alsace. Reims and Verdun are doable by car as stops between Paris and Colmar, if you're speedy. Train travelers with only one day between Colmar and Paris must choose Reims or Verdun.

Northern France

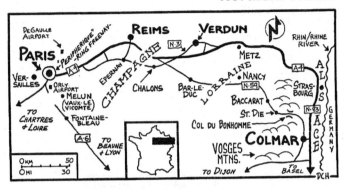

Cuisine Scene—Alsace

Alsatian cuisine is a major tourist attraction in itself. You can't miss the German influence. This is the place for *choucroute* (sauerkraut and sausage—although it seems a shame to eat it in a fancy restaurant), smelly Münster cheese, pretzels, and *baeckeanoffe* (potato, meat, and onion stew). The native *tarte à l'oignon* (like an onion quiche but better), *tarte flambée*, fresh trout, *foie gras*, and Alsatian cheesecake will bring you back to France.

Alsatian Wines

The local grapes produce these fine white wines: Sylvaner (fairly light, fruity, and inexpensive); Riesling (more robust than Sylvaner but drier than the German style you're probably used to); Gerwurtztraminer (spicy with a powerful bouquet, good with pâtés and local cheeses); Muscat (very dry with a distinctive bouquet and taste, best as a before-dinner wine); Tokay/Pinot Gris (more full-bodied than Riesling but fine with many local main courses); Pinot Noir (the local red is overpriced; very light and fruity, generally served chilled); and the tasty Crèmant d'Alsace (the region's good and inexpensive champagne). You'll also see Eaux-de-Vie, a powerful fruit-flavored brandy; try the *framboise* (raspberry) flavor.

COLMAR

There isn't a straight street in Colmar. Thankfully, it's a lovely town to be lost in. Navigate by the high church steeples and the helpful signs directing visitors to the various sights.

Colmar is a well-pickled old place of 70,000 residents, offering heavyweight sights in a warm small-town package.

Historic beauty was usually a poor excuse to be spared the ravages of World War II, but it worked for Colmar. The American and British military were careful not to bomb the half-timbered old burghers' houses, characteristic red and green tiled roofs, and cobbled lanes of Alsace's most beautiful city.

Today Colmar thrives with colorful buildings, impressive art treasures, and popular Alsatian cuisine. Schoolgirls park their rickety horse carriages in front of the city hall, ready to give visitors a clip-clop tour of the old town. Antique shops welcome browsers, and hotel managers run down the sleepy streets to pick up fresh croissants in time for breakfast.

Orientation

Tourist Information: The TI is next to the Unterlinden Museum on place Unterlinden, the gateway to the old town. Pick up a city map and Route du Vin map. If you lack wheels, ask for *Colmar Actualités*, a booklet with bus schedules. Ask about wine festivals and Colmar's Folklore Tuesdays (with folk dancing at 20:30 each Tuesday mid-May through mid-September on place de l'Ancienne). The TI organizes public town walks of the old town and of the Unterlinden Museum (20F, 1 hour, usually Tuesday, Thursday, and Saturday in summer), reserves hotel rooms, and has *chambre d'hôte* listings for the region and Colmar. (TI open Monday–Saturday 9:00–18:00, until 19:00 in the summer, Sunday 10:00–14:00, tel. 03 89 20 68 92.) There's a public WC 20 yards to the left of the TI.

Tours: You can hire a private guide for a walking tour (430F, ask at TI). A minibus tour company, Les Circuits d'Alsace, organizes day trips around the Alsace (tel. 03 89 41 90 88).

Helpful Hints: Place Unterlinden (a 15-minute walk from the train station) is the visitors' town center, where you'll find the TI, a major museum, and a huge and handy Monoprix department store (8:30–20:30, closed Sunday, supermarket and cafétéria). Every city bus starts or finishes on place Unterlinden.

Colmar is most crowded from June through September. For ten days in early August the local wine festival rages, and Sauerkraut Days are celebrated on the first or second weekend in October. Open-air markets take place on Thursday and Saturday.

Self-service laundromats are at rue Turenne near Petite Venise and at 1 rue Ruest (just off the pedestrian street rue Vauban, usually open daily 8:00–21:00).

Colmar

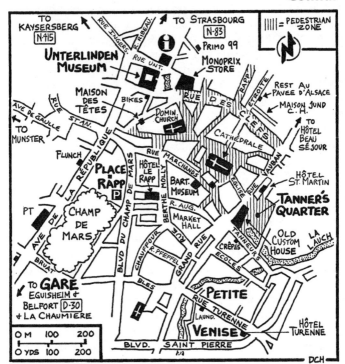

Arrival in Colmar

By Train or Bus: To reach Colmar's center city from the bus or train station (they're side by side), walk straight out, turn left on the avenue de la République, and keep walking. Allow 15 minutes. Buses 1, 2, and 3 each go from the station to the TI (5F, pay the driver).

By Car: Follow signs to *centre-ville*. There are several handy pay lots (place Rapp) and a huge free lot at "parking du Musee Unterlinden" (across from Primo 99 hotel).

Sights—Colmar

▲**Old Town**—The importance of 15th- to 17th-century Colmar is clear as you wander its pedestrian-friendly old center, which is decorated with 45 buildings classified as historic monuments. Back in feudal times, when most of Europe was fragmented into chaotic little princedoms and dukedoms, merchant-dominated cities (natural proponents of the formation of large nation-states) banded together to form "trading leagues." The Hanseatic League was the super-league of northern Europe. Colmar was a member of a smaller league of ten Alsatian cities called the Decapolis (founded 1354). Delegates of this group met in Colmar's **Old Custom House** (Koïfhus). You'll see both Gothic and Renaissance in its circa 1840 architecture.

Passing under the Custom House, you'll find yourself facing the place de l'Ancienne Douane and a Bertholdi statue—arm raised, *à la* Statue of Liberty. The half-timbered commotion of higgledy-piggledy rooftops just beyond marks the **Tanners' Quarters**. These 17th- and 18th-century rooftops each struggled to get space in the sun to dry their freshly tanned hides. The place de l'Ancienne Douane is the festive site of outdoor wine-tasting many summer evenings. The "Petite Venise" quarter just beyond is quaint but probably not worth your time.

Rather, wander the scenic lanes between the Koïfhus and the TI. The most photographed houses in town are the Pfister House (a richly decorated merchant's house from 1537 with an external spiral staircase turret and painted walls showing the city folk's taste for Renaissance humanism) and the House of Heads (1609, decorated with 105 faces and masks).

▲▲▲**Unterlinden Museum**—Colmar's touristic claim to fame, this is one of my favorite museums in Europe. Its extensive yet manageable collection ranges from Roman Colmar to medieval wine-making exhibits, and traditional wedding dresses to paintings that give vivid insight into the High Middle Ages.

The highlight of the museum (and, for me, the city) is Grünewald's gripping Isenheim Altarpiece, actually a series of three different paintings on hinges that pivot like shutters (study the little model on the wall, explained in English). Designed to help people in a medieval hospital endure horrible skin diseases (St. Anthony's Fire, later called rye ergotism) long before the age of painkillers, it's one of the most powerful paintings ever produced.

Stand medieval in front of the centerpiece and let the agony and suffering of the Crucifixion drag its fingers down your face. The point—Jesus' suffering—is drilled home: the weight of his body bending the crossbar, his elbows pulled from their sockets by the weight of his dead body, his mangled feet, the grief on Mary's face. In hopes that the intended

viewers—the hospital's patients—would know that Jesus under-
stands their suffering, he was even painted looking like he, too,
had a skin disease. Study the faces and the Christian symbolism.

The three scenes of the painting changed with the seasons
of the church year. The happy ending—a psychedelic explosion of Resurrection joy—is the spiritual equivalent of jumping
from the dentist's chair directly into a Jacuzzi.

There's more to the museum. Ringing the peaceful cloister
is a fine series of medieval church paintings and sculpture and a
room filled with old wine presses. Downstairs you'll find Roman
and prehistoric artifacts. The upstairs contains local and folk history, with everything from medieval armour to old-time toys.
(30F, open April–October 9:00– 18:00, off-season 9:00–12:00
and 14:00–17:00, closed Tuesday, tel. 03 89 41 89 23.)

▲▲**Dominican Church**—Here is another medieval mind-
blower. In Colmar's Église des Dominicains, you'll find Martin
Schongauer's angelically beautiful *Virgin in the Rosebush* (from
1473, but looking like it was painted yesterday) holding court on
center stage. The text in Mary's halo tells the theme of the painting: "Pick me also for your child, O very Holy Virgin." Jesus
clings to his mother, reminding the viewer of the possibility of
an intimate relationship with Mary. And Mary is painted as a
paragon of maternal security. The contrast provided by the simple Dominican setting heightens the flamboyance of this late-
Gothic masterpiece. Dominican churches were particularly
austere, as the 13th-century Catholic Church was combating a
wave of heretical movements, such as the Cathars, whose message was a simpler faith (8F, open daily 10:00–18:00, winter
10:00–13:00 and 15:00–18:00). This Dominican austerity is more
apparent after a visit to Colmar's fancier—and Franciscan—St.
Martin's cathedral.

Bartholdi Museum—This interesting little museum recalls the
life and work of the local boy who gained fame by sculpting the
Statue of Liberty. Several of his statues, usually with one arm
raised high, grace Colmar's squares (20F, March– December
10:00–12:00 and 14:00–18:00, closed Tuesday and off-season, in
the heart of the old town at 30 rue des Marchands).

Sleeping in Colmar
(5F = about $1, postal code: 68000)
Sleep Code: **S** = Single, **D** = Double/Twin, **T** = Triple,
Q = Quad, **b** = bathroom, **t** = toilet only, **s** = shower only,

CC = Credit Card (**V**isa, **M**asterCard, **A**mex), **SE** = Speaks English, **NSE** = No English, * = French hotel rating system (0–4 stars).

Hotels are jammed on weekends in June, September, and October. July and August are busy, but there are always rooms—somewhere.

Maison Jund offers my favorite budget beds in Colmar. This magnificent half-timbered home is a medieval treehouse soaked in wine and filled with flowers. The rooms are equipped with kitchenettes, and some have full bathrooms. Rooms are generally available only from April to mid-September (D-160F, Db/Tb-200F, 12 rue de l'Ange, tel. 03 89 41 58 72, fax 03 89 23 15 83). Mr. Jund also offers wine-tasting.

Hôtel Turenne** is a fine historic hotel in a great location offering bright pastel and modern rooms with all the comforts (Sb-230F–340F, Db-250F–385F, Tb-385F–550F, garage 20F, CC:VMA, 10 route du Bale, tel. 03 89 41 12 26, fax 03 89 41 27 64, SE). The rooms on the street are cheaper and noisier. Half of its 85 rooms are nonsmoking.

Hôtel Le Rapp** with 40 simple rooms and a small basement pool, is beautifully located and well-run (Sb-285F–310F, Db-285F–410F, extra person-80F, CC:VMA, 1 rue Berthe-Molley, tel. 03 89 41 62 10, fax 03 89 24 13 58, Bernard and his staff SE). The alley rooms can be noisy. Its pricey restaurant serves a classy Alsatian menu with impeccable service. You can dine for less in the Rapp's low-key brasserie.

Hôtel Beau Séjour** is upscale and cushy, with a pleasant garden and a well-respected restaurant (Sb-250F–360F, Db-300F–500F, Tb-330F–600F, private parking for drivers or a 15-minute walk from the center, 25 rue du Ladhof, tel. 03 89 41 37 16, fax 03 89 41 43 07).

Primo 99 is a French prefab hotel—a modern, cheap, efficient, bright, nothing-but-the-plastic-and-concrete-basics place to sleep for those to whom ambiance is a four-letter word and modernity is next to godliness. It's one of Colmar's best budget deals (S-140F, Sb-220F, D-200F, Db-280F, add 50F for a third person, family discounts, CC:VM, 5 rue des Ancêtres, free parking in the big square in front, rooms held for a phone call until 18:30, tel. 03 89 24 22 24, fax 03 89 24 55 96, SE). Half the beds have footboards—a problem if you're more than 6'2".

Hotel St. Martin*** is a classy, family-run place right in the old center with a history as a coaching inn going back to 1361. It's small with Old World–yet-modern rooms woven into its antique frame. Half of its 24 rooms are in a second building opposite a peaceful courtyard. While just as comfortable and characteristic, these are with showers rather than baths and no elevator or air conditioning, thus cheaper (Sb-290F–550F, Db-350F–650F, Tb-550F–830F, CC:VMA, free parking nearby, 38 Grand Rue, tel. 03 89 24 11 51, fax 03 89 23 47 78, the Winterstein family SE). For about the same money but without a hint of the Old World or a family, you can sleep comfortably and centrally in the slick **Hotel Mercure** (Db-510F, three rooms for disabled people, air-con, CC:VMA, rue Golbery, tel. 03 89 41 71 71, fax 03 89 23 82 71, SE).

La Chaumière*, while frumpy and on a big characterless street, offers cheap beds by the train station. The sleepable rooms surround a courtyard above a smoky local café (St-155F, Sb-180F, D-180F, Db-240F, T-245F, CC:VM, 74 avenue de la République, tel. 03 89 41 08 99).

The best cheap beds (40F, in large rooms) in Colmar are at the **Maison des Jeunes** (near the station in a comfortable and fairly central location, Camille-Schlumberger 17, tel. 03 89 41 26 87). The desk is open 7:00–12:00 and 14:00–23:00. The less central **youth hostel**, open March–October until midnight, has dorm beds (64F, breakfast included, 15-minute walk from station and downtown, 2 rue Pasteur, tel. 03 89 80 57 39).

Sleeping near Colmar in Eguisheim
(5F = about $1, postal code: 68420)

Colmar is getting crowded and pricey, but the nearby wine villages remain a good deal. If you prefer the village scene, try Eguisheim or any of the hundreds of good-value *chambres d'hôte* that line the Route du Vin.

The enchanting village of Eguisheim offers several fine CHs and is almost a walk from Colmar, convenient for train travelers (who can catch a bus from Colmar) and for those with cars. **Madame Dirringer's** fine rooms are trés Alsatian, spacious, and clean (D-150F, Db-180F, breakfast included, 11 rue Riesling, tel. 03 89 41 71 87). A nearby vineyard mansion experience can be had at the **Hertz-Meyers** (Db-250F– 270F, Tb-355F, 3 rue Riesling, tel. 03 89 23 67 74). The friendly **Stockys** offers comfortable rooms for 150F (24 rue de Colmar, tel. 03 89 41 68 04). If it's a hotel you want, the very comfortable **L'Auberge Alsacienne*****, with a fine restaurant, gives three stars for the price of two (Db-270F– 310F, Tb-380F, 12 Grand Rue, tel. 03 89 41 50 20, fax 03 89 23 89 32).

Eating in Colmar

In the Tanners Quarter/Petite Venise area, Colmar's most scenic dining locale, you'll find several reasonable restaurants and cafés. For crêpes with atmosphere, eat at **Crêperie Tom Pouce** (daily, inexpensive, 10 rue des Tanneurs). Next door, the **Restaurant des Tanneurs Weinstub** is a bit more upscale, with Alsatian menus from 100F (closed Wednesday, indoor and outdoor seating, tel. 03 89 23 72 12). For canal-front dining, head into La Petite Venise to the bridge on rue Turenne, where you'll find a pizzeria, a *weinstube*/café (both cheap), and a fine but pricey canal-level restaurant, **Les Bateliers**.

The **Hôtel Restaurant Le Rapp** is a good place to savor a slow, elegant meal served with grace and fine Alsatian wine (menus start at 95F). Its **Rappstub Bistrot** offers a cheaper menu from the same kitchen (60F to 70F plate of the day, closed Friday, air-conditioned, 1 rue Berthe-Molley, tel. 03 89 41 62 10, SE).

Two good self-services dish up low-stress meals in sterile settings. **Flunch**, on place Rapp, is more pleasant but pricier than the **Monoprix caféteria**, downstairs in the Monoprix market, across from the Unterlinden Museum.

Transportation Connections—Colmar

By train to: Strasbourg (hrly, 50 min), **Reims** (4/day, 5 hrs, with probable transfers in Strasbourg, Nancy, and Chalons-sur-Marne or Epernay), **Dijon/ Beaune** (5/day to Dijon, 4 hrs, transfer in Belfort; it's another 30 min to Beaune), **Paris'** Gare de l'Est (10/day, 6 hrs, transfer in Mulhouse), **Amboise** (go first to Paris, then catch direct train from Paris' Gare d'Austerlitz, allow all day), **Basel, Switzerland** (8/day, 1 hr), **Karlsruhe, Germany** (3/day, 90 min, via Strasbourg; from Karlsruhe, it's 90 min to Frankfurt, 3 hrs to Munich).

The Wine Road (Route du Vin)

Alsace's Route du Vin is an asphalt ribbon tying 90 miles of vineyards, villages, and feudal fortresses into an understandably

Alsace

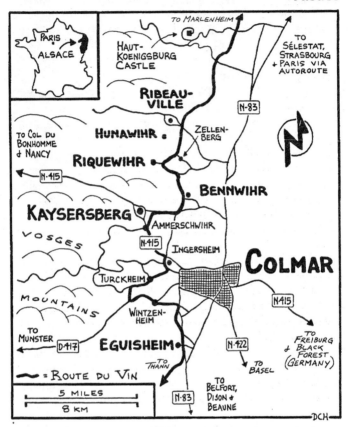

popular tourist package. The dry, sunny climate has made for good wine and happy tourists since Roman days. Colmar and Eguisheim are ideally located for exploring the 30,000 acres of vineyards blanketing the hills from Marlenheim to Thann. If you have only a day, focus on towns within easy striking range of Colmar. Top ones are Eguisheim, Kaysersberg, Riquewihr, and Hunawihr. Get a map of the Route du Vin from any TI.

Throughout Alsace you'll see *Dégustation* signs. *Dégustation* means "come on in and taste," and *gratuit* means "free"; otherwise, there's a small charge. Most towns have wineries that give tours; those in Eguisheim and Riquewihr are good. The modern cooperatives at Bennwhir, Hunawihr, and Ribbeauville, created after the destruction of World War II, provide a good look at a more modern and efficient method of production. Your hotel receptionist or the Colmar TI can give you advice, or even telephone a winery for you to confirm tour times. You may have to wait for a group and tag along for a tour and free tasting. Be sure to try Crèmant, the Alsatian "champagne." It's very good—and much cheaper. The French term for headache, if you really get "Alsaced," is *mal à la tete*.

Getting Around the Wine Road

Pick up a Michelin regional map before heading out.

By Bus: Public buses connect Colmar with most of the villages along the Route du Vin. The schedules are fairly convenient (Eguisheim #303, 6/day, 5 min; Kaysersberg #13, hrly, 30 min; Riquewihr #6, 6/day, 30 min). Buy tickets from the driver. Get schedules from the TI.

By Bike: The Wine Road's level terrain makes biking a very good option. You can rent a bike at the Peugeot bike store in Colmar (40F/5 hrs, 70F/day, Visa number for security, open 8:30–12:00 and 14:00–18:00, closed Monday and Sunday) next to the Unterlinden Museum or at the station (ask at the TI for other locations). Kaysersberg and Eguisheim are fine biking destinations.

By Car: The easiest approach to the Wine Road is to leave Colmar on the N-83 toward Belfort; you'll soon see signs to Eguisheim—from there you're on your own.

By Foot: Well-signed walking trails connect Route du Vin villages through the vineyards, and serious walkers can climb to the higher ruined castles of the Vosges. Kayserberg to Riquewihr is a pleasant two-hour walk (use the bus to return). Get more information at a local TI.

Sights—The Wine Road

Eguisheim—Just a few miles (a flat and easy bike ride) from Colmar, this scenic little town is best explored by walking around its circular road, then cutting through the middle. (See hotel recommendations under Sleeping near Colmar.) Visit the Eguisheim Wine Cooperative (Cave vinicole d'Eguisheim, 6 Grand Rue, tel. 03 89 22 20 20, folklore and tastings in summer on Wednesday 17:00–19:00, open daily 10:00–12:00 and 14:00–19:00). If you have a car, follow signs straight up to Les Husseren and Les Châteaux for a pleasant walk to the ruined castle towers and a fine view to the Vosges above and vineyards below.

Kaysersberg—Albert Schweitzer's hometown is larger and more crowded but just as cute as Eguisheim. Climb to the castle (under long-term renovation), browse through the art galleries, enjoy the colorful bundle of 15th-century houses and the stork's nest near the fortified town bridge, visit Dr. Schweitzer's house (10F, closed 12:00–14:00), check out the church with its impressive 400-year-old altarpiece, taste some wine, and wander into nearby vineyards. Kaysersberg's TI is inside the Hôtel de Ville (tel. 03 89 78 22 78). Walking trails through the vineyards to other Route du Vin towns are well-marked; walk toward the castle (75 yards to the right of the TI as you face it) and you'll see signs.

Riquewihr—Too cute, commercial, and overrun, this little walled village is crammed with shops, cafés, art galleries, cobblestone streets, and flowers. Tastings and tours can be found at Caves Dopff et Irion (Cour du Château, tel. 03 89 47 92 51, TI tel. 03 89 47 80 80).

Hunawihr—Here's another bit of wine-soaked Alsatian cuteness, complete with a 16th-century fortified church and great views. This small town is possibly the most beautiful on the Route du Vin, is less touristed, and has a few *chambres d'hote*. Taste at the wine cooperative, wander up to the fortified church (fine view from the cemetery), and delight in the brightly painted homes.

STRASBOURG

Sitting right on the Rhine river, Strasbourg provides an urban blend of Franco-Germanic culture, architecture, and ambiance. It's home to the European Parliament and a fascinating *vielle ville* (old city) of pedestrian streets, canals, and half-timbered homes. If it's a big-city fix you need, come here.

Tourist Information: The TI is in front of the train station (park there). Pick up a city map and walk 15 minutes straight up rue Marie Kuss to rue Gutenberg to find the old city and cathedral.

Sights—Strasbourg

▲▲**Strasbourg Cathedral**—This uniquely Alsatian cathedral, with its tall, slender spire, multicolored tile, and red stone roof is well worth a side trip. Approach the cathedral on foot from place Gutenberg and rue Mercière. It's particularly stunning in the late afternoon light. Don't miss the doomsday pillar, the 15th-century astronomical clock inside, or the walk up the tower. The view is worth the struggle (10F, tower open 8:30–18:30). After touring the cathedral, take a stroll through Strasbourg's enchanting La Petite France—follow signs from place Gutenberg.

Transportation Connections—Strasbourg

Strasbourg is an easy side trip from Colmar or a stop en route to or from Paris. **By train to: Colmar** (hrly, 50 min), **Paris'** Gare de l'Est (13/day, 4.5 hrs), **Karlsruhe, Germany** (3/day, 50 min), **Basel, Switzerland** (hrly, 2 hrs).

VERDUN

Little remains in Europe today to remind us of World War I. Verdun provides a fine tribute to the more than a million lives lost in the World War I battles fought here. While the lunar landscape of WWI is now forested over, the craters remain—along with millions of undetonated bombs in vast cordoned-off areas. Drive through the eerie moguls that surround the city of Verdun, stopping at melted sugar-cube forts and plaques marking where towns once existed. With two hours and a car, or a full day and a bike, you can see the most impressive sights and appreciate the awesome scale of the battles. The town of Verdun is not your destination but a springboard into the battlefields surrounding it.

   Tourist Information: The TI is on place Nation (daily 8:30–19:00 May–September, otherwise closed from 12:00–14:00 and at 18:00, tel. 03 29 86 14 18).

Arrival in Verdun

By Train: Walk straight out of the station and down avenue Garibaldi for the town center.

   By Car: Follow signs to *centre-ville*, place Nation, and Porte Chatel, and you'll pass the TI just before crossing the river.

Getting Around the Verdun Battlefields

The TI has good maps of the battlefields. French-language minivan tours of the battle sites are available June–September, leaving the TI around 14:00 (occasionally in English—ask). To reach the battlefields by car or bike (about 20 miles round-trip), follow the N-3 toward Etain and turn left on the D-913 to Champs de Bataille, Rive Droite. You can rent a bike at Cycles Flavenot, 10 rue de la Marne.

Verdun

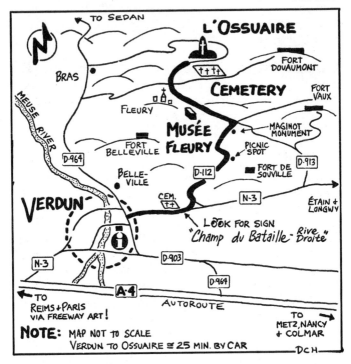

The battlefield remains are situated on two sides of the Meuse River; the Rive Droite is the more interesting. Follow signs to Fort Douaumont and the Ossuaire, and you'll pass the Musée Fleury en route.

Sights—Verdun

▲▲**Battlegrounds**—Start with the interesting **Mémorial-Musée de Fleury**, where you'll see reconstructed scenes and models of the battles that raged for more than four years. (18F, open mid-March to mid-September 9:00–18:00; off-season 9:00–12:00 and 14:00–18:00.)

Don't miss **l'Ossuaire**, the tomb of the 130,000 French and Germans whose last home was the muddy trenches of Verdun (same hours as the museum). Look through the low windows for a boney memorial to those whose political and military leaders asked them to make the "ultimate sacrifice" for their countries. Enter the monument and experience a humbling and moving tribute. Ponder a war that left half of all the men in France aged 15–30 dead or wounded. See the thought-provoking 20-minute film (15F) in the basement; ask for the English version. You can climb the tower (6F) for a territorial view. The little 1F picture boxes in the gift shop are worth a look (turn through all the old photos before your time expires).

Before leaving, walk to the cemetery and listen for the eerie buzz of silence and peace. You can visit the nearby **Tranchée des Baionnettes**, where an entire division of soldiers was buried alive in their trench—though it's mostly covered with bushes (many of the soldier's bayonets remained above ground until recently). A visit to the nearby **Fort Douaumont** (15F) is mildly interesting. Here you'll tour an underground fort, a bunker, and tunnels, and see the remains of a World War I command control center.

Citadelle Souterraine—In downtown Verdun, this is a disappointing train ride through the tunnels of the French Command. While it tries to recreate the Verdun scene, it's not worth your time or money.

Transportation Connections—Verdun
By train to: Colmar (4/day, 5 hrs, transfers in Chalons-sur-Marne and Strasbourg), **Reims** (4/day, 3 hrs, transfer in Chalons-sur-Marne), **Paris'** Gare de l'Est (5/day, 3 hrs, transfer in Chalons-sur-Marne).

REIMS
Deservedly famous for its cathedral and champagne, contemporary Reims is a modern, bustling city with little character. Just an hour and a half by car or train from Paris, it makes a good day trip or handy stop for travelers en route elsewhere. Most sights of interest (champagne caves included) are within a 20-minute walk from the cathedral.

Tourist Information: The TI is immediately to the left of the cathedral as you face the front (open Easter–June 9:00–20:00; closes earlier off-season, tel. 03 26 77 45 25). Their free city map shows the champagne caves.

Arrival in Reims
By Train: Walk out of the station, look up, and follow the cathedral's spire; a 15-minute walk.

By Car: A piece of cake—just follow the *cathédrale* signs and park as close to it as possible. You may find parking easier behind the cathedral.

Sights—Reims

▲▲▲**Cathedral**—The cathedral of Reims is a glorious example of Gothic architecture, with the best west portal (inside and outside) anywhere. (Medieval churches always face east; the end you enter is the west portal.) The coronation place of 800 years for French kings and queens, it houses many old treasures, great medieval stained glass, and a lovely modern set of Marc Chagall stained-glass windows filling the east end. (Open daily from 7:30–19:30.)

▲**Champagne Tours**—Reims is the capital of the Champagne region, and while the bubbly stuff's birthplace was Epernay, you can tour a champagne cave right in Reims. All charge for tastings (20F–30F, most close 12:00–14:00 and 16:30–17:30). The **Taittinger Company** does a great job trying to convince you they're the best (walk ten minutes up rue de Barbatre from the cathedral to 9 place St. Nicaise, tel. 03 26 85 45 35). After seeing their movie (in very comfortable theater seats), follow your guide down into some of the 3 miles of chilly, chalk caves, many dug by ancient Romans. Popping corks signal when the tour's done and the tasting's begun (20F, tour includes a tasting, 9:30–12:00 and 14:30–16:30).

One block beyond Taittinger, on place des Droits de l'Homme, you'll find several other champagne caves. **Piper Heidsieck** offers a remarkable train-ride tour and tasting (35F, refunded if you buy, 51 boulevard Henri-Vasnier, tel. 03 26 84 43 44, call first). You can simply drop by for a tour without a reservation at both Piper Heidsieck and Taittinger.

Champagne purists will go directly to Epernay (26 km away, well-connected to Paris and Reims) where **Moet Chandon** offers tours (20F with tasting, tel. 03 26 51 21 00). This is the original champagne—where the monk Dom Perignon, after much fiddling with his wine, stumbled onto this bubbly treat. On that happy day he shouted, "Brothers, come quickly . . . I'm drinking stars!"

Transportation Connections—Reims

By train to: Epernay (8/day, 30 min), **Verdun** (8/day, 3 hrs, transfer in Chalons sur Marne), **Paris'** Gare de l'Est (10/day, 90 min), **Colmar** (3/day, 5 hrs, transfer in Vitry and Strasbourg).

BELGIUM

- 12,000 square miles (a little smaller than Maryland)
- 10 million people (830 people per square mile)
- 30 Belgian francs = about $1

Belgium falls through the cracks. Nestled between Germany, France, and Britain, and famous for waffles, sprouts, and endive, it's no wonder many travelers don't even consider a stop here. But as many who visit remark that Belgium is one of Europe's best-kept secrets. There are tourists but not as many as the country's charms merit.

The country is split between the French-speaking Walloons in the south and the Dutch-speaking Flemish people (60 percent of the population) in the north. The capital city, Brussels, while mostly French-speaking, is officially bilingual. There is a small minority of German-speaking people and, because of Belgium's international importance, more than 20 percent of its residents are foreigners.

It is in Belgium that Europe comes together: where Romance languages meet Germanic languages, Catholics meet Protestants, and the Benelux union was established, planting the seed 40 years ago that, today, is sprouting into the unification of Europe. Belgium flies the flag of Europe as vigorously as any place you'll visit.

Bruges and Brussels are the best two first bites of Belgium. Brussels is one of Europe's great cities and the capital of the European Community. Bruges is a medieval gem, a wonderfully preserved town that expertly nurtures the tourist industry, bringing it a prosperity it hasn't enjoyed since it helped lead northern Europe out of the Middle Ages 500 years ago.

Belgians brag that they eat as much as the Germans and as well as the French. They are the world's leading beer consumers and among the world's leading carnivores. In Belgium, never bring chrysanthemums to a wedding. And tweaking little kids on the ear is considered rude.

Ten million Belgians pack into 12,000 square miles (the size of Maryland). At 830 people per square mile, it's the second most densely populated country in Europe (after the Netherlands). This population concentration, coupled with a dense and well-lit rail and road system, causes Belgium to actually shine at night when viewed from space, a phenomenon NASA astronauts call the "Belgian Window."

Belgium's rail system is tops, and its various rail deals are worth considering. The second-class Multipass gives groups of three to five people any two trips in Belgium. Three people pay 1,190BF, four pay 1,340BF, and five pay 1,490BF; at least one of the Multipass users must be age 26 or older. (The one-way fare from Brussels to Bruges is 360BF per person.) Seniors age 60+ can get any six rides for 1,190BF (second class) or 1,850BF (first class). Anyone traveling on the weekend should ask for the weekend discount (40 percent reduction for one person, 60 percent off for any traveling companions).

BRUGES (BRUGGE)

With Renoir canals, pointy gilded architecture, time tunnel art, and stay-awhile cafés, Bruges is a heavyweight sightseeing destination, as well as a joy. Where else can you ride a bike along a canal, munch mussels washed down with the world's best beer, savor heavenly chocolate, and see Flemish Primitives and a Michelangelo, all within 300 yards of a bell tower that rings out "don't worry, be happy" jingles every 15 minutes? And there's no language barrier.

The town is Brugge (broo-gha) in Flemish. It's Bruges (broozh) in French and English. Before it was Flemish or French, the name was a Viking word for "wharf" or "embarkment." Right from the start, Bruges was a trading center. By the 14th century, Bruges' population was 35,000, in a league with London, and the city was the most important cloth market in northern Europe. By the 16th century, the harbor had silted up and the economy had collapsed. In the 19th century, a new port, Zeebrugge, brought renewed vitality to the area. But today, Bruges prospers mainly because of tourism: it's a uniquely well-preserved Gothic city and a handy gateway to Europe. It's no secret, but even with the crowds, it's the kind of city where you don't mind being a tourist.

The tourists' Bruges (you'll be sharing it) is contained within a 1-kilometer-square canal, or moat. Nearly everything of interest and importance is within a cobbled and convenient swath between the train station and the Market Square (a 15-minute walk).

Planning Your Time

Bruges needs at least two nights and a full, well-organized day. Even nonshoppers enjoy browsing here, and the Belgian love of life makes a hectic itinerary seem a little senseless.

With one day, the speedy visitor could do this—9:30, climb the belfry; 10:00, catch the minibus orientation town tour; 11:00, tour the Burg sights (visit the TI if necessary); 12:15, walk to the brewery, have lunch, and catch the 13:00, tour; 14:30, walk through the Beguinage; 15:00, tour the Memling Museum (six paintings); 15:45, see the Michelangelo in the church; and 16:00, tour the Groeninge Museum (closes at 17:00). Rent a bike for an evening ride through the quiet back streets (or take a 900BF half-hour horse-and-buggy tour or catch a canal-boat tour). Lose the tourists and find a dinner. (If that seems insane, skip the belfry and the brewery.)

Orientation

(tel. code: 050)

Tourist Information: The main office (on Burg Square, daily 9:30–18:30, Saturday and Sunday 10:00–12:00 and 14:00–18:30; off-season closed at 17:00, tel. 050/448686) and the train station office (daily 10:30–18:30; off-season closed Sunday) sell a great 25BF all-inclusive Bruges visitors' guide with a map and listings of all sights, hours, and services. The free *Exit* includes a monthly calendar of the many events the town puts on to keep its hordes of tourists entertained. It's entirely in Dutch but almost readable (i.e., *Harmonieconcert*). Skip the TI's "combo" museum ticket. They also have train schedule information and specifics on the various kinds of tours available.

Arrival in Bruges

By Train: From the train, you'll see the square belfry tower on the main square. Upon arrival, pick up the city info booklet/map at the station TI. Most buses (#1, #3, #4, #6, #8, #11, #13, #16) go right to the Market Square (40BF ticket, buy from driver, good for an hour). Taxi fare to most hotels is 200BF. It's a scenic 15-minute walk from the station to the center: cross the busy street and canal in front of the station and have people direct you to the Market Square via the Beguinage. You could rent a bike at the station for the duration of your stay (325BF/day with hefty 1,500BF deposit).

By Car: Drivers should park in the underground t'Zand parking garage near the station and pretend they arrived by train.

Helpful Hints

Change traveler's checks at Brussel Lambert Bank (Monday–Friday 9:00–12:30 and 13:30–16:30, Saturday 9:00–12:00, on the Market Square). Shops are open 9:00– 18:00; a little later on Friday. Grocery stores are usually closed on Sunday. Market day is Wednesday morning (Burg) and Saturday morning (t'Zand). Saturday and Sunday afternoons there is a flea market along Dijver (in front of Groeninge Museum). October through March is off-season (when some museums close on Tuesday). A botanical garden blooms in the center at Astrid Park.

Sights—Bruges

An Orientation Tour on Foot—Bruges' sights are listed in walking order: from the Market Square, to the Burg, to the cluster of museums around the Church of Our Lady to the Beguinage (a ten-minute walk from begining to end). Like Venice, the ultimate sight is the town itself, and the best way to enjoy that is to get lost on the back streets away from the lace shops and ice-cream stands.

The Market Square (Markt)—Ringed by banks, the post office, lots of restaurant terraces, great old gabled buildings, and the belfry, this is the modern heart of the city. Most city buses go from here to the station. Under the belfry are two great Belgian french-fry stands and a quadralingual braille description and model of the tower. In its day, a canal went right up to the central square of this formerly great trading center.

▲▲The Belfry (Belfort)—This bell tower has towered over Market Square since 1300. In 1486, the octagonal lantern was added, making it 83 meters high—that's 366 steps (daily 9:30–17:00, October–March closed 12:30–13:30, WC in courtyard). The view is worth the climb and the 100BF. Survey the town. On the horizon you can see the towns along the coast. Just before you reach the top, peek into the carillon room. The 47 bells can be played mechanically with the giant barrel and movable tabs (as they do on each quarter-hour) or with a manual keyboard (as it does for regular concerts) with fists and feet rather than fingers. Be there on the quarter-hour when things ring. It's *bellissimo* at the top of the hour. Carillon concert times are listed at the base of the belfry (usually Wednesday and Saturday 21:00–22:00,

Bruges

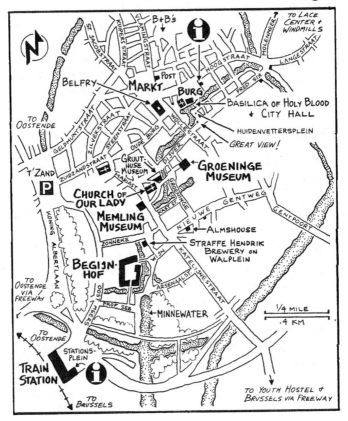

Sunday at 14:15). From Markt and the belfry, Breidelstraat leads
to Burg Square.

▲▲**Burg Square**—The opulent square called Burg is Bruges'
civic center, historically the birthplace of Bruges and the site of
the ninth-century castle of the first Count of Flanders. Today
it's the scene of outdoor concerts, a parking place for horse
buggies, and home of the TI (with a public WC). It's surrounded by six centuries of architecture. Sweeping counterclockwise 360 degrees, you'll go from Romanesque (the round
arches and thick walls of the basilica in the corner, best seen
inside the lower chapel), to the pointed Gothic arches of the
Town Hall (with its "Gothic Room"), to the well-proportioned
Renaissance windows of the Old Recorder's House (next door,

under the gilded statues), past the TI and the park to the elaborate 17th-century Baroque of the Provost's House.

▲**Basilica of the Holy Blood**—Originally the Chapel of Saint Basil, it is famous for its relic of the blood of Christ, which, according to tradition, was brought to Bruges in 1150, after the Second Crusade. The lower chapel (through door labeled "Basiliek") is dark and solid—a fine example of Romanesque (with some beautiful statues). The upper chapel (separate entrance, climb the stairs) is decorated Gothic and is often filled with appropriately contemplative music. An English flier tells about the relic, art, and history. The Basilica Museum is small but sumptuous and contains the gem-studded hexagonal reliquary that carries the relic on its yearly Ascension Day trip through the streets of Bruges (museum is next to the upper chapel, 40BF, open daily 9:30–12:00 and 14:00–18:00; shorter hours and closed Wednesday off-season).

▲**City Hall's Gothic Room**—Built around 1400, this is the oldest in the Low Countries. Your ticket gives you a room full of old town maps and paintings, and a grand "Gothic Hall" beautifully restored. Its painted and carved wooden ceiling features "hanging arches" (explained by an English flier). The free ground-level lobby is a picture gallery of Belgium's colonial history, from the Spanish Bourbon king to Napoleon (60BF, open daily 9:30–17:00, off-season closed 12:30–14:00, Burg 12).

Provincial Museum (Brugse Vrije)—This is just one ornate room with an impressive Renaissance chimney. If you're into heraldry, the symbolism, explained in the free English flier, makes this worth a five-minute stop. If you're not, you'll wonder where the rest of the museum is (20BF, open 10:00–12:00 and 13:30–17:00, closed Monday, entry in corner of square).

Fish Market—From Burg, walk under the Goldfinger family down Blinde Ezelstraat, to the persistent little fish market and Huidevettersplein, a tiny, picturesque, and restaurant-filled square. Continue on to Roezenhoedkaai, from which you can get a great photo of the belfry reflected in the canal. Can you see its tilt? It leans about 4 feet. Down the canal (past a flea market on weekends) looms the huge brick spire of the Church of Our Lady (tallest spire in the Low Countries). Between you and the church are the next three museums.

▲▲▲**Groeninge Museum**—This diverse and classy collection shows off mostly Flemish art from Memling to Magritte. While it has plenty of worthwhile modern art, the highlights are its vivid and pristine Flemish Primitives. ("Primitive" here means before the Renaissance.) Flemish art is shaped by its love of detail, its merchant patrons' egos, and the power of the Church. Lose yourself in the halls of Groeninge: gaze across 15th-century canals, into the eyes of reassuring Marys, and through town squares littered with leotards, lace, and lopped-off heads (200BF, open daily 9:30–17:00; October–March closed 12:30–14:00 and Tuesday, Dijver 12). The Brangwyn Museum, next door, is only interesting if you are into lace or the early 20th-century art of Brangwyn (80BF, daily 9:30–17:00; off-season closed 12:30–14:00 and Tuesday, Dijver 16).

▲Gruuthuse Museum—A wealthy brewer's home, this is a sprawling smattering of everything from medieval bedpans to a guillotine. There's no information inside, so to understand the crossbows, dark old paintings, and what a beer merchant's doing with box seats peeking down on the altar of the Church of Our Lady next door, you'll have to buy or browse through the 600BF guidebook (130BF, daily 9:30–17:00, shorter hours off-season, Dijver 17).

▲▲Church of Our Lady—The church stands as a memorial to the power and wealth of Bruges in its heyday. Just inside the door is a delicate Madonna and Child by Michelangelo. It's said to be the only Michelangelo statue to leave Italy in his lifetime (cloth money). If you like tombs and church art, pay to wander through the apse (60BF, Michelangelo free, art-filled apse Monday–Friday 10:00–11:30 and 14:30–17:00, closes at 16:00 on Saturday; Sunday open 14:30–17:00; off-season it closes at 16:30 Sunday–Friday; on Mariastraat).

▲▲St. Jans Hospital/Memling Museum—Just beyond the Church of Our Lady is a medieval hospital with six much-loved paintings by the greatest of the Flemish Primitives, Hans Memling. The fascinating medieval hospital might reopen in 1997, but the Memling art is wide open. His *Mystical Wedding of St. Catherine* triptych deserves a close look. Catherine and her "mystical groom," the baby Jesus, are flanked by a headless John the Baptist and a pensive John the Evangelist. The chairs are there so you can study it. If you understand the Book of Revelations, you'll understand St. John's wild and intricate vision. The Reliquary of St. Ursula, an ornate little minichurch in the same room, is filled with impressive detail (100BF, open daily 9:30–17:00; off-season closed 12:30–14:00 and Wednesday, Mariastraat 38).

▲▲**Straffe Hendrik Brewery Tour**—Belgians are Europe's beer connoisseurs. This fun and handy tour is a great way to pay your respects. The happy gang at this working family brewery gives entertaining and informative 45-minute/three-language tours (usually by friendly Inge, 120BF including a beer, piles of very steep steps, a great rooftop panorama, daily on the hour 11:00–17:00, occasionally skipping 14:00, October–March 11:00 and 15:00 only, 1 block past church and canal, take right down skinny Stoofstraat, bordering the Beguinage towards the center on the square called Walplein, #26, tel. 332697). Originally "Henri Maes," this delicious brew is now known as Straffe Hendrik (strong Henry). They remind their drinkers: "The components of the beer are vitally necessary and contribute to a well-balanced life-pattern. Nerves, muscles, visual sentience, and a healthy skin are stimulated by these in a positive manner. For longevity and life-long equilibrium, drink Straffe Hendrik in moderation!"

Their bistro, where you'll be given your included-with-the-tour beer, serves a quick and hearty lunch plate (the 150BF "bread with paste and vegetables" is the best value, although the 250BF "meat selection and vegetables" is a beer-drinker's picnic for two). You can eat indoors with the smell of hops or outdoors with the smell of hops. This is a great place to wait for your tour or to linger afterwards—just watch out for the medieval whoopee cushions on the tables.

▲▲**Beguinage**—For military (and various other) reasons, there were more women than men in the medieval Low Countries. Towns provided Beguinages, a dignified place in which these "Beguines" could live a life of piety and service (without having to take the same vows a nun would). You'll find Beguinages all over Belgium and Holland. Bruges' Beguinage almost makes you want to don a habit and fold your hands as you walk under its wispy trees and whisper past its frugal little homes. For a thin slice of Beguinage life, walk through the simple museum (Beguine's House, 60BF with English flier, open daily 10:00–12:00 and 13:45–17:30, closes at 18:00 on Sunday, open much less off-season).

Minnewater—Beyond the Beguinage is Minnewater, an idyllic, clip-clop world of flower boxes, canals, swans, and tour boats packed like happy egg cartons. Beyond that is the train station.

Almshouses—Walking from the Beguinage back to the center, you might detour along Nieuwe Gentweg to visit one of about 20 almshouses in the city. At #8, go through the door (free) into the peaceful courtyard. This was a medieval form of housing the poor. The rich would pay for someone's tiny room here in return for lots of prayers.

Lace and Windmills by the Moat—A ten-minute walk from the center to the northeast end of town brings you to three windmills strung out along a pleasant grassy setting on the "big moat" canal (between Kruispoort and Dampoort, on the Bruges side of the moat). One of the windmills (St. Janshuys-molen) is open for visitors (40BF, 9:30–12:45 and 13:45–17:00, closed October through April), and a fourth windmill may be completed in 1997. Bruges used to have 27 windmills.

To actually see lace being made, drop by the nearby Lace Centre, where ladies toss bobbins madly as their eyes go bad (40BF includes demonstration and a small lace museum, Kant-centrum, next to the Jerusalem church, weekdays 10:00–12:00 and 14:00–18:00, closes at 17:00 Saturday, closed Sunday, Peper-straat 3). The Folklore Museum, in the same neighborhood, is cute but forgettable (80BF, open daily 9:30–17:00, less off-season, Rolweg 40). To find either place, ask for the Jerusalem church.

▲▲**Rent a Bike**—While the sights are close enough for easy walking, the town is a treat to bike through, and you'll be able to get away from the tourist center. Consider a peaceful evening ride through the back streets and around the outer canal. Rental shops have maps and ideas. The TI sells a handy "5X On The Bike Around Bruges" map/guide, narrating five different bike routes through the idyllic nearby countryside. The best basic trip is 30 minutes along the canal out to Damme and back. The Netherlands/Belgium border is a 40-minute pedal beyond Damme. Two shops rent bikes under the belfry on Hallestraat (70BF/1 hour, 150BF/4 hours, 250BF/day, free child seats). At either shop, you can pick up a bike at 18:00, and drop it back the next morning for the four-hour rate. Popelier Eric's doesn't require a deposit (#14 Hallestraat, daily 10:00–20:30, tel. 343262, free bike maps), but the shop at Hallestraat 4 does (1,000BF, passport, or credit-card imprint).

Tours of Bruges

Bruges by Bike—The Backroad Bike Company leads daily bike tours through the nearby countryside (450BF, 30 km, 2–4 hrs, tel 050/343045).

Bruges by Boat—The most relaxing and scenic (if not inform-ative) way to see this city of canals is by boat, with the captain narrating. Boats leave from all over town (copycat 35-minute rides, 170BF, 10:00–18:00).

City Minibus Tours—"City Tour Bruges" gives 50-minute/330BF rolling overviews of the town in a 13-seat, three-skylight minibus, with dial-a-language headsets and ear-phones. The tour leaves hourly (on the hour, 10:00–19:00 in summer, 18:00 spring and fall) from the Market Square. The audio is clean, and the narration gives a good history as you tour the town the lazy way.

Bus Tours of Countryside—Quasimodo Tours is a hip outfit offering those with extra time two all-day tours through the rarely visited Flemish countryside. You can do "Flanders Fields" on Tuesday and Thursday from 9:00–16:30 (possibly Sunday upon request) and see WWI battlefields, trenches, memorials, and poppy-splattered fields. On Monday, Wednesday, and Friday, it's "Triple Treat": the port of Damme, a castle, monastery, brewery, and chocolate factory, and sampling the treats—a waffle, chocolate, and beer. Tours are in English only (22-seat bus, canceled if eight don't sign up, lots of walking, pickup at your hotel or the train station, no smoking, 1,300BF, 1,000BF for backpackers, tel. 050/370470 to book, fax 374960).

Walking Tours—Local guides walk small groups through the core of town daily in July and August (120BF, depart from TI at 15:00, 1,200BF for a private guide). The tours, while earnest, are heavy on history and in two languages, so they may be less than peppy. Still, to propel you beyond the pretty gables and canal swans of Bruges, they are good medicine.

Self-Guided Chocolate Tastebud Tours—Bruggians are connoisseurs of fine chocolate. You'll be tempted by chocolate-filled display windows all over town. Godiva is the best big factory/high-price/high-quality local brand, but for the finest small-family operation, drop by Maitre Chocolatier Verbeke. While Mr. Verbeke is busy downstairs making chocolates, Mrs. Verbeke makes sure customers in the shop get the chocolate of their dreams. Ask her to assemble a small 100-gram bag (80BF, about seven pieces, the smallest amount sold) of your favorites. Most are "pralines," which means they're filled. While the "hedgehogs" are popular, be sure to get a "pharaoh's head." Pray for cool weather, since it's closed when it's very hot. (Open at least in the mornings on Tuesday, Wednesday, Friday, and Saturday, a block off the Market Square at Geldmuntstraat 25, tel. 334198.)

Sleeping in Bruges
(30BF = about $1, tel. code 050, zip code: 8000)

Sleep Code: **S** = Single, **D** = Double/Twin, **T** = Triple,
Q = Quad, **b** = bathroom, **t** = toilet only, **s** = shower only,
CC = Credit Card (Visa, MasterCard, Amex). Everyone
speaks English.

Listed from most expensive to cheapest (not by value or
preference), all places are located between the train station and
the old center, with the most distant (and best) being a few blocks
beyond the Market to the north and east. All include breakfast,
are on quiet streets, and (with two exceptions) keep the same
prices throughout the year. Assuming you'll arrive at the Market
Square by foot or bus, I'll give hotel directions using a 12-hour
clock, as if you were standing with your back to the belfry.

Hotels

Hansa Hotel offers 20 rooms in a completely modernized old
building. It's bright and tastefully decorated in elegant pastels.
This is a great splurge, with best prices Sunday through
Thursday nights (Sb-2,700BF–3,500BF, Db-3,000BF–
3,800BF, extra bed 1,250BF, price varies with size of room,
elevator, run by Johan and Isabelle, CC:VMA, a block north of
Market, Niklaas Desparsstraat 11, tel. 338444, fax 334205, E-
mail: information@hansa.be). Head for Vlamingstraat at 1:00
and take the first left.

Hotel Aarendshuis, an old merchant's mansion, is a place
to luxuriate. Family run with spacious rooms, chandeliered
public places, and a small garden, it's both kid-friendly and
classy (prices vary with size and luxury: Sb-1,700BF–2,000BF,
Db-2,500–3,500BF, Tb-3,500BF, Qb-4,000BF, kids under 10
free, grand boil-your-own-eggs buffet breakfast included,
300BF carpark, elevator, CC:VMA, 2 blocks off the Burg at
Hoogstraat 18, tel. 337889, fax 330816). Immediately to your
right at 4:00, take Briedelstraat, which becomes Hoogstraat.

Hans Memling gets more interesting as its owner, Gilbert,
does. The parrot speaks Flemish, while the first king and queen
of an independent Belgium (Leopold I and Louise Marie, 1835)
peer down on you through the chandeliers as you breakfast.
There's Mozart in the morning and Beethoven in the afternoon. The giant living/breakfast room is literally palatial, while
the 17 huge upstairs bedrooms are decorated with a man's
touch (Sb-1,750BF, Db-2,300BF, Tb-2,800BF, Qb-3,400BF,

cheaper in winter, skimpy breakfast, elevator, 2 blocks north of Market, Kuipersstraat 18, tel. 332096, easy phone reservations if arriving before 18:00). At 11:00, take Sint Jakobsstraat for 1 block, angle right through Eiermarkt square to Kuipersstraat. Across the street, **Hotel Cavalier** is tall and skinny with less charm, but serves a hearty buffet breakfast in a royal setting (Sb-1,800BF, Db-2,300BF, Tb-2,800BF, Qb-3,200BF, two lofty "backpackers doubles" on the fourth floor for 1,600BF, run by friendly Viviane De Clerck, CC:VM, Kuiperstraat 25, tel. 330207, fax 347199).

Hotel St. Christophe is like a medieval motel overlooking a garden (D-1,800BF, Db-2,600BF, Nieuwe Gentweg 76, CC:VMA, tel. 331176, fax 340938). The annex in back has garden views but cheap-feeling rooms. At 5:00 (to the right behind you), take Wollestraat a ten-minute walk to Nieuwe Gentweg.

Hotel Rembrandt-Rubens has 18 rooms in a creaky 500-year-old building, with tipsy floors, throw rugs, elephant tusks, a gallery of creepy old paintings, and probably the holy grail in a drawer somewhere (S-1,000BF, Ss-1,400BF, one D-1,500BF, Ds-2,000BF, Db-2,300BF, Tb-2,900BF, Qb-3,800BF, locked up at 24:00, on a quiet square between the Memlings and the brewery at Walplein 38, tel. 336439). The breakfast room (which must have been the knights' hall) overlooks a canal (while Rembrandt and Rubens overlook you from an ornately carved and tiled 1648 chimney). There's a little warmth behind Mrs. DeBuyser's crankiness. She's run the place for 44 years. At 8:00, take Steenstraat 2 blocks to the square, turn left on Mariastraat, then right on Walstraat.

The **Hotel Karel de Stoute**, run by smiling Ray Weewauters, is a 15th-century house with carved railings, a huge chandelier, and comfortable rooms (Sb-2,400BF, Db-2,850BF, Tb-3,400BF, double beds cheaper than twins, some rooms are smoky, CC:VMA, Moerstraat 23, tel. 343317, fax 344472). Take Sint Jakobsstraat at 11:00, first left on Geldmuntstraat, first right on Geerwiynstraat, then left on Moerstraat.

Hotel t'Keizershof is a doll house of a hotel that lives by its motto, "Spend a night, not a fortune." It's simple and tidy, with eight small, cheery rooms split between two floors, a shower and toilet on each (S-925BF, D-1,300BF, T-1,900BF, run by Stefaan and Hilda, a block in front of the train station, Oostmeers 126, easy parking, tel. 338728).

Bed and Breakfasts

These places offer the best value. Each is central, run by people who enjoy their work, and offers three or four doubles you'd pay 2,000BF–2,200BF for in a hotel. **Yvonne De Vriese** rents three B&B rooms on a corner overlooking two canals (S-1,000BF, D-1,500BF, Db-1,800BF, plus 500BF for third or fourth person, breakfast served in your room, all with fridge, TV, stereos, and little libraries, CC:VMA, free parking, 4 blocks east of Burg, Predikheren-straat 40, bus #6 or #16 from station, tel. 334224). The Db-room is smaller, on the ground floor, and closer to traffic. D-rooms are big and bright, one overlooks both canals, and the other is on the quiet back side. At 4:00, take Briedelstraat to the Burg Square, go through archway, pass fish market, turn left on Braambergstraat, which becomes Predikherenstraat. A block away, **Jan Degeyter** rents two spacious rooms on a quiet street (Db-1,800BF, Tb- 2,300BF, lots of stairs, CC:VMA, Waalsestraat 40, tel./fax 331199).

Koen and Annemie Dieltiens are a young couple who enjoy translating for the guests who eat a hearty breakfast around a big table in their bright, homey, comfortable house (S-1,100BF, Sb-1,400BF, D-1,400BF, Db-1,800BF, T-1,900BF, Tb-2,300BF, Qb-2,800BF, no smoking, lots of steep stairs, 3 blocks east of Market, Sint-Walburgastraat 14, tel. 334294, fax 335230). They are a friendly wealth of information on Bruges. At 1:00, take Philipstockstraat, turn left on Wapenmakersstraat, then take first right. Around the corner you'll find **Paul and Roos Gheeraert**, who live on the first floor, while their guests take the second. Lots of stairs but with bright, comfy rooms, this is a fine value (Sb-1300BF, larger Sb-1500BF, Db-1,600BF, larger Db-1,800BF, Tb-2,300BF, 4 blocks east of Market, Rid-derstraat 9, tel. 335627, fax 345201).

Chris Deloof's rooms are another good value in the old center. The ones with showers are more elegant, but the upstairs A-frame lofty room is fun (Ss-1,100BF, D-1,00BF, Ds-1,900BF, small shared kitchen available, Geerwijnstraat 14, tel. 340544, fax 059/803472). Chris, who teaches cooking, will cook up a good dinner for you (price depends on menu). At 11:00, take Sint Jakobsstraat, to the first left on Geldmuntstraat, then first right on Geerwijnstraat.

Youth Hostels

Bruges has several good hostels offering beds for around 350BF in three- to seven-bed rooms. Pick up the hostel info sheet at the station TI. Smallest, loosest, and closest to the center are: **Snuffel Travelers Inn** (Ezelstraat 47, tel. 333133), **Bauhaus International Youth Hotel** (Langestraat, 135, tel. 341093), and **Passage** (Dweerstraat 26, tel. 340232, its hotel next door has 1,200BF doubles). Bigger, more modern, and less central are: **International Youth Hostel Europa** (Baron Ruzettelaan 143, tel. 352679), **IYH Herdersbrug** (Louis Coiseaukaai 46, tel. 599321), and the **Merkenveld Scout Center** (Merkenveldweg 15, tel. 277698).

Eating in Bruges

Specialties include mussels cooked a variety of ways (one order can feed two people), fish dishes, grilled meats, and french fries. Every local has a favorite bistro. Touristy places on the square are affordable, while candle-cool bistros flicker on back streets.

Wittekop is very Flemish, specializing in the beer-soaked equivalent of *beef bourgignon* (18:00–24:00, closed Sunday and Monday, 14 Sint Jakobsstraat). **De Kluiver** offers great "seasnails in spiced bouillon" simmered in a whispering jazz ambiance (12 Hoogstraat, closed Wednesday and Thursday). For jazz and hearty budget spaghetti, head for **Estaminet**, in front of peaceful Astrid Park (open from 11:00 on, closed Monday afternoon and all day Thursday, Park 5). Another jazzy place to join locals for dinner is **De Versteende Nacht Jazzcafe** on 11 Langestraat (19:00–02:00, closed Sunday and Monday). Locals like **La Dentelliere** for its good food, service, and prices (33 Wijngaardstraat) and **Vlissinghe 1515**, a pub on Blekersstraat, for its friendly atmosphere.

Picnics: Geldmuntstraat is a handy street when you're hungry. A block off the Market Square at Geldmuntstraat 1, the **Fresh Spegelaere** shop serves sandwiches and salads by weight (100g is a tiny tub, open 7:00–18:30, closed Sunday, counter seating). Across the street is **Pickles Frituur,** for the best sit-down fries in town. A block further, past the Verbeke chocolate shop, the **Nopri Supermarket** is great for picnics (push-button produce pricer lets you buy as little as one mushroom, open 9:00–18:30, closed Sunday). The small **Delhaize** grocery store is on the Market Square opposite the belfry (8:00–12:00 and 13:30–18:00, opens at 9 on Saturday, closed Sunday). For your midday "daily bread," enjoy a huge selection of sandwiches at **Dagelijks Brood** on 21 Philipstockstraat (7:00–18:00, closed Tuesday). For midnight munchies, head to the tiny **Nightshop** grocery across the street (14:00–02:00, closed Monday, 14 Philipstockstraat).

Frietjes: These local french fries are a treat. Proud and traditional *frituurs* serve tubs of fries and various local-style shish kebabs. Belgians dip their *frietjes* in mayonnaise, but ketchup is there for the Yankees (along with spicier sauces). For a quick, cheap, and scenic meal, hit a *frituur* and sit on the steps or benches overlooking the Market Square, about 50 yards past the post office.

Beer: Belgium boasts more than 350 types of beer. Straffe Hendrik (strong Henry), a potent local brew, is, even to a Bud Lite kind of guy, obviously great beer. Among the more unusual of the others to try: Kriek (a cherry-flavored beer), Dentergems (with coriander and orange peel), and Trappist (a dark, monk-made beer). Non-beer-drinkers enjoy Kriek and Frambozen (the cherry and raspberry-flavored beers). Each beer is served in its own unique glass. Any pub carries the basic beers, but for a selection of 300 types, drink at **t'Brugs Beertje** (5 Kemelstraat, open 16:00–1:00, closed Wednesday). When you've finished those, step next door, where **Dreupel Huisje "1919"** serves more than 100 Belgian gins and liqueurs (closed Tuesday). Another good place to gain an appreciation of the Belgian beer culture is **de Garre**, off Breidelstraat (between Burg and Markt) on the tiny Garre alley (open 12:00–24:00; off-season closed Wednesday).

Transportation Connections—Bruges

From Brussels, all of Europe is at your fingertips (see Brussels Connections, below). Train information, tel. 382382.

By train to: Brussels (2/hr, 1 hr), **Ghent** (3/hr, 20 min), **Oostende** (3/hr, 15 min), **Köln** (6/day, 4 hrs), **Paris** (6/day, 4 hrs, via Brussels), **Amsterdam** (hrly, 3.5 hrs).

Trains from England: Bruges is an ideal "welcome to Europe" stop after crossing the English Channel. Catch the London/Victoria–Ramsgate train (2 hrs), then the Ramsgate–Oostende boat (4.5 hrs) or jetfoil (90 min, $14 extra), and then the Oostende–Bruges train (15 min). Five boats run daily (cost of ferry crossing: 800BF one way, same price for the cheap five-day return ticket, one overnight boat, 24:00–6:00; 1,000BF cabins for two, tel. 059/559955). Or you can take the English Channel tunnel Eurostar train from London to Brussels, then transfer to Bruges.

BRUSSELS

Brussels, the capital of Belgium, is also the capital of Europe. This is where Europe comes together. Since WWII, it has been the convenient home of both NATO and the "government of Europe," working busily to move things towards unity. It's the linguistic hinge as well (60 percent of all Belgians speak the Germanic Flemish and 40 percent speak the Romantic French). It's easy to miss Brussels as you zip from Amsterdam to Paris on the train, but those who stop are pleasantly surprised.

Brussels, like Belgium, is officially a bilingual country. Most maps and signs here list place names in French and Flemish (Dutch). Since 80 percent of the people in Brussels speak French, I have normally listed only the French names in this chapter.

Planning Your Time
Brussels is low on great sights and high on ambiance. On a quick trip, a day and a night are enough for a good first taste. It could even be done as a day trip from Bruges (an hour away by train) or a stopover on the Amsterdam–Paris ride (nearly hourly trains). The main reason to stop—La Grand Place—takes only a few minutes to see. With very limited time, skip the indoor sights and enjoy a coffee or a beer on the square. Even travelers not "into art" can spend an enjoyable three hours at Brussels' ancient- and modern-art museums. If you do the auto and military museums (side by side), plan on a three-hour trip from the town center. Most important, this is a city to browse and wander.

Brussels

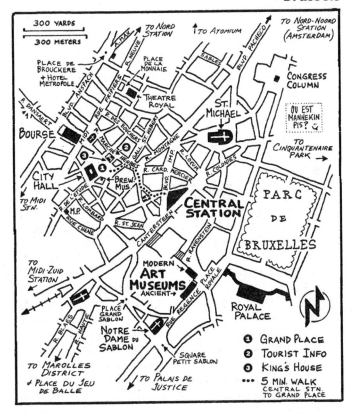

300 YARDS
300 METERS

PLACE DE
BROUCKERE
+ HOTEL
METROPOLE

TO NORD
STATION

TO ATOMIUM

TO NORD-NOORD
STATION
(AMSTERDAM)

PLACE
DE LA
MONNAIE

SABLES

BLVD PACHECO

CONGRESS
COLUMN

R. DANSAERT

R. NEUVE

THEATRE
ROYAL

ST.
MICHAEL

OU EST
MANNEKIN
PIS? ☺

BOURSE

CITY
HALL

TO MIDI
STN.

BLVD ANSPACH

R. ANTSACH

RUE FRITIERS

R. DES BOUCHERS

MARCHÉ AUX HERBES

RUE AU BEURRE

GALL. ST. HUBERT

R. MONTAGNE

IMP. COUDENBERG

R. COLONIES

R. CARD. MERCIER

R. DE L'ETUVE

RUE LOMBARD

M.P.

RUE CHENE

R. ST. JEAN

CAANTERSTEEN

BREW.
MUS.

CENTRAL
STATION

R. RAVENSTEIN

PARC
DE
BRUXELLES

TO
CINQUANTENAIRE
PARK

TO
MIDI-ZUID
STATION

MODERN
ART
MUSEUMS
ANCIENT→

PLACE
ROYALE

RUE REGENCE

PLACE
GRAND
SABLON

NOTRE
DAME DU
SABLON

ROYAL
PALACE

N

R. BLAES

R. HAUTE

SQUARE
PETIT SABLON

TO MAROLLES
DISTRICT
+ PLACE DU JEU
DE BALLE

TO PALAIS DE
JUSTICE

❶ GRAND PLACE
❷ TOURIST INFO
❸ KING'S HOUSE

••• 5 MIN. WALK
CENTRAL STN.
TO GRAND PLACE

Orientation
(tel. code: 02)

Central Brussels is defined by a ring of roads (which replaced the old city wall) called the Pentagon. All hotels and nearly all the sights I mention are within this circle. The center of this center is the main square (La Grand Place), Tourist Office, and the Central Station (3 blocks away). Leaving the Central Station, walk downhill (through the arch in the curved Le Meridien Hotel across the street), turn right, and you'll soon reach a small square with a fountain. To get to the Grand Place, turn left at the far end of the square; to get to the TI, continue straight past the square for 1 block.

Tourist Information: Although the office at 63 rue du Marche-aux-Herbes is for all of Belgium, it does Brussels just

fine (downhill 3 blocks from the Central Station, open daily
9:00–19:00, closes Saturday and Sunday from 13:00–14:00,
closes off-season at 18:00, tel. 02/504-0390). There's also an
office in the city hall in the Grand Place (open daily 9:00–18:00
in-season, tel. 513 8940). Among their countless fliers, pick up
"Destination Brussels," "What's On," a city map, and a public
transit map. The 80BF *Brussels Guide & Map* booklet is worthwhile if you want a series of neighborhood walks and a more
complete explanation of the city's many museums.

Arrival in Brussels

By Train: Brussels can't decide which of its three stations is
the main one. Most international trains leave and land at the
Nord or Midi Stations. The Midi Station (also called Zuid or
South) is the place to catch the speedy Eurostar train that gets
you to London in three hours. The area around the Midi Station is a rough-and-tumble immigrant neighborhood (with a
towering Ferris wheel), and the area around the Nord Station
is a dangerous red-light district. Trains zip under the city, connecting all three stations every two minutes or so. Ask on
board if your train stops at Central. If not, it's a free and easy
three-minute chore to connect from Nord or Midi. As you
wait for your train, look at the track notice board that tells
which train is on deck. They zip in and out constantly. Anxious
travelers often board the wrong train on the right track. The
Central Station has handy services (grocery store, info desks,
waiting rooms, etc.) and is nearest to the sights.

By Plane: Shuttle trains run between the Central and
Nord stations to Brussels International Airport 14 km away
(85BF, 3/hour, 20 min). Airport info: tel. 723-6010.

Helpful Hints

Laundry: Laundromat "Washing 65" is handy to my recommended hotels and has plenty of machines (65 rue du Midi,
open daily 7:00–21:00, good change machine, soap machine,
clear English instructions).

Off-Season Hours: Museums usually close one hour earlier off-season.

Getting Around Brussels

Most of Brussels' sights are walkable. For a few of the sights,
like the auto and military museums, take the Métro. The TI's

La Grand Place

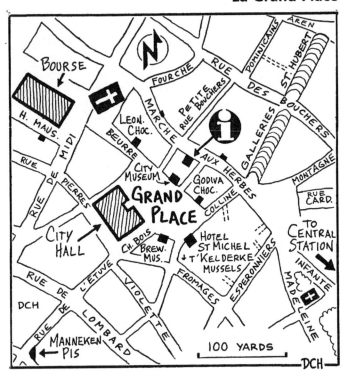

excellent "Métro Tram Bus Plan" is free. The integrated system uses one 50BF ticket that is good for one hour (notice the time when you first stamp it, buy tickets on bus or at Métro stations). The deals (five tickets for 230BF, ten tickets for 320BF) are available at newsstands and Métro stations, and TIs sell the one-day ticket for 125BF (cheaper than three rides).

Sights—Brussels

▲▲▲**La Grand Place**—Brussels' main square, aptly called La Grand Place, is the heart of the old town and the greatest sight Brussels has to offer. Any time of day it's worth swinging by to see what's going on. Concerts, flower markets, sound-and-light shows, endless people-watching—it entertains (as do the streets around it).

The museums on the square are pretty dull. You'll see them advertised and featured in the travel literature, but only because there's precious little else in town with a turnstile worth paying to use. The **Hôtel de Ville**, or city hall, with the tallest spire, is the square's centerpiece (80BF, visits only by 30-minute tours, Tuesday 11:30 and 15:15, Wednesday 15:15, and Sunday 12:15) but no big deal to see. The **City Museum**, opposite the city hall, is in a neo-Gothic building (1875) called "the King's House" (in which no king ever lived). The top floor has an entertaining room full of costumes the Manneken has pissed through, the middle floor features maps and models of old Brussels, and the bottom floor has a few paltry pieces of art (80BF, open 10:00–12:30 and 13:30–17:00, closed Friday). Opposite the King's House, the **Brewery Museum** with one room of old brewing paraphernalia and one room of new (all explained in Flemish and French), is really bad (100BF with a beer, open daily 10:00–17:00). The **Lace and Costume Museum** has not a word of English and is worthwhile only to those who have devoted their lives to the making of lace (80BF, open 10:00–12:30 and 13:30–17:00, closed Wednesday, 4 Violette, a block off the square).

For many, the best thing about the Grand Place is **chocolate** at Godiva's or Leonidas. The Godiva shop offers the very best (120BF for 100 grams). But most locals sacrifice 10 percent in quality to double their take by getting their fix at Leonidas (50 BF for 100 grams). The smallest amount sold is 100 grams—six to eight pieces.

Manneken-Pis—Brussels is a great city, but its mascot (apparently symbolizing the city's irreverence) is a statue of a little boy urinating. For the story about this little squirt, read a postcard stand. It's 3 short blocks off the Grand Place, but for exact directions, I'll let you ask a local *"Ou est le Manneken-Pis?"* He may be wearing some clever outfit. By tradition, costumes are sent to Brussels from around the world. Cases full of these are on display in the City Museum (described above).

▲▲▲**Museum of Ancient Art**—This museum, featuring Flemish and Belgian art of the 14th to 18th centuries, is packed with a dazzling collection of masterpieces by Van der Weyden, Breughel, Bosch, and Rubens (free, worthwhile 20BF map of ancient- and modern-art museum complex, open 10:00–12:00 and 13:00–17:00, closed Monday, rue de la Regence 3, tel. 508-3211). Start your visit with the free 30-minute audiovisual lesson in Flemish art appreciation. This show features a handful of pieces, enabling you to go through the museum with an ability to understand these as if you were an art historian. Or get headsets at the info desk and take a Walkman tour (100BF). For more information and a good souvenir, consider the 100BF *Twenty Masterpieces of the Art of Painting—A Brief Guided Tour* guide booklet. Tour the rooms of this (and the modern) museum in numerical order.

▲**Museum of Modern Art**—Take a look at Belgium's contribution to the art of the 19th and 20th centuries (free, connected to the ancient-art museum by underground escalator, open 10:00–13:00 and 14:00–17:00, closed Monday, place Royale 1). Each section is well-described in English. David's neoclassical work (e.g., *Death of Morat*) is a treat, as are the surreal fantasies of René and Georgette Magritte. Enjoy riding the living room from one floor to the next.

▲**The Park of the Cinquantenaire**—This park sprawls out from under a massive triumphal arch, which was built in 1880 to celebrate the 50th anniversary of Belgian independence. While there's precious few of the governmental buildings of the European Union (EU) to get visually excited about, you can emerge from the Métro at the Schuman stop to be surrounded by the political headquarters of a more or less united Europe. The huge, star-shaped Berlaymont building (built in 1963 to house the Commission of the European Union) was polluted by asbestos insulation and is now empty and awaiting renovation. From there, walk ten minutes through the park to the AutoWorld and military museums (under the giant arch). The next Métro stop (Merode) is much a closer shot to the museums.

▲▲**AutoWorld**—This is a delight for any car enthusiast and even worthwhile for people who think a Studebaker is some kind of French cannibal dish (150BF, open daily 10:00–18:00, in the Palais Mondial, Cinquantenaire, Métro: Merode, tel. 736-4165). Starting with Mr. Benz's motorized tricycle of 1886, you'll walk through a giant hall filled with 400 historic cars. It's well-described in English. There is a one-hour/100BF Walkman tour available.

▲**The Royal Museum of the Army and Military History**— Wander through a vast collection of 19th-century weaponry and uniforms and a giant hall dedicated to airplanes of war (free, open 9:00–12:00 and 13:00–16:30, closed Monday, tel. 733-4493). There's a good display from the Belgian struggle for independence (early 1800s). Personnel shortages mean the WWI and WWII wings might be closed.

Belgian Centre of the Comic Strip—This strip joint is housed in an industrial warehouse designed by Horta, the local Art Nouveau great. It's free to get inside to visit the brasserie and bookstore. Upstairs, the comics are interesting only to the Belgians (180BF, 10:00–18:00, closed Monday, rue des Sables 20, tel. 219-1980).

Royal Museum of Central Africa—Remember the Belgian Congo? Brussels has an excellent museum of the Congo and much more of Africa (ethnography, sculptures, jewelry, colonial history, flora and fauna) an hour from the center by Métro (Métro 1A to "Montgomery"), then take tram #44 to its final stop, "Tervuren." Finally, walk 200 meters through the park to a palace (80BF, 10:00–17:00, weekends 10:00–18:00, tel. 769-5200).

Atomium—This giant atom, with escalators connecting the various "molecules" and a restaurant with a view in the top sphere, was the symbol of the 1958 Universal Exhibition held in Belgium (200BF, daily 9:00–20:00, open less off-season, Métro: Heysel, tel. 477-0977). Today it's the cheesy nucleus of a park on the edge of town that has the kid-pleasing **Mini-Europa,** with 1:25 scale models of 300 famous European buildings (380BF, discounts for kids, daily 9:30–18:00, tel. 478-0550).

Shopping, Markets, and Colorful Neighborhoods

Place du Grand Sablon—Near the ancient-art museum, this square is famous for its antique shops and its classy open-air antique market (Saturday 9:00–16:00, Sunday 9:00–12:00). The Wittamer bakery, also on the square, is known throughout Belgium for its elegant little pies and cakes. The Notre Dame of the Sablon Church is a good example of 15th-century flamboyant Gothic. Across the street (uphill from the church), the more cozy Place du Petit Sablon is surrounded by 48 statues representing the traditional professions that made this city a power in her day. A five-minute walk to the south brings you to the massive Palace of Justice (the largest, bulk-wise, of anything built in 19th-century Europe), towering like a giant hammer over the bars and junk dealers of this vibrant community. Nearby, a five-minute walk past the Palace, Europe's most enjoyable flea markets thrives at place du Jeu de Balle (daily from 7:00).

North of La Grand Place—A block north of the square is Grasmarkt/Marche-aux-Herbes. This was where the ancient trade route from London split (with one branch heading to Germany and the other branch to Italy). It's filled with people-watching fun. While there's not much to see of the EU buildings, an entertaining way to celebrate the unification of Europe is to drop into one of the Euroshops across the street from the TI and browse through all the Euro knickknacks.

The elegant Galeries Royales Saint-Hubert claims to be the first commercial gallery in Europe. Browse through the touristy restaurant streets as you head to the shopping center at place de la Monnaie. From there, follow rue Neuve, a pedestrian shopping street leading up to place Rogier near Gare du Nord. Detour over to place de Brouckere to wander through the turn-of-the-century splendor of Hotel Metropole (the hotel's story is told in a folder lying around on most tables). A coffee in the hotel's bar or on their terrace is a classy splurge.

Tours of Brussels

Chatterbus Tours (Bus Bavard, Babbelbus) offers the best organized insight into Brussels. This creative minibus tour makes hard-to-understand Brussels more than a collection of sights. The groups are small and the guides seem to care. The Chatterbus slogan is "Our guides are not parrots, our groups are not crowds." Guides expertly explain the delicate balance between French and Flemish through the architecture and art of the city. Starting with medieval and moving through modern styles, this is a study in how a region in an almost perpetual state of flux until the last century somehow managed to find some cohesion and create a modern state. Of special interest is the late-19th-century Art Nouveau style, especially as pioneered by Belgian Victor Horta. You'll see several of his buildings on the tour (daily mid-June through mid-September 10:00, meet your guide at Galeries Saint-Hubert, 90 rue Marche-aux-Herbes near the Grand Place, 300BF, cheaper for hostelers, tel. 673-1835). De Boeck's City Tours, a typical three-hour, tape-recorded bus tour, provides the handiest way to get the grand perspective on Brussels (780BF, discounted to 630BF with a Chunnel ticket, starts with a walk around the Grand Place at rue de la Colline 8, daily in-season at 10:00, 11:00, 14:00, and 15:00; off-season at 10:00 and 14:00; tel. 513-7744). You'll see (and learn about) the Royal Palace, Atomium, and the EU headquarters.

Sleeping in Brussels
(30BF = about $1, tel. code: 02, zip code: 1000)
Sleep Code: **S** = Single, **D** = Double/Twin, **T** = Triple, **Q** = Quad, **b** = bathroom, **t** = toilet only, **s** = shower only, **CC** = Credit Card (**V**isa, **M**asterCard, **A**mex). Everyone speaks English.

Like everything else, hotel prices are high in central Brussels. You have three budget options: modern youth hostels with double rooms, safe but dingy old places, and business hotels offering summer or weekend specials. September is very crowded, and finding a room without a reservation can be impossible.

Business Hotels with Summer Rates
The fancy (5,000BF–6,000BF) hotels of Brussels live off the business and diplomatic trade. They are desperately empty in July or August and on weekends (most Friday, Saturday, and Sunday nights). While many pay full fare during summer, if you ask for a summer rate you'll save about a third. If you go through the tourist office, you'll save even more—up to two-thirds. Four-star hotels in the center abound with summer rates of 2,000BF–2,500BF. If you persist and are willing to sink as low as three stars, you'll probably get a double with enough comforts to keep a diplomat happy, plus a fancy breakfast for as low as 1,500BF.

While the TI assured me that every day in July and August there are always tons of business-class hotel rooms on the push list, you can book in advance by calling the BTR room-booking service (tel. 513-7484). In these months, I'd arrive without a reservation, walk from the Central Station down to the TI, and let them book me a room within a few blocks of there. These seasonal rates apply only to business-class hotels. Budget accommodations charge the same throughout the year.

Moderate Hotels on or near the Grand Place
Hôtel L'Auberge Saint Michel, overlooking Europe's greatest square, features a royal setting and a family feel. Of its 15 rooms, some are old, some are new, either quiet in the back or grand with a view (overlooking the square, Sb-3,700BF, Db-4,200BF; without view, Sb-2,300BF, Db-2,700BF, breakfast in room-300BF, elevator, view comes with noise on weekends, run by the Calas family, CC:VMA, Grand Place 15, tel. 511-0956, fax 511-4600).

Hôtel La Madeleine, on the small square between the station and the Grand Place, is comfortable, hotelesque, and professionally run (S-1,300BF but no shower available, Sb-1,900BF, Db-2,800BF–3,300BF, Tb-3,900BF, elevator, CC:VMA, rue de la Montagne 22, tel. 513 2973, fax 502 1350).

Hôtel Opera, on a great people-filled street near the Grand Place, is professional, dark, and classy, with all the comforts and an elevator (Sb-1,950BF, Db-2,350BF, Tb-3,200BF, 200BF more in September, includes breakfast, CC:VMA, rue Gretry 53, tel. 219-4343, fax 219-1720).

Hotel Welcome, run by a bundle of hospitality energy named Meester Smeester, offers small but business-class rooms. With just ten rooms, it brags it's the smallest hotel in Brussels (small Sb/Db-2,200BF, Db-2,600BF–3,000BF, family deals, breakfast-250BF, free parking, reserve a week in advance, CC:VMA, at Ste. Catherine Métro stop on a characteristic old square, 23 Quai au Bois a Bruler, tel. 219 9546, fax 217 1887).

Atlas Hotel has bright, modern rooms with all the comforts but is not worth its winter rates (weekend and summer prices: Sb-2,700BF including breakfast, Db-2,900BF without breakfast, extra person-1,100BF, breakfast-400BF, CC:VMA, rue du Vieux Marche aux Grains 30, tel. 502 6006, fax 502 6935). Prices are 30 percent higher on off-season weekdays.

Hotel Pacific is gently run by Paul Powells, whose motto is "safe, clean, and cheap." While the charming breakfast room is 19th-century, the ramshackle upstairs is tree camp–deco. Still, the rooms are clean and spacious (if well-worn), the location is excellent, and Paul gives the place an enjoyable calmness (S-950BF, D-1,550BF, Ds-1,600BF–2,000BF, including a cheese omelet breakfast, showers-100BF, elevator, easy trusting phone reservations, rue Antoine Dansaert 57, tel. 511 8459).

Youth Hostels

Three classy modern hostels, in buildings that could double as small state-of-the-art minimum security prisons, are within a ten-minute walk of the Central Station. Each accepts people of all ages and charges about the same: S-660BF, D-1,080BF, beds in quads-440BF, beds in bigger dorms-400BF, sheets-120BF; nonmembers pay up to 100BF extra. All rates include breakfast and showers down the hall. These places serve cheap meals, and rooms are locked up from 10:00 to 14:00. The **Breughel Hostel**, a fortress of cleanliness, is handiest and most comfortable (18 of its rooms are bunk-bed doubles, midway between the

Midi and Central Stations, behind the Notre Dame de la Chapelle church, rue de St. Esprit 2, tel. 511-0436, open 7:00–10:00 and 14:00–24:00). The new **Sleepwell**, surrounded by highrise parking lots, is also comfortable (offers morning walking tour at 10:00, 22 rue de Damier, tel. 218-5050). **Jacques Brel** is a little farther out but still a reasonable walk to everything (rue de la Sablonniere 30, tel. 218-0187).

Eating in Brussels

Eat mussels in Brussels. They're served everywhere. You get a bucket and a pile of fries. Use one empty shell to tweeze out the rest of the mussels. When the mollusks are in season, from about July 10 through April, you'll get the big Dutch mussels. Locals take a break in May and June, when only the puny Danish variety is available. For an atmospheric cellar just off the Grand Place, step into the **t'Kelderke** (Grand Place 15, tel. 513-7344, open daily 12:00–02:00), serving local specialties, especially mussels (a splitable 2-kilo bucket of "*moules*" for 625BF). Breakfast in your hotel is expensive. Consider the 125BF breakfast special at the art deco **Falstaff** restaurant (daily 7:00–11:30, Rue Henri Maus 25, across from the Bourse, 511-9877). If Brussels puts you in an Art Nouveau mood, have a meal or coffee at the city's most atmospheric hangout, **De Ultieme Hallucinatie** (exotic 500BF meals, 316 rue Royale, 11:00– 03:00, Saturday and Sunday from 16:00, tel. 217-0614).

Transportation Connections—Brussels

By train to: Amsterdam (hrly, 3 hrs), **Paris** (6/day, 3 hrs), **Berlin** (7/day, 9 hrs), **Bern** (4/day, 8 hrs), **Frankfurt** (9/day, 5 hrs), **Munich** (9/day, 8 hrs), **Rome** (4/day, 17–20 hrs). Train info: tel. 219-2880.

To London: Brussels and London are now just three 140-mph hours apart by Eurostar train (under the English Channel in 20 minutes; 5/day, $154, or $75 with 14 days advance purchase, call 1-800-EUROSTAR in the U.S.A. to book). If you buy your Eurostar tickets in Brussels, you'll get your tickets immediately at the train station; travel agencies can't deliver until the next day.

Another option is the sloooow train and ferry combination (8/day, 4.5–7.5 hrs). Or save a little money by riding a Eurolines bus ($62 one-way, tel. 02/203-0707).

THE NETHERLANDS

- 13,000 square miles (the size of Maryland)
- 15 million people (1,150 per square mile, 15 times the population density of the U.S.)
- 1 guilder = about 70 cents

The Netherlands, Europe's most densely populated country, is also one of its wealthiest and best-organized. Efficiency is a local custom. The average income is higher than that in the United States. Though only 8 percent of the labor force are farmers, they cultivate 70 percent of the land, and you'll travel through vast fields of barley, wheat, sugar beets, potatoes, and flowers.

Holland is the largest of 12 states that make up the Netherlands. A generation ago, Belgium, the Netherlands, and Luxembourg formed the nucleus of a united Europe when they joined economically to form Benelux.

The word "Netherlands" means "lowlands." Half the country is below sea level, reclaimed from the sea (or rivers). That's why the locals say, "God made the Earth, but the Dutch made Holland." Modern technology and plenty of Dutch elbow grease have turned much of the sea into fertile farmland. While a new 12th state—Flevoland, near Amsterdam—has recently been drained, dried, and populated, Dutch reclamation projects are essentially finished.

The Dutch generally speak English, pride themselves on their frankness, and like to split the bill. Traditionally, Dutch cities have been open-minded, loose, and liberal (to attract sailors in the days of Henry Hudson), but they are now paying the price of this easygoing style. Amsterdam has become a bit too seedy for many travelers' tastes. Enjoy more sedate Dutch evenings by sleeping in a small town nearby and side-tripping into the big city.

The Dutch guilder (f, for its older name, florin) is divided into 100 cents (c). There are about f1.50 in a U.S. dollar (f1.50 = $1). To find prices in dollars, simply cut the price in guilders by a third (e.g., f60 = $40). The colorful Dutch money has Braille markings and classy watermarks.

The country is so small, level, and well-covered by trains and buses that transportation is a snap. Major cities are connected by speedy trains that come and go every ten or 15 minutes. Connections are excellent, and you'll rarely wait more than a few minutes. Round-trip tickets are discounted. Buses take you where trains don't, and bicycles take you where buses don't. Bus stations and bike-rental shops cluster around train stations. The national bus system (both within and between cities) runs on a uniform "strip card" system. You can buy various strip cards on the bus or more cheaply (15 strip cards, f11) at train stations, post offices, and some tobacco shops. If you're caught riding without a card, you have to take off your clothes.

Holland is a biker's dream. The Dutch, who average four bikes per family, have put small bike roads (with their own traffic lights) beside every big auto route. You can rent bikes at most train stations and drop them off at most others. (You can take bikes on trains, outside of rush hour, for f9.)

Smaller shops are open 9:00–18:00 and until 21:00 on Thursday (closed Sunday). The larger stores and supermarkets are open weekdays 8:00–20:00, and until 17:00 on Saturday (closed Sunday). The businesslike Dutch know no siesta, but many shopkeepers take Monday mornings off.

The best "Dutch" food is Indonesian (from the former colony). Find any Indisch restaurant and experience a *rijsttafel* (rice table). With as many as 30 spicy dishes, a *rijsttafel* can be split and still fill two hungry tourists. *Nasi rames* is a cheaper miniversion of a *rijsttafel*. Local taste treats are cheese, pancakes (*pannenkoeken*), Dutch gin (*jenever*, pronounced "ya nayver"), light Pilsner beer, and "syrup waffles" (*stroopwafel*). Yogurt in Holland (and throughout northern Europe) is delicious and drinkable right out of its plastic container. *Broodjes* are sandwiches of fresh bread and delicious cheese—cheap at snack bars, delis, and *broodje* restaurants. For cheap fast-food, try a Middle Eastern *shwarma*, roasted lamb in pita bread. Breakfasts are big by continental standards. Lunch and dinner are served at American times.

Experiences you owe your tongue in Holland: a raw herring (outdoor herring stands are all over), a slow coffee in a "brown café," an old *jenever* (smooth, local gin) with a new friend, and a giant *rijsttafel*. Tipping is not expected, but locals round the bill up (never more than 5 percent) as thanks for good service.

AMSTERDAM

Amsterdam is a progressive way of life housed in Europe's most 17th-century city. It's a city built on good living, cozy cafés, great art, street-corner jazz, stately history, and a spirit of live and let live. It has 800,000 people and as many bikes, with more canals than Venice—and as many tourists. While Amsterdam may box your Puritan ears, this great, historic city is an experiment in freedom.

Planning Your Time

While I'd sleep in nearby Haarlem, Amsterdam is worth a full day of sightseeing on even the busiest itinerary. While the city has a couple of must-see museums, its best sight is its own breezy ambiance. And the greatest way to experience that is Dutch-style: on two wheels.

Consider this plan for Amsterdam in a day:

Rent a bike at the station. Head west down Haarlemmer-straat, working your wide-eyed way through the Prinsengracht (along the canal) and gentrified Jordan area to Westerkerk, with the tallest spire in the city. Tour Anne Frank's House.

Pedal past the palace, through the Dam Square, down Kalverstraat (the city's bustling pedestrian mall), and poke into the sleepy Begijnhof. Roll down tacky Leidsestraat. Lunch at the Atrium (behind Spui) or a salad bar in the American Hotel (on Leidseplein).

Tour the Rijksmuseum and the Van Gogh Museum. Bike Spiegelstraat to Muntplein. Catch the hourlong canal-boat tour at Spui.

Pedal back down Damrak to the train station. For a detour through seedy, sexy, pot-smoking Amsterdam, roll down Damstraat, then down Oudezijds Voorburgwal through the land of Rastafarian "coffee shops," red lights over black tights, and sailors lost without the sea.

For Amsterdam in a day without a bike, consider riding the tram to the Rijksmuseum and Van Gogh Museum. After touring the museums, walk to Spui for a canal-boat tour, then walk to Anne Frank's House before returning to the station.

With two days in Holland, I'd side-trip by bike, bus, or train to an open-air folk museum and visit Edam or Haarlem. For a third day, I'd do the other great Amsterdam museums. With four days, I'd do the "historic triangle" or visit the Hague.

Orientation (tel. code: 020)

The central train station is your starting point (tourist information, bike rental, and trolleys and buses fanning out to all points). Damrak is the main street axis, connecting the station with Dam Square (people-watching and hangout center) and the Royal Palace. From this spine, the city spreads out like a fan, with 90 islands, hundreds of bridges, and a series of concentric canals (named "Princess," "Gentleman's" and "Emperor's") laid out in the 17th century, Holland's Golden Age. The city's major sights are within walking distance of Dam Square.

Tourist Information

Try to avoid Amsterdam's inefficient VVV office across from the train station. (VVV is Dutch for tourist-information office; open daily 9:00–17:00 or later; the TI in train station open 8:00–19:30). Most people wait 30 minutes just to pick up the information brochures and get a room. Avoid this line by studying the wall display of publications for sale and going straight to the cash window (where everyone ends up anyway, since any information of substance will cost you). Consider buying: a city map (f3.50), any of the four walking tour brochures (f4), and *What's On* (f3.50, monthly entertainment calendar listing all the museum hours and much more).

The TI on Leidsestraat is much less crowded and is open daily 9:00–19:00, closing at 17:00 on Sunday. But for 75 cents a minute, you can save yourself a trip by calling the tourist information toll-line at 06-3403-4066 (Monday–Saturday 9:00–17:00). If you're staying in nearby Haarlem, use the

uncrowded Haarlem TI (see Haarlem section, below) to
answer most of your Amsterdam questions and provide you
with the brochures.

Don't use the TI to book a room. The phone system is
easy, everyone speaks English, and the listings in this book are
a better value than the potluck booking you'd be charged for at
the TI.

Helpful Hints

Many shops close all day Sunday and Monday morning. A *plein*
is a square, *gracht* means canal, and most canals are lined by
streets with the same name. Handy telephone cards (f10 or f25)
are sold at the TI, GVB transit office, tobacco shops, post
office, and train stations. Beware of the bogus telephone offices
dressed up like government outlets but ready to rip you off.
Tourists are considered green and rich, and the city has more
than its share of hungry thieves.

Arrival in Amsterdam

By Train: Amsterdam swings, and the hinge that connects it to
the world is its perfectly central Central Station. Walk out the
door and you're in the heart of the city. You'll nearly trip over
trams ready to take you anywhere your feet won't. Straight
ahead is Damrak street, leading to Dam Square. With your
back to the entrance of the station, the TI and GVB are to
your left, just across the bus lanes.

By Plane: From Schiphol Airport, take the train to Amsterdam (4/hr, 20 min, f6). If you'll be staying in Haarlem, take a
direct express bus to Haarlem (#236 or #362, 2/hour, 30 min, f9).

Getting Around Amsterdam

The uncrowded and helpful transit-information office (GVB)
is next to the TI (in front of the train station). Its free multilingual "Tourist Guide to Public Transport" includes a transit
map and explains ticket options and tram connections to all
the sights.

By Bus and Tram: Individual tickets cost f3 (pay as you
board) and give you an hour on the system. "Strip cards" are
cheaper. Any downtown ride costs two strips (good for an hour
of transfers). A card with 15 strips costs f11 at the GVB, train
stations, post offices, airport, or tobacco shops throughout the
country. These strips are good on buses all over Holland (e.g.,

six strips for Haarlem to the airport), and you can share them with your partner. For f12, a Day Card gives you unlimited transportation for a 24-hour period from 06:00–06:00. If you get lost, ten of the city's 17 trams take you back to the central train station.

By Foot: The longest walk a tourist would take is 45 minutes from the station to the Rijksmuseum. Watch out for silent but potentially painful bikes, trams, and curb posts.

By Bike: One-speed bikes, with "brrringing" bells and two locks, rent for f8 per day at the central train station (6:00–22:00 weekdays, 8:00–22:00 weekends; deposit of f200, $150, or your credit card imprint required; entrance to the left down the ramp as you leave the station, tel. 624 8391). In the summer, arrive early or make an easy telephone reservation. The f1 flier shows a fun countryside bike ride starting with the free shuttle ferry behind the station. To take advantage of their (unadvertised) rate of four hours for f5, have the time of your checkout noted on the receipt.

By Boat: While the city is great on foot or bike, there are a "Canal Bus" and a similar "Museum Boat," with an all-day ticket that shuttles tourists from sight to sight. Tickets cost f22 (with discounts that'll save you about f5 on admissions). A sales booth is in front of the central train station, offering handy free brochures with museum times and admission prices. The narrated ride takes 90 minutes if you don't get off (every 30 minutes in summer, every 45 minutes off-season, seven stops, live quadrilingual guide, 10:00–17:00, discounted after 13:00, tel. 6222181).

Sights—Amsterdam

▲▲▲Rent a Bike—A day enjoying the bridges, bike lanes, and sleepy off-the-beaten-path canals on your own one-speed is the essential Amsterdam experience. The real joys of Europe's best-preserved 17th-century city are the countless intimate glimpses it offers: the laid-back locals sunning on their porches under elegant gables, rusted bikes that look as if they've been lashed to the same lamppost since the '60s, wasted hedonists planted on canalside benches. To escape to the countryside, hop on the free ferry behind the Amsterdam station. In five minutes, Amsterdam will be gone, and you'll be rolling through your very own Dutch painting. (See Getting Around Amsterdam, above, for bike rental info, and Planning Your Time for a suggested daylong bike tour of Amsterdam.)

Amsterdam

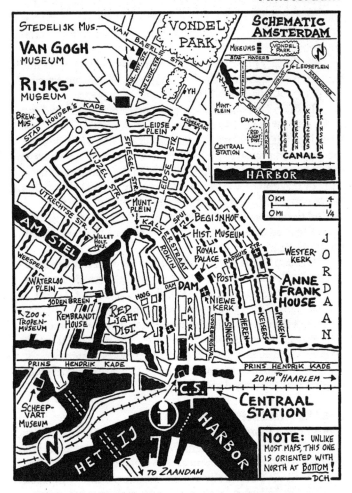

▲▲▲Rijksmuseum—Focus on the Dutch masters: Rembrandt, Hals, Vermeer, and Steen. For a list of the top 20 paintings, pick up the cheap (f1) leaflet "A Tour of the Golden Age" and plan your attack (or follow the self-guided tour, one of 20, in my *Mona Winks* guidebook). Audiotaped tours are available (f7.50, more than 200 paintings described, shortcuts advisable).

Follow the museum's chronological layout to see painting evolve from narrative religious art, to religious art starring the

Dutch love of good living and eating, to the Golden Age, when secular art dominates. With no local church or royalty to commission big canvases in the post-1648 Protestant Dutch republic, artists specialized in portraits of the wealthy city class (Hals), pretty still lifes (Claesz), and nonpreachy slice-of-life art (Steen). The museum has four quietly wonderful Vermeers. And, of course, a thoughtful brown soup of Rembrandt. Study the *Night Watch* history room before you see the real thing. Other works by Rembrandt show his excellence as a portraitist for hire (*De Staalmeesters*) and offer some powerful psychological studies, such as *St. Peter's Denial*—with Jesus in the murky background (f12.50, daily 10:00–17:00, great bookshop, decent cafeteria, tram 2 or 5 from the station, tel. 673 2121).

▲▲▲**Van Gogh Museum**—Next to the Rijksmuseum, this outstanding and user-friendly museum is a stroll through a beautifully displayed garden of van Gogh's work and life (f12.50, open daily 10:00–17:00, tel. 570 5200).

Stedelijk Modern Art Museum—Next to the Van Gogh Museum, this place is fun, far-out, and refreshing, with mostly post-1945 art, but also a permanent collection of Monet, van Gogh, Cézanne, Picasso, and Chagall (f8, daily 11:00–19:00, closes at 17:00 November–March, tel. 573-2911).

▲▲**Anne Frank House**—A fascinating look at the hideaway where young Anne hid when the Nazis occupied the Netherlands. Pick up the English pamphlet at the door and don't miss the thought-provoking neo-Nazi exhibit in the last room. Fascism smolders on (f10, open Monday–Saturday 9:00–17:00, Sunday 10:00–17:00, summer until 19:00, 263 Prinsengracht, tel. 556 7100). For an interesting glimpse of Holland under the Nazis, rent the powerful movie *Soldier of Orange* before you leave home.

Westerkerk—Near Anne Frank's House, this landmark church, with a barren interior and Amsterdam's tallest steeple, is worth climbing for the view (f3, ascend only with a guide, departures on the hour, April–September 10:00–16:00, closed Sunday, tel. 624 7766).

Royal Palace Interior—It's right on Dam Square, built when Amsterdam was feeling its global oats, and worth a look (f5, open daily mid-May through early September, 12:30–17:00).

▲▲**Canal-Boat Tour**—These long, low, tourist-laden boats leave continually from several docks around the town for a good, if uninspiring, 60-minute quadrilingual introduction to the city (f12, 2/hr). One very central company is at the corner of Spui and Rokin, about five minutes from Dam Square (9:30–22:00, tel. 623-3810). No fishing allowed but bring your camera for this relaxing orientation. Some prefer to cruise at night when the bridges are illuminated.

Biking and Walking Tours—The Yellow Bike Tour company offers bike tours (f29, three hours, choose between city or country) and city walking tours (f15, two hours) daily April through November (Nieuwezijds Kolk 29, near central station, tel. 620 6940).

Brewery Tour—The infamous Heineken brewery tours are in full slosh Monday–Friday 9:30–11:00 (f2, Stadhouderskade 78).

▲Begijnhof—Step into this tiny, idyllic courtyard in the city center to escape the crazy 1990s and feel the charm of old Amsterdam. Notice house #34, a 500-year-old wooden struc- ture (rare since repeated fires taught city fathers a little trick called brick). Peek into the hidden Catholic church, opposite the English Reformed church, where the pilgrims worshiped while waiting for their voyage to the New World (marked by a plaque near door). Be considerate of the people who live here (free, on Begijnensteeg Lane, just off Kalverstraat between #130 and #132, pick up English info flier at office near entrance).

Amsterdam History Museum—Offering the town's best look into the age of the Dutch masters, this creative and hardworking museum features Rembrandt's paintings, fine English descrip- tions, and a carillon loft. The loft comes with push-button recordings of the town bell tower's greatest hits and a self-serve carillon "keyboard" to ring a few bells yourself. The museum is next to the Begijnhof, 92 Kalverstraat (f8, weekdays 10:00–17:00, Saturday and Sunday 11:00–17:00, good-value restaurant). Its free pedestrian corridor is a powerful teaser.

Rembrandt's House—Interesting only to his fans, with 250 etchings (f7.5, Monday–Saturday 10:00–17:00, Sunday 13:00–17:00, 15-minute English audiovisual presentation upon request, Jodenbreestraat 4).

Holland Experience—Opening in 1997, this multimedia pres- entation uses 3-D effects, a movable floor, and "aroma manip- ulation" to highlight Holland's waterworks, flowers, and art (daily 9:00–22:00, Jodenbreestraat 8, near Rembrandt's House, tel. 422 2233).

▲Tropenmuseum (Tropical Museum)—As close to the Third World as you'll get without lots of vaccinations, this imaginative museum offers wonderful re-creations of tropical-life scenes and explanations of Third World problems (f10, weekdays 10:00–17:00, Saturday and Sunday 12:00–17:00, tram 9 to 2 Linnaeusstrasse).

Netherlands Maritime (Scheepvaart) Museum—This kid-friendly museum is fascinating if you're into Henry Hudson or *scheepvaarts* (f12.50, open daily 10:00–17:00, Sunday 12:00–17:00, closed Monday off-season, English explanations, bus #22 or #28 to Kattenburgerplein 1).

▲Herengracht Canal Mansion (Willet Holthuysen Museum)—This 1687 patrician house offers a fine look at the old rich of Amsterdam, with a good 15-minute English introductory film and a 17th-century garden in back (f5, open weekdays 10:00–17:00, Saturday and Sunday 11:00–17:00, tram 4 or 9 to Herengracht 605).

Our Lord in the Attic—Near the station, in the red-light district, you'll find a 17th-century merchant's house–turned-museum (Amstelkring museum), with a fascinating hidden church. This dates from 1661, when post-Reformation Dutch Catholics were not allowed to worship in public. The church fills the attics of several homes (f5, weekdays 10:00–17:00, Saturday and Sunday 13:00–17:00, O.Z. Voorburgwal 40).

▲Red-Light District—Europe's most high-profile ladies of the night shiver and shimmy in display-case windows along Voorburgwal, between the station and the Oudekerk. It's dangerous late at night but a fascinating walk at any other time after noon.

According to CNN statistics, more than 60 percent of Amsterdam's prostitutes are HIV-positive (but a naive tourist might see them as just hard-working girls from Latin America or Africa trying their best to build up a bank account—f35 at a time).

Amsterdam has two sex museums, one in the red-light district and one a block in front of the train station on Damrak. While visiting one can be called sightseeing, visiting both is a bit obsessive. Here's a comparison:

The red-light district sex museum is less offensive, with five sparsely decorated rooms relying heavily on badly dressed dummies acting out the roles that women of the neighborhood play. It also has videos, phone-sex phones, and a lot of uninspired paintings, old photos, and sculpture (f5, along the canal at Oudezijds Achterburgwal 54).

The Damrak sex museum goes much deeper, with many more rooms. It tells the story of pornography from the 1860s through today, starting with early French porno photos. Every sexual deviation is uncovered in its various displays, and the nude and pornographic art is a cut above the other sex museum's. Also interesting is the international sex art and memorabilia from Europe, India, and Asia. You'll find a Marilyn Monroe tribute and some S&M displays, too (f4, Damrak 18, a block in front of the station).

Vondelpark—This huge and lively city park gives a fragrant look at today's Dutch youth, especially on sunny summer weekends.

Leidesplein—Brimming with cafés, this people- and pigeon-watching square is an impromptu stage for street artists, accordionists, jugglers, and even kids playing piano. Sunny days are liveliest. Stroll nearby Lange Leidsedwarsstraat (1 block away) for a tastebud tour of ethnic eateries from Greece to Indonesia.

Shopping—Amsterdam brings out the browser even in those who were not born to shop. Ten general markets, open six days a week, keep folks who brake for garage sales pulling U-ies. Shopping highlights include Waterlooplein (flea market), the huge Albert Cuyp street market, various flower markets (daily along Singel Canal near the mint tower, or Munttoren), diamond dealers (free cutting and polishing demos at shops behind the Rijksmuseum and on Dam Square), and Kalverstraat, Amsterdam's teeming walking/shopping street (parallel to Damrak).

Sleeping in Amsterdam
(f1 = about 70 cents, tel. code: 020)
Sleep Code: **S** = Single, **D** = Double/Twin, **T** = Triple, **Q** = Quad, **b** = bathroom, **t** = toilet only, **s** = shower only, **CC** = Credit Card (Visa, MasterCard, Amex). Nearly everyone speaks English in the Netherlands, and prices include breakfast unless noted.

While I prefer sleeping in cozy Haarlem (see below), those into more urban charms will find that Amsterdam has plenty of beds. For a f5 fee, the VVV (tourist office) can find you a room in the price range of your choice.

Sleeping near the Station
Amstel Botel, the city's only remaining "boat hotel," is a ship-shape, bright, and clean, floating hotel with all the comforts in 175

rooms (Sb-f120, Db-f140, Tb-f180, f10 extra for canalside view, f10 breakfast, f25/day parking pass, CC:VMA, 400 yards from the station, on your left as you leave, you'll see the sign, Oosterdok-skade 2-4, 1011 AE Amsterdam, tel. 626 4247, fax 639 1952).

Sleeping between Dam Square and Anne Frank's House

Hotel Toren is a chandeliered historic mansion in a pleasant, canalside setting in downtown Amsterdam. This splurge is classy, quiet, and 2 blocks from Anne Frank's (S-f85, Sb-f165 to f185, three unadvertised D-f155, Db-f180, Tb-f230, bridal suites for f275 to f375 make you want to get married, CC:VMA, 164 Keizersgracht, 1015 CZ Amsterdam, tel. 622 6352, fax 626 9705). Well-heeled readers will prefer the pricier, fancier 17th-century **Canal House Hotel** a few doors down (Sb-from f210, Db-f225 to f265, CC:VMA, Keizersgracht 148, 1015 CX Amsterdam, tel. 622 5182, fax 624 1317).

Cheap hotels line the noisy main drag between the town hall and Anne Frank's House. These are all up a long, steep, and depressing stairway, with quieter rooms in the back. None serves breakfast. **Hotel Pax** is the cheapest, with generally large, plain but airy, and pleasant rooms, carefully managed by Mr. and Mrs. Veldhuizen (tiny D-f70, D-f85, T-f105, showers down the hall, Raadhuisstraat 37, tel. 624 9735), but the **Hotel Aspen**, a few doors down, is a better value. It's tidy and simple, with firmer beds and double-paned windows (S-f50, D-f75, Db-f100, Tb-f120, Qb-f160, CC:MA, Raadhuisstrasse 31, 1016 DC Amsterdam, tel. 626 6714).

Sleeping in the Leidseplein Area

The area around Amsterdam's museum square (Museumplein) and the rip-roaring nightlife center (Leidseplein) is colorful, comfortable, convenient, and affordable. These two hotels are on a quiet street, easy to reach from the central station (tram 1, 2, or 5 to Leidseplein, walk to canal and turn right), and within easy walking distance of the Rijksmuseum. **Kooyk Hotel** is a homey place with 19 rooms, four on the ground floor. Halls are narrow, some top rooms are dumpy, some canalside rooms are bright and cheery, bedspreads are faded, but beds and carpeting are new (S-f75, D-f115, T-f150, Q-f185, Quint-f225, run by Pierre, CC:VM, Leidsekade 82, 1017 PM Amsterdam, tel. 623 0295, fax 638 8337). **Hotel Maas**, with a phone, TV, and coffeepot in every room and an elevator, is a big, well-run, classy, quiet, and hotelesque place (S-f100, one D-f125, Db-f195 to f295, extra person-f50, CC:VMA, Leidsekade 91, 1017 PN Amsterdam, tel. 623 3868, fax 622 2613).

Hotel Keizershof is a wonderfully Dutch place, with six bright, airy rooms in a 17th-century canal house. You'll climb a steep spiral staircase to rooms named after old-time Hollywood stars. The friendly De Vries family makes this a treat and has plenty of fine eating advice (S-f65, D-f110, Ds-f130, Db-f140, T-f150, family deals, discounts for stays longer than two nights, includes classy breakfast, CC:VM, where Keizers canal crosses Spiegelstraat at Keizersgracht 618, 1017 ER Amsterdam, tel. 622 2855, fax 624 8412). It's a ten-minute walk from Leidseplein.

Hotel De Leydsche Hof is in a fine canalside locale with simple, quiet rooms. Its peaceful and friendly demeanor helps you overlook the dirty old carpets and flimsy cots (D-f85, Db-f95, Tb-f130, Qb-f170, no breakfast, Mr. Piller, 14 Leidsegracht, 1016 CK Amsterdam, tel. 623 2148). Also a ten-minute walk from Leidseplein.

Sleeping near Vondel Park
Weekend B&B, at the home of Karen McCuster, is a homey option. It's run as a B&B on Friday, Saturday, Sunday (three-day stay required) and as a B without the breakfast the rest of the week (no minimum stay required). Advance reservations are necessary (D-f75 to f100 for B&B weekend, 20 percent cheaper rest of week). Tram 2 from the station gets you to Zeilstraat 22 (third floor, 1075 SH Amsterdam, tel. 679 2753).

Youth Hostels
The **Christian Youth Hostel Eben Haezer** is scruffy, with 20-bed women's dorms and a 40-bed men's dorm. Friendly, well-run, in a great neighborhood, it has Amsterdam's best rock-bottom budget beds (f15 per bed with sheets and breakfast, maximum age 35, near Anne Frank's House, Bloemstrasse 179, tel. 624 4717). It serves cheap, hot meals, runs a snack bar, offers lockers to all, leads nightly Bible studies, and closes the dorms from 10:00 to 14:00. The hostel will happily hold a room for a phone call (ideally three–seven days in advance). Its sister Christian hostel, **The Shelter** (in the red-light district, open to any traveler, f18 for a bed, tel. 625 3230), is similar but definitely not preaching to the choir.

Amsterdam's two IYHF youth hostels are **Vondelpark**
(f28 with breakfast, f6 sheets, f5 extra for nonmembers, S-f66,
D-f77, Amsterdam's top hostel, lots of school groups, six to 22
beds per dorm, right on the park at Zandpad 5, tel. 683 1744,
fax 616 6591) and **Stadsdoelen YH** (f26 with breakfast, just
past Dam Square, March–October, Kloveniersburgwal 97, tel.
624 6832).

Eating in Amsterdam
Dutch food is basic and hearty. *Eetcafés* are local cafés serving
budget sandwiches, soup, eggs, and so on. Cafeterias, *broodje*
(sandwich shops), and automatic food shops are also good bets
for budget eaters. Picnics are cheap and easy. A central supermarket is Albert Heijn, near the flower market, at the corner of
Koningsplein and Singel canal (Monday–Saturday 9:00–20:00).

Eating near Spui in the Center
The city university's **Atrium** is a great, cheery budget cafeteria
(f8 meals, Monday–Friday 12:00–14:00 and 17:00–19:00, from
Spui, walk west down Landebrug Steeg past the canalside Café
t' Gasthuys 3 blocks to Oudezijds Achterburgwal 237, go
through arched doorway on the right, tel. 525-3999). Even
better (and more expensive) is the **La Place cafeteria** in the
Vroom Dreesmann department store (daily 9:30–18:00, Thursday until 21:00, Sunday 12:00–5:00, near Mint Tower, corner
of Rokin and Muntplein). The locals splurge for Dutch food at
Restaurant Haesje Claes (f25 entrees, daily 12:00–24:00,
Spuistraat 275, tel. 624 9998).

Eating in or near the Train Station
Keuken van 1870 has been cooking very simple meals in a
simple setting since, you guessed it, 1870 (cheap cafeteria, open
weekdays 12:30–20:00, weekends 16:00–21:00, 4 Spuistraat,
several blocks west of station, tel. 624 8965). The train station
has a surprisingly classy budget self-service **Stationsrestau-
rantie** on platform 1 (daily 8:00–22:00).

Eating near Anne Frank's House
For pancakes in a smoky but family atmosphere, try the **Pancake Bakery** (f15 pancakes, splitting is OK, offers an Indonesian pancake for those who want two experiences in one, daily
12:00–22:00, Prinsengracht 191, several blocks north of A.F.

House, tel. 625 1333). Across the canal, **DeBolhoed** serves
great vegetarian food (daily 12:00–22:00, Prinsengracht 60).

Eating near the Rijksmuseum, on Leidseplein

The art deco **American Hotel** dining room serves an elegant
all-you-can-eat f12.50 salad bar (weekdays 7:00 a.m.–1:00 a.m.,
where Leidseplein hits Singel canal). The **Theater Café** offers
classy and tasty f25 meals (next to Hotel Maas, 50 meters down
Singel canal from the American Hotel). On the café-packed
street called Lange Leidsedwarsstraat, you'll find **Bojo**, a good
Indonesian restaurant, at #51 (Monday–Wednesday 16:00–
01:30, Thursday–Sunday 12:00–01:30, 622 7434).

Bars

Try a *jenever* (Dutch gin), the closest thing to an atomic bomb
in a shot glass. While cheese gets harder and sharper with age,
jenever grows smooth and soft. Old *jenever* is best.

Drugs

Amsterdam, Europe's counterculture Mecca, thinks the concept of a "victimless crime" is a contradiction in itself. While
hard drugs are definitely out, marijuana causes about as much
excitement as a bottle of beer. A "pot man" with a worldly
menu of f25 baggies is a fixture in many bars (walk east from
Dam Square on Damstraat for a few blocks, then down to
Nieuwmarkt). While several touristy Bulldog cafés are very
popular with tourists, less glitzy smaller places (farther from
the tourists) offer a better value and a more comfortable
atmosphere. The Easy Times Coffee Shop and the brighter
Tops Coffee Shop next door (near the corner of Leidsestraat
and Prinsengracht) dangle their menus from a string at the bar.
For a complete rundown on this side of the town, look for a
copy of the soon-to-be-resurrected "Mellow Pages." Another
interesting place to get information on the marijuana scene in
Amsterdam is the American-run KGB office (Kannabis Genet-
ics Bureau), formerly the CIA office (Cannabis in Amsterdam),
located in the Hempire State Building (1 Droogbak, afternoons, closed Tuesday, tel. 627-1646).

▲**The Marijuana and Hemp Museum**—This is a collection
of dope facts, history, science, and memorabilia (f6, daily
11:00–22:00, Sunday until 17:00, at Oudezijds Achterburgwal
148). While quite small, it has a shocker finale: the high-tech

grow room in which tens of varieties of marijuana are cultivated in optimal hydroponic (among other) environments.
Some plants stand 5 feet tall and shine under the intense grow
lamps. The view is actually through glass walls into the neighboring "Sensi Seed Bank" Grow Shop (which sells carefully
cultivated seeds and all the gear needed to grow them). Pot
should never be bought on the street in Amsterdam. Well-
established coffee shops are considered much safer. Up to 10
grams of marijuana can be possessed but not sold here—not
the law but an accepted local standard.

Transportation Connections—Amsterdam

Amsterdam's train-information center requires a long wait.
Save lots of time by getting train tickets and information in a
small-town station or travel agency. For phone information,
call 06-9292 for local trains or 06-9296 for international (50
cents/minute, daily 7:00–24:00). To get international train
information for the price of just the long-distance call, call
030/332555 (daily 8:00–22:00).

By train to: Schiphol Airport (4/hr, 20 min, f6), **Haarlem** (6/hr, 15 min, f10.25 round-trip), **The Hague** (4/hr, 45
min), **Rotterdam** (2/hr, 1 hr), **Brussels** (hrly, 3 hrs), **Oostende** (hrly, 4 hrs, change in Roosendaal), **Paris** (5/day, 5 hrs,
required fast train from Brussels with f21 supplement), **London** (4/day, 10–12 hrs), **Copenhagen** (5/day, 11 hrs), **Frankfurt** (10/day, 5 hrs), **Munich** (8/day, 8 hrs, change in
Mannheim), **Bonn** (10/day, 3 hrs), **Bern** (8/day, 9 hrs, change
in Basel).

Amsterdam's Schiphol Airport: The airport, like most
of Holland, is English-speaking, user-friendly, and below sea
level. Its banks (daily 6:00–24:00) offer fair rates. Schiphol
Airport has easy bus and train connections (7 miles) into
Amsterdam or Haarlem. The airport also has a train station
of its own. (You can validate your Eurailpass and hit the rails
immediately; or, to stretch your train pass, buy the short
ticket today and start the pass later.) Schiphol flight information (tel. 06-350 340 50, 75 cents/minute) can give you flight
times and your airline's Amsterdam number for reconfirma-
tion before going home (a guilder a minute to climb through
its phone tree).

HAARLEM

Cute, cozy yet real, handy to the airport, and just 15 minutes by train from downtown Amsterdam, Haarlem is a fine home base, giving you small-town, overnight warmth with easy access to wild and crazy Amsterdam.

Haarlem is a busy Dutch market town, buzzing with shoppers biking home with fresh bouquets. Enjoy Saturday (general) and Monday (clothing) market days, when the square bustles like a Brueghel painting with cheese, fish, flowers, and families. You'll feel comfortable here. Buy some flowers to brighten your hotel room.

Orientation (tel. code 023)

Tourist Information: Haarlem's VVV, at the train station, is friendlier, more helpful, and less crowded than Amsterdam's. Ask your Amsterdam questions here (Monday–Saturday 9:00–5:30, closed Sunday; closes at 4:00 on off-season Saturdays, tel. 06-320 24043, f1 a minute).

Arrival in Haarlem: As you walk out of the train station, the TI is on your right and the bus station is across the street. Two parallel streets flank the train station (Kruisweg and Jansweg). Head up either one and you'll reach the town square and church within ten minutes. If uncertain of the way, ask a local person, "*Grote Markt?*" ("Main square?"), and you'll get pointed in the right direction.

Helpful Hints: The handy GWK change office at the station offers decent exchange rates (8:00–20:00, Thursday and Friday until 21:00, Sunday 9:00–17:00). The train station rents

Haarlem

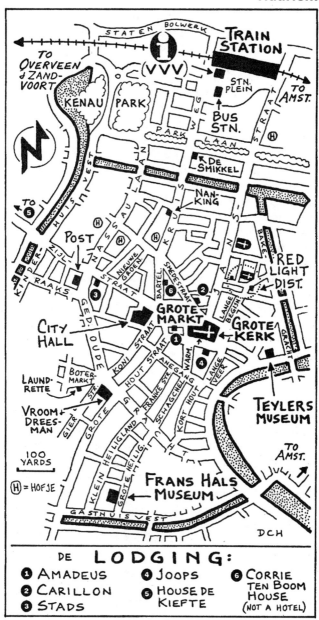

TO OVERVEEN & ZANDVOORT

STATEN BOLWERK

TRAIN STATION

(VVV)

KENAU

PARK

STN. PLEIN

TO AMST.

BUS STN.

PARK LAAN

DE SMIKKEL

NAN-KING

TO ⑤

RED LIGHT DIST.

POST

GROTE MARKT

GROTE KERK

CITY HALL

LAUNDRETTE

BOTER-MARKT

VROOM-DREES-MAN

TEYLERS MUSEUM

TO AMST.

100 YARDS

Ⓗ = HOFJE

FRANS HALS MUSEUM

GASTHUIS VEST

DCH

DE LODGING:

❶ AMADEUS
❷ CARILLON
❸ STADS
❹ JOOPS
❺ HOUSE DE KIEFTE
❻ CORRIE TEN BOOM HOUSE (NOT A HOTEL)

bikes cheaply and easily (f5/4 hours, f8/day, f100 deposit, daily 6:00–24:00). My Beautiful Laundrette is handy, self-service, and cheap (daily 8:30–20:30, near Vroom Dreesman at 20 Boter Markt, f10 wash and dry). The VVV and local hotels have a helpful parking brochure.

Sights—Haarlem

▲▲**Frans Hals Museum**—Haarlem is the hometown of Frans Hals, and this delightful museum displays many of his greatest paintings in a glorious old building (f7.50, open 11:00–17:00, Sunday 13:00–17:00, tel. 516 4200). Enjoy take-me-back paintings of old-time Haarlem. Peter Brueghel the Younger's painting *Proverbs* (outside room 24) shows 72 old Dutch proverbs; the handy English-language key gives you a fascinating peek into the Dutch old days. The museum across the street features the architecture of old Haarlem.

Corrie Ten Boom House—As many Americans (but few Dutch) know, Haarlem is also home to Corrie Ten Boom (popularized by *The Hiding Place*, an inspirational book and movie about the Ten Boom family's experience hiding Haarlem Jews from the Nazis). The Ten Boom House, at 19 Barteljorisstraat, is open for 45-minute English tours (donation requested; Tuesday–Saturday 10:00–16:00; November through April 11:00–15:00, same days; only one tour/day off-season; tel. 531 0823). Some of the guides do more preaching than teaching.

Grote Kerk (Church)—You'll see (and maybe hear) Holland's greatest pipe organ (regular free concerts, summer Tuesdays at 20:15, some Thursdays at 15:00, TI office has schedule). The church is open and worth a look, if only to see its Oz-like organ (f2.50, Monday–Saturday 10:00–16:00; closes at 15:00 in winter). Note how the organ, which fills the west end, seems to have stolen the show from the altar. (But there is a handy public WC in the east end.) To enter the church, look for the small entrance marked "*Entree*" behind the church, kitty-corner from La Plume restaurant.

▲**Teylers Museum**—Famous as the oldest museum in Holland, it used to be interesting mainly as a look at a 200-year-old museum. New exhibition halls (with rotating exhibits) and a café have brought new life to the dusty exhibits. So if you enjoy mixing, say, Renaissance sketches with pickled coelecanths, drop by (f7.50, Tuesday–Saturday 10:00–17:00, Sunday 13:00–17:00, Spaarne 16).

Red Lights—For a little red-light district precious as a Barbie doll, wander around the church in Haarlem's cutest Begijnhof (2 blocks northeast of the big church, off Lange Begijnestraat, f50, no senior or student discounts). Don't miss the mall marked by the red neon sign, *t'Steegje*. The nearby *t'Poortje*, "office park," costs f7.50.

Nightlife in Haarlem

Haarlem's evening scene is great. The bars around the Grote Kerk and Lange Veerstraat are colorful, lively, and always full of music.

The **Studio** (next to the Hotel Carillon), jammed with Haarlem's 30-something crowd, has a pleasant ambiance. **Café Brinkman**, on the square, is a good people-watching perch. **Café 1900** (across from the Corrie Ten Boom House) is classy by day and draws a young crowd with live music on Sunday nights. Lange Veerstraat (behind the church) is probably the best bar street in town. The **Crack** (32 Lange Veerstraat) is the wild and leathery place to go for loud music and smoking. Pot's for sale across the street (#47) at **High Times**. The **Imperial Café and Bar** has live music every night except Sunday (a few doors down from the Crack, at 3 Korte Veerstraat).

Don't be shocked if locals drop into a bar, plunk down f25 for a baggie of marijuana, and casually roll a joint. (If you don't like the smell of pot, avoid "coffee shops" sporting Rastafarian yellow, red, and green colors; wildly painted walls; or plants in the windows.)

Sleeping in Haarlem
(f1 = about 70 cents, tel. code: 023)

The helpful Haarlem tourist office ("VVV" at the train station, Monday–Saturday 9:00–17:30, f1/minute, tel. 06/320-24-043) can nearly always find you a f30 bed in a nearby private home (for a f9-per-person fee plus a cut of the hotel's money). Haarlem is most crowded in April, on Easter weekend, May, and August, but if you phone ahead, my recommended hotels will happily hold a room without a deposit (though they may ask for a credit-card number). Nearly every Dutch person you'll encounter speaks English. The listed prices include breakfast (unless otherwise noted) but do not include a f3 per-person-per-day tourist tax. To avoid this town's louder than normal street noises, forego views for a room in the back. Don't needlessly use the TI's room-finding service.

Hotel Amadeus has 15 small, bright rooms, all with simple modern furnishings, TV, private shower, and toilet. Some have views of the square. This hotel, ideally located above an Italian restaurant in a characteristic building on the market square, is relatively quiet and has an elevator. The lush old lobby is on the second floor in a "pianola bar" (Sb-f85, Db-f110, Tb-f150, nicer rooms cost a little more, seconds-on-everything-welcome buffet breakfast, kid-friendly, a 12-minute walk from train station, brothers Dave and Mike run the place for their family, CC:VMA, use credit card to secure reservations, Grote Markt 10, 2011 RD Haarlem, tel. 532 4530, fax 532 2328, E-mail: amadeus@euronet.nl).

Hotel Carillon, also right on the town square, has ste-e-e-p stairs. The location is ideal, many of the well-worn rooms are small, and front rooms come with great town square views, lots of street noise, and double-paned windows (22 rooms, tiny loft singles-f52.50, Db-f115, Tb-f160, no elevator, 12-minute walk from train station, CC:VMA, Grote Markt 27, 2011 RC Haarlem, tel. 531 0591, fax 531 4909). For 1997, the Carillon is opening another hotel a five-minute walk away (similar prices, check in at Carillon).

The rollicking **Stads Café** has big, bright, and cheery rooms, most with TV and solid modern wood furniture. Its restaurant hops at night (see Eating, below), but most of its rooms are in the back and quiet (13 rooms, S-f50 to f60, D-f75, Db-f100, Tb-f130, Qb-f160, breakfast f9, CC:VMA, 2 blocks off the marketplace, Zijlstraat 56-58, 2011 TP Haarlem, tel. 532 5202, fax 532 0504).

Hotel Joops is an innovative concept. A well-organized central office, just behind the church in the town center, administers a corral of apartments and rooms, totaling 200 beds in 20 buildings (all within 2 blocks of the church). They have bright and spacious rooms (S-f45, D-f75, T-f110) and elegant fully furnished apartments with kitchen facilities and the lived-in works (Db-f125 to f145, Tb-f165 to f190, six-bed apartments-f235, discounts for weeklong stays, rates are 30 percent cheaper mid-September to March, office at Oude Groenmarkt 12, 2011 HL Haarlem, tel. 532 2008, fax 532 9549).

Bed and Breakfast House de Kiefte, your cozy, get-into-a-local-home budget option, epitomizes the goodness of B&Bs.

Marjet (mar-yet) and Hans, a young couple who speak fluent American, rent four bright and cheery nonsmoking rooms (with a hearty breakfast and plenty of travel advice) in their 100-year-old home on a quiet neighborhood street (S-f45, Sb-f65, Db-f85, T/Tb-f125, Qb-f160, Quint/s-f185, five-minute walk from the center, minimum two nights, family loft sleeps up to five, very steep stairs, kid-friendly, 15-minute walk or f11-taxi from train station; from Market Square walk straight out Zijlstraat, past Stads Café, over bridge, fourth street on left, Coornhertstraat 3, 2013 EV Haarlem, tel. 532 2980, cellular phone 06/5474-5272).

Family Dekker B&B is in a fine, quiet neighborhood near the station. For 25 years Mrs. Dekker has given her guests a cheery welcome in her clean but well-worn place (small D-f50, D-f60, T-f90, Q-f120, 2 blocks from the station at Ripperdastraat 9, 2011 KG Haarlem, tel. 532 0554).

Hotel Lion D'Or is a classy business hotel with all the professional comforts, an attached restaurant, and a very handy location (Sb-f200, Db-f260, extra beds-f50, request a "weekend package" at least three days in advance to get substantial weekend discounts June through September and in winter months; CC:VMA; across the street from the station at Kruisweg 34, 2011 LC Haarlem, tel. 532-1750, fax 532-9543).

The 300-room, very American **Hotel Haarlem Zuid** is sterile but a good value for those interested only in sleeping and eating (Db-f90–f115, Tb-f120, breakfast-f13, elevator, easy parking, inexpensive hotel restaurant, in an industrial zone, a 20-minute walk from the center on the road to the airport, CC:VMA, Toekenweg 2, 2035 LC Haarlem, tel. 536 7500, fax 536 7980). Buses easily connect it to the station and town square.

Sleeping near Haarlem

The **Hotel Fehres** offers eight rooms in a quiet, kid-friendly, garden-filled, residential setting (bus #7 from Haarlem station or Market Square, or a five-minute walk from the Overveen station, one stop west of Haarlem with twice-an-hour train connections to Amsterdam). Friendly Mrs. Fehres pampers her guests (D-f90, Db-f100, Tb-f120, Qb-f140, 299 Zijlweg, 2015 CM Haarlem, tel. 527 7368). **Pension Koning**, a ten-minute walk north of the station or quick hop on bus #71, has five simple rooms in a row house in a residential area (S-f35, D-f70, T-f105 with breakfast, Kleverlaan 179, 2023 JE, tel. 526 1456).

274   *Rick Steves' France, Belgium & the Netherlands*

Youth Hostel Jan Gijzen, with f23 beds in 20-bed dorms, charges f5 extra for nonmembers (includes breakfast, Jan Gijzenpad 3, 2 miles from the Haarlem station bus #2, or a five-minute walk from the Samtpoort Zuid train station, 7:00–24:00, closed November–February, tel. 537 3793, fax 537 1176).

Eating in Haarlem

All restaurants listed below are just a few blocks off the Market Square.

Enjoy a memorable Indonesian *rijsttafel* feast at the **Nanking Chinese-Indonesian Restaurant** (Kruisstraat 16, tel. 532 0706, daily until 22:00). Couples eat plenty, heartily, and more cheaply by splitting a (f24.50) Indonesian rice table for one. (Each eater should order a drink.) Say "hi" to gracious Ai Ping and her daughter, Fan. Don't let them railroad you into a Chinese (their heritage) dinner. They also do cheap and tasty take-out. For more expensive and impressive meals, try **Mooi Java** (they don't mind diners splitting a f33 *rijsttafel*, across from the station, tel. 532 3121, daily 17:00–22:00) or **De Lachende Javaan** ("The Laughing Javanese," closed Monday, Frankestraat 25, tel. 532 8792). **Toko Nina** has take-out Indonesian food (Koningstraat 48).

Going Dutch? How about pancakes for dinner at **Pannekoekhuis "De Smikkel"** (open daily until 20:00, 2 blocks in front of station, Kruisweg 57, tel. 532 0631)? Dinner and dessert pancakes cost f12 each (f2.50 per person cover charge, so splitting pancakes is OK).

For a "bread line" experience with basic/bland food, well-worn company, and the cheapest price in town (f9), eat at **Eethuis St. Vincent** (22 Nieuwe Groenmarkt, Monday–Friday 12:00–13:30 and 17:00–19:00).

For good food, classy atmosphere, and f30 dinners, try the **Bastiaan** (closed Monday, CC:VMA, Lange Veerstraat 8). **La Plume** is a less expensive steak house (open daily, CC:VMA, 1 Lange Veerstraat). For a candlelit dinner of cheese and wine, consider **In't Goede Uur** (Korte Houtstraat 1), or eat well and reasonably (surrounded by trains) in a classy Old World **Stations Restaurant**, between tracks 5 and 6, in the Netherlands' oldest train station (open daily 12:00–20:00). Popular with locals, **Jacobus Pieck** is a classy hole in the wall offering a varied menu selection during the day and just one f15 dinner special in the evening (9:00–20:00, until 18:00 on Saturday, closed Sunday, Warmoesstraat 18, tel. 532 6144).

Eko Eet Café is great for a cheery, tasty vegetarian meal in Haarlem (f18 menu, Zijlstraat 39, daily 17:30–21:30).

The **Stads Café** has fun being a restaurant (daily until midnight, Zijlstraat 56-58, tel. 532 5202), a three-ring circus of reasonable food (f12.5 dinner special, f23 cheese or meat fondue buffets, salad bar, or "meat on a hot rock sizzling at your table"), with a stained-glass, candlelit, honky-tonk atmosphere, and piano music (Friday–Sunday).

For a healthy budget lunch with Haarlem's best view, eat on the top floor or roof garden of the **Vroom Dreesman** department store (9:30–18:00, Thursday until 21:00, closed Sunday, on Grote Houtstraat). For a (f2) cone of old-fashioned local french fries, drop by **Friethuis de Vlaminck** on Warmoesstraat 3 (closed Sunday and Monday), just behind the church.

Transportation Connections—Haarlem

By train to: Amsterdam (6/hr, 15 min, f10.25 same-day return), **Delft** (2/hr, 45 min), **Hoorn** (2/hr, 55 min), **The Hague** (3/hr, 40 min), **Alkmaar** (2/hr, 30 min), **Schiphol Airport** (2/hr, 40 min, f10, transfer at suburban Amsterdam-Sloterdijk). The direct express buses #236 and #362 to the airport are faster (2/hr, 30 min, f9). By taxi, it's a f70 ride.

Sights—Near Haarlem and Amsterdam

The Netherlands are tiny. The sights listed below are an easy day trip by bus or train from Haarlem or Amsterdam. Match your interest with the village's specialty: choose from flower auctions, folk museums, cheese markets, Delft porcelain, resort beaches, and modern art.

▲▲**Zuiderzee Museum**—As far as open-air folk museums go, this one in the salty old town of Enkhuizen is particularly lively, with a "Living on Urk" village populated by people who do a very convincing job of role-playing no-nonsense 1905 Dutch villagers. No one said "Have a nice day" back then. You can eat herring hot out of the old smoker, see barrels and rope made, and enjoy children enjoying the dress-up chest, the old-time game zone, and making sailing ships out of old wooden shoes (f15, daily early April–late October 10:00–17:00, free tours at 11:30, private guide for f75, tel. 0228/310291). Trains zip from Amsterdam directly to Enkhuisen, where a shuttle boat will take you to the museum, avoiding a pleasant 15-minute walk.

▲**Zaanse Schans**—At this 17th-century Dutch village turned open-air folk museum, you can see and learn about everything Dutch, from cheese making to wooden-shoe carving. Take an inspiring climb to the top of a whirring windmill (get a group of people together and ask for a tour), or buy a small jar of fresh, windmill-ground mustard for your next picnic. Located in the town of Zaandijk, this is your easiest one-stop look at traditional Dutch culture and the Netherlands' best collection of windmills. (Free, daily 8:30–18:00, until 17:00 in winter, tel. 075/616-8218.) Fifteen minutes by train north of Amsterdam: take the Alkmaar-bound train to Station Koog-Zaandijk and walk following signs—past a fragrant chocolate factory—for ten minutes.

▲▲**Aalsmeer Flower Auction**—This is your best look at the huge Dutch flower industry. About half of all the flowers exported from Holland are auctioned off here in six huge auditoriums. Visitors are welcome to wander on elevated walkways (through what is claimed to be the biggest building on earth), over literally trainloads of fresh-cut flowers (f5, Monday–Friday 7:30–11:00, it's pretty dead after 9:30 and on Thursday, bus #172 from Amsterdam's station; from Haarlem, take bus #191, 2/hr, 60 min; tel. 0297/393939). Aalsmeer is close to the airport and a handy last fling before catching a morning weekday flight.

▲▲▲**Keukenhof**—The greatest bulb flower garden on earth—each spring 6 million flowers conspire to make even a total garden-hater enjoy them. This 70-acre park is packed with tour groups daily from about March 27–May 22 (f16, 8:00–19:30, last tickets sold at 18:00, bus from Haarlem to Lisse, where you catch a free shuttle bus, tel. 0252/465-555). Go very late in the day for the best light and the fewest groups.

Zandvoort—For a quick and easy look at the windy coastline in a shell-lover's Shangri-La, visit the beach resort of Zandvoort, a breezy 45-minute bike ride, or ten minutes by train or car west of Haarlem (from Haarlem, follow signs to Bloemendaal). Between posts 68 and 70, beach bathers work on all-around tans.

Volendam, Marken, and Monnikendam—These famous towns are quaint as can be (although Volendam is too touristy). De Rijp is a fine, sleepy, untouristy town to visit when driving around the area north of Amsterdam.

▲**Hoorn**—This is an elegant, quiet, and typical 17th-century Dutch town north of Amsterdam. Its TI can rent you a bike or give you a walking tour brochure. Any TI has a flier describing the "Historic Triangle," an all-day excursion from Amsterdam that connects Hoorn, Medemblik, and Enkhuizen by steam train and boat (f25, tel. 0229/318344).

▲**Alkmaar**—This town is Holland's cheese capital—especially fun (and touristy) during its weekly cheese market (Friday 10:00–12:00).

▲**Delft**—Peaceful as a Vermeer painting (he was born here) and lovely as its porcelain, Delft is a typically Dutch town with a special soul. Enjoy it best by simply wandering around, watching people, munching local syrup-waffles, or daydreaming from the canal bridges. The town bustles during its Saturday antique market. Its colorful Thursday food and flower market (9:00–17:00) attracts many traditional villagers. The TI, on the main square, has a f3 brochure outlining Delft's sights and a do-it-yourself "Historical Walk through Delft" (open weekdays 9:00–18:00, Saturday 9:00–17:00, Sunday 10:00–15:00, tel. 015/212 6100). The town is a museum in itself, but if you need a turnstile, it has an impressive Army Museum. Or you can tour the Royal Porcelain Works (f3.50, daily 9:00–17:00, Sunday 10:00–17:00, tel. 015/256 9214) to watch the famous 17th-century blue Delftware turn from clay into art.

▲▲**Edam**—For the ultimate in cuteness and peace, make tiny Edam your home base. It's very sweet but palatable, and 30 minutes by bus from Amsterdam (2/hour). Don't miss the Edam Museum, a small, quirky house offering a fun peek into a 400-year-old home and a floating cellar (10:00–16:00, Sunday 14:00–16:00, on main square). Wednesday is the town's market day (9:00–1:00). In July and August, market day includes a traditional cheese market (10:00–12:00).

Consider making Edam your home base. **Hotel De Fortuna,** an eccentric canalside mix of flowers, cats of leisure, a pet turtle, and duck noises, offers steep stairs and low-ceilinged rooms in several ancient buildings in the old center of Edam (Db-f162, including breakfast, garden patio, attached restaurant, CC:VMA, Spuistraat 3, 1135 AV Edam, tel. 0299/371727, fax 71469). The **Damhotel,** centrally located (on a canal around the corner from the TI), has attractive, comfortable rooms with a plush feel (Sb-f80, Db-f120, Tb-f180, including breakfast, attached restaurant, CC:VMA, Keizersgracht 1, 1135 ZG Edam, tel. 0299/371766, fax 374031). The

TI (tel. 0299/371727) has a list of cheaper rooms in private homes. **De Harmonie**, with simple small rooms above a bar, is a last resort (f40 per person, shower and toilet down the hall, Voorhaven 92, 1135 GW Edam, tel. 0299/371664). **Tai Wah** has reasonable take-out (eat in the De Fortuna garden) or eat-in Chinese/Indonesian food (12:00–22:00, closed Tuesday, Lingerzijde 62, tel. 02993/71088).

▲**Rotterdam**—This city, the world's largest port, bounced back after being bombed flat in World War II. See its towering Euromast, take a harbor tour, and stroll its great pedestrian zone. It's an easy train connection to Amsterdam (TI tel. 06-34034065, toll call-f1 per two minutes).

▲▲**The Hague**—Locals say the money is made in Rotterdam, divided in the Hague, and spent in Amsterdam. The Hague (or "Den Haag" in Dutch) is the Netherlands' seat of government and the home of several engaging museums. The Mauritshuis' delightful, easy-to-tour art collection stars Vermeer and Rembrandt (f10, Tuesday–Saturday 10:00–17:00, Sunday 11:00– 17:00, Korte Vijverberg 8, tel. 070/3469244). Across the pond, the Torture Museum (Gevangenpoort) shows the medieval mind at its worst (f5, Monday–Friday 10:00–16:00, Sunday 13:00–16:00, required tours on the hour; confirm with ticket-taker if film and talk will be in English before committing, tel. 070/346 0861). For a look at the 19th century's attempt at virtual reality, tour Panorama Mesdag, a 360-degree painting of the town of Scheveningen in the 1880s, with a 3-D sandy beach foreground (f3, Monday–Saturday 10:00–17:00, Sunday 12:00–17:00, Zeestraat 65, tel. 070/310 6665). The nearby Peace Palace, a gift from Andrew Carnegie, houses the International Court of Justice (f5, Monday–Friday 10:00–16:00, required guided tours at 10:00, 11:00, 14:00, 15:00, or 16:00; tram 7 or 8 from the station; tel. 070/302 4137, closes without warning, call ahead or check at TI). Scheveningen, the Dutch Coney Island, is liveliest in summer (take tram 7); and Madurodam, a mini-Holland amusement park, is a kid-pleaser (f20, discounts for kids, daily 9:00–17:00, until 22:00 in summer, tram 1 or 9, tel. 070/355 3900). The Hague's TI is at the train station (9:00–17:30, later in summer, Sunday 10:00–17:00, tel. 06-34035051, 75 cents a minute).

▲▲**Arnhem's Open-Air Dutch Folk Museum**—An hour east of Amsterdam, Arnhem has a home show in a time tunnel: Holland's first and biggest folk museum. You'll enjoy a huge park of windmills, old farms, traditional crafts in action, and a pleasant education-by-immersion in Dutch culture. The English guidebook (f7.50) explains each historic building (f16, daily April–October 10:00–17:00, tel. 026/357 6111, fax 357 6147). The park has several good budget restaurants and covered picnic areas. Its rustic **Pancake House** serves hearty (splittable) Dutch flapjacks.

Trains make the 70-minute trip from Amsterdam to Arnhem twice an hour. At Arnhem station, take bus #3 or #13 (faster) to the Openlucht Museum. By car from Haarlem, skirt Amsterdam to the south on E9, following signs to Utrecht, then take A12 east to Arnhem. Just before Arnhem, take the Arnhem Nord exit (you'll see the white *"Openluchtmuseum"* sign) and follow the signs to the nearby museum. For the Kröller-Müller Museum, follow the white signs to Hoge Veluwe.

▲▲**Kröller-Müller Museum, Hoge Veluwe National Park**—Also near Arnhem, the Hoge Veluwe National Park is Holland's largest (13,000 acres) and is famous for its Kröller-Müller Museum. This huge and impressive modern-art collection, including 55 paintings by van Gogh, is set deep in the natural Dutch wilderness. The park has lots more to offer, including hundreds of white-painted bikes you're free to use to make your explorations more fun. (Museum entrance f8, easy parking, Tuesday–Sunday 10:00–17:00, tel. 055/3781441.) Pick up more information at the Amsterdam or Arnhem TI (tel. 026/4420330). Bus #12 connects the Arnhem train station with the Kröller-Müller Museum (summer only). Consider combining a visit to the park and the open-air museum for a great day trip from Amsterdam.

APPENDIX

"La Marseillaise"
There's a movement in France to soften the lyrics of their national anthem. Sing it now . . . before it's too late.

Allons enfants de la Patrie, (Let's go, children of the fatherland,)
Le jour de gloire est arrivé. (The day of glory has arrived.)
Contre nous de la tyrannie (The blood-covered flagpole of tyranny)
L'étendard sanglant est levé, (Is raised against us,)
L'étendard sanglant est levé. (Is raised against us.)
Entendez-vous dans nos campagnes (Do you hear what's happening in our countryside?)
Mugir les féroces soldats? (The ferocious soldiers are groaning)
Qui viennent jusque dans nos bras (They're coming nearly into our grasp)
Egorger nos fils et nos compagnes. (They're slitting the throats of our sons and our women.)
Aux armes citoyens, (Grab your weapons, citizens,)
Formez vos bataillons, (Form your battalions,)
Marchons, marchons, (March on, march on,)
Qu'un sang impur (So that their impure blood)
Abreuve nos sillons. (Will fill our trenches.)

French History in an Escargot Shell
Around the time of Christ, Romans "Latinized" the land of the Gauls. With the fifth-century fall of Rome, the barbarian Franks and Burgundians invaded. From this unique mix of Latin and Celtic cultures evolved today's France.

While France wallowed with the rest of Europe in medieval darkness, it got a head start in its development as a nation-state. In 507, Clovis established Paris as the capital of his Christian, Merovingian dynasty. Clovis and the Franks would eventually become Louis and the French. Charles Martel stopped the spread of Islam by beating the Spanish Moors at the battle of Poitiers. And Charlemagne, the most important of the "Dark Age" Frankish kings, was crowned Holy Roman Emperor in 800 by the pope. Charles the Great presided over the "Carolingian Renaissance" and effectively ruled a vast-for-the-time empire.

The treaty which, in 843, divided Charlemagne's empire among his grandsons, marks what could be considered the birth of Europe. For the first time, a treaty was signed in the vernacular languages (French and German) rather than in Latin. While this split established a kind of Franco/Germanic divide, it also heralded an age of fragmentation. While petty princes took the reigns, the Frankish king ruled only the Île-de-France, a small island of land around Paris.

Vikings, or Norsemen, settled in what became Normandy. Later, in 1066, these "Normans" invaded England. The Norman king, William the Conqueror, consolidated his English domain, accelerating the formation of modern England. But his rule also muddied the political waters between England and France, kicking off a centuries-long struggle between the two nations.

In the 12th century, Eleanor of Aquitaine (a separate country in southwest France) married Louis VII, king of France, bringing Aquitaine under French rule. They divorced and she married Henry of Normandy, soon-to-be Henry II of England. This marital union gave England control of a huge swath of land from the English Channel to the Pyrénées. For 300 years, France and England would struggle over control of Aquitaine. Any enemy of the French king would find a natural ally in the English king.

In 1328, a French king (Charles IV) died without a son. The English king was his nephew, and naturally was interested in the throne. The French resisted. This pitted France, the biggest and richest country in Europe, against England, with the biggest army. They fought from 1337 to 1453, in what was modestly called the Hundred Years' War. Since it involved nearly all of Europe, many consider it the first world war.

Regional powers from within France sided with England. Burgundy actually took Paris, captured the royal family, and recognized the English king as heir to the French thrown. England controlled France from the Loire north, and things looked bleak for the French king.

Enter Joan of Arc, a 16-year-old peasant girl driven by religious voices. France's national heroine left home to support the dauphin Charles VII (boy prince, heir to the throne but too young to rule). Joan rallied the French, inspiring them to ultimately throw out the English. In 1430, Joan was captured by the Burgundians, who sold her to the English, who convicted her of heresy and burned her at the stake in Rouen. But the inspiration of Jeanne d'Arc lived on and by 1453, English holdings on the Continent had dwindled to the port of Calais.

By 1500, a strong centralized France had emerged with borders close to today's borders. Her kings (from the Renaissance François I, through the Henrys and all those Louises) were model divine monarchs, setting the standards for absolute rule in Europe.

Of course these excesses, coupled with the modern thinking of the Enlightenment—whose leaders were the French *philosophes*—led to the French Revolution (1789) and the end of the Old Regime and its notion that some are born to rule while others are born to be ruled.

But the excesses of the Revolution led to the rise of Napoleon, who ruled the French empire as a dictator, until his excesses ushered him into a south Atlantic exile and a compromise king returned. The modern French king was himself ruled by a constitution. Rather than leotards and powdered wigs, he went to work in a suit with a briefcase.

The 20th century spelled the end of France's reign as a military and political superpower. Devastating wars with Germany in 1870, 1914, and 1940 and the loss of her colonial holdings have left France with not quite enough land, people, or production to be a top player on a global scale.

Still, France is the cultural capital of Europe and a leader in the push to integrate Europe into one unified economic power. When that happens, Paris will once again emerge as a superpower capital.

Camping

Here are some good campgrounds for the French destinations recommended in this book. All provide free hot showers and clean bathroom facilities, and average 60F for two per night. Campers should pack sleeping bags, tent, tarp, sleeping pads, thongs for the showers, a camping *gaz* stove (no Coleman fuel here), a light pot, plastic plates, and silverware. Consider buying cheap fold-up camping chairs (40F), available at big French *supermarchés*.

Paris: Avoid camping here. It's too hard to reach the city center. Still, if you must, try Camp du Bois du Boulogne, allée du Bord de l'Eau in the Bois (woods) de Boulogne (tel. 01 45 24 30 00). It's the only campground "in" Paris, but it is not strong on security and is generally crowded. Open all year and fully equipped.

Rouen: Municipal Camping. Ten minutes by car or bus from Rouen, in Deauville, on the N-15 toward Le Havre (tel. 02 35 74 07 59). Nice but small area, immaculate bathrooms.

Honfleur: Camping du Phare. A scruffy facility with a great location—a few minutes' stroll from the heart of Honfleur. It's just outside the city as you head to Trouville. Open April–October 15. A far nicer facility, but a five-minute drive to town, is Camping Domaine Catinière, in Fiquefleur (tel. 02 32 57 63 51, open April–September).

Bayeux: Municipal Camping. Very friendly, small sites, but a terrific facility and a ten-minute walk to the city center (blvd. Eindhoven, tel. 02 31 92 08 43, open March–October 31).

D-Day Beaches: You'll see small campgrounds every-where. The area between Arromanches and the Pointe du Hoc is best.

Mont St. Michel: Camping du Mont St. Michel (Pb. 8/50116 Le Mont St. Michel, tel. 02 33 60 09 33, check in at the Motel Vert). It's 1.5 miles from Le Mont and 50 yards from great views of it. Otherwise, nothing to write home about. Open year-round.

Amboise: Camping de L'Île d'Or. On the island across the bridge from the city center, you can't miss it. Scenic location and easy walk into Amboise. Minigolf and pool (tel. 02 47 57 23 37).

Sarlat: Camping Les Perieres. A 15-minute walk downhill to Sarlat. This resort sports a pool, tennis courts, store, café, and lovely setting. Call ahead in the summer or forget it (Rd. 47, tel. 05 53 59 05 84, open April–September 30).

Albi: Parc de Caussels. One mile east of town. Crowded but friendly, with a huge supermarket across the street (tel. 05 63 60 37 06, open April–November).

Carcassonne: Camping de la Cité. Brand new site and facility; 15-minute walk to la Cité. Inquire at TI for information or follow signs from the *ville basse*, the newer part of the city (tel. 04 68 25 11 77).

Arles: Camping City. The best and most convenient of several in the area. Fifteen-minute walk into the city center, a new pool, poolside café, and hairy umbrellas (on the road to Crau, tel. 04 90 93 08 86, open March–October 31).

Avignon: Camping Bagatelle. Right across the Pont (bridge) Daladier from Avignon. Great city views, popular, but lots of sites and a great café (tel. 04 90 86 30 39).

Cagnes-sur-Mer (Nice): Camping Panoramer. Meet the friendly owners and admire the best Riviera view around. It's a long walk to the Nice-bound bus stop, but buses run often (chemin des Gros Buaux, tel. 04 93 31 16 15, follow chemin du Val Fleuri from the N-7 in Cagnes-sur-Mer, open Easter–September 20, call ahead in summer).

Antibes: Camps are everywhere; you'll see signs. There's easy access to Nice via bus. Be sure to arrive by noon in the summer.

Annecy: Campgrounds line each side of the lake.

Chamonix: Camping les Rosières. Comfortable site, wonderful views, and a beautiful 20-minute walk to town—follow the stream. Funky trailers for rent 1 mile from Chamonix on route du Praz, tel. 04 50 53 10 42, open all year).

Beaune: Camping les Cent Vignes. This is my favorite campground in France, a 15-minute walk to the city center, fully equipped (great restaurant), individual sites, and campers from all over Europe (10 rue Dubois, tel. 03 80 22 03 91, follow signs toward Dijon and watch for camping signs, open March 15–October 31).

Dijon: Camping Municipal du Lac. Streamside location and a short waddle to the lake. Fine facilities (1 mile from Dijon, follow signs from the station in the direction of Paris, tel. 03 80 43 54 72, open April–November 15).

Colmar: Camping intercommunal de l'Île. A few miles from the city center, but a nice riverfront location and good facilities (Plage de L'Île, follow the N-415 toward Fribourg, open February–November 30, tel. 03 89 41 15 94).

Let's Talk Telephones

Smart travelers use the telephone every day—for making hotel reservations, calling tourist information offices, and phoning home. In Europe, card-operated public phones are speedily replacing coin-operated phones. Each country sells telephone cards good for use in that country. Get a phone card at any post office. To make a call, pick up the receiver, insert your card in the slot in the phone, dial your number, make your call, then retrieve your card. The price of your call is automatically deducted from your card as you use it. If you have phone-card phobia, you'll usually find easy-to-use "talk now-pay later" metered phones in post offices. Avoid using hotel room phones, which are major rip-offs, for anything other than local calls or calling-card calls (see below).

Calling Card Operators
Calling home from Europe is easy from any type of phone if you have a calling card. From a private phone, just dial the toll-free number to reach the operator. Using a public phone, first insert a small-value coin or a phone card. Then dial the operator, who will ask you for your calling card number and place your call. You'll save money on calls of three minutes or more. When you finish, your coin should be returned (or if using a card, no money should have been deducted). Your bill awaits you at home (one more reason to prolong your vacation). For more information, see Introduction: Telephones and Mail.

	AT&T	**MCI**	**Sprint**
France	0800 99 00 11	0800 99 00 19	0800 99 00 87
Belgium	0800-100-10	0800-10012	0800-100-14
Netherlands	06-022-9111	06-022-9122	06-022-9119

Dialing Direct
Calling Between Countries: First dial the international access code, then dial the country code, followed by the area code (if it starts with zero, drop the zero), then the local number.

   Calling Long Distance Within a Country: First dial the area code (including its zero), then the local number.

   Some of Europe's Exceptions: In Spain, area codes start with nine instead of zero (just drop or add the nine instead of a zero, as in other countries). A few countries, such as Denmark, Norway, and France, lack area codes. You still use the above sequence and codes to dial, just skip the area code. Within France, dial the ten-digit telephone number direct throughout the country.

International Access Codes
When dialing direct, first dial the international access code of the country you're calling from.

Austria:	00	France:	00	Norway:	00
Belgium:	00	Germany:	00	Portugal:	00
Britain:	00	Ireland:	00	Russia:	810
Czech Rep:	00	Italy:	00	Spain:	07
Denmark:	00	Latvia:	00	Sweden:	009
Estonia:	800	Lithuania:	810	Switzerland:	00
Finland:	990	Netherlands:	09	U.S.A./Canada:	011

Country Codes
After you've dialed the international access code, then dial the code of the country you're calling.

Austria:	43	France:	33	Norway:	47
Belgium:	32	Germany:	49	Portugal:	351
Britain:	44	Ireland:	353	Russia:	7
Czech Rep:	42	Italy:	39	Spain:	34
Denmark:	45	Latvia:	371	Sweden:	46
Estonia:	372	Lithuania:	370	Switzerland:	41
Finland:	358	Netherlands:	31	U.S.A./Canada:	1

Telephone Directory
Useful Parisian Phone Numbers and Addresses
American Church: 01 47 05 07 99
American Express: 11 rue Scribe, Métro: Opéra. 01 47 70 77 07
American Hospital: 01 47 47 53 00
American Pharmacy: 01 47 42 49 40
Emergency: Dial 17 for police, otherwise 01 42 60 33 22
English tourist information recording: 01 47 20 88 98
Office of American Services (lost passports, etc.): 01 42 96 12 02
Paris and France Directory Assistance (they speak some English): 12
Sunday Banks: 115 and 154 avenue des Champs-Élysées
U.S. Embassy: 01 43 12 22 22

Airline Offices in Paris
Orly Airport Information: 01 48 84 32 10 or 01 49 75 52 52
Roissy–Charles de Gaulle Airport Information: 01 48 62 22 80

Air Canada: 01 44 50 20 20
Air France: 01 43 35 61 61 or 01 44 08 22 22
American: 01 42 89 05 22
British Air: 01 47 78 14 14
British Midland: 01 48 62 55 65
Continental: 01 42 99 09 09
Delta: 01 47 68 92 92
Iberia: 01 40 47 80 90
KLM: 01 44 56 18 18
Lufthansa: 01 42 65 37 35
Northwest: 01 42 66 90 00
Olympic: 01 42 65 92 42
SAS: 01 47 42 06 14
TWA: 01 49 19 20 00
United: 01 48 97 82 82

Useful Phone Numbers

	Tourist Info	Train Info	Zip Code
France			
Paris	01 47 23 61 72 (usually speak English)	several stations (often do not speak English)	750XX (last 2 digits ar *arrondissement*)
Albi	05 63 49 48 80	05 63 54 45 51	81000
Amboise	02 47 57 09 28	02 47 23 18 23	37400
Annecy	04 50 45 00 33	04 50 66 50 50	74000
Antibes	04 92 90 53 00	04 93 99 50 50	06600
Arles	04 90 18 41 20	04 90 82 50 50	13200
Avignon	04 90 82 65 11	04 90 82 50 50	84000
Bayeux	02 31 92 16 26	02 31 83 50 50	14400
Beaune	03 80 26 21 30	03 80 41 50 50	21200
Beynac	05 53 29 43 08	05 53 59 00 21	24220
Carcassonne	04 68 25 07 04	04 68 47 50 50	11000
Chamonix	04 50 53 00 24	04 50 53 00 44	74400
Chinon	02 47 93 17 85	02 47 20 50 50	37500
Collioure	04 68 82 15 47	04 68 82 05 94	66190
Colmar	03 89 20 68 92	03 89 41 66 80	68000
Dijon	03 80 44 11 44	03 80 41 50 50	21000
Dinan	02 96 39 75 40	02 93 69 22 39	22100
Honfleur	02 31 89 23 30	02 31 44 77 44	14600
Mont St. Michel	02 33 60 14 30	02 33 60 00 35	50016

	Tourist Info	Train Info	Zip Code
Nice	04 93 87 07 07	04 93 87 50 50	06000
Reims	03 26 77 45 25	03 26 88 50 50	51084
Rouen	02 32 08 32 40	02 35 98 50 50	76000
Sarlat	05 53 59 27 67	05 53 59 00 21	24200
Verdun	03 29 86 14 18	03 29 45 50 50	55100
Villefranche	04 93 01 73 68	04 93 87 50 50	06230

Belgium

Bruges	050/448686	050/448686	8000
Brussels	02/504-0390	02/219-2880	1000

Netherlands

Amsterdam	06-3403-4066	030/332555	multiple

Climate Chart

First line, average daily low; second line, average daily high; third line, days of no rain.

Paris

J	F	M	A	M	J	J	A	S	O	N	D
34°	34°	39°	43°	49°	55°	58°	58°	53°	46°	40°	36°
43°	45°	54°	60°	68°	73°	76°	75°	70°	60°	50°	44°
16	15	16	16	18	19	19	19	19	17	15	14

Nice

40°	41°	45°	49°	56°	62°	66°	66°	62°	55°	48°	43°
56°	56°	59°	64°	69°	76°	81°	81°	77°	70°	62°	58°
23	20	23	23	23	25	29	26	24	22	23	23

Brussels

30°	32°	36°	41°	46°	52°	54°	54°	51°	45°	38°	32°
40°	44°	51°	58°	65°	72°	73°	72°	69°	60°	48°	42°
9	13	13	12	14	15	13	12	17	13	10	11

Amsterdam

31°	31°	34°	40°	46°	51°	55°	55°	50°	44°	38°	33°
40°	42°	49°	56°	64°	70°	72°	71°	67°	57°	48°	42°
8	11	14	14	16	16	13	12	11	10	9	9

Numbers and Stumblers

•Europeans write a few of their numbers differently than we do.
$1 = 1$, $4 = 4$, $7 = 7$. Learn the difference or miss your train.
•In Europe, dates appear as day/month/year, so Christmas is
25-12-97.
•Commas are decimal points and decimals commas. A dollar
and a half is 1,50 and there are 5.280 feet in a mile.
•When pointing, use your whole hand, palm downward.
•When counting with fingers, start with your thumb. If you
hold up your first finger to request one item, you'll probably
get two.
•What we Americans call the second floor of a building is the
first floor in Europe.
•Europeans keep the left "lane" open for passing on escalators
and moving sidewalks. Keep to the right.

The French Rail System

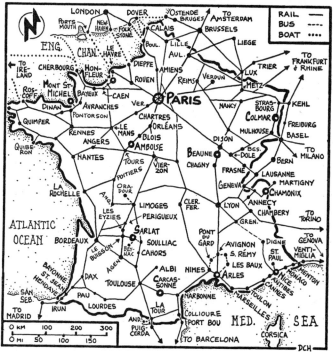

Basic French Survival Phrases

English	French	Pronunciation
Hello (good day).	Bonjour.	bohn-zhoor
Do you speak English?	Parlez-vous anglais?	par-lay-voo ahn-glay
Yes. / No.	Oui. / Non.	wee / nohn
I'm sorry.	Désolé.	day-zoh-lay
Please.	S'il vous plaît.	see voo play
Thank you.	Merci.	mehr-see
Goodbye.	Au revoir.	oh vwahr
Where is...?	Où est...?	oo ay
...a hotel	...un hôtel	uhn oh-tehl
...a youth hostel	...une auberge de jeunesse	ewn oh-behrzh duh zhuh-nehs
...a restaurant	...un restaurant	uhn rehs-toh-rahn
...a grocery store	...une épicerie	ewn ay-pee-suh-ree
...the train station	...la gare	lah gar
...the tourist info office	...l'office du tourisme	loh-fees dew too-reez-muh
Where are the toilets?	Où sont les toilettes?	oo sohn lay twah-leht
men / women	hommes / dames	ohm / dahm
How much is it?	Combien?	kohn-bee-an
Cheaper.	Moins cher.	mwan shehr
Included?	Inclus?	an-klew
Do you have...?	Avez-vous...?	ah-vay-voo
I would like...	Je voudrais...	zhuh voo-dray
...a ticket.	...un billet.	uhn bee-yay
...a room.	...une chambre.	ewn shahn-bruh
...the bill.	...l'addition.	lah-dee-see-ohn
one	un	uhn
two	deux	duh
three	trois	twah
four	quatre	kah-truh
five	cinq	sank
six	six	sees
seven	sept	seht
eight	huit	weet
nine	neuf	nuhf
ten	dix	dees
At what time?	À quelle heure?	ah kehl ur
Just a moment.	Un moment.	uhn moh-mahn
Now.	Maintenant.	man-tuh-nahn
today / tomorrow	aujourd'hui / demain	oh-zhoor-dwee / duh-man

For more user-friendly French phrases, check out *Rick Steves' French Phrase Book and Dictionary* and *Rick Steves' French/German/Italian Phrase Book and Dictionary*.

Road Scholar Feedback for
FRANCE, BELGIUM, & THE NETHERLANDS 1997

We're all in the same travelers' school of hard knocks. Your feedback helps us improve this guidebook for future travelers. Please fill this out (attach more info or any tips/favorite discoveries if you like) and send it to us. As thanks for your help, we'll send you our quarterly travel newsletter free for one year. Thanks! **Rick**

I traveled mainly by: ___ Car   ___ Train/bus tickets
___ Railpass   Other (please list _____)

Number of people traveling together:
___ Solo   ___ 2   ___ 3   ___ 4   ___ Over 4   ___ Tour

Ages of traveler/s (including children):

_____

I visited _____ countries in _____ weeks.

I traveled in: ___ Spring   ___ Summer   ___ Fall   ___ Winter

My daily budget per person (excluding transportation):
___ Under $40   ___ $40–$60   ___ $60–$80   ___ $80–$120
___ over $120   ___ Don't know

Average cost of hotel rooms: Single room $_____
Double room $_____   Other (type _____) $_____

Favorite tip from this book:

_____

Biggest waste of time or money caused by this book:

_____

Other Rick Steves books used for this trip:

_____

Hotel listings from this book should be geared toward places that are:
___Cheaper   ___More expensive   ___About the same

Of the recommended accommodations/restaurants used, which was:

Best _____

    Why? _____

Worst _____

    Why? _____

I reserved rooms:

___from USA   ___in advance as I traveled

___same day by phone   ___just showed up

Getting rooms in recommended hotels was:

___easy   ___mixed   ___frustrating

Of the sights/experiences/destinations recommended by this book, which was:

Most overrated _____

    Why? _____

Most underrated _____

    Why? _____

Best ways to improve this book:

_____

I'd like a free newsletter subscription:

___ Yes   ___ No   ___ Already on list

_____

Name

_____

Address

_____

City, State, Zip

Please send to:
Europe Through the Back Door,
Box 2009, Edmonds, WA 98020

Faxing Your Hotel Reservation

Most hotel managers know basic "hotel English." Faxing is the pre-
ferred method for reserving a room. It's more accurate and cheaper
than telephoning and much faster than writing a letter. Use this
handy form for your fax. Photocopy and fax away.

One-Page Fax

To: _____ @ _____
            hotel   *fax*

From: _____ @ _____
            name   *fax*

Today's date: ___ /____ /___
              day *month* *year*

Dear Hotel _____,

Please make this reservation for me:

Name: _____

Total # of people: _____   # of rooms: _____   # of nights: _____

Arriving: ___ /____ /___   My time of arrival (24-hr clock): _____
          day *month* *year*   (I will telephone if I will be late)

Departing: ___ /____ /___
           day *month* *year*

Room(s): Single___ Double___ Twin___ Triple___ Quad___

With: Toilet___ Shower___ Bath___ Sink only___

Special needs: View___ Quiet___ Cheapest Room___

Credit card: Visa___ MasterCard___ American Express___

Card #: _____

Expiration Date:_____

Name on card: _____

You may charge me for the first night as a deposit. Please fax or mail me
confirmation of my reservation, along with the type of room reserved,
the price, and whether the price includes breakfast. Thank you.

_____
Signature

_____
Name

_____
Address

_____
City   *State*   *Zip Code*   *Country*

INDEX

Rick Steves' Phrase Books

Unlike other phrase books and dictionaries on the market, my well-tested phrases and key words cover every situation a traveler is likely to encounter. With these books you'll laugh with your cabby, disarm street thieves with insults, and charm new European friends.

Each book in the series is 4" x 6", with maps.

RICK STEVES' FRENCH PHRASE BOOK & DICTIONARY
U.S. $5.95/Canada $8.50

RICK STEVES' GERMAN PHRASE BOOK & DICTIONARY
U.S. $5.95/Canada $8.50

RICK STEVES' ITALIAN PHRASE BOOK & DICTIONARY
U.S. $5.95/Canada $8.50

RICK STEVES' SPANISH & PORTUGUESE PHRASE BOOK & DICTIONARY
U.S. $7.95/Canada $11.25

RICK STEVES' FRENCH, ITALIAN & GERMAN PHRASE BOOK & DICTIONARY
U.S. $7.95/Canada $11.25

Other Books from John Muir Publications

Rick Steves' Books

Asia Through the Back Door, $17.95
Europe 101: History and Art for the Traveler, $17.95
Mona Winks: Self-Guided Tours of Europe's Top Museums, $18.95
Rick Steves' Baltics & Russia, $9.95
Rick Steves' Europe, $18.95
Rick Steves' France, Belgium & the Netherlands, $15.95
Rick Steves' Germany, Austria & Switzerland, $14.95
Rick Steves' Great Britain, $15.95
Rick Steves' Italy, $13.95
Rick Steves' Scandinavia, $13.95
Rick Steves' Spain & Portugal, $13.95
Rick Steves' Europe Through the Back Door, $19.95
Rick Steves' French Phrase Book, $5.95
Rick Steves' German Phrase Book, $5.95
Rick Steves' Italian Phrase Book, $5.95
Rick Steves' Spanish & Portugese Phrase Book, $7.95
Rick Steves' French/German/Italian Phrase Book, $7.95

A Natural Destination Series

Belize: A Natural Destination, $16.95
Costa Rica: A Natural Destination, $18.95
Guatemala: A Natural Destination, $16.95

City•Smart™ Guidebook Series

City•Smart Guidebook: Cleveland, $14.95
City•Smart Guidebook: Denver, $14.95
City•Smart Guidebook: Minneapolis/St. Paul, $14.95
City•Smart Guidebook: Nashville, $14.95
City•Smart Guidebook: Portland, $14.95
City•Smart Guidebook: Tampa/St. Petersburg, $14.95

Travel+Smart™ Trip Planners

American Southwest Travel+Smart Trip Planner, $14.95
Colorado Travel+Smart Trip Planner, $14.95
Eastern Canada Travel+Smart Trip Planner, $15.95
Florida Gulf Coast Travel+Smart Trip Planner, $14.95
Hawaii Travel+Smart Trip Planner, $14.95
Kentucky/Tennessee Travel+Smart Trip Planner, $14.95
Minnesota/Wisconsin Travel+Smart Trip Planner, $14.95
New England Travel+Smart Trip Planner, $14.95
Northern California Travel+Smart Trip Planner, $15.95
Pacific Northwest Travel+Smart Trip Planner, $14.95

Other Terrific Travel Titles

The 100 Best Small Art Towns in America, $15.95
The Big Book of Adventure Travel, $17.95

Indian America: A Traveler's Companion, $18.95
The People's Guide to Mexico, $19.95
Ranch Vacations: The Complete Guide to Guest and Resort, Fly-Fishing, and Cross-Country Skiing Ranches, $22.95
Understanding Europeans, $14.95
Undiscovered Islands of the Caribbean, $16.95
Watch It Made in the U.S.A.: A Visitor's Guide to the Companies that Make Your Favorite Products, $16.95
The World Awaits, $16.95
The Birder's Guide to Bed and Breakfasts: U.S. and Canada, $17.95

Automotive Titles

The Greaseless Guide to Car Care, $19.95
How to Keep Your Subaru Alive, $21.95
How to Keep Your Toyota Pickup Alive, $21.95
How to Keep Your VW Alive, $25

Ordering Information

Please check your local bookstore for our books, or call **1-800-888-7504** to order direct and to receive a complete catalog. A shipping charge will be added to your order total.

Send all inquiries to:
John Muir Publications
P.O. Box 613
Santa Fe, NM 87504